Migrant Marginality

This edited book uses migrant marginality to problematize several aspects of global migration. It uses case studies from Western and Eastern Europe, North America and the Caribbean to examine how many societies have defined their national identities, cultural values and terms of political membership through (and in opposition to) constructions of migrants and migration.

The first section of the book examines the limitations of multicultural policies that have been used to incorporate migrants into the host society. The second section examines anti-immigrant discourses and get-tough enforcement practices that are geared toward excluding and removing criminalized "aliens". The third section examines some of the gendered dimensions of migrant marginality. The fourth section examines the way that racially marginalized populations have engaged the politics of immigration, constructing themselves as either migrants or natives.

The book offers researchers, policy makers and students an appreciation for the various policy concerns, ethical dilemmas and political and cultural antagonisms that must be engaged in order to properly understand the problem of migrant marginality.

Philip Kretsedemas is an Associate Professor of Sociology at the University of Massachusetts-Boston.

Jorge Capetillo-Ponce is presently Director of Latino Studies, Associate Professor of Sociology and Research Associate at the Mauricio Gaston Institute at University of Massachusetts-Boston.

Glenn Jacobs is Professor of Sociology at the University of Massachusetts-Boston and head of the Umass-Boston, Trotter Institute research consortium on immigrant community-based organizations.

Routledge Advances in Sociology

For a list of full titles in this series, please visit www.routledge.com.

Migrant Marginality

A Transnational Perspective

**Edited by Philip Kretsedemas,
Jorge Capetillo-Ponce and Glenn Jacobs**

Routledge
Taylor & Francis Group

NEW YORK   LONDON

First published 2014
by Routledge
711 Third Avenue, New York, NY 10017

Simultaneously published in the UK
by Routledge
2 Park Square, Milton Park, Abingdon, Oxon OX14 4RN

*Routledge is an imprint of the Taylor & Francis Group,
an informa business*

© 2014 Taylor & Francis

Library of Congress Cataloging-in-Publication Data
    Migrant marginality : a transnational perspective / edited by Philip
Kretsedemas, Jorge Capetillo-Ponce and Glenn Jacobs. — 1st Edition.
      pages cm. — (Routledge advances in sociology ; 98)
    Includes bibliographical references and index.
  1. Immigrants—Cultural assimilation. 2. Women immigrants—Legal
status, laws, etc. 3. Emigration and immigration—Government
policy. 4. Transnationalism. I. Kretsedemas, Philip, 1967–
    JV6342.M5294 2013
    305.9'06912—dc23
    2013005295

ISBN: 978-0-415-89317-6 (hbk)
ISBN: 978-0-203-54970-4 (ebk)

Typeset in Sabon
by IBT Global.

SUSTAINABLE
FORESTRY
INITIATIVE
SFI label applies to the text stock

Certified Sourcing
www.sfiprogram.org
SFI-01234

Printed and bound in the United States of America
by IBT Global.

Contents

PART III
Gendered Peripheries: Emigrants, Asylum Seekers
and the Feminization of Migrant Marginality

PART IV
Immigrant Identities and the Politics of Race and Nativity

PART V
Where To, Beyond the Margin?

Figures

Tables

1 Introduction
The Problem of Migrant Marginality

Jorge Capetillo-Ponce
and Philip Kretsedemas

There is a long history in the social sciences of using the migrant experience to explore marginal conditions. As many theorists have explained, margins are also border zones, and migrants straddle many kinds of borders, be they ethno-cultural, geopolitical, gendered, sexualized, legal-juridical or racial.[1] Furthermore, these borders are constantly being redefined by acts of migration. The migration process forces the emigrant to renegotiate his or her relationship to the inherited culture and homeland. Meanwhile, the migrant's arrival leads the host society to redefine its own cultural, economic and geopolitical borders.

The old world isn't entirely left behind and the new land isn't entirely welcoming (and to borrow a line from Jeffrey Reitz,[2] the warmth of this welcome has become increasingly guarded over the past few decades). The migrant may have a foothold in both worlds, but he or she also inhabits a liminal space that does not quite belong to either. The ethnic enclaves and 'immigrant ghettoes' of the late nineteenth century were one such space, being physically located within the nation's borders, but on the cultural and social margins of the mainstream society.[3] These spaces still exist today, but immigration law has also created new kinds of marginal conditions.

Illegalized migrants, for example, are incorporated into the economic life of the nation as deportable people. In this case, the marginality of the migrant manifests itself as a precarious legal situation that travels with him or her. Instead of associating migrants with a particular kind of urban space (like the ethnic enclave), illegality describes a type of person who could be hiding within this space. This makes for a more fluid kind of marginality—one that has no clearly defined social or geographic limits, but that provides a guiding rationale for the policing of migrant bodies within all of the spaces that compose the national territory.[4]

Illegality is just one of the many kinds of migrant marginality that is discussed in this book. It is a good place to start, however, because it draws attention to an ethical and conceptual tension that runs through the heart of migrant marginality. For example, illegality can be framed as a marginal condition that is inflicted on the migrant. But illegality carries its own kind of moral stigma, which leads the migrant to be viewed as a 'law breaker' and 'tax burden'. In this case, it is the migrant who is blamed for marginalizing other people, by taking jobs and resources that are presumed to be the rightful property of natives and legal residents.

Marginality may be a problem, but for whom? The very act of defining marginality poses a problem, because it is a shifting and contested construct. Can we presume that the socioeconomic marginality of the migrant is any worse than that of the native (considering that, in many nations, the employment rate of the migrant population is higher than that of the native born[5])? And by framing migrant marginality as a problem, are we implying that marginality is not a problem for citizens and natives, or that citizens are insulated from the problem of marginality simply because they are citizens?[6]

The short answer to all of these questions is no. The contributions to this book explore many kinds of migrant marginality. But the goal is not to show that migrants have a privileged claim to marginality above all other populations. When marginality is viewed in this light, it devolves into a competitive claims-making strategy. Marginality is rendered visible as a kind of deprivation that legitimizes demands for rights and resources, and the more extreme the deprivation the more compelling the claim. As a result, the analysis of marginality gets focused on documenting empirically verifiable conditions of immiseration. But as the chapters in this book show, the analysis of marginal conditions can be used to do much more than this.

Marginalities raise questions about the way that national identities, immigration policies, migrant recruitment practices and migrant/native distinctions have been constructed. This line of inquiry draws attention to the kind of marginality described by Georg Simmel's writing on the stranger.[7] Marginality is not just a deprivation that people have to be rescued from. Marginalities expose the antagonisms of existing social arrangements, and they define the conditions under which society works through these antagonisms. From this vantage point, marginalities can also be understood as transition spaces that shed light on new problems (or that help us to see 'old' problems in 'new' ways). This is, arguably, the most valuable thing about marginal conditions. As Gilles Deleuze has explained, a well-posed problem is more powerful than an efficient solution.[8] Solutions usually terminate at a single end point. Problems open up new horizons for thought, social organization and interaction that can be populated by many kinds of solutions, and that are not exhausted by any of them.

This creative and critical process of posing problems is the common thread that runs through all of the chapters in this book. In many respects, this is not a book about the 'immigrant experience'. It is a book that examines how many societies have defined their national identities, cultural imaginaries and terms of political membership through (and in opposition to) constructions of migrants and migration. All of the chapters in this book interrogate these constructions in one way or another. And they don't just use these interrogations to shed light on problems that are specific to migrants. They show how the critical analysis of marginalities can be used to raise questions about the shared social condition in which migrants and natives encounter one another.

This line of inquiry is both practical and theoretical. It is premised on the understanding that you can't explain migrant marginality without examining how migrant populations have been constructed in the popular imagination and by the policies and practices of powerful institutions. Or in other words, the empirical 'reality' of the migrant experience cannot be extricated from the fields of discourse through which the migrant has been rendered visible, as an object of 'public concern' and as a subject of the law and state policy.

(RE)FRAMING TRANSNATIONALITY

The research presented in this book draws from a diverse array of methodologies. including ethnography, textual analysis, qualitative interviews and quantitative survey methods (and sometimes including bits and pieces of all of these methods). The geopolitical and analytical scope of the book's contents is also very diverse. Many of the chapters explore the politics and policies of nations that you might not expect to find in a book on immigration—like Slovenia, Portugal, Ireland, the Dominican Republic, Sweden and the US Virgin Islands. Some of the chapters focus on the reception of migrants by the host society. Other chapters examine the dynamics of emigration from the vantage point of the sending nation, and still other chapters examine how migrants construct their identities in response to the way they have been perceived and received by the host society.

There is also, clearly, a transnational scope to this collection of case studies, but they are not united by a geographic focus or national typology. We are not trying to provide a representative survey of the politics of immigration in a particular kind of receiving nation (focusing on traditional nations of immigration versus new hubs of global migration) or a particular region (focusing on immigration in the global North or the global South, or in Asia as opposed to Europe). And unlike much of the recent research on transnationalism, this book does not focus its attention on the way that migrants straddle multiple national contexts.[9] Although some of the chapters provide insights into these transnational migrant networks and identities, most of the chapters illustrate how migrant identities are being adapted to the culture and politics of a single, national context.

The book's transnational character is defined, primarily, by the marginalities that are explored in all of its chapters. It explores the transnational scope of a diverse array of problems that are bound up with the political, economic and cultural dynamics of global migration. This is why the book's contents are not organized into geographic regions. Instead, the book is organized into thematic sections that illustrate how different aspects of migrant marginality have unfolded across several national contexts. The first section of the book takes a look at the limitations of discourses on multiculturalism; the second section examines anti-immigrant discourses and get-tough enforcement practices that are geared toward excluding and removing criminalized aliens; the third section examines some of the gendered dimensions of migrant marginality; and the fourth section examines the way that racially marginalized populations have engaged the politics of immigration, constructing themselves as migrants or natives (and sometimes, as both).

TESTING THE LIMITS OF MULTICULTURALISM

The book begins its investigation of migrant marginality in a rather counterintuitive way, by exploring the limitations of policies and practices that have been used to incorporate migrants into the host society. The book starts off this way because we want to underscore the complexity of migrant marginality.

As Bhikhu Parekh and William Connolly have explained, a truly egalitarian multiculturalism requires an ongoing, open-ended, democratic dialogue about the meaning of multiculturalism.[10] The most important part of this process is the dialogue itself. Multicultural discourses and policies can furnish the public sphere with compelling symbols of inclusion, but with little substantive input from migrant populations. When this happens, multiculturalism devolves into a discussion that members of the majority culture are having among themselves *about* migrant populations—instead of being a dialogue that they are having *with* migrant populations. Unfortunately, this is not an unusual problem, because the dialogue between migrants and the mainstream society is undergirded by a majority/minority power dynamic (especially for racialized migrant populations). As a result, discourses on multiculturalism can get caught in the trap of reproducing the racial and cultural common sense of the majority culture—making it that much more difficult to comprehend the barriers being experienced by migrant populations.

It may be tempting to view these antagonisms as less important than the more explicit forms of anti-immigrant xenophobia examined later in the book. It's worth noting, however, that anti-immigrant ideologies tend to focus on the cultural difference of the immigrant. Consider the Oslo shootings of 2011, that were carried out by a gun man protesting the multicultural policies of the Norwegian state, or the Wisconsin shootings of 2012, carried out by a white supremacist who targeted worshippers at a Sikh Temple.[11] Terrorist attacks like those of September 11, 2011 or the Boston Marathon bombing of 2013, only add more fuel to the fire, creating a field of visibility that is defined by extremist elements in the immigrant and native-born population. Once this begins to happen, the possibility of initiating a multicultural dialogue among populations that want to live peacefully together slips further into the background. Instead of seeing that long term peace and security will be defined by the quality of the intercultural communication between these populations, it becomes tempting to dismiss multiculturalism as an impossibility, that can only undermine the security of the nation.

Understandably, this is a daunting challenge, and this is, perhaps, why many Western nations view the mere adoption of multicultural policies—no matter how symbolic—as a major achievement. But as the chapters in the first section of the book show, the problem of marginality is always resurfacing within the politics and discourse of multiculturalism.

Marta Araujo engages this dilemma in Chapter 2 by deconstructing the discourse on immigrants and multiculturalism in Portugal. Araujo argues that Portuguese multiculturalism is still in denial about the relationship between Portuguese colonialism and the migration flows of the current era. She explains that the racial hierarchies that were established during the colonial era continue to inform the dehistoricized fascination with immigrant culture that is reflected in Portuguese multiculturalism. As a result, it is difficult to see that there is a relationship between the de facto segregation of black/African immigrants in Portugal today and a history of antiblack racism that can be traced to the colonial era—because the black immigrant (and immigration in general) has been constructed as an exotic, 'new' presence in Portuguese society.

In Chapter 3, Valentina Pagliai examines the multicultural discourse of the pro-immigrant, Italian left. She explains that within these left-leaning, pro-immigration circles there was an insufficient awareness of the scope and severity of Italian cultural racism—until the far right, anti-immigrant movement began making its presence felt in the mainstreams of Italian politics. Pagliai explains, however, that the progressive discourse on multiculturalism is still lacking. She observes that this discourse participates in the same romanticization of authentic types that informed colonial era discourses on culture and community.

On one hand, the cultural difference of racialized migrants is embraced by Italian progressives, but on the other hand migrants find themselves boxed in by these sympathetic constructions, because of their latent essentialism. Instead of entering into a dialogue with the native population about their cultural identity and political interests, the migrant gains acceptance by adhering to a set of performance standards that have been defined in advance by the native population. The perverse result is that the migrant ends up distorting his or her culture in order to communicate effectively with their supporters in the majority culture. Pagliai uses this dilemma to explain how the civic participation of migrants can be inhibited by the very same multicultural policies and programs that have been designed to include them in Italian society.

One of the common strands running through chapters 2 and 3 is their critique of essentialized constructions of immigrant community and culture. In this case, the problem lies in the way that immigrant culture is rendered visible and 'embraced' by the mainstream society. Chapter 4 takes this critique in a different direction, by examining the ways that multicultural policies can inadvertently homogenize migrant cultures. In this chapter. Gwendolyn Alexis analyzes the legal and scholarly discourse on religious pluralism in Sweden. Alexis focuses on the burial rites of Muslim immigrants, explaining how Swedish laws and regulations make it nearly impossible for these rites to be respected. She explains that, in order for Muslim burial rites to enjoy the same recognition as those of Christian populations, it is necessary to renegotiate the meaning and terms of the religious neutrality that is affirmed by the Swedish state. Alexis's discussion draws attention to the transnational scope of this dilemma, through comparisons with similar debates over Muslim burial rites and the establishment of Hindu and Muslim worship centers in the US. She also provides a comparative review of conceptual models of religious diversity that highlight legal norms and multicultural principles that have been affirmed, to varying degrees, by most Western nations. As a result, she uses the Swedish case study to draw attention to a body of discourse that extends far beyond Sweden. She is describing an encounter not just between Muslim immigrants and the Swedish state, but also between non-Western, non-Christian immigrants and the political culture and legal norms of the West.

All of these chapters make a point that is elaborated further in the rest of the book. Migrant marginality and migrant incorporation are not mutually exclusive phenomena. Migrants can become marginal through the *way* they are incorporated into the host society. What may look like inclusion to the mainstream society could look like a barrier to inclusion to migrant populations. And there is no Archimedean vantage point that can be used to put these contrasting interpretations in proper perspective. The normative framework for these negotiations has to be constructed by the same parties who are negotiating the meaning of multiculturalism, while they are engaged in these negotiations.

MANUFACTURING EXCLUSION: ANTI-IMMIGRANT POLITICS AND POLICIES

There are other varieties of marginality that lend themselves to a more conventional, empirical description of disparities and inequalities. There is ample evidence, for example, that the immigration policies of most advanced industrialized nations have become more security- and enforcement-oriented.[12] This shift toward the securitization of immigration policy can also be understood as a transnational phenomenon. It has been shaped by a trend toward policy convergence and cross-national coordination in the migrant recruitment practices, economic priorities and border security strategies of the nation-states of the global North.[13]

One practical result of this transformation is that more migrants are being detained and deported than ever before. But the rise of this securitized immigration regime has also taken shape in the context of the post–Cold War era expansion of global migration (although economic globalization has been mainly focused on expanding and trade and investment flows, we shouldn't lose sight of the fact that there has been a real increase in the flow of international migrants over the past few decades[14]).

So it would appear that migrants are 'needed' but not necessarily 'wanted'. The expansion of migrant flows has occurred during the same time that receiving nations have become more invested in policing, detaining and deporting migrant populations. For some immigration scholars this apparent contradiction is a direct result of the policy priorities of Western industrialized nations. From this vantage point, migration flows are not being controlled for the purpose of restricting immigration, but to better manage an expanding flow of mostly desirable migrant workers, tourists and business visitors.

There are some important differences at play within this body of argument. Some scholars have argued that these controls are pragmatic attempts at minimizing actually existing hazards like 'unwanted' low-skilled migration, terrorist networks, human trafficking and so on.[15] Others have argued that this recruitment-control dynamic is a regulatory strategy that is used to maximize the productivity (and exploitability) of migrants, which is integral to the functioning of the global economy.[16] Either way, there is an interest in showing how immigration controls have been conditioned by a utilitarian rationality that is deeply embedded within the economic priorities and institutional culture of the modern state.

Other theorists have explained how the desire to control immigration has been conditioned by a more visceral body of sentiments. From this vantage point, exclusionary and racialized national identities are the core motivating factor.[17] Xenophobic (nativist) perceptions of migrants overdetermine the way that debates over immigration policy unfold in the public sphere. Etienne Balibar has produced one of the most influential explanations of these exclusionary sentiments (which is referenced by many of the contributors to this book).[18] Balibar uses the concept of cultural racism to describe how immigrants can be stigmatized by a coded racial discourse that focuses on their cultural difference. In France, for example, anti-immigrant racism can immerse itself in a discourse on national identity that makes distinctions between assimilable and unassimilable migrants (these distinctions being an indirect way of rationalizing the exclusion of darker-skinned, non-European, non-Christian migrants).

In Chapter 5, Ana Kralj explains how these exclusionary sentiments have played out within the immigration policies and media discourse of Slovenia. She points out that Slovenian cultural racism is more transparently 'cultural' than that of other European nations. Most of the migrants that have entered Slovenia in recent years are displaced populations from other parts of Eastern Europe (as opposed to being nonwhite migrants from Africa and Asia). But despite these differences, the discursive architecture of Slovenian nativism is similar to the rest of Europe. The exclusion of the immigrant Other is justified by a discourse on crime and illegality, which delineates the outer limits of Slovenian nationality (whereby the illegalized migrant becomes symbolic of everything the Slovenian national is not). Kralj observes how this nativist common sense has shaped Slovenian immigration law, but she concentrates her attention on the discourse of the print media—which openly expresses sentiments that are usually concealed by the exclusionary policies of the state.

In Chapter 6, Mark Dow provides a critical examination of the practices and (extra)legal rationales that are used to detain and deport racialized migrants in the US. As other scholars have observed, these practices are informed by an immigration control discourse that is less overtly xenophobic than most European nations (Michael Welch and Liza Schuster have described the anti-immigrant discourse of the US as deploying a "quieter" kind of framing strategy[19]). Even within the rhetoric of the US immigration control movement, the racialized migrant is often stigmatized by a color-blind discourse on illegality.[20] Dow explains that this discourse, which holds the migrant accountable to an individual standard of legal culpability, is also a defining feature of the US detention system. Dow also explains how anti-immigrant sentiments that target racialized migrants can be enabled by enforcement practices that operate in the grey space of the law. These are spaces of indeterminacy that void the migrant's rights—not because these rights have been restricted but because they have not been clearly defined. Dow uses his critical analysis to recover some important ethical and policy questions that have been buried within the slippage between the formal goals of the detention system and its informal, day-to-day workings.

In Chapter 7, Barbara Faedda offers a complementary analysis of anti-immigrant discourse and the criminalization of immigrants in Italy. Her study reviews the transformation of Italian immigration law from the late 1980s to the present. She observes that, like the US, Italian immigration policy and immigration discourse have become increasingly concerned with restricting the entry of criminalized 'undesirables'.

Faedda explains that the link between nativist populism and institutional discrimination against immigrants in Italy is articulated in a more open fashion than in the US. She also explains how the struggle to define Italian immigration law (and the place of the migrant in Italian society) is bound up with a struggle over the meaning of Italian national identity.

GENDERED PERIPHERIES: EMIGRANTS, ASYLUM SEEKERS AND THE FEMINIZATION OF MIGRANT MARGINALITY

The next section of the book explores the gendered dimensions of migrant marginality. As some immigration and race scholars have observed, it is no coincidence that global migration flows have been illegalized and criminalized during the same period of time that these migration flows have become increasingly nonwhite.[21] But it's just as important to note that these migration flows are composed of a growing number of female migrants, who are concentrated in the illegalized, low-wage migrant force.[22] This change isn't important just because of what it reveals about the sex composition of global migration flows. It also indicates that gender roles and gendered power dynamics are playing an important role in shaping the way that global migration works.

Cinzia Solari explores these gendered dynamics in Chapter 8. Her discussion focuses on the emigration of Ukrainian women to Italy (who are mainly recruited as low-wage domestics, and are often recruited as 'illegal' workers). Solari explains how these women are positioned as the subjects of a nation-building project that is heavily informed by discourses on masculinity/femininity and familial, gender roles. She also shows how this Ukrainian national imaginary shapes the migration process (defining the way migration happens, the kinds of jobs these women work and the expectations placed on them to support the "homeland").

Although these female migrants are playing an important role in sustaining the globalizing economies of Italy and the Ukraine, they are also engaging in a kind of labor that is stigmatized through its association with migration. Cultural authenticity is associated with territorial sovereignty. The migrant who goes elsewhere to support others back home compromises this principle of territorial sovereignty (because the nation should, ideally, be able to sustain itself—keeping in mind the masculinized subtext that is laced through discourses on economic self-sufficiency[23]). It's also notable that female migrants (and, in the case of Ukraine, older female migrants) are deemed the most appropriate type of person to undertake this stigmatized form of labor. This stigma is reinforced by Italian anti-immigrant racism, which targets illegalized migrant workers, but it is also normalized by the gendered construction of post-Soviet, Ukrainian identity.

In Chapter 9, Tamar and Tinatin Zurabishvili provide another look at the dynamics of Eastern European emigration, focusing on post-Soviet Georgia. Like Solari, they describe an emigration process that is mainly driven by the movement of women, who are incorporated into the labor markets of wealthier European nations as illegalized, low-wage workers. The Zurabishvilis also focus on the impact that these emigration flows have had on the sending nation. They explain, for example, that Georgian emigrants from Daba Tianeti are generally viewed as doing better for themselves than the people who have stayed back home. But female emigrants also tend to earn less than men, although they remit a larger proportion of their income than male emigrants.

So it would appear that female emigrants are caught in a bundle of contradictions that has been conditioned, in part, by the gendered roles and expectations imposed on them. They may be quietly resented for being 'better off' than Georgian natives who didn't emigrate, but they are also performing stressful, low-status, domestic work in the receiving nation.

Moreover, as the Zurabishivilis point out, the remittances of these migrants have done little to reenergize the Georgian economy. Remittances have kept many families from slipping into poverty, but they have also widened income and wealth disparities within the Georgian population. Unfortunately, female emigrants are easy targets for popular frustrations about this economic situation. And as Solari has observed in the case of Ukraine, female migrants who send large amounts of remittances back home are often stigmatized more so than those who send smaller remittances.[24]

The last two chapters in this section focus on the situation of female asylum seekers. In Chapter 10, Jacqueline Polanco discusses the difficulties that lesbian, transvestite and transgender persons from the Dominican Republic have faced in gaining asylum in the US. One of the most compelling things about Polanco's analysis is that it operates at the nexus of gender, sexuality, national identity, class and racialization. But it is also notable that she begins her analysis with a gender disparity, observing that gay males have been more successful than lesbians in being granted asylum by the US courts.

So it would appear that lesbian asylum seekers are not well served by gender asylum advocacy[25] that has protected heterosexual women from abuse by their male spouses, and they are also at a disadvantage in appealing to a standard of persecution for sexual minorities that has been defined, primarily, by gay males. Polanco explains that it is difficult for lesbians to prove that they belong to an oppressed category of persons, because the homophobic culture of the Dominican Republic forces sexual minorities—and especially lesbians—to hide their orientation. Polanco also shows how the inability of asylum law to fully recognize the persecution and marginality of gay, lesbian and transgender persons in the Dominican Republic reinforces their marginality under the law, and that the advocacy groups attempting to engage these issues have themselves been marginalized within the rather narrow space that exists for this activism in the US. Gendered power dynamics are not the only factor at work in this process, but they play a role, nonetheless, in shaping (and undermining) the credibility of lesbian asylum seekers.

In Chapter 11, Deirdre Conlon examines the process through which female refugees make asylum claims in Ireland. She explains how asylum seekers are pulled into a web of power dynamics that require them to produce confessional narratives that are often based on selective interpretations of the conditions that led them to flee their home nation. Conlon grounds her analysis in a Foucauldian understanding of how subjectivities are produced by disciplinary mechanisms and micropractices that can be articulated and reinforced in many institutional settings. Conlon also demonstrates how female migrants become sympathetic figures by allowing themselves to be constructed as deserving victims. This is a different kind of subjectivity than that of the female emigrants discussed by Solari and the Zurabishivilis. Conlon also focuses on a different kind of dilemma than Polanco, who is more concerned with explaining why lesbian asylum seekers are unable to produce credible narratives of persecution (as opposed to explaining how their refugee experience is distorted through the way they "become credible"). Underlying these differences, however, there are important continuities. All of these chapters illustrate how female migrants can be maneuvered into marginal conditions that lead them to be viewed as objects of pity, suspicion or scorn.

These chapters also describe a political field that's more complex than the one's outlined in the prior sections. Female migrants don't just belong to a minority population whose culture is being essentialized or homogenized by the mainstream culture. They also have to struggle with gendered and sexualized power dynamics that are directed at them from their 'fellow nationals' (lesbian and transgender migrants, in particular, can find themselves mutually excluded by the host society and their own 'communities'). In this case, it's not possible to romanticize immigrant culture as a place of refuge from an indifferent society. Immigrant culture has to be understood as a site of contestation that can be populated by many different political projects, that are not necessarily 'friendly' to one another. We also shouldn't think about marginality solely in terms of a majority/minority power dynamic. It's also important to consider how marginalities can be mediated (for better or worse) by power dynamics and interactions that unfold within and between minoritized populations. The last section of the book explores this subject in more depth.

IMMIGRANT IDENTITIES AND THE POLITICS OF RACE AND NATIVITY

The fourth section of the book explores how racialized populations have appropriated discourses on race, ethnicity and nativity in the US and the Caribbean. The first chapter in this section explores a kind of anti-immigrant discourse that is very different from the ones examined in the first two sections of the book. In Europe, blackness and immigrant otherness are closely related (see Chapters 2 and 3).[26] In the Caribbean, on the other hand, black identity politics has been incorporated within a discourse on nativity and local resistance.

Chapter 12 provides one insight into this black, native identity politics, with a case study of migration and the tourist industry in the US Virgin Islands. Jorge Capetillo-Ponce and Luis Galanes explain that the native-born population of the US Virgin Islands is predominantly composed of black/Afro-Caribbean persons and the foreign-born population is mainly composed of white absentee landowners and tourists, and black migrant workers. Capetillo-Ponce and Galanes examine the discourse on local residency which is used by the native population to make sharp distinctions between "indigenous" residents and recent arrivals. They also explain that this local identity politics is being used to challenge a neoliberal economic agenda that is deeply engrained in the history, politics and economic structures of the Caribbean. This discussion also invites some compelling questions about the social and political meaning of nativity.

Capetillo-Ponce and Galanes describe the structural economic and political inequalities that have stimulated the native identity politics of US Virgin Islanders. They also describe this identity politics as a variety of nativist discourse. Their account of this nativist discourse raises the question of how Afro-Caribbean nativism compares and contrasts with the nativist movements of the global North (which are predominantly white). On one hand, Capetillo-Ponce and Galanes indicate that there is a kind of nativist politics that cannot be reduced to white racism and that provides a valid way for marginalized populations to express their grievances. On the other hand, they draw attention to the contradictions of this kind of politics, which uses national political membership to challenge an economic agenda that is being advanced by the very same national governments that have defined the discourse on nation and citizenship they are trying to mobilize on their behalf (hence the efforts of US Virgin Islanders to provide constitutional protections for native residents were rejected by the US government, which is still the sovereign authority that presides over the islands).

Is the Western nation-state a political entity that is obligated to protect the native-born citizenry? Or as world systems theorists have argued, is it best understood as one of the historic coordinating centers for a global process of capital accumulation (which includes the recruitment and exploitation of migrant labor)?[27] These antagonisms raise another important question: how do you go about defining the local? In Chapter 13, Ryan Mann-Hamilton explores this question further. He traces the history of an African American migrant community that settled on the island of Hispaniola in the late nineteenth century. Mann-Hamilton explains that these migrants were recruited when the entire island was under the control of the postrevolutionary Haitian state. But when their portion of the island came under the control of the Dominican Republic, the blackness of these migrants became a problem for the state.

Mann-Hamilton describes a black identity politics which has been shaped by a long history of conflict with the nation-state. He shows how Dominican national identity was constructed in opposition to blackness and how this led to the dismantling of the African American migrant community. Mann-Hamilton also explains that the present-day descendants of these African American migrants have developed a discourse on local resistance that is opposed to the incursions of global capital and the developmental agenda of the Dominican state.

It's also worth considering how this localized identity politics articulates (or not) with other discourses on blackness. For example, Mann-Hamilton draws attention to the continuity between the antiblack racism directed at Haitian migrants in the Dominican Republic today, and the earlier history of antiblack racism that led to the dismantling of the community in the early 1900s. In both cases, blackness functions as a symbol of that which is external to the national self-concept. A big difference, however, is that Haitian migrants, in the present day, are subjected to racialized constructions of 'illegality' that alienate them from the very same discourse on grounded locality that is claimed by the descendents of the African American community that Mann-Hamilton interviewed. Furthermore, all migrants (legal or 'illegal') can be constructed as tools of the very same globalist, developmental agenda that is being resisted by the present-day descendents of this migrant community (in the same way that the US Virgin Islanders, discussed by Capetillo-Ponce and Galanes, have resisted the incursions of tourists, migrants and other non-natives, whether black or white). So it remains an open question whether blackness, as a discourse on local resistance, can be articulated in sympathy with another kind of blackness that is associated with the racialized foreigner.

This dilemma sheds some more light on the issues that are explored in the first section of the book, concerning the challenge of multiculturalism. The chapters in the opening section interrogated the way that migrants negotiated their interests and identities with those of the majority culture. But there is also the question of how racialized migrants negotiate their interests and identities with those of native-born minorities. The last five chapters in this section take a closer look at this issue, focusing on the politics of race and immigration in the US.

Unlike the Caribbean, black populations in the US cannot lay claim to a majoritarian identity. But unlike most of their European counterparts, it's still possible for the US black population to be constructed as natives. The antecedents for this discourse on black nativity are deeply engrained features of US political and popular culture, which stretch into the late nineteenth century.[28] In recent years, US immigration control advocates have appealed to this body discourse, in their efforts to frame migrants (and Latinos especially) as economic predators who are taking jobs away from native blacks.[29]

On the other hand, a large body of critical race scholarship has shown that the US mainstream has a history of favorably contrasting nonwhite migrants (especially Asians) to black, native-born minorities.[30] The nonwhite migrant assimilates by identifying with the majority culture, which leads him or her to adopt a racial and political identity that is defined in opposition to native-born minorities. Some researchers have shown that racialized migrants (typically the second-generation offspring) can choose a different pathway by identifying with native-born minorities. This line of inquiry has spun off in different directions, with some researchers depicting these acts of solidarity as indicators of downward mobility (typified by the segmented assimilation thesis[31]) and others showing how these acts of solidarity allow for a different kind of mobility that is defined by the political interests and socioeconomic networks of the native-born minority population.[32]

This situation draws attention to the complex context in which migrants and native-born minorities encounter one another. Migrants can be encouraged to distance themselves from the native minority population. Native minorities, on the other hand, can be exposed to discourses that construct migrants as the new problem facing the nation. The challenge facing both of these populations is whether they are capable of sorting through their similarities and differences, and in a way that respects the epistemic validity of their varying narratives and identities.

Chapter 14 provides a good introduction to this social terrain, because it explores the identity politics of a migrant population that straddles the borderline between blackness and immigrant otherness. In this chapter, Jennifer Jones describes the situation of Afro-Mexican migrants in North Carolina. Jones acknowledges that some Afro-Mexicans can minimize the hazards of immigrant racial profiling by adopting a black identity. But she also explains that these black identities are not adopted for instrumental reasons. Because of the history of antiblack racism in Latino cultures (and the antiblack racism that is reinforced by the process of immigrant incorporation in the US[33]) Afro-Mexicans are usually isolated from other Latino populations. As a result, Afro-Mexicans tend to view native-born black populations in the US as their natural allies. Jones observes that the affinity that Afro-Mexicans have for African Americans is also shared by many nonblack Mexicans, who have been alienated by the anti-Latino racism of the white mainstream society.

Jones's analysis adds an important perspective to the scholarly literature on black/Latino relations, which has tended to focus on tensions between these populations.[34] Jones concludes that Mexicans are, by and large, drawing closer to native blacks—and not drawing away. But her analysis also raises some equally compelling questions about how this process can be interpreted.

Between 2000 and 2010, for example, the US Census showed that the white identifications of the US Latino population actually increased (from 48 to 53 percent), whereas the black identifications remained roughly the same—at less than 3 percent.[35] Ironically, this increase in white identifications occurred during the same period of time that anti-Latino racism and nativist anxieties about 'illegal aliens' have been on the rise in the US. Although it may appear otherwise, these trends don't contradict Jones's thesis that Mexicans are drawing closer to the black/African American population.

A number of studies have shown that Latinos who are sensitized to the problem of racial discrimination are more likely to see themselves as racial minorities.[36] These Latinos identify as Puerto Rican, Mexican American or Dominican, with the understanding that these are nonwhite cultural identities. But as several Latino studies scholars have shown, the US racial classification system has never been receptive to these kinds of identities, which complicate the meaning of nonwhiteness.[37] The US government has a long history of trying to make the Latino population conform to the white/nonwhite binary. So the tendency of Latinos to identify as white, on one hand, or to model their racial identities after native minorities, on the other hand, is not so contrary as it first appears. These are both examples of how racialized migrants adapt their identities to the racial binary that has defined the meaning of race in the US. In many respects, this is an inevitable result of the 'assimilation' process, but it can have a debilitating side effect for some racialized migrants. It leaves no room for considering that there is a kind of marginality that leads migrants to be alienated from both poles of the US racial binary.

Chapters 15 and 16 provide two very different perspectives on this dilemma. In Chapter 15, P. Khalil Saucier examines the racial identities of male Cape Verdean youth (both migrants and native-born). He explains that most of these young men articulate their Cape Verdean identities in solidarity with the African American population and that they do not like being 'confused' with Latinos. Saucier also reflects on the ambiguous relationship between Cape Verdean culture and Latino culture. Because Cape Verde is an African nation that has been defined by a legacy of Portuguese colonization, it can lay claim to a pan-Africanist cultural politics. On the other hand, Cape Verdeans can also lay claim to a Lusophone diaspora culture that has been shaped by many of the same influences as the diaspora cultures of Latin America and the Caribbean. But in the identity politics of Saucier's respondents, 'Latino' is treated as a separate racial-cultural category from that of 'Cape Verdean'.

Saucier explains that this is mainly because his respondents found black identities to be more relevant to their experiences of race and racism in the US. He also explains that these youth don't use black identity politics to hide their Cape Verdean identities (the way that some black migrants have adopted African American 'cover up' identities[38]). But Saucier also indicates that Cape Verdean youth prefer to be seen as Americans, and that they are aware of the stigma of immigrant otherness—and want to distance themselves from it.

These observations open up some important questions. Although many Cape Verdean youth articulate their identities in opposition to whiteness, they are also distancing themselves from an immigrant otherness that is racialized in its own way. So they are, arguably, rejecting an undesirable otherness, that is specific to the racialized foreigner and different from 'American blackness', but which is not explicitly described in racial terms. It's also possible that black identities are valuable to Cape Verdean youth because there is a tacit understanding that they have more credibility, in the public sphere and especially among other minority youth, as a way of performing race and making claims about racial injustice. But this also means that experiences of racial discrimination that cannot be rendered legible through a discourse on blackness could be left 'unspoken'.

In Chapter 16, Tiffany Joseph provides a different perspective on this dilemma. Her study focuses on the identities of Brazilian migrants to the US.

Unlike Cape Verdeans, Brazilians are less likely to gravitate toward a black identity. Even so, Joseph shows that the Brazilian migrants in her study were more likely to identify as black (or white) than as Latino (when using open-ended classifications, see Table 16.1). One reason for the relative popularity of these black identifications may have to do with the racial demographics of Brazil (because Brazil is host to the largest population of African-descent persons living outside of Africa). But Joseph also demonstrates how the identifications of these migrants change as they become acculturated to the meaning of race and ethnicity in the US. She explains that the efforts of Brazilians to distance themselves from other Latinos have been shaped by their perceptions of the stigma associated with Latino otherness in the US. These sorts of maneuvers corroborate the arguments of other scholars that the Latino (and especially the Mexican) immigrant has become the focal point of anti-immigrant racism in the US.[39] They also shed light on a kind of marginality that is specific to the situation of the racialized foreigner.

The last chapter in this section situates all of these issues in a broader, historical context. In this chapter, Rachel Rubin and Jeff Melnick examine contrasting portrayals of black and immigrant racial otherness in the US popular media, and they use these depictions to shed light on the changing relationship between immigrants, racial minorities and the majority society over the course of the twentieth century. They explain how immigrants have been historically pitted in competition against native minorities in the US. But Rubin and Melnick also explain how immigrants have changed the mainstream culture, with creative interventions that have been influenced by a black cultural aesthetics. They close the chapter by recounting how Asian immigrants have been favorably compared to black populations, while being subjected to stereotypes that distinguish them from other racial minorities.

WHERE TO, BEYOND THE MARGIN?

As we cautioned earlier, this book is more concerned with describing problems than it is with formulating tidy solutions. Its main goal is to provide the reader with a richer understanding of the challenges facing migrant populations, and the challenge that migration poses for both sending and receiving nations. So it should not be surprising that it leaves the reader with more questions than it answers. It's also fitting that the book closes by posing even more questions.

In Chapter 18, Sharif Islam considers how immigration scholars can conduct research that does a better job of grappling with the marginalities explored throughout the book. He explains that immigration scholars need to spend more time reflecting on the normative framework guiding their research and insists that there is much to learn from the interdisciplinary writing on research ethics. For an example, Islam reviews some of the recent theory on decolonizing methodologies and explains how it relates to immigration research.

Islam's discussion grapples with the challenge of creating an inclusive dialogue that is sensitive to the micropolitics of interpersonal communication. He explains that it is not sufficient that research be conducted on behalf of migrant populations. Migrants should play a more active role in defining the goals of the research, and researchers should put more effort into describing migration from the vantage point of the migrant. Islam also offers some suggestions for engaging the problem of locality that was surfaced by Chapters 12 and 13. He encourages immigration researchers to explore the "shared spaces" in which migrants and natives encounter one another, and he observes that these spaces can be used to advance a discourse on locality that transforms migrant/native and citizen/noncitizen distinctions.

Although this discussion provides some refreshing insights into the dilemmas explored earlier in the book, it's just as important to consider the aporias that it opens up. The research agenda that Islam describes has to be guided by a normative commitment to inclusion, respect for difference and democratic communication. But this process also requires the participants to be open to renegotiating the moral-ethical framework that they bring to the encounter (if they are genuinely interested in validating the perspectives of others). As a result, the normative framework is transformed into a metalevel commitment to having an egalitarian discussion about how to negotiate our varied values and identities, as opposed to grounding the discussion in a predefined consensus about what these values and identities should be. This is a process in which all parties are inevitably going to be transformed in some way, but in which the terms of this transformation are mutually negotiated. There is both an integrationist and pluralistic dimension to this process, but it also differs from both of these conceptual schemas in some important ways. Differences can merge together at one point in time, while setting the stage for a new field of differences that emerge later on. And there is no clear expectation of what the final outcome will be, because the main concern is with the dynamics of the process, not the end point.

Understandably, Islam's discussion does not resolve all of the questions that it raises. He also reminds us that there is nothing especially new about the decolonizing methodologies research agenda and the normative arguments that he reviews in the course of his discussion. But he does provide some novel insights into how these questions and considerations can be connected to immigration research.

In Chapter 19 Glenn Jacobs provides a summary discussion of the book's contents and situates this discussion in the scholarly literature on globalization. He points out that globalization hasn't erased the salience of the local or of the national. As many of the book's chapters demonstrate, the desire to refortify national borders has intensified in tandem with the expansion of global migration. Jacobs also raises the question of whether a postnational paradigm of citizenship and cultural identity could mediate these tensions. He reflects on the potential limitations of postnationalism, leaving the reader with more questions to ponder. Does postnationalism open up a new horizon that offers a way out of the quagmire of migrant marginality? Or does it create yet another social and discursive space, in which the hazards of marginality will resurface in a new form? Both of these possibilities are lurking within the discourse on postnationalism. In any event, Jacobs shows that, like so many of the other topics explored in this book, the most valuable thing about postnationalism is the kind of conversation that it opens up.

NOTES

1. For some examples of this broad and diverse body of inquiry see: Jafari Allen, "Black/Queer/Diaspora at the Current Conjuncture," *GLQ: A Journal of Lesbian and Gay Studies* 18, no. 2–3 (2012): 211–248; Robin Cohen, *Migration and Its Enemies: Global Capital, Migrant Labor and the Nation-State* (Abingdon, UK: Ashgate, 2006); Ambreen Hai, "Border Work, Border Trouble: Postcolonial Feminism and the Ayah in Bapsi Sidhwa's Cracking India," *MFS Modern Fiction Studies* 46, no. 2 (2000): 379–426; Hastings Donnan and Thomas Wilson, *Borders: Frontiers of Identity, Nation and State* (Oxford: Berg, 1999); David Johnson and Scott Michaelson, eds., *Border Theory: The Limits of Cultural Politics* (Minneapolis: University of Minnesota Press, 1997); Shahram Kosravi, *"Illegal" Traveller: An Auto-Ethnography of Borders* (Basingstoke, UK: Palgrave MacMillan, 2010); Jonathon Moses, *International Migration: Globalization's Last Frontier* (London: Zed Books, 2006); and Felicity Schaeffer-Grabiel, "Flexible Technologies of Subjectivity and Mobility across the Americas," *American Quarterly* 58, no. 3 (2006): 891–914.
2. Excerpted from the title of Reitz's cross-national study of immigrant integration. Jeffrey Reitz, *Warmth of the Welcome: The Social Causes of Economic Success for Immigrants in Different Cities and Nations* (Toronto: Toronto University Press, 1999).
3. These spaces are a central focus of 'classical era' assimilation theory and cultural pluralist theory, which continue to have a marked influence on immigration studies (reemerging today through theories of transnational migrant communities and ethnic diaspora). For various accounts see Richard Alba and Victor Nee, *Remaking the American Mainstream: Assimilation and Contemporary Immigration* (Cambridge, MA: Harvard University Press, 2003); Peter Kivisto, ed., *Incorporating Diversity: Rethinking Assimilation in a Multicultural Age* (London: Paradigm, 2005); and Ewa Morawska, *Sociology of Immigration: (Re)making Multifaceted America* (Basingstoke: Palgrave Macmillan, 2009).
4. For a theoretical and empirical introduction to these enforcement practices, see the following edited volumes: David Brotherton and Philip Kretsedemas, eds., *Keeping Out the Other: A Critical Introduction to Immigration Enforcement Today* (New York: Columbia University Press, 2008), and Nicholas De Genova and Nathalie Peutz, *The Deportation Regime: Sovereignty, Space and the Freedom of Movement* (Durham: Duke University Press, 2010).

5. This shouldn't be surprising because workforce replenishment is one of the principal aims of immigrant recruitment. There is a long-standing debate over the 'displacement effect' that migrants have on native labor. Although many studies have concluded that this effect is not very large and is off-set by the positive economic contributions of migrant populations, there is also evidence that migrants can have a negative impact on wage levels and employment for lower-skilled native workers. See Timothy Hatton and Jeffrey Williamson, *Global Migration and the World Economy: Two Centuries of Policy and Performance* (Cambridge, MA: MIT, 2008), 289–312.

6. Margaret Somers has argued that the problem of de facto statelessness has become a growing problem for the native-born citizenry, and that reactionary populist movements that utilize a discourse on national belonging (which can be mobilized against immigrants) are responding, in part, to the evisceration of their own legal, political and social rights. Margaret Somers, *Genealogies of Citizenship: Markets, Statelessness, and the Right to Have Rights* (Cambridge: Cambridge University Press, 2008), 118–144.

7. Robert Park's writing made a more direct connection between migration and marginality than Simmel, but his understanding of the dynamics of social change was largely derived from Simmel (who Park studied under for several years in Berlin). Park's thesis on the marginal man—which offered some compelling insights into how marginal conditions can be understood as threshold states that are on the frontiers of progressive social change—eventually fell out of favor with social theorists. This is largely because subsequent interpretations of Park's theory of marginality became mired in essentializing notions of race difference and personality traits (themes that also appeared in Park's writing, although he warned about the dangers of reducing marginality to a "social type"). See Robert Park, "Human Migration and the Marginal Man," *American Journal of Sociology* 33, no. 6 (1928): 881–893; *Race and Culture* (Glencoe: Free Press, 1950), v–x and 372–376; and Georg Simmel, "The Stranger," *Georg Simmel on Individuality and Social Forms* (1908; Chicago: University of Chicago Press, 1971), 143–149. Also see Philip Kretsedemas, *The Immigration Crucible: Transforming Race, Nation and the Limits of the Law* (New York: Columbia University Press, 2012), 117–134.

8. This is a theme in Deleuze's writing that is closely related to his understanding of the creation of new concepts. See Gilles Deleuze and Felix Guattari, *What Is Philosophy?* (New York: Columbia University Press, 1994), 1–34. For a more involved discussion of how Deleuze and Guattari's writing can be applied to the analysis of migrant marginalities, see Philip Kretsedemas, *Migrants and Race in the US: Territorial Racism and the Alien/Outside* (New York: Routledge, 2013).

9. For some examples, see: Stephen Castles, "Migration and Community Formation under Conditions of Globalization," *International Migration Review* 36, no. 4 (2002): 1143–1168; Nina Glick Schiller, Linda Basch and Cristina Szanton Blanc, "From Immigrant to Transmigrant: Theorizing Transnational Migration," *Anthropological Quarterly* 68, no. 1 (1995): 48–63; and Robert Smith, "Migrant Membership as an Instituted Process: Transnationalization, the State and the Extra-Territorial Conduct of Mexican Politics," *International Migration Review* 37, no. 2 (2003): 297–343.

10. William Connolly, *Pluralism* (Durham: Duke University Press, 2005), and Bhikhu Parekh, *Rethinking Multiculturalism: Cultural Diversity and Political Theory* (Cambridge, MA: Harvard University Press, 2002).

11. James Ridgeway, "Oslo Shooting: Read Anders Behring Breivik's Internet Comments Here," *Mother Jones*, July 23, 2011, accessed December 7, 2012: http://www.motherjones.com/politics/2011/07/anders-behring-breiviks-online-

comments; Matt Pearce, "Sikh Temple gunman played in supremacist rock band called End Apathy," *LA Times*, August 6, 2012, accessed December 7, 2012: http://www.latimes.com/news/nation/nationnow/la-na-nn-sikh-temple-gunman-end-apathy-20120806,0,7628363.story.

12. For various accounts see Antje Ellerman, *States against Migrants: Deportation in Germany and the United States* (Cambridge: Cambridge University Press, 2007); Wayne Cornelius, Takeyuki Tsuda, Philip Martin and James Hollifield, eds., *Controlling Immigration: A Global Perspective* (Stanford: Stanford University Press, 2004); De Genova and Peutz, *Deportation Regime*; and Kretsedemas, *Immigration Crucible*.

13. Wayne Cornelius and Takeyuki Tsuda, "Controlling Immigration: The Limits of Government Intervention," in *Controlling Immigration: A Global Perspective*, ed. Wayne Cornelius et al. (Stanford: Stanford University Press, 2004), 3–50.

14. Hatton and Williamson have observed that the relationship between global trade and migration in the current era is the inverse of what it was in the late nineteenth century (in which an era of open migration and protective economic measures has been displaced by a new concern for expanding global trade and controlling migration flows; Hatton and Williamson, *Global Migration and the World Economy*, 393–404). But they also observe that immigration policy has become more restrictive, in part because it is much easier for people to migrate today than in the nineteenth century. In this regard, the restrictive emphasis of present-day immigration policy is better understood as an attempt to control an expanding migrant flow, leading to the paradoxical situation in which immigration controls and migration flows have expanded in tandem with one another. The US is a good case in point. From the late 1980s onward, US migration flows returned to peak levels that had not been seen since the 'boom era' of the 1890s and 1910s (and it has sustained these highs, more consistently and for a longer period of time). Meanwhile, the flow of 'nonimmigrants' or temporary visitors has grown exponentially—and now outpaces the flow of 'regular' immigrants (who are recruited as long-term residents) by over thirty to one. For a detailed discussion see Philip Kretsedemas, "The Limits of Control: Neoliberal Priorities and the US Nonimmigrant Flow," *International Migration* 50, no. s1 (2012): e1–18, accessed April 9, 2013, http://onlinelibrary.wiley.com/doi/10.1111/j.1468–2435.2011.00696.x/full, and Douglas Massey and Katherine Bartley, "The Changing Legal Status Distribution of Immigrants: A Caution," *International Migration Review* 39, no. 2 (2005): 469–484.

15. See James Hollifield, "The Emerging Migration State," *International Migration Review* 38, no. 3 (2004): 885–912, and Christian Joppke, "Why Liberal States Accept Unwanted Migration" *World Politics* 50, no. 2 (1998): 266–293.

16. These arguments all take a critical, political-economy approach to the study of immigration policy—but they are also rather diverse in their own right. Saskia Sassen, who is one of the most influential of these theorists, has produced explanations that have been informed, at different points in time, by world systems theory and also by post-Marxist complexity theory. See Saskia Sassen-Koob, "Towards a Conceptualization of Immigrant Labor," *Social Problems* 29, no. 1 (1981): 65–85, and idem, *Territory, Authority, Rights: From Medieval to Global Assemblages* (Princeton, NJ: Princeton University Press, 2008), 277–322. There are other explanations of immigration policy that take a Foucauldian approach to the analysis of neoliberalism and the control of migrant labor. See Mark Duffield, "Racism, Migration

and Development," *Progress in Development Studies* 6, no. 1 (2006): 68–79; Jonathan Inda, *Targeting Immigrants: Government, Technology, and Ethics* (New York: Wiley-Blackwell, 2005); and Philip Kretsedemas, "Immigration Enforcement and the Complication of National Sovereignty: Understanding Immigration Enforcement as an Exercise in Neoliberal Governance," *American Quarterly* 60, no. 3 (2008): 553–573.

17. Brian Fry has produced one of the few typological summaries of theories on nativism. The kinds of sentiments that I have just described are most relevant to the "nationalism" and "prejudice" models of nativism described by Fry. See Brian Fry, *Nativism and Immigration: Regulating the American Dream* (New York: LFB Scholarly, 2006), 9–34. Robert Chang's theory of nativistic racism provides another very compelling and widely influential account of these exclusionary anti-immigrant sentiments. See Robert Chang, *Disoriented: Asian Americans, Law and the Nation-State* (New York: NYU Press, 1999). For other perspectives see Leo Chavez, *The Latino Threat* (Stanford: Stanford University Press, 2009); Bill Hing, *Defining America through Immigration Policy* (Philadelphia: Temple University Press, 2003); Lisa Lowe, *Immigrant Acts: On Asian Americans and Cultural Politics* (Durham: Duke University Press, 1996); and Maggie Ibrahim, "The Securitization of Migration: A Racial Discourse," *International Migration* 43, no. 5 (2006): 163–187.

18. Etienne Balibar, "Is There a Neo-racism?" in *Race, Nation, Class: Ambiguous Identities*, ed. E. Balibar and I. Wallerstein (New York: Verso, 1991), 17–28. But there are other permutations of anti-immigrant racism that are informed by a racialized geopolitical imaginary, more so than the racialization of cultural difference. See Kretsedemas, *Migrants and Race in the US*.

19. Michael Welch and Liza Schuster, "Detention of Asylum Seekers in the UK and US: Deciphering Noisy and Quiet Constructions," *Punishment and Society* 7, no. 4 (2005): 397–417.

20. Jonathan Inda's discussion of how immigration enforcement deploys a neoliberal discourse on "prudentialism" provides a broader conceptual framework for understanding these color-blind tendencies. See Inda, *Targeting Immigrants*. Also see Robin Dale Jacobson, *The New Nativism: Proposition 187 and the Debate over Immigration* (Minneapolis: University of Minnesota Press, 2008).

21. Hing, *Defining America through Immigration Policy*, and Ibrahim, "Securitization of Migration."

22. Seyla Benhabib and Judith Resnik, eds., *Migrations and Mobilities: Citizenship, Borders and Gender* (New York: NYU Press, 2009); Eleonore Kofman, "Female 'Birds of Passage' a Decade Later: Gender and Immigration in the European Union," *International Migration Review* 33, no. 2 (1999): 269–299; and Saskia Sassen-Koob, "Notes on the Incorporation of Third World Women into Wage-Labor through Immigration and Off-Shore Production," *International Migration Review* 18, no. 4 (1984): 1144–1167.

23. As many feminist scholars have observed, liberal discourses on individuality, economic self-sufficiency and political agency reformulated a much older set of patriarchal and masculinized distinctions that have historically informed the Western discourse on citizenship and public life. See Nancy Fraser and Linda Gordon, "Contrast versus Charity: Why Is There No Social Citizenship in the United States?," in *The Citizenship Debates*, ed. Gerson Shafir (Minneapolis: University of Minnesota Press), 113–130, and Carole Pateman, *The Disorder of Women: Democracy, Feminism and Political Theory* (Stanford: Stanford University Press, 1990).

24. Cinzia Solari, "Prostitutes' and 'Defectors': Gendered Migration and the Ukrainian State" (paper presented at the annual meeting of the American Sociological Association, Atlanta, August 2010). Solari also briefly touches on this issue in Cinzia Solari, "Resource Drain vs. Constitutive Circularity: Comparing the Gendered Effects of Post-Soviet Migration Patterns in Ukraine," *Anthropology of East Europe Review* 28 (2010): 215–238.

25. Connie Oxford, "Protectors and Victims in the Gender Regime of Asylum," *NWSA Journal*, 17, no. 3 (2005): 18–38, and Patricia Seith, "Escaping Domestic Violence: Asylum as a Means of Protection for Battered Women," *Columbia Law Review* 97, no. 6 (1997): 1804–1843.

26. In many European nations, blackness has become associated with the most undesirable kind of immigrant (typified by public outrage over asylum seekers who 'drain' pubic resources). But blackness has also become a conspicuous symbol of a more general kind of racial otherness that has been introduced to the nation by recent migration flows. For various accounts see Gilroy, *Ain't No Black in the Union Jack*; Frances Henry and Carol Tator, eds., *The Colour of Democracy: Racism in Canadian Society*, 4th ed. (Toronto: Nelson-Thomson, 2004); Manuelo Sanches, Fernando Clara, Joao Duarte and Leonor Martins, eds., *Europe in Black and White: Immigration, Race and Identity in the "Old Continent"* (Bristol: Intellect, 2010); and Welch and Schuster, "Detention of Asylum Seekers in the UK and US."

27. For one example of this line of argument see Sassen-Koob, "Towards a Conceptualization of Immigrant Labor."

28. Some of the earliest examples of this tendency emerged in the legal-juridical sphere. One example is the body of jurisprudence that held that the antidiscrimination protections of the 14th amendment did not apply to Latinos and Asians (as well as "mixed race" persons); another is the amendment to the 1875 Naturalization Act that allowed black minorities to become citizens, but initially neglected to extend this same right to Chinese and Mexican persons. These trends and their manifestations within popular media and political discourse are discussed in more depth in Kretsedemas, *Migrants and Race in the US*. See also, Martha Menchaca, *Recovering History, Constructing Race: The Indian, Black and White Roots of Mexican Americans* (Austin: University of Texas Press, 2001), 279–285.

29. For some examples see Peter Brimelow, *Alien Nation: Commonsense about America's Immigration Disaster* (New York: Harper Perennial, 1996), 63–86 and 173–175; Julianne Hing, "Rep. Cleaver: GOP Manufactures Black-Brown Tensions," *Colorlines News for Action*, Mar. 2, 2011, accessed Jan. 4, 2012, http://colorlines.com/archives/2011/03/rep_cleaver_gop_manufacturing_black-brown_tension_for_anti-immigrant_policies.html; Elahe Izade, "Buchanan on How to Lower Black Unemployment," DC Centric: Race, Class, the District, Oct. 25, 2011, accessed Jan. 4, 2012, http://dcentric.wamu.org/2011/10/pat-buchanan-on-how-to-lower-black-unemployment/; Mark Krikorian, "Get Serious: More Immigrants Means Fewer Jobs for Blacks," *Urban League Opportunity Journal*, Summer 2007, accessed Jan. 5, 2012, http://www.cis.org/node/452; Rob Sobhani, "A Plan to Boost Black Unemployment: We Must Stem the Tide of Immigration," Philly.com, Dec. 8, 2011, accessed Jan. 5, 2012, http://articles.philly.com/2011–12–08/news/30490807_1_illegal-immigrants-immigration-policies-immigration-system; and Charlotte Williams, "African Americans Targeted by Another Anti-immigrant Front Group," *Imagine 2050*, Oct. 3, 2011, accessed Jan. 4, 2012, http://imagine2050.newcomm.org/2011/10/03/african-americans-targeted-by-another-anti-immigrant-front-group/.

30. For some examples see Moon-Kie Jung, "The Racial Unconscious of Assimilation Theory," *Du Bois Review* 6, no. 2 (2009): 375–395; Michael Omi and Howard Winant, *Racial Formation in the United States: From the 1960s to the 1990s* (New York: Routledge, 1994), 14–23; and David Roediger, *Working toward Whiteness: How America's Immigrants Became White: The Strange Journey from Ellis Island to the Suburbs* (New York: Basic Books, 2006).

31. Alejandro Portes and Min Zhou, "The New Second Generation: Segmented Assimilation and Its Variants," *Annals of the American Academy of Political and Social Science* 530 (1993): 74–96, and Herbert Gans, "Second-Generation Decline: Scenarios for the Economic and Ethnic Futures of the Post-1965 American Immigrants," *Ethnic and Racial Studies* 15, no. 2 (1992): 174–192.

32. Jose Itzigsohn and Carlos Dore-Cabral, "Competing Identities? Race, Ethnicity and Panethnicity among Dominicans in the US," *Sociological Forum* 15, no. 2 (2000): 225–247; Katherine Neckerman, P. Carter and J. Lee, "Segmented Assimilation and Minority Cultures of Mobility," *Ethnic and Racial Studies* 22 (1999): 945–965; and Tekle Woldemikael, "A Case Study of Race Consciousness among Haitian Immigrants," *Journal of Black Studies* 20 (1989): 224–239.

33. See Jung, "Racial Unconscious of Assimilation Theory," and Silvio Torres-Saillant, "The Tribulations of Blackness: Stages in Dominican Racial Identity," *Callaloo* 23, no. 3 (2000): 1086–1111.

34. For two examples, see Tatcho Mindiola, Yolanda Flores Niemann and Nestor Rodriguez, eds., *Black-Brown Relations and Stereotypes* (Austin: University of Texas Press, 2003), and Nicolas Vaca, *Presumed Alliance: The Unspoken Conflict between Latinos and Blacks and What It Means for America* (New York: Harper Collins, 2004).

35. Sharon Ennis, Merarys Rios-Albert and Nora Vargas, *The Hispanic Population, 2010* (Washington, DC: US Census Bureau, 2011), accessed April 9, 2013, http://www.census.gov/prod/cen2010/briefs/c2010br-04.pdf, and Betsy Guzman, *The Hispanic Population Census 2000 Brief* (Washington, DC: US Census Bureau, 2001), accessed May 19, 2012, http://www.census.gov/prod/2001pubs/c2kbr01-3.pdf.

36. Much of the research on US Latino identity has observed that these identities operate at the nexus of race, ethnicity and culture; they are not simply one or the other. Adrián Félix, "New Americans or Diasporic Nationalists? Mexican Migrant Responses to Naturalization and Implications for Political Participation," *American Quarterly* 60, no. 3 (2008): 601–624; Tanya Golash-Boza, "Dropping the Hyphen? Becoming Latino(a)-American through Racialized Assimilation," *Social Forces* 85, no. 1 (2006): 27–55; Itzigsohn and Dore-Cabral, "Competing Identities?"; Nancy Landale and Salvatore Oropesa, "White, Black or Puerto Rican?" *Social Forces* 81, no. 1 (2004): 231–254; and Clara Rodriguez and Hector Cordero-Guzman, "Placing Race in Context," *Ethnic and Racial Studies* 15, no. 4 (1992): 523–542.

37. See Juan Perea, "The Black/White Paradigm of Race: The 'Normal' Science of American Racial Thought," *California Law Review* 85, no. 5 (1997): 1213–1258, and Clara Rodriguez, *Changing Race: Latinos, the Census and the History of Ethnicity in the United States* (New York: NYU Press, 2000). But the US Census also appears to be veering away from this historic tendency. In August 2012 it announced its intentions to convert "Hispanic" back into a "race-specific" category for the 2020 Census (which is how it was treated prior to 1980). This means that "Hispanic" will be treated as a

distinct racial-ethnic identification, instead of being a multiracial ethnic identification (which allows Hispanics to identify as white, black or some other race). Hope Yen, "Census Bureau Proposes Changes: Hispanics as Distinct Category and Use of Term 'Negro,'" *Huffington Post*, Aug. 9, 2012, accessed Nov. 11, 2012, http://www.huffingtonpost.com/2012/08/09/census-bureau-changes-race-hispanics-negro_n_1760467.html.

38. See Alex Stepick, *Pride against Prejudice: Haitians in the United States* (New York: Allyn and Bacon, 1998), 1–15.

39. See Leo Chavez, *The Latino Threat: Constructing Immigrants, Citizens, and the Nation* (Stanford: Stanford University Press, 2008).

Part I

Testing the Limits
of Multiculturalism

2 Challenging Narratives on Diversity and Immigration in Portugal

The (De)Politicization of Colonialism and Racism

Marta Araújo

[In the early 2000s] immigration issues were not a priority in the research agenda of academics and little of that knowledge was being applied to public policies. We were receiving a large flow of Ukrainians, Brazilians and others; we had had a radical change of conditions and of the social groups of immigration. It was necessary to study and understand this immigration, which no longer was just the traditional coming of Africans. It was also urgent to understand how we, Portuguese, were to rethink ourselves in the face of this reality. . . . I think the Observatory on Immigration would make a good service if it could further deepen the question of intercultural dialogue of which Portugal has been a pioneer, and could again be, in the sense of opening a new phase of that dialogue, because that is the future of humanity. (Roberto Carneiro, Director of the Observatory on Immigration)[1]

In this chapter, I argue that there are a number of problematic aspects in contemporary narratives on immigration and diversity in Portugal—mostly in politics, but which are also being circulated and legitimated by academic discourse. First, drawing on an assumed Portuguese *specificity* and especially on Gilberto Freyre's idea of Lusotropicalism, these narratives depoliticize colonialism in order to attest a national historical *vocation* for interculturality, thus evading racism. Second, they posit Portugal as a homogenous-turned-heterogeneous country due to globalization, subsuming (post)colonial dynamics into the push-and-pull logic of contemporary immigration flows, and obscuring colonial legacies in contemporary sociopolitical constructions of 'race'. Third, they contribute to the self-assuring idea of the country as modern and developed, by overemphasizing immigration and downplaying emigration in Portuguese society. Finally, they imply a causal relationship between recent demographic change and institutional response, implicitly seeing the visibilization of *difference* as a necessarily positive—and sufficient—achievement.

After presenting the main contours of these hegemonic narratives, I provide some critical reflections that are informed by my experience as a researcher who is engaged in understanding the production, maintenance and challenges to racism in education. Education is a particularly interesting context for analysis as many institutional responses to cultural diversity and collective struggles for equality have been rehearsed therein.[2] I draw on three research projects in which I have been recently involved: a) a postdoctoral project (2003–2007)[3] exploring the schooling of racially and ethnically marked[4] students in a context seen as homogeneous; b) collaborative research (2008–2012)[5] on Eurocentrism in Portuguese history textbooks—seeing these at the intersection of broader political, social and cultural debates; and c) a comparative project on the semantics of racism and anti-racism in civil society organisations, public institutions and policies in different European contexts (2010–2013)[6], with an empirical focus on employment and education.

DEPLOYING MAINSTREAM NARRATIVES ON IMMIGRATION AND DIVERSITY

Mainstream accounts of diversity and immigration in Portugal advance narratives that are used to legitimate contemporary policy interventions. In this section, I discuss crucial features of these mainstream accounts, which have been advanced within the social sciences, political debates and the realm of policy making. In the subsequent sections I explore these features in more detail and consider their impact for the debate on (anti-)racism—with a focus on education.

From the 1990s, "Portugal ceased to be a traditional country of emigration and became a country of immigration and a host country for foreign citizens looking for better standards of living."[7] These demographic changes in Portuguese society were accompanied by the creation of institutional bodies, such as the *Secretariat for the Coordination of Multicultural Education Programs* in 1991, the figure of the *High Commissioner for Immigration and Ethnic Minorities* in 1996, the *High Commissariat* in 2002 and the *Observatory on Immigration* in 2003. In the last two decades, new institutional responses have been formulated to address education for a diverse society, most notably *interculturality*—seen as overcoming the shortcomings of *multicultural education*, common in Anglophone societies: "Whereas the multicultural approach fosters a preservation of identities and often places minority groups in a 'ghetto-situation', the intercultural approach emphasizes personal enrichment due to the exchange of experiences and knowledge with others."[8] These national-led initiatives have been rehearsed mainly in the Lisbon metropolitan area (where the vast majority of the foreign population is located[9]), and especially with 'youth at risk'. Locally, schools have welcomed *new* students and started showing a concern to include *all*. Diversity is now celebrated in festivals and other special events, enabling ethnically marked students to enhance their *self-esteem*; teachers provide additional support to help them with *their language difficulties.* Schooling in Portugal has changed and has new democratic concerns. Although *still* lagging behind many European policies and practices, the gap is narrowing. According to the *experts*, Portugal provides a "model of good practice,"[10] being rated second in the 2007 and 2011 *Migrant Integration Policy Index* (MIPEX),[11] and the "most generous" country in an international study by the United Nations in 2009.[12] The *success* of 'integration' policies in Portugal can be explained, according to official and academic authorities, by the history of *soft* colonialism and the *miscegenation of multiple cultural traditions* and cultures.[13] Racism is thus a marginal phenomenon:[14] "the Portuguese are in favor of equal civic rights and a multicultural society."[15]

Portugal is, nowadays, a diversified and a modern, *multicultural* country. Youngsters dance to the sound of *kuduro* and people learn *capoeira*; in the cinema. New *Lisboners* are exhibited. Supermarkets and restaurants sell *ethnic* food. *African* prints are fashionable. Diversity is now literally *consumed*.[16] And yet, like commonly stated, "not too spicy" as "around here, people don't like odd stuff." Thus, in reality there is a domesticated fusion of *ethnic* sounds to make them more sophisticated, *exotic* flavors conveniently shelved in specific supermarket areas, and Portuguese Roma pupils occasionally *contained* in separate classrooms under the pretext of their special educational needs and cultural idiosyncrasies.[17]

CHANGING THE NARRATIVE AND ENLARGING THE RESEARCH AGENDA

The examples just described are aspects of common narratives that depict Portugal as a nation *at ease* with difference. These narratives, with their nuances and changing contours, have emerged from discourses that are not value-free. Yet the naturalization and depoliticization[18] of many of the assumptions on which it rests make it difficult to hold a meaningful debate on (anti-)racism in political and academic discussions. I thus argue that more critical and sophisticated analyses of ethno-racial equality need to broaden the debate and take into account its historical, political and contextual dimensions. In the remainder of this chapter I examine the intertwined aspects that are being naturalized or concealed by such narratives.

Rewriting the Nation: Colonial History, Power and Racism

In Portugal, political discourse on immigration and diversity is obscuring the centrality of colonialism in ideological constructions of 'race'. The official rhetoric centered on interculturality (re)produces a *myth of tolerant conviviality*, whereby the history of Portuguese colonialism becomes an available symbolic resource to demonstrate the tolerant character of the nation, while being disallowed to debate contemporary racism. While it is significant that colonialism—key to the proliferation of pseudoscientific racial ideologies—is publicly evoked to attest to the tolerant character of the Portuguese nation,[19] it should be noted that many other societies have their own myths of tolerance (e.g., US 'color-blindness', British 'fairness', Brazilian 'racial democracy').

This myth of colonial conviviality became politically relevant in Portugal via the appropriation, throughout the 1950s, of Gilberto Freyre's work on Lusotropicalism,[20] which tried to demonstrate the exceptionality of Portuguese *benevolent* colonialism. Freyre believed that the Portuguese were open to biological miscegenation and cultural interpenetration with people from the tropics, which would lead to the creation of harmoniously integrated multiracial societies.[21] He explained this aptitude as resulting from the miscegenated nature of *the Portuguese people*, following the long history of *contact* with Muslims and Jews in the Iberian Peninsula, in precolonial times.

In the 1930s and 1940s, Freyre's ideas on miscegenation met strong resistance in Portugal. The idea of biological miscegenation was not appropriated officially. The mixing of different 'races' was linked to ideas of 'degeneration', thus jeopardizing an imperial project strongly anchored in 'race'.[22] It was in the 1950s—in the context of struggles by national liberation movements and international pressure from the United Nations to decolonize—that Lusotropicalism became politically significant in Portugal. The dictator Salazar, partially appropriating Freyre's ideas (with his approval), advertised the idea that Portugal was a harmonious multicontinental and multiracial nation so as to render decolonization uncalled-for.[23]

Although Freyre's ideas were seen as innovative, because they decoupled 'race' from culture and interrupted social Darwinist thought,[24] other bodies of political discourse and practices of colonial domination were revealing of the prevailing racial asymmetries in power.[25] Salazar's *New State* regime continued to affirm the supremacy of European civilization and the positioning of black Africans as inferior.[26] By hierarchically categorizing the population of Portugal's then multicontinental territory by 'race,' it endlessly postponed the possibility of racially marked populations becoming truly *assimilated*.[27] Lusotropicalism was therefore more an aspiration than an accurate depiction of Portuguese colonial *race relations*.[28]

Lusotropicalism was not a new idea, being anchored in nineteenth-century views on national identity that emphasized the *softness of character* and the *adventurous spirit* of the Portuguese.[29] The support that these ideas received from the elites of the right and left—and the capability of an authoritarian regime to diffuse them, namely through education—helps to explain how they endured after the restoration of democracy and the independencies in the mid-1970s. In contemporary discourse, two main ideas seem to persist: 1) a national identity strongly anchored in Portugal's imperial past and in the supposed exceptionality of its history of 'expansion'; and 2) the universalistic values of Portuguese society, seen as less racist than other European societies.

Significantly, it is within the rhetoric on interculturality that the discursive field of Lusotropicalism seems to be reactivated. Adriano Moreira,[30] who was a key actor both in Salazar's 'overseas'/colonial policies in the early 1960s and in the contemporary official endorsement of Lusotropicalism stated, "unexpectedly, the Gilbertian problematic that was defined around the intervention of the Europeans in the tropics seems now to be reedited due to the presence of the tropics in the European territory."[31] This official narrative has been visible at least since the 1990s, as evident in the preface to the legislation that created the *Secretariat for the Coordination of Multicultural Education Programs*:

> Portuguese culture, distinguished for its universalism and its awareness thereof and for its long links with other cultures which, over the centuries, have made it welcome diversity, comprehend differences and great particularity with open arms, is an open and varied culture enriched by the diffusion of a people which has sought overseas a further dimension to its identity. Today, Portugal is proud to be the chance product of a mysterious alchemy which found in the sea, that great unknown, its ideal medium and its path to adventure.[32]

Serving a political agenda that reinforces the idea of Portugal as a *tolerant* country, this narrative has a wide-reaching significance, including in school contexts:

> . . . integration is easy . . . We . . . We have that advantage and I tell them [the students] that so that they can see . . . Which were the countries that integrated black people like Portugal did? . . . So, the Portuguese may have some flaws. Weren't there any racist Portuguese, *aren't* there? Fine. Weren't there any Portuguese who enslaved black people, who treated them badly? I have no doubt! I met some. But no one gets along with any other race like the Portuguese do (Teacher 1, School 1)

In official discourses on immigration and diversity, history has recently started being more systematically mobilized to promote a sanitized account of Portugal's colonial past that consecrates its *pioneering* role in the management of diversity. The contemporary renarration of colonialism and empire is not specific to the Portuguese case. For instance, Anne-Marie Fortier explores how, in the New Labor era of the mid-2000s, the refusal of the British government to address its legacy of imperialism was linked to the forging of a "multicultural nationalism, that is, the reworking of the nation as inherently multicultural." Accordingly, Fortier proposes that there was "a shift away from linear narratives of nations moving *from* monoculture and exclusivity *to* multiculture and inclusivity, in favor of a narrative that posits multiculture and diversity at the heart of the nationalistic project."[33] Fortier's "multicultural nationalism" helps to elucidate how history is being deployed to legitimate certain national heritages and destinies across different contexts.

In a similar fashion, in the last decade we have witnessed the consolidation of a *historicized* narrative that reconstructs the Portuguese nationalistic project through the idea that friendly interracial/intercultural coexistence took place both in the colonies and in the metropolis, and attests to a national *vocation* for interculturality. This is evident, for instance, in the rationale for a book series launched by the *High Commissariat for Immigration and Intercultural Dialogue* entitled *Intercultural Portugal*: "History can have a crucial role in the projection envisaged for the future of a society marked by the richness of cultural diversity."[34] The first volume, *Interculturality in Portuguese Expansion: 15 to 18th Centuries*, presents a historical narrative that shows the presumed success of Portuguese society in managing cultural *contact* with Others (highlighting as exemplary the *civilizatory missions* in Eastern Asia). The account is depoliticized in such a way that slavery—a paradigmatic illustration of the operation of power through the deployment of racial categories—is framed as "mother of many intercultural societies."[35] Consider the following extract:

The social status and the economy of slaves were so similar to those of poor and free men from Lisbon that the interaction between these two groups was necessarily very close (Saunders, 1994: 198). Far from any color prejudice, workers in Ribeira, free whites and black slaves used to sit all together at the same table to eat. This fraternal conviviality, born of a labor held under conditions of equality, is documented since the sixteenth century, and lasted until the nineteenth century (Tinhorão, 1988: 118).[36]

> While attempting to find examples that demonstrate racial conviviality (proving interculturality), this account sanitizes and legitimates the colonial system of slavery based along racial lines (disproving racism). Accordingly, interculturality is historicized, but not racism. Rather than being seen as embedded in the colonial project, racism is reduced to "color prejudice." Therefore, we can argue that history has become an official resource, helping to consecrate the privilege of a *specific* national community (and its historical narratives),[37] while making illegitimate and competing political claims. This is particularly evident in the retractions made by those in positions of power while debating the legacies of slavery and racism, or in the refusal of the Portuguese state to recognize the Roma as a *national* minority (a population that has been residing in the territory for at least five centuries).

Evading 'Race' in Presentist Accounts on Immigration and Education

A second aspect of these hegemonic narratives that requires closer inspection and debate is one that posits Portugal as having been suddenly transformed from a homogenous into a heterogeneous nation, as a result of contemporary globalization. This narrative rests on the assumption of the *presumed* homogeneity[38] of the national population.

Portugal has been constructed through political and academic discourse as one of Europe's first nation-states, with ancient and stable borders: the perfect textbook example of the nation as the natural coincidence of a territory, a community and a culture.[39] These statements have often sustained the idea of national homogeneity while evading how such homogeneity was achieved, managed and policed. Any process of imposing national homogeneity entails violence, however symbolic. Only through the *invisibilization of violence* can presumed homogeneity be reinforced. This is particularly evident in education, most notably in history curricula and textbooks.[40] The naturalization of a foundational white, Christian, national 'we' goes hand in hand with the invisibilization of the violent governance of Others through death, expulsion, exploitation or exclusion (e.g., the Muslims, the Jews, the Roma or the black enslaved). This narrative, which excludes Others from the national project while implicitly naturalizing the privilege of a foundational 'we', fails to critically engage with *securitization*—initially focused on the national territory, but now transposed to national identity.[41] This results in commonsense views of a stable white, Christian, national identity under the threat of external pressures—that is, immigration as a new global phenomenon that suddenly transformed homogeneous countries into heterogeneous ones, causing national (white) citizens to react—sometimes with hostility—to *difference*. This thinking pervades much research and many policy initiatives on immigration and racism in Europe.[42]

Most contemporary accounts of immigration are heavily influenced by dehistoricized globalization theories. They tend to offer a presentist analysis, in which the past has the span of a few decades, making postcolonial dynamics irrelevant and sidelining considerations of 'race' and racism. In Portugal, for instance, most official accounts of immigration take the early 1990s as a key moment in contemporary immigration. These accounts decouple migration from the history of colonialism and subsume it into an economic logic of "push and pull factors."[43]

Much contemporary work that operates within this framework fails to consider that twentieth-century migrations into the metropolitan territory started to become noticeable in the late 1960s, when workers were recruited from the Cape Verdean archipelago to fill the demand for labor created by white Portuguese emigration and also by white Portugese recruitment to the ongoing wars against national liberation movements in Angola, Guinea-Bissau and Mozambique. The inward movement of people from several areas of Africa, which had been constructed as part of the Portuguese nation during the colonial era, was intensified with the end of formal colonial administration in the mid-1970s. While nationality law became significantly more restrictive from 1981, espousing a *jus sanguinis* rationale—that denied Portuguese citizenship to many youth who were born in the national territory—immigration from the former African colonies continued to increase throughout the 1980s and 1990s. In 1999, these African migrant flows still represented almost half of the total *foreign* population of Portugal[44]—a figure that excludes people from postcolonial populations who obtained citizenship.

It is true that the dynamics of Portugese immigration changed in the 1990s. During this time the geographic origins of Portugese immigrants became more diversified. This increase in immigration remained generally steady until the mid-2000s.[45] After this time, immigration from Portugal's former African colonies became statistically less significant, mainly due to an increase in immigrants from the former Soviet bloc. However, the current emigration of Eastern Europeans from Portugal and the slowing down of immigration into Portugal[46]—effects of the so-called contemporary *economic crisis*—illustrate the persisting significance of the postcolonial contexts that are still shaping Portugese immigration, and the persisting significance of the historical processes and cultural formations that are associated with these postcolonial contexts[47]

In official narratives, although postcolonial (*postindependence*) migration might be acknowledged, it is not sufficiently discussed and debated. This lack of discussion is paving the way to the renarration of Portugal as a country where immigration is recent and divorced from its colonial past. The following example by the *European Monitoring Centre on Racism and Xenophobia* is illustrative:

> Several EU Member States have had migrants and minorities in the education system for a longer period of time. There are countries with a colonial past and also an early experience with foreign workers (e.g. France, UK, the Netherlands). Many of the minority members in these countries have attained citizenship. . . . The education system of several countries has to deal with the effects of more recent immigration (e.g. Greece, Italy, Spain, Portugal, Finland, Ireland, and, to some extent, Denmark).[48]

The downplaying of colonialism has also been reinforced by the fact that much of the recent, political and academic concern with diversity in Portugal happened at a time when newly arriving migrants were no longer equated with the colonized subject, but rather with the white 'Eastern European'—often used as 'model minority'—hindering a debate on racism. Indeed, as a report by the *European Commission against Racism and Intolerance*[49] on Portugal indicated, a 'two-speed' integration process has been taking place. One side of this process involves those arriving more recently from Eastern Europe, who have been better received possibly because they have relatively higher academic and professional qualifications—and significantly, in my view, are white. The other side of this process involves black people coming from African countries, who face enduring difficulties 'integrating' into Portuguese society. Yet the prevalence of a discourse that is evasive on matters of 'race'/power is downplaying the operation of 'race', under the pretext of job skills and qualifications:

Carlos Trindade [responsible for migration issues as an executive member of the national trade union federation, the CGTP] however, puts such discrimination down to the issue of job qualifications held by immigrants. He said a recent influx of Ukrainian immigrants had been a success story because they usually hold good qualifications. He said black immigrants often came from countries with a poorer social infrastructure. Out on the street, three Cape Verdean men disagreed. Joseph Armando, Pedro Gonçalves and Paolo Nazolini said that they all had professional backgrounds, but felt that colour was an issue when they went for jobs or housing. By day, they camped and cooked on a city square, parking cars for odd change. By night, they slept in shelters or hostels.[50]

Throughout the 1980s and the 1990s, black high-skilled workers in low-skilled jobs did not enjoy as much public sympathy as white Eastern European immigrants. Nowadays, the position of the white 'immigrant' is often used as a depository and model for official solutions (e.g., professional requalification), while the black colonized immigrant is assumed to have been *assimilated*—or else blamed for *failure to integrate*.

In education, these color-blind narratives have helped to naturalize racism. This is evident in the perceptions many educators have of the Portuguese fluency of students from African countries in which Portuguese is the official but not the national language. The (political) nonrecognition of the diversity of the Portuguese language has often resulted in labeling those forms of Portugese spoken in various African contexts as 'ignorant.' The expression 'to speak like an Angolan', in one teacher's words, and the older colonial expression 'to speak *pretoguês*' (*preto* + *português*, a derisory *Portuguese of the black*) are both grounded on the conflation of 'race' and language. Language skills are thus used as a proxy for cognitive ability in a way that masks the use of racial criteria. The same does not seem to apply to the children of British or French parents, whose foreign accents are not associated with cognitive-skill deficits. Thus racism is perpetuated by keeping hidden the criteria for academic success.

Other minoritized groups also face discrimination. For instance, Chinese and Eastern Europeans are often perceived as being *too industrious*. Yet, in relation to schooling, stereotypes of these groups seem to work in different ways than for black students. A common view among teachers is that Eastern European and Chinese students are very motivated, disciplined and hardworking children, who quickly learn the language and whose parents are very committed to education. This enables Eastern European and Chinese youth to be constructed as 'model students'. Black students, on the other hand, are more often perceived as lazy, talkative or undisciplined, and as culturally and linguistically deprived. The following examples are illustrative:

Now, regarding the other, if we can say this, nationalities, this year I am having a student and I really like her and I already realized she's committed, for example . . . one of Chinese origin. I have a Russian and I see that she, really, has a different academic background . . . she already reasonably speaks Portuguese and I am convinced she is going to be a good student. (Teacher 1, School 2) He can't, he can't express himself and then he makes mistakes, he speaks really . . . when he writes it's really like an Angolan and . . . he doesn't understand what he reads, he doesn't. And then he doesn't make an effort and he himself once told me, "I am dumb" [laughs], literally, those were his words, "I am dumb and, so, I can't." (Teacher 2, School 1)

The positioning of Eastern Europeans and Asians as 'model minorities' helps to prove the effectiveness of official integration policies and to shift blame for academic failure onto the culture and families of underachievers.[51] Such discourses effectively exclude racism as an explanation for academic and social inequalities. We thus need further contextualized research that engages with the history of 'race' ideas and challenges the cliché binary *poor, black student* versus *intelligent, motivated Eastern European* that persists in many approaches to education.

The Thesis of Migration Transition: Recentering Portugal, Amplifying Difference

Closely related to the view of diversity as a recent phenomenon are the narratives that characterize Portugal as having changed from a traditional country of *e*migration into one of *im*migration in the early 1990s—this being the "thesis of migration transition."[52] The thesis of migration transition has downplayed the structural role that emigration still plays in the country.[53] Nowadays, Portugal is a 'receiving' *and* 'sending' society. According to official data,[54] it is estimated that over five million Portuguese people live outside the country—the equivalent to half its territorial residents. This figure is on the increase, and new forms of emigration are often statistically invisible, relating to temporary work or intra–European Union countries and therefore not officially registered. Although structural factors—rather than mere individual dynamics—continue to play a key role in Portuguese emigration,[55] it was only in the current context of the so-called *economic crisis* that it became publicly acceptable to utter this. A few decades ago,

> In Portugal, in the context of EU integration, [in 1986] it made no sense to continue to admit emigration because this was always associated with, in our case [Portugal], the misery in standards of living, the economic aspects of the Monarchy and the beginning of the Republic, a severe economic situation in the country that naturally led the people out of the

country. And so emigration was an epithet to be associated with the New State [Estado Novo], to the past, and not to the democratic state.[56]

The wide circulation of the *e/immigration transition thesis* has resulted in a substantial increase in political and academic interest in Portugese diversity, now constituting a real *immigration industry*. Significantly, the way in which immigration began to be accentuated in the 1990s plays an ambiguous role in the representations of Portugal. As Vale de Almeida[57] suggests, an overemphasis on immigration in Portugal has helped to create an imaginary in which the country is positioned as "center." Although immigration might be still perceived as a threat, these narratives help us to imagine Portugal as a desirable destination for immigrants, valuing the national identity by locating it alongside other rich and modern European countries. This thesis is explicit in the following academic narrative that was produced inthe mid-1990s:

> The existence of ethnic groups in Portugal presents, nowadays, a noticeable statistical dimension and an increased socio-cultural diversity, conferring on the country a truly multicultural profile, a characteristic that it shares with many European and world countries.[58]

Moreover, the overemphasis on the role of immigration helps to reinforce a binary vision of development: the global South as poor, wrecked by disease and poverty, aspiring to emigrate to the rich, developed and modern North. This is best understood as the operation of an "immigrant imaginary." Salman Sayyid[59] developed this idea, of the "immigrant imaginary" to analyze contemporary discourses on immigration and the postcolonial subjects of imperial colonialism in the British context. According to Sayyid, this imaginary works by consecrating and amplifying an ontological distinction between *host society* and *immigrants*. In the national context, the prevalence of this "immigrant imaginary" secures the self-assuring idea that 'tolerant' Portugal is a desirable destination for migrants due to its positioning in *Europe*—that is, in the modern and developed world—disproving nineteenth-century views that *Africa begins at the Pyrenees*. Conversely, it naturalizes the idea that the African continent is premodern and underdeveloped, which informs much political, scholarly and commonsense thinking. In education, this imaginary circulates in the generalizations made by many teachers about the various African contexts from which recent migrant students come, and their assumptions about their inferior education systems and attitudes to schoolwork:

> I don't see that [ethnic difference] is a problem. The only need that emerges is . . . in terms . . . say, intellectual terms . . . They actually need, for example, our Africans . . . They need much more support at that level, not due to an ethnic difference, because that's not it, but due

to a large difference in the work attitudes, and in the set of contents that they should have . . . now acquired, and they haven't. . . . They are here, out of their countries, and take in customs and lifestyles that are not theirs, but with which they have to live and, to a certain extent, get used to so they can progress, isn't it? (Teacher 3, School 1)

Poor expectations of these students are compounded by teachers' assumptions about assimilation into Portuguese culture and education as a necessary road for academic success—with 'race' deferring the possibility of becoming truly assimilated. Hence the relation between racism and educational success is masked by assumptions of inferior early-academic experiences and qualifications, even when—as in this case—students were known to come from socioeconomically privileged backgrounds.

Associating Demographic Change with Positive, Political Visibility

A final aspect of these narratives that I wish to explore is the presumption of a causal relationship between increased demographic diversity, political visibility and institutional response. Drawing on Andrea Brighenti's work on the concept of *visibility*, I argue that such cause-and-effect relation needs to be made problematic.

Considering that the "invisible is what is *here without being an object*,"[60] Brighenti invites us to explore the construction of diversity as a nonissue—that is, something that is not accorded social and political relevance. In democratic Portugal, there is a time lapse of about two decades (roughly from the mid-1970s to the 1990s) in which diversity did not receive significant political attention. In religion, debates were polarized between secularists and Catholics without any concern with religious pluralism. Culture and language were not seen as deserving special attention or provisions: the formerly colonized were supposed to speak Portuguese and to have assimilated into Portugese language and culture. A "no problem here" approach[61] pervaded, and it went undisputed both academically and politically by the left and right. Diversity issues were ignored in politics, including diversity in education, until the period in which changes to the demographic composition of the national population became increasingly more evident. It was only in the early 1990s, following Portuguese integration in the European Union, that such concerns were put on the political agenda.[62] although in a conservative fashion (not concerned with or requiring structural reform). Yet most official and academic accounts conceal this. Chronological narratives continue to depict policy making on these matters as an arena governed by good will rather than power relations: Portugal became an immigration country, and institutional bodies and policy interventions were formulated to respond to this *new* scenario. These narratives conflate a demographic question with a political one, failing to consider when and how the state started showing a public concern with (the not-so-new) diversity.

We must also consider the role of other actors in dealing with aspects of immigration and diversity that had not yet gained public visibility in democratic Portugal. The problematic association between demographic change and political response has rendered local initiatives and struggles invisible. Despite the absence of state initiatives or debates, the social problems faced by minoritized people—particularly in the housing and employment sectors and in access to the law—were being addressed by local associations at least since the 1970s.[63] Meanwhile, cultural diversity has gained more political visibility, but politicians and other public officials have also reasserted the idea of a welcoming nation, making it difficult to speak of inequalities and racism. This challenge is being currently met by political activists and grassroots movements, but it is a particularly difficult task given the depoliticization of the wider debate over these issues. While European public policies have supported local projects aimed at socioeconomic integration, these policies have also neutralized the political agendas of grassroots associations and NGOs.[64]

Finally, as Brighenti suggests, visibility is not necessarily liberating. The process of making diversity more visible may simply function as "a strategic resource for regulation."[65] This raises fundamental questions about what kinds of diversity-related political agendas have been incorporated as "legitimate concerns" and what has remained off the agenda. For example, the *Secretariat for the Coordination of Multicultural Education Programs* was Portugal's first institution to address cultural diversity. It was created in 1991 to "coordinate, foster and promote, within the education system, programs and events which aim for conviviality, tolerance, dialogue and solidarity between different peoples, ethnicities and cultures" (Statutory Regulation 63/91, of March 13). The emergence of the secretariat was related to the intensification of racism across Europe during that period. Yet racism was recognized only in its most violent forms, which were seen as marginal phenomena in Portuguese society and not a school matter. Official discourses and practices have been anchored in a conception of racism as prejudice,[66] rather than as a historical and political process, structurally embedded in modern societies.[67] Accordingly, it has been proposed that racism may be *treated* by emphasizing the value of different cultures and developing skills in intercultural communication.[68] By leaving concerns with structural amd political equality aside, it has merely made *difference* visible, rather than challenging inequities in power.

This silence on matters of power and inequality is particularly evident in the Portuguese education system. The main state structures have remained broadly unchanged, with the Ministry of Education continuing to rest its policies on assumptions of the *presumed homogeneity* of its school population. According to the annual European reports published over the last decade by the *European Monitoring Centre on Racism and Xenophobia* and its successor the *Fundamental Rights Agency*, the overall situation of education policy and practice for diversity in Portugal is bleak. Initiatives tend to be centered in the capital, Lisbon, and there is insufficient provision for Portuguese as an additional language, a total absence of state-endorsed bilingual education, few training opportunities for teachers, underachievement in some minority groups and persistent, explicit school segregation.[69] All of these problems are aggravated by the ineffectiveness of the equality body that was established to monitor and tackle racism in Portugal.[70] These problems also raise serious questions about the self-proclaimed 'success' of Portuguese 'integration policies'. Moreover, the depoliticization of debate is preventing a meaningful discussion of ethno-racial inequalities in education. Rather, diversity is being viewed through the lens of exoticizing narratives, epitomized by the multicultural festival. For example, when asked about the activities developed at his school, one teacher replied:

> In our festivities when, for instance, our Africans . . . when we do something to do with music, or with dance . . . Indeed, it's wonderful to see them dance! And to see, to make . . . the Africans dance or the Europeans . . . They are perfectly different things! And to us, it brings us a huge joy . . . I remember, for instance, the dances, the songs in which they make instruments with a tin can if necessary . . . moments of theater in which . . . in which they put . . . hmmm . . . their way of speaking, their language or dialect. And so, it's moments like this of enormous enrichment and of cultural interchange that benefits all. (Teacher 4, School 1)

In education, engagement with diversity is still seen as taking place outside the classroom. Inside the class, Eurocentrism in the curricula and textbooks goes unchallenged[71] and the perception that racially and ethnically marked students have cultural and linguistic deficits prevails.[72] These contrary tendencies are revealing of Sayyid's "immigrant imaginary,"[73] in which immigrant experiences are read from either an exoticized or a banalized register—celebrating and exaggerating difference and overemphasizing sameness and denying racism. In sum, while making *difference* visible, current approaches are not moving beyond a 'benevolent' or 'celebratory' multiculturalism,[74] even when deploying the intercultural rhetoric. Diversity is conceptualized as an educational *problem* rather than a resource, and considerations of structural inequalities and enduring Eurocentric canons of knowledge are sidelined.

CONCLUSIONS

Portugal has joined the growing list of Western countries that include concerns about immigration and diversity in their political and research agendas. Even so, the Portugese state is still failing in its efforts to tackle racism at the institutional level. This situation has been naturalized by the hegemony of the political, academic and commonsense assumptions that were analyzed in this chapter. In these political narratives—which have been endorsed by sectors of the Portugese academia—there is a tendency to historicize the *tolerant nation* and to attest a vocation for interculturality that circulates presentist accounts of immigration and evades the historical roots of contemporary, Portugese racism. In both cases, the debate over the legacies of colonial 'race' thinking is made irrelevant. Although historically informed perspectives are paramount for understanding how 'race' has been configured across time, it is crucial to note the emergence of a narrative that *historicizes* diversity as a deterrent for a discussion on racism. In turn, the constitution of the *immigration industry* of the last decade in Portugal is erasing 'race' and concealing (post)colonial dynamics within a logic of push-and-pull factors.

Academic work needs to challenge this overemphasis on national *specificities* regarding racism, which characterizes the Portugese discourse on immigration and diversity. Mainstream accounts tend to overestimate the specific national contours of the management of diversity and immigration, losing sight of a common, European (post)colonial legacy of 'race'. Contrary to treating the Portuguese case as exceptional or peculiar, I argue for the need to develop theoretical approaches that open up the possibility of in-depth international comparisons. A contextualized, comparative approach can also overcome the temporal linearity evident in the reductionist construction of certain contexts as *not yet awakened* to normative multiculturalism—implicit in many accounts of southern European societies. This comparative approach can also be used to overcome the assumption that multiculturalist policy formulations and interpretations are unavoidably progressive (evolving from assimilation to integration to multiculturalism/interculturality), or as bringing paradigmatic change.

Research must also disrupt discourses on diversity which presume that the achievement of visibility is necessarily positive, and it must engage the the cumulative effect of successive invizibilizations, which have made alternatives to the current, depoliticized public debate over immigration and diversity, hard to imagine. There are many struggles against colonialism, slavery and racism that have not just been marginalized, but made invisible. Likewise, the struggles by radical intellectuals, political activists and grassroots movements for an antiracist education have a long history of questioning Eurocentric canons of knowledge and the inequities (re)produced by school structures, arrangements and practices.[75] A more productive research stream could be achieved by engaging these critiques and alternatives to the enduring shortcomings of hegemonic approaches.

Finally, research needs to overcome naive ideas about the relationship betweeen policy-making and knowledge, and particularly, the notion that official policies fail at tackling racism because of insufficient knowledge about better solutions or models. As Lesko and Bloom have argued, "ignorance is an effect of particular knowledge, not an absence of knowledge."[76] In the

Portuguese context, it is commonly suggested that there was a slow apropria-
tion of debates on diversity and immigration–which became more visible in
the early 1990s. Meanwhile,public bodies and academics have tacitly ignored
institutional racism and antiracist struggles in a number of other contexts, in
favour of a culturalist approach to *difference* that tends to evade questions of
'race'/power. This is a political choice, not an accident or forgetfulness.

NOTES

1. ACIDI, *BI: Boletim Informativo* 92 (Oct.–Dec. 2011): 8–9.
2. Cameron McCarthy, "After the Canon Knowledge and Ideological Representation in the Multicultural Discourse on Curriculum Reform," in *Race,
   Identity, and Representation in Education*, ed. Cameron McCarthy and
   Warren Crichlow (New York: Routledge, 1993), 289–305.
3. This was a qualitative study of compulsory education in a private and a state
   school in 'white areas' (using interviews, classroom observation and analysis
   of official documents). (Funding body: Foundation for Science and Technology, FCOMP-01–0124-FEDER-007554)
4. Salman Sayyid, *"Slippery People*: The Immigrant Imaginary and the Gram-
   mar of Colours," in *Institutional Racism in Higher Education*, ed. Ian Law,
   Deborah Philips and Laura Turney (Stoke-on-Trent: Trentham Books, 2004),
   149–159.
5. The project "'Race' and Africa in Portugal: A Study on History Textbooks"
   (accessed Nov. 13, 2012, www.ces.uc.pt/projectos/rap) is centered on three
   moments: the analysis of textbooks and education policy, interviews with a
   variety of institutional actors and participatory workshops. (Funding body:
   Foundation for Science and Technology, PTDC/CED/64626/2006)
6. The project TOLERACE was funded by the 7th Framework Programme of
   the European Community (Grant Agreement no. 244633). I draw particularly on the analysis of European reports on racism, especially on education. Project TOLERACE, "The Semantics of Tolerance and (Anti-)Racism
   in Europe: Public Bodies and Civil Society in Comparative Perspective,"
   accessed April 12, , 2013, http://www.ces.uc.pt/projectos/tolerace
7. Speech by Nuno Severiano Teixeira (2001), who was then the minister of
   internal affairs, cited by Vanda Santos, *O Discurso Oficial do Estado sobre
   a Emigração dos anos 60 a 80 e Imigração dos anos 90 à actualidade* (Lisbon: OI/ACIME, 2004), 107.
8. EUMC, *Migrants, Minorities and Education* (Vienna: EUMC, 2004),
   92, accessed Jan. 11, 2009, http://fra.europa.eu/fraWebsite/products/
   publications_reports/comparative_reports/pub_cr_education_04_en.htm.
9. SEF, *Relatório de Actividades: Imigração, Fronteiras e Asilo* (Lisbon: SEF,
   2007), accessed Mar. 21, 2009, http://www.sef.pt/portal/v10/PT/aspx/
   estatisticas/relatorios.aspx?id_linha=4265&menu_position=4141#0.
10. ACIDI, *BI: Boletim Informativo* 52 (Sept. 2007).
11. The MIPEX is a monitoring tool for measuring "the integration of migrants
    into society," resulting from the collaboration of the British Council and
    the Migration Policy Group, and receiving funding by the European Union.
    Accessed Nov. 13, 2012, http://www.mipex.eu/.
12. Clara Viana, "Imigração: Portugal é o mais 'generoso' em políticas de inte-
    gração," *Público*, Oct. 5, 2009, accessed Oct. 5, 2009, http://ultimahora.
    publico.clix.pt/noticia.aspx?id=1403698.

13. ACIME, *Imigração: Os mitos e os factos* (Lisbon: ACIME, 2005), 21.
14. ME, normative dispatch 63/91, *Dário da República*, N° 60—Série I-B, Mar. 13, 1991.
15. Lucinda Fonseca, Jorge M. Malheiros and Sandra Silva, "Portugal," in *Current Immigration Debates in Europe: A Publication of the European Migration Dialogue*, ed. Jan Niessen, Yongmi Schibel and Cressida Thompson (Brussels: MPG, 2005), 5.
16. Sayyid, *"Slippery People."*
17. Marta Araújo and Silvia Rodríguez Maeso, "The 'Prudent' Integration of Roma/Gypsy Pupils: Segregation and White Flight in Portuguese Compulsory Schooling" (TOLERACE working paper, Coimbra, 2012), accessed Apr. 5, 2012, http://www.ces.uc.pt/projectos/tolerace/pages/en/publications/working-papers/february-2012.php.
18. Wendy Brown, *Regulating Aversion: Tolerance in the Age of Identity and Empire* (Princeton, NJ: Princeton University Press, 2006).
19. Miguel Vale de Almeida, *Um Mar da Cor da Terra: 'Raça', Cultura e Política da Identidade* (Oeiras: Celta, 2000).
20. Gilberto Freyre, *Em torno de um novo conceito de tropicalismo* (Coimbra: Coimbra Editora, 1952). See also Gilberto Freyre, *Casa Grande e Senzala* (1933; Lisbon: Livros do Brasil, 2003).
21. This could be seen in the existence of friendly social contacts or in the possibility of having sexual intercourse with 'native' women. See Cláudia Castelo, *O modo português de estar no mundo': O luso-tropicalismo e a ideologia colonial portuguesa (1933–1961)* (Porto: Edições Afrontamento, 1998), and Valentim Alexandre, "O Império e a Ideia de Raça" in *Novos Racismos*, ed. Jorge Vala (Oeiras: Celta, 1999), 133–144.
22. Castelo, *O modo português.*
23. Ibid., and Alexandre, *O Império e a Ideia de Raça.*
24. Almeida, *Um Mar da Cor da Terra*, and Margarida C. Ribeiro, *Uma História de Regressos: Império, Guerra Colonial e Pós-Colonialismo* (Porto: Afrontamento, 2004).
25. Also, contestation of the rhetoric during that period should not be overlooked. See, Charles Boxer, *Race Relations in the Portuguese Colonial Empire, 1415–1825* (Oxford: Clarendon, 1963); James Duffy, *Portuguese Africa* (London: Oxford University Press, 1959).
26. Almeida, *Um Mar da Cor da Terra*; Carlos Cardoso, "The Colonialist View of the African-Origin 'Other' in Portuguese Society and Its Education System," *Race, Ethnicity and Education* 1, no. 2 (1998): 191–206; and Ribeiro, *Uma História de Regressos.*
27. Lorenzo Macagno, "Um antropólogo norte-americano no «mundo que o português criou»: Relações raciais no Brasil e Moçambique segundo Marvin Harris," *Lusotopie* (1999), 143–161, and Maria Paula Meneses, "Os espaços criados pelas palavras: Racismos, etnicidades e o encontro colonial," in *Um olhar além das fronteiras—educação e relações raciais*, ed. Nilma L. Gomes (Belo Horizonte, Brazil: Autêntica Editora, 2007), 55–76.
28. Castelo, *O modo português.*
29. João Leal, *Etnografias Portuguesas (1870–1970): Cultura Popular e Identidade Nacional* (Lisbon: Publicações Dom Quixote, 2000).
30. Adriano Moreira was overseas minister (1961–1963) in Salazar's regime. However, in some segments of Portuguese society, his political responsibilities have been broadly sanitized, and he is often invited to participate in academic debates on issues of interculturality.
31. Joaquim Pires Valentim, "Luso-tropicalismo e Lusofonia: Uma perspectiva psicossocial," *Via Latina* 6, no. 2 (2005): 68.

32. ME, normative dispatch 6391, translated in Cardoso, "Colonialist View," 198.
33. Anne-Marie Fortier, *Multicultural Horizons: Diversity and the Limits of the Civil Nation* (London: Routledge, 2008), 22.
34. ACIDI, *Apresentação de Estudo OI: A Interculturalidade na Expansão Portuguesa* (2007), accessed May 9, 2007, http://www.oi.acidi.gov.pt/modules.php?name=News&file=article&sid=1377.
35. João Paulo Oliveira Costa and Teresa Lacerda, *A Interculturalidade na Expansão Portuguesa (Séculos XV–XVIII)* (Lisbon: ACIME, 2007), 23, 86–87.
36. Ibid., 104.
37. This has been most visible in the depoliticization of colonialism and slavery in the contest titled *"7 Wonders of Portuguese Origin in the World."* This program was broadcast by the public television channel RTP1 (June 10, 2009) to mark the Day of Portugal, Camões and the Portuguese Comunities. Salazar's regime used this date to celebrate the Day of Race. The contest listed 27 buildings (22 of which classified as World Heritage by UNESCO) related to the history of 'Portuguese Expansion', and received support from the Portuguese Institute for Architectural Heritage (IPPAR), the Ministry of Education and the Ministry of Culture. A public petition by international academics was launched to denounce the rewriting of the Portuguese colonial past. RTPI, *"7 Wonders of Portuguese Origin in the World,"* accessed Nov. 13, 2012, http://www.petitiononline.com/port2009/petition.html.
38. David Theo Goldberg, *The Threat of Race: Reflections on Racial Neoliberalism* (Malden, MA: Wiley-Blackwell, 2009).
39. Shiv Visvanathan, "Nation," *Theory, Culture & Society* 23, no. 2–3 (2006): 533–538.
40. Marta Araújo and Silvia Rodriguez Maeso, "History Textbooks, Racism and the Critique of Eurocentrism: Beyond Rectification or Compensation," *Ethnic and Racial Studies* 35, no. 7 (2012): 1266–1285.
41. AbdoolKarim Vakil, "Heróis do Lar, Nação Ambi-Valente: Portugalidade e Identidade Nacional nos tempos dos pós," in *30 Anos de Democracia em Portugal*, ed. Manuel Loff (Porto: FLUP, 2006), 73–101.
42. Silvia Rodríguez Maeso and Marta Araújo " Understanding the logics of racism in contemporary Europe—Booklet presenting key findings and recommendations" (Coimbra: Centre for Social Studies, 2013), accessed Apr. 12, 2013, http://www.ces.uc.pt/projectos/tolerace/pages/pt/dissemination-materials-activities/documents.php, and Araújo and Maeso, "'Prudent' Integration."
43. Barnor Hesse and Salman Sayyid, "Narrating the Postcolonial Political and the Immigrant Imaginary," in *A Postcolonial People: South Asians in Britain*, ed. Nasreen Ali, Virinder S. Karla and S. Sayyid (London: Hurst, 2006), 13–31.
44. Maria Ioannis Baganha and José C. Marques, *Imigração e Política: O caso português* (Lisbon: Fundação Luso-Americana para o Desenvolvimento, 2001).
45. SEF, *Relatório de Actividades: Imigração, Fronteiras e Asilo* (Lisbon: SEF, 2007), accessed Mar. 21, 2009, http://www.sef.pt/portal/v10/PT/aspx/estatisticas/relatorios.aspx?id_linha=4265&menu_position=4141#0.
46. Natália Faria, "Regresso de imigrantes está a deixar o país mais pobre e envelhecido," *Público*, May 25, 2009, accessed May 25, 2009, http://ultima-hora.publico.clix.pt/noticia.aspx?id=1382690&idCanal=62.
47. Hesse and Sayyid, "Narrating the Postcolonial Political," 21.
48. EUMC, *Migrants, Minorities and Education*, 10.

49. ECRI, *Second Report on Portugal* (Strasbourg: Council of Europe, 2002), accessed Nov. 13, 2012, http://www.coe.int/T/E/human_rights/Ecri/1-ECRI/2-Country-by country_approach/Portugal/Portugal_CBC_2en.asp# TopOfPage.
50. Charies Dunn-Chan, "Portugal Sees Integration Progress," *BBC News*, Nov. 14, 2005, accessed Mar. 21, 2009, http://news.bbc.co.uk/2/hi/europe/ 4436276.stm.
51. Discourses on 'model immigrants' can be found more widely in political discourses. Eastern Europeans are often constructed as 'good immigrants', integrating easily across the country. On the contrary, black Africans are often seen as self-excluding, creating ghettos in metropolitan areas with high unemployment rates, and thus causing 'discomfort' (e.g., António Vitorino's interventions in the RTP1 TV show *Prós e Contras*, Episode 17: "A Imigração: Os novos colonizadores," May 8, 2006).
52. José Carlos Marques, *Os Portugueses na Suíça: Migrantes Europeus* (Lisbon: ICS, 2008).
53. Miguel Vale de Almeida, "Comentário," in *"Portugal não é um País Pequeno": Contar o 'Império' na Pós-colonialidade*, ed. Manuela R. Sanches (Lisbon: Cotovia, 2006), 361–397.
54. MNE, *Comunidades Portuguesas e Comunidades Luso-descendentes* (2007), accessed Apr. 27, 2008, http://www.mne.gov.pt/mne/pt/infocidadao/ comunidades/.
55. Marques, *Os Portugueses na Suíça*.
56. Observatório da Emigração, "A emigração evoluiu em modalidades distintas, mas no decurso da nossa história fomos tendo sempre saídas," Oct. 11, 2011, accessed Nov. 13, 2012, http://www.observatorioemigracao.secomunidades.pt/np4/2659.html.
57. Almeida, *Comentário*, 363–364.
58. Maria Beatriz Rocha-Trindade, *Sociologia das Migrações* (Lisbon: Universidade Aberta, 1995), 204.
59. Sayyid, *"Slippery People"*; also in Hesse and Sayyid, "Narrating the Postcolonial Political."
60. Andrea Brighenti, "Visibility: A Category for the Social Sciences," *Current Sociology* 55, no. 3 (2007): 328, original emphasis.
61. Chris Gaine, *No Problem Here: A Practical Approach to Education and 'Race' in White Schools* (London: Hutchinson, 1987).
62. Cardoso, "Colonialist View."
63. Rosana Albuquerque, "Dinâmicas Associativas e Comunidades Imigrantes," in *A Imigração em Portugal: Os movimentos humanos e culturais em Portugal*, ed. SOS Racismo (Lisbon: SOS Racismo, 2002), 366–381.
64. Ibid.
65. Brighenti, "Visibility," 339.
66. Julian Henriques, "Social Psychology and the Politics of Racism," in *Changing the Subject, Psychology, Social Regulation and Subjectivity*, ed. Julian Henriques, Wendy Hollway, Cathy Urwin, Couze Venn and Valerie Walkerdine (London: Routledge, 1984), 60–90.
67. David Theo Goldberg, *The Racial State* (Oxford: Blackwell, 2002).
68. Entreculturas, *O que quero dizer quando penso em Educação Intercultural?*, 2009, accessed Mar. 12, 2009, http://www.entreculturas.pt/DiariodeBordo. aspx?to=214.
69. See also Araújo and Maeso, "'Prudent' Integration."
70. EUMC, *Migrants, Minorities and Education*; EUMC, *Annual Report 2006* (Vienna: EUMC, 2006), accessed Jan. 11, 2009, http://fra.europa.eu/fraWebsite/products/publications_reports/annual_report/ar2006_part2_en.htm;

FRA, *Annual Report 2007* (Vienna: FRA, 2007), accessed Feb. 12, 2009, http://fra.europa.eu/fraWebsite/products/publications_reports/annual_report/ar2007_part2_en.htm; and FRA, *Annual Report 2008* (Vienna: FRA, 2008),, accessed Feb. 12, 2009, http://fra.europa.eu/fraWebsite/products/publications_reports/annual_report/ar2008_part2_en.htm.

71. Araújo and Maeso, "History Textbooks."
72. Marta Araújo, "O silêncio do racismo em Portugal: O caso do abuso verbal racista na escola," in Gomes, *Um olhar além das fronteiras*, 77–94. For a discussion of the construction of minoritized populations as cultural and linguistic deficits in the academia see Philomena Essed, "Ethnicity and Diversity in the Dutch Academia," *Social Identities 5*, no. 2 (1999): 211–225.
73. Sayyid, *"Slippery People"*;
74. See Barry Troyna, *Racism and Education* (Buckingham: Open University Press, 1993), and Boaventura de Sousa Santos and João Arriscado Nunes, "Para ampliar o cânone do reconhecimento, da diferença e da igualdade," in *Reconhecer para libertar: Os caminhos do cosmopolitismo multicultural*, ed. Boaventura de Sousa Santos (Porto: Edições Afrontamento, 2004), 20–51.
75. See, for instance, Carter G. Woodson, *The Mis-Education of the Negro* (Washington: The Associated Publishers, 1933).
76. Nancy Lesko and Leslie Bloom, "Close encounters: truth, experience and interpretation in multicultural teacher education", *Journal of Curriculum Studies*, vol. 30, no. 4 (1998): 375–395 at 380.

3 Politics, Citizenship and the Construction of Immigrant Communities in Italy[1]

Valentina Pagliai

One evening during my fieldwork in Tuscany,[2] I was invited to a Senegalese dinner feast held in Prato. When we arrived we found that the food was (as far as I know) Senegalese, and so were its cooks, and even the DJ playing music. But most of the people eating were local Italians. They were people working in antiracist associations, local politicians and other social workers dealing with immigration. There were very few immigrants present, and even fewer from Africa, although the feast was organized by African activists and part of a series of events held every Friday. Each Friday a different immigrant group from a particular national origin would prepare a feast.

Mauro,[3] a local politician from the Social Observatory of the Province of Prato, a part of the local government, sat with me and eventually started complaining about the absence of immigrants among the crowd. He told me that he went to another feast organized by African immigrants and found that there were hundreds of them. There, he felt like the only local (white) person around. Why then, did they not come to this one, although they had been invited? He had asked this same question of an African lady, herself an activist, and she had told him: "because that party was for us. This one we make for you." This answer bewildered him: why, he asked me, because the whole purpose of these feasts was to have Italians and immigrants get together and know each other, facilitating a multicultural and intercultural relationship, why didn't the Africans come?

Part of the answer could be that these multicultural feasts were lived by the immigrants fundamentally as a display, part of how they managed the relationship with the local leftist politicians. The Senegalese who organized the feast and participated were involved in political action, but probably their motives were different from the motives of the Italian politicians who sponsored them. For the Italian politicians and social workers, the feasts were about creating a new, multicultural society and fighting racism—where racism was understood mainly as intolerance of cultural differences due to ignorance. In this work, the local antiracist activists and politicians focused on cultural exchange and mutual integration between the locals and the immigrant 'communities'.[4]

For the Senegalese activists involved, the feast fostered their own personal political influence vis-à-vis the local authorities, influence that they could later use to help other immigrants. It allowed them, for example, to get funding for other initiatives they eventually wanted to do. To obtain this increased power, they managed their presentation of the self through the homology of culture/nation/community, which, as I will argue in this article, is the homology through which immigrants are perceived and categorized by the local political establishment. In other words, immigrants can acquire political influence by catering to the dominant paradigm in the antiracist movement in Italy—namely, the multiculturalist one. What made Mauro uncomfortable, I surmise, was the sudden realization of the presence of the display. In a sense, he yearned to find an authenticity (the authentic Senegalese party) that he perceived as being willingly hidden elsewhere and kept from him.

Antiracist activists and liberal politicians like Mauro often expressed discouragement as they thought that the immigrants were unwilling to 'communicate' and were isolating themselves, notwithstanding all the efforts made to help them establish meaningful ties and relationships in the receiving society. In a sense, the immigrants appeared unwilling to participate in their own 'development'.

But part of the problem, I believe, is due to the presuppositions themselves inherent in the multiculturalist approach adopted: first, the multiculturalist approach leads to a reification of cultural boundaries, which are also problematically conflated with national = racial = ethnic = community boundaries.[5] Second, the multiculturalist approach tends to see racism as a problem of single individuals, due to simple ignorance, which can be solved by giving to the racist person information about cultural differences. But, as Silverman notes, "racism is not an external evil which periodically plagues the body politic; it is an integral part of the very constitution of modern nation-states."[6] In fact, the multiculturalist approach, with its reification of culture, may contribute to create prejudice and justify discrimination. Finally, the focus on immigrant 'cultural communities' as the privileged targets of integrationist efforts, and as the basic unit of immigrant political agency and civic participation, can become a limit to the immigrants' ability to participate in their new country as active citizens. Ironically, as I will show ahead, this undermines the efforts of those liberal politicians and activists (both immigrants and nonimmigrants) that use multiculturalism exactly to foster that civic participation.

CULTURE, RACISM AND THE *MULTICULTURA*

According to Étienne Balibar,[7] a *new racism* is emerging in Europe in which cultural differences have become naturalized. As Paul Gilroy argues,[8] cultural racism has substituted the previous biologically based racism. Racist claims are hidden under assertions of "civilizational differences"[9] so that "the convenient argument that some cultural differences are so profound that they cannot be bridged has become commonplace."[10] According to Gerd Baumann,[11] these cultural differences have been naturalized in dominant discourse, whereas the concept of culture has been transformed into "a reified entity that has a definite substantive content and assumes the status of a thing that people 'have' or 'are members of.'"[12] "This reification," writes Baumann, "is the very cornerstone that holds the dominant discourse together across all political divides."[13] And Nora Räthzel notes[14] that celebration of diversity per se is no warranty against racism since the New Right's argument has become "that in order to preserve the variety of cultures, people from different cultures need to stay in their respective places."[15] Cultural boundaries have come to be identified with ethnic boundaries and community boundaries, each in turn reified and naturalized.[16]

Connected to this naturalization of cultural difference is a substitution of the term 'ethnicity' to replace the scorned term 'race'. The term 'racism' itself is rarely used to identify the problems faced by immigrants in Italy. I was often corrected when I used it and invited to use the term 'discrimination', or 'ethnic discrimination', instead. 'Race' is also a term carefully avoided (contrarily to the US), almost to the point of being unpronounceable. Instead the term 'ethnic group' is used, which is generally conflated with citizenship in a nation-state. As Verena Stolcke[17] notes, ethnicity was supposed to be connected to culture, but it immediately came to be naturalized and connected to descent. Ethnicity thus "tended to downplay or side-step racism, that is, discriminations and exclusions ideologically justified as resulting from supposedly really existing racial, and hence hereditary, moral or intellectual deficiencies."[18]

In Europe, race and racism are directly associated with Nazism and the Holocaust. Because of such association, particularly painful to European states that came out of the war in ruins, after World War II the term 'race' was if not prohibited at least to a large extent erased. The word would not be used in public discourse, in politics and not even in academia. 'Race' and 'racism' in a sense had to have no place in Europe. This was particularly true in Italy, where 'racism' and 'race' were associated with Fascism and thus with a past from which the new democratic republic wanted to disassociate itself completely. In addition, the Italian Left saw 'race' and 'racism' as something belonging to the ways of thinking of the Right, of the conservative parties, something they had fought against during the war and that had been eradicated with the death of Mussolini. The Left did recognize that racism still existed, but it belonged to other capitalist nation-states, such as the US and South Africa, not to 'us'. This state of denial stifled any study of racism in Italy and any debate of it in the larger society to the present, and caused a lack of open discussion of racism in the Italian Left.

The outcome of this denial and erasure can be seen in Tuscany today. The Left, traditionally governing the regional and local governments in

Tuscany since after World War II, appears unprepared to face the growing racism and hostility against immigrants, especially when it comes from inside its ranks. It literally is scrambling for a plan to answer the racism and discriminatory discourses that the Right is voicing against immigrants. The Left, ineffectively attempting to protect immigrant rights while maintaining consensus from a population increasingly bent on negating and reducing those rights, is losing votes and control of the local governments for the first time.

In this relative intellectual and political void, both the Left and the antiracist movements have adopted a multiculturalist approach.[19] During my research, I saw this approach articulated into the following general discourse: the immigrants are our[20] brothers and sisters and fellow members of the working class (*proletari*); therefore we need to be in solidarity with them; they are not stealing our jobs because they do the jobs we do not want to do;[21] their cultures are different from ours and a reciprocal lack of knowledge about them creates problems and misunderstandings; however, we can both change and learn to live together if we make an effort to get to know each other better.

Gilroy[22] and Baumann[23] note that both the conservatives and the Left, including antiracism groups, accept the vision of culture as reified and naturalized, albeit in different ways and with different goals and priorities. The effect is to focus antiracist effort on multiculturalism without encouraging a parallel discussion of institutional and political racism. Italian activists and politicians fighting against racism and to protect immigrant rights see the desirable goal to be achieved in the *multicultura* (multiculturalism), or in the *intercultura* (interculturalism).[24]

Activists and antiracist groups in Tuscany operate under the multicultural/intercultural paradigm. They mostly see the solution to racism and discrimination in allowing the local population to become more informed about the beauty and wisdom of the cultural ways of the immigrants. As a consequence, they often focus on organizing cultural events such as movie series in the original language, presentations on cultures, art displays, music concerts, dances and even a beauty contest for the election of a 'Miss Multicultural,' soccer games, parties and especially food sharing in organized dinners. Elements of reified immigrant cultures (in particular music, language, food and dress) are increasingly accepted and adopted by Italian progressive youth.[25] As Alana Lentin notes, "the idea that knowledge of the histories and customs of other cultures would engender a greater degree of tolerance . . . continues to underpin a form of anti-racism that sees racism as prejudicial behavior."[26] This multicultural approach tends to fix, reify and essentialize cultural and ethnic identities and can be easily co-opted to reinforce racist discourses.[27]

In addition to the previously mentioned issues, the multiculturalist approach is very much centrally created and directed from above (by the Tuscan Left). The presence of people of immigrant origin among the events' organizers is still limited. As such, concerns that may be closer to the immigrants' needs—such as finding jobs, accessing educational programs geared toward adult learners, getting certifiable training to find better jobs and protection from housing discrimination—are not always treated as priorities. Instead, cultural forms of antiracist protest and programs are favored. For example, an immigrant activist I interviewed in Florence[28] told me that a plan proposed to the Province of Florence to use funds to cover tuition for selected young immigrant teenagers to attend a local technical high school had been denied. However, these funds had been readily spent in a successively proposed multicultural festival.

An awareness that their efforts were not leading anywhere and were not contributing to a diminishing of racism was present among the antiracist activists I contacted and interviewed. Yet, instead of reexamining the multiculturalist paradigm itself, they felt at a loss and tended to see the problem in some kind of "absence or lack" from the immigrant part: at times an absence of communities, other times a lack of knowledge of the working of democratic institutions or the absence of a will to communicate.

Lest I paint a too negative and limiting portrait of these activists (who, it must not be forgotten, included immigrants and people of immigrant origins, who also tended to believe in the multiculturalist approach), I must say that the cultural events are not the only activities that they sponsor. The activists and politicians in the local administrations do much more to help immigrants *orient*: free law consultations, helping them find housing, interventions in cases of actual discrimination, consultation with schools, creation of bilingual education programs for Italian teachers, etc. However, this is not understood as fighting racism, but simply as protecting the individual rights of particular immigrant persons. There is often a lack of recognition of particular inequities as part of structural racism. This lack of recognition, I believe, dooms these activists to work always on the defense, in a sense, solving one at a time the cases of discrimination affecting individual immigrants, but lacking a way to articulate a wider political action.

THE NECESSITY OF IMMIGRANT COMMUNITIES

The Tuscan local politicians and activists I interviewed generally referred to immigrants in terms of communities: the Chinese community, the Romanian community and so on. Each of these communities is supposed or expected to have a spokesperson or representative, somebody who can relay the information coming from local authorities to the whole of the 'community' and who knows and is able to communicate the needs of the same 'community'. This may be a person or, very often, an association. Immigrants are imagined as belonging to communities automatically, as if the fact of coming from the same country would immediately warrant the existence of a community of some kind. This imagination is one-sided. When speaking to persons of immigrant origins, I found them wary to use the term 'community', and they would point out that, even when there is a group of people identifying themselves, for example, as a Romanian community, this does not necessarily include all of the people of Romanian citizenship or origin living in a certain area. At times, the way people related to each other was through much more restricted and at the same time porous networks of friends and families, loosely connected to other networks that may span across cultures or countries of origin. Other times, they identified with much larger units, such as 'Eastern European' or simply 'immigrant'. This renders the term *community* unsuitable to describe the situation and the relationships among immigrants in Tuscany.

However, many local politicians and activists were absolutely convinced of the presence and necessity of communities, and when they did realize their absence, they complained they should be there. One activist went as far as to tell me, "All other immigrants have communities. What's wrong with ours that they do not have them?" Why was the presence of communities so important? I think the answer is to be sought in the need to maintain control, both political-economic and ideal, of immigrants. It is a way of binding and categorizing that may also reinforce racial formation processes.

The concept of community is a complex one, and yet it is too often invoked without a discussion of its meaning. As Baumann has shown,[29] the concept can be extremely problematic. Benedict Anderson's[30] proposal to consider communities as *imagined* already interrogates an older view of them as fixed and bounded groups, pointing instead at the historical and social processes through which people come to see themselves as a community. However, one must be careful not to attribute to this *imagination* an absolute value, assuming that it is completely shared and relevant to people at all times. As Baumann argues,[31] communities may be invoked or denied by people at different times and for different purposes: people do not necessarily imagine themselves as belonging to communities, or at least not at all times. Moreover, one needs to pay careful attention to who does the invoking, or the 'imagining'—if it is done by people who perceive themselves as outsiders with respect to such 'communities', or from the perspective of those who perceive themselves as members. This is particularly appropriate to the Tuscan case, where, and I will return to this ahead, immigrant communities have been imagined to a large degree from outside and above.

The possibility that communities may be *imagined*—or created/produced—from outside and above is important as it forces an interrogation of the relationship between the concept of community and political power. Suggestive, in this regard, is Harold Morris's[32] proposal that the concept of community as it is used in social sciences originated in a colonial context. In his study of Indians in Uganda during the British colonial period, Morris sees 'community' as a colonial construct and conceptualization of the world, created to *organize* the subjects of the colonial state. A propos, Baumann notes:

> The South Asian ethnic minorities—even in East Africa—lived in a society characterized by cross-cutting cultural, economic, political, and other social cleavages. In the colonial context, the community discourse itself can be seen as a denial of these cross-cutting cleavages in the interests of a ruling elite. Those who were not meant to belong to it were conveniently parceled up into communities, there to mind their own business under community supervision. . . . The discourse about ethnic minorities as communities defined by a reified culture bears all the hallmarks of dominance.[33]

One has to wonder then if the concept of community can really be applied without considering the possibility of such colonial origin. In Tuscany today, it still risks being used as an instrument of control and regimentation.

This view of community is fortified when one considers that the label 'community' often entails a sense of otherness: it is the social or cultural other who is perceived as having 'communities'—the working class, the immigrants, the exotic subjects of anthropological research. Similarly, as Renato Rosaldo has argued,[34] 'culture' is also a concept connected to otherness—the 'we' is rarely perceived as having 'culture' in the present.[35] 'Our' culture is removed to the past or seen as endangered, something to be preserved in museums, revitalized or protected through some kind of purism. There is a sense of endangerment. Immigrants' cultures appear to flourish instead—they are strong and resilient, deterministically shaping immigrants' actions. Their communities, by contrast, appear too weak. In my interviews and in focus group discussions I recorded, Tuscans complained about the absence of 'communities' among the immigrants or, in a more benign key, they forecasted that such communities needed time and would form in the future. This contrast is meaningful: communities need to be strong to circumscribe and allow control of the phantasmatic 'strong culture' of the Other, so that culture will not 'overflow' to smother 'us'. Significantly, traditionally scholars have associated the creation of immigrant communities with the first step toward 'assimilation': a necessary step in fact.[36] An example is Joseph Fitzpatrick, who argued:

> If people are torn too rapidly away from the traditional cultural framework of their lives, and thrown too quickly as strangers into a cultural environment which is unfamiliar, the danger of social disorganization is very great. They need the traditional social group in which they are at home, in which they find their psychological satisfaction and security, in order to move with confidence toward interaction with the larger society. The immigrant *community* is the *beachhead* from which they move with strength.[37]

Note the metaphor: the community as "beachhead" indexes that immigrants' arrival is seen as an invasion, a penetration of the host society, at the same time as it supposedly assures that such penetration will be carried on in orderly fashion, without the 'out-of-controllness' that would create further disruptions.

Scholars studying language, especially in the field of contact linguistics,[38] have long realized the trouble with 'community'. These scholars have examined the idea of 'speech community' in their attempt to identify and or describe the speakers of a certain language. A 'speech community' has been defined in various ways—for example, as the people that interact using a common language,[39] or as a group of people sharing a common set of communicative norms.[40] However, it has become increasingly clear that such speech communities are abstract entities that do not correspond to actual bounded social groups.[41] Correspondingly, the concept of language as a bounded code has been brought under scrutiny. A main problem lies with the definition of 'sharing'—a person's knowledge of diverse codes and varieties is always unique and so is a person's language, his or her *idiolect*. Multiple unbounded codes are shared to various degrees among speakers. A concept such as speech community, relying on some kind of boundary, is fundamentally problematic.[42] Rather than separate languages spoken by separate speech communities, one finds a series of "zones of contact,"[43] continua and gradients. Speech communities then, and (imagined) communities, are used to section, categorize, name and possibly control social groups.

THE POLITICAL ECONOMY OF COMMUNITY REPRESENTATION

From the end of the nineties, in Tuscany, the local governmental authorities openly expressed the desire to interact with immigrants through immigrants' associations representing ethnic communities (such as 'the Albanian immigrant association' or similar). They did so, among other reasons, to find a way to make sure, in allocating funds or starting programs to help immigrants, that they were not just helping single individuals, but that they were helping the whole of the immigrants. To better understand this, one needs to understand how the Italian institutions allocate money through the city councils, the provinces and the regions. Here, on the one hand, large amounts of funds are earmarked for particular programs—funds that may appear or disappear in the short run and depending on changes in the political situation—and on the other hand the services to the wider population (including services to the immigrant population) have been progressively decentered from direct state control and from being operated by the institutions themselves. These services have been progressively decentralized, and their operation has been turned over to private organizations, including cooperatives or associations—with a statute and membership—that can demonstrate their capacity to furnish such services.[44]

To obtain information about the felt needs of the immigrants, activists and politicians working in governmental institutions try to identify some spokesperson or some association that can tell them what those are. They try to identify somebody who can speak for the immigrants or for some particular groups of immigrants, such as those of Chinese or Romanian descent. By relating to immigrants as 'communities' in effect the local authorities actively engage in the fabrication of those immigrant communities. One of the important means through which they have done this is by allocating recognition (and thus political power), authority and economic funds to particular individuals and associations seen as *representing* the 'community'. As a response, such associations have mushroomed.

Angela Xhani, a cultural mediator for *Le Api*, an immigrant women's cooperative, who has worked with several of these immigrants' associations, told me that several were created over time with 'community' defined in various ways: either as cultural group, national group, or even supranational group. Most of these associations-cum-communities were short-lived, continuously shifting and changing, often as a consequence of the availability or nonavailability of earmarked funds.

In my research, I found that Tuscan activists in local institutions reacted to this instability with a discontent toward immigrants' associations in general. At times, they felt that the 'spokespersons' they had contacted were phony. In conversations with me, some expressed the feeling that the immigrants were "cheating" in a sense, creating false association to gain money personally. Some doubted that the associations they were in contact with were "the real communities."

Some activists felt burned out and cynical toward immigrant associations. Some felt that whereas they themselves were trying to do good for the immigrants, the immigrants themselves were trying to get favors for themselves or their friends. They wondered how immigrants could be made to think unselfishly about the good of *all* immigrants. Some got to the point of perceiving immigrant associations almost like small mafias that tried to help only their own members. One of the local activists, when interviewed, wondered why, whereas Italians were trying to do good for all immigrants and all people—acting by following principles and ideals of justice—the immigrants could not be brought to do the same, and seemed unable to follow the same ideal principles and help their whole 'community,' trying instead to increase their own personal benefit.

Undoubtedly many immigrants expressed their personal entrepreneurship, and tried to create better employment opportunities for themselves, through the creation of 'associations-representing-communities'. Although they did start associations on the basis of ideas and principles, intending to express immigrant voices and help other immigrants orient themselves in the Italian society, people in these associations also perceived the association as a means of finding a job or making a living. The way in which institutions allocate funds encourages this kind of associationism that is partially interested in ideal principles and partially interested in economic opportunities. However, this is true of local Italians as well, who create the same kinds of associations and cooperatives based partly on ideals and partly on economic needs. For example, cooperatives that offer legal services to immigrants may be staffed by Italian social activists who want to be socially useful while at the same time making a living.[45] Why is this considered acceptable for Italians but not for immigrants? The answer is probably in the way 'community' is idealized.

'Community' invokes feelings of selflessness and brotherhood. Compared to other associations, 'associations-representing-communities' are expected to abide by higher moral principles rather than simple economic need. As Baumann notes,[46] the word 'community' is invariably positive, and more strikingly, as Raymond Williams argues, "unlike all other terms of social organization (*state, nation, society,* etc.) it seems never to be used unfavourably, and never to be given any positive opposing or distinguishing term."[47] Thus community implies a *moral system*. Better still: it is imagined as the fountainhead of the moral system itself. 'Communities' must reassure the majority of the fundamental benevolence—or even meekness—of the minority.[48]

Tuscans in institutions and NGOs rarely questioned the concept of community itself. For them the 'real' immigrant community was out there, but unreachable. The expectation that the community should exist and that it is possible for people in it to have the same needs, goals and agendas remains at the root of the problem. By insisting on having national/ethnic/cultural communities as their interlocutors, the activists are imagining a *subject* into existence, but imagining it as inferior to the Self.

In sum, both the need of institutions to relate to communities and the possibility for institutions to give funding to the communities that present themselves lead the immigrants to produce organisms that can claim to represent or be communities. As I noted earlier, over time this may have the negative effect of creating distrust between the institutions and the immigrants, in which people in institutions start perceiving the 'fabrication' (or inauthenticity) of these communities, whereas, on the other side, they continue to imagine the existence of 'real communities' that they cannot reach (and put the fault for that inability on the immigrants' associations).

COMMUNITIES AND NATIONS

The multiculturalist/interculturalist discourses not only reify cultural differences but also are based on a reification of 'national identities'. A homology is imagined between being citizens of a certain nation-state, belonging to a certain ethnicity/race and being part of a 'community'. I will give two examples. The first regards the organization of international soccer tournaments in Pistoia and Florence, and the second the creation of the Foreigners' Council in Florence.

In Pistoia, a primary association helping immigrants is the *Associazione Pantagruel*, which, since its origins, had the goal of fostering positive relationships among immigrants and between them and the larger society. During an interview there with a social worker, Donato,[49] I asked about the center's activities to fight racism and foster the orientation of immigrants into the local society. Donato narrated in great detail how his association organized a soccer tournament among immigrants.[50] In the tournament, immigrants from the same country played on the same team, and there was also an Italian team included. The soccer tournament thus replicated the multiculturalist idea of 'separate but equal'. It was supposed to foster friendliness between the groups involved and to allow immigrants to "get to know" locals.

The teams' categorization reifies the cultural differences between groups while erasing the differences inside each group. In addition, soccer is a zero-sum game, not one that fosters cooperation between people on opposing teams.[51] Instead, it invokes and reinforces opposing allegiances. In this case, the cultures = communities = nations = teams become in effect engaged as oppositional parties struggling against each other.[52] When I asked Donato about the effectiveness of the tournament, he declared it had been a success, and then expressed admiration toward a similar tournament in Florence that included many more national teams. He took that as an example of Florence's advancement in the *multicultura*.

A similar reasoning was applied to the creation of the *Foreigners' Council* of the Common of Florence. In this case the reification of national identities, paired with an assumption of homogeneous communities—directly mapped onto race/ethnicity—led to the ultimate failure (and falling apart) of the council itself as a democratic and political institution.

In recent years the Italian Left has attempted to pass a law that would grant the vote in local election to all residents, independent of citizenship (thus including immigrant residents). This law proposal was refused by the Italian Right and in the end was not passed. In the meantime, some commons and provinces moved autonomously to grant voting rights to immigrants in local elections.[53] These attempts were blocked by the central government as unconstitutional. Then various commons and provinces resorted to creating the foreigners' councils as alternative ways to give immigrants the possibility of voting and voicing their opinions. Several of the local governments in Tuscany, in opposition to the national government,[54] enacted this option. Among them, the Commons of Florence decided to create the Florence Foreigners' Council, investing it with the power of speaking[55] and advising the city council on matters related to immigration.

However, this decision was made from above, to a large degree in disregard of the opinions coming from the immigrant residents themselves. Moreover, the Foreigners' Council was organized on the basis of a categorization of voters into nationalities, with the underlying understanding that these corresponded to homogenous cultures = communities. At the first elections, lists of candidates were created and divided into national parties, instead of political ones. Also each immigrant could vote only for candidates from his or her own country (Peruvians only for Peruvians, Chinese only for Chinese and so on). South Saharan Africans were lumped together, showing that in this case race, understood here as 'being Black', was equated to culture = community. The immigrants' interests, thus, were understood and imagined to follow the interest of 'their own' racialized nationality. A further assumption was that only an Albanian, for example, could represent an Albanian's point of view and that any Albanian could do it successfully.

The result was disastrous. First, the voting turnout was very low, about 12 percent of eligible immigrants, although one could surmise that immigrants would be interested in electing a representative and making their voice heard. As a consequence, the voting results were skewed toward electing those individuals who had the ability to reach out to large groups from their own country. This meant that the elected representatives did not necessarily have political experience. They often did not have a plan or platform that could be of use and that could command respect from the city council. These newly elected councilors soon found themselves unable to work. Finally, when their first term expired after three years, instead of electing new representatives, Florence's city council unilaterally prolonged the term for an unclear number of years,[56] imposing a very undemocratic understanding of 'representation'. In effect, the originally elected representatives became the all-purpose representatives for the whole of the immigrants. Instead of democratically representing voters, they represent homogeneous units (cultures) that supposedly determine and reflect the interest and wants of their interchangeable members.

Many immigrant activists disassociated themselves from these elections, feeling that the original purpose of the Foreigners' Council had not been well served. One of them, belonging to the COSPE NGO, himself a Nigerian Italian, was quite critical of the elections when I interviewed him. He said:

Interviewee: How can they call it a list [of candidates]? I mean, I would tell them [the elected candidates]: if you had a minimum of political competency, the first thing that you would do is—since you have been elected, the first proposal to the City Council of the Common, [should be] "we are politically mature persons; we want to vote on the basis of ideas, aggregate around ideas." But not—and I told them: I do not live in Florence, but if I were a resident of Florence I would not have voted, I would not have participated, because this is no more than a show of paternalism.

Researcher: Presupposing that all have the same interests?

Interviewee: Not only, but that I do not have the political awareness to recognize in a Peruvian the person that can reflect my interests, and that I would prefer a person of my ethnic group or maybe even worse, of my tribe!

Where immigrants from one country are imagined as acting as a whole, as an 'ethnos', where ethnicity is racialized and homologous to nationality, *individual immigrants' independent political agency is erased.* Although the idea of creating a foreigners' council was a positive idea, and an important experiment toward fostering new forms of social engagement and citizenship, the faulty assumptions about national identities and the reification of culture and ethnicity were an obstacle to its success.

In conclusion a multiculturalist approach, among those people who are trying to fight racism and protect immigrants' rights in Tuscany, leads to overlooking structural racism, focusing instead on activities that reify culture. Such an approach leads to a naturalization of culture and its homologation to ethnicity/race/nationality. This in turn creates obstacles to the immigrants' fuller participation in Italian social life, dooming the action of activists to failure. This analysis urges a rethinking of the concept of community, not toward further discussion of what constitutes a community, but rather toward a critique of how 'community' is being used in certain contexts, by whom, to obtain which goals, and what kinds of effects this concept has on the life of people and on the relationships between them, the institutions and the wider society.

NOTES

1. This chapter was made possible by a fellowship from the Remarque Institute at New York University, and by research grants from the Wenner-Gren Foundation, the National Science Foundation and Oberlin College. It was done under the sponsorship of the Antidiscrimination Center of the Province of Pistoia and the Social Observatory of the Provinces of Pistoia and Prato. I am indebted to Robert Garot, Erika Hoffman, Chantal Tetreault and Angela Xhani for their suggestions on previous versions of this chapter.

2. My research focused on racial formation processes in discourse and immigration in Tuscany, Italy. I conducted fieldwork in Tuscany in the metropolitan area of Florence-Prato-Pistoia from 2005 through January 2009. In these areas immigrants reach 8–12 percent of the total population. I videotaped everyday conversations among groups of people in close networks (such as families, groups of friends or acquaintances, clients in barbershops, etc.); I conducted seventy-nine unstructured interviews with a theoretical sample of the population, fifty-three interviews with social service specialists and volunteers working with immigrants, and eight group focus interviews with members of ARCI recreational clubs. Thanks to my collaboration with Professor Robert Garot (CUNY) I have access to an additional ninety-five interviews with immigrants living in the area and thirty-five interviews with

immigrant service providers. Participant observation with fieldnotes was used to record spontaneous exchanges. I conducted a period of systematic media watch during summer 2006 (mid-June to mid-August), and again in 2008 (March–April).

3. A pseudonym.
4. Apart from governmental agencies, other kinds of agencies working with immigrants are the trade unions, associations and cooperatives, NGOs and the Caritas. Italian trade unions have become increasingly concerned with immigrants' rights in an attempt to stop illegal work practices that hinder both immigrant and Italian workers. Associations—created by immigrants, by locals or both—do specific work (for example, sport associations, music associations, etc.). The largest Italian association, the Association of Italian Recreational Clubs (ARCI), includes offices and agencies that work actively on social causes, including protecting immigrants' rights, fighting racism, helping immigrants to find a job or housing and mediating conflict at the local levels. The ARCI fosters multiculturalism (through events, concerts, dinners, etc.) and furnishes a point of aggregation for intellectual and activists. NGOs working with immigrants include the COSPE (*Cooperazione per lo Sviluppo dei Paesi Emergenti*—Co-operation for the Development of Emerging Countries), which does advocacy for immigrant rights, research on racism and discrimination, media relation monitoring, training programs for teachers and mediators, and courses of Teaching Italian as a Second Language. The Caritas is the Vatican's main caregiving agency. Finally, cooperatives may work independently or be hired by the local government to furnish services related to immigration, such as educational programs, Italian language classes for adults, foreign language courses, conflict mediation courses for social workers, and legal services.
5. See also Cornelius F. Delaney, *The Liberalism-Communitarianism Debate: Liberty and Community Values* (Lanham, MD: Rowman & Littlefield, 1994).
6. Maxim Silverman, *Deconstructing the Nation: Immigration, Racism and Citizenship in Modern France* (London: Routledge, 1992), 26.
7. Étienne Balibar, "Is There a "Neo-Racism"?" in *Race, Nation, Class*, ed. Etienne Balibar and Immanuel Wallerstein (New York: Verso, 1991), 17–28.
8. Paul Gilroy, "Foreword: Migrancy, Culture, and a New Map of Europe," in *Blackening Europe: The African American Presence*, ed. Heike Raphael-Hernandez (New York: Routledge, 2004), xii.
9. Ibid., xiii.
10. Ibid., xv.
11. Gerd Baumann, *Contesting Culture: Discourses of Identity in Multi-ethnic London* (Cambridge: Cambridge University Press, 1996).
12. Ibid., 12.
13. Ibid., 11.
14. Nora Räthzel, "Developments in Theories of Racism," in *Europe's New Racism? Causes, Manifestations, and Solutions*, ed. Events Foundation (New York: Berghahn Books, 2002), 9.
15. Ibid., 7.
16. Baumann, *Contesting Culture*, 16–17; see also Unni Wikan, *Generous Betrayal: Politics of Culture in the New Europe* (Chicago: University of Chicago Press, 2002).
17. Verena Stolcke, "Is Sex to Gender as Race Is to Ethnicity?" in *Gendered Anthropology*, ed. Teresa del Valle (London: Routledge, 1993), 24.
18. Ibid., 24.

19. See also Alana Lentin, *Racism and Anti-racism in Europe* (London: Pluto, 2004).
20. Here meaning 'us locals, us Tuscans'.
21. This argument assumes that immigrants actually want to do those undesirable jobs. But their doing them is already a product of racism and discrimination. Moreover, in the current stagnant economy immigrants and locals are in competition for the same jobs.
22. Paul Gilroy, "The End of Racism," in *'Race,' Culture and Difference*, ed. James Donald and Ali Rattansi (London: SAGE in association with The Open University, 1992), 50.
23. Baumann, *Contesting Culture*, 24–25.
24. The two terms are kept distinct in debates over them in Tuscany, but they are used interchangeably in everyday conversations. Multiculturalism is understood as a state of several cultures living together in respect of each other's differences. Interculturalism is understood as a further step in which these various cultures freely mix to create a unique hybrid. Some activists see the second as the most desirable state, whereas the first is seen as fostering and fixing divisions among human beings. They are both distinguished from *assimilation*, which is understood as an undesirable one-way process in which the receiving society does not change. The term *integration* is often avoided as a synonym for assimilation. *Orientamento* (orientation) or *inserimento* (insertion) are the preferred terms used to describe the process whereby immigrants gain the competence needed to live successfully in the receiving society.
25. The reappropriation of symbols of African culture, in particular, is mediated by a view of Africa as symbol of resistance to oppression.
26. Lentin, *Racism*, 81.
27. Ibid., 22.
28. The name will remain confidential.
29. Baumann, *Contesting Culture*.
30. Benedict R. O'G. Anderson, *Imagined Communities: Reflections on the Origins and Spread of Nationalism* (London: Verso, 1983).
31. Baumann, *Contesting Culture*.
32. Harold S. Morris, *The Indians in Uganda: A Study of Caste and Sect in a Plural Society* (London: Weidenfeld & Nicholson, 1968).
33. Baumann, *Contesting Culture*, 30.
34. Renato Rosaldo, "Ideology, Place and People without Culture," *Cultural Anthropology* 3, no. 1 (1988), 77–87.
35. In Tuscany, a common perception was that 'our' culture was lost or dying. Thus Tuscans see themselves as belonging to a postmodern world of cultural 'loss'.
36. See, for example, Florence Kluckhohn, "Family Diagnosis: Variations in the Basic Values of Family Systems," *Social Casework* 39 (1958), 63–73; Eugene Litwak, "Geographic Mobility and Extended Family Cohesion," *American Sociological Review* 25, no. 3 (1960), 385–394; and Abraham Weinberg, *Migration and Belonging* (The Hague: Martinus Nijhoff, 1961).
37. Joseph P. Fitzpatrick, "The Importance of 'Community' in the Process of Immigrant Assimilation," *International Migration Review* 1, no. 1 (1966): 8, emphasis mine.
38. Mary Louise Pratt, "Linguistic Utopias," in *The Linguistics of Writing: Arguments between Writing and Literature*, ed. Nigel Fabb et al. (Manchester: Manchester University Press, 1987), 48–66.
39. Leonard Bloomfield, "A Set of Postulates for the Science of Language," *Language* 2 (1926): 153.

40. William Labov, *Language in the Inner City: Studies in Black English Vernacular* (Philadelphia: University of Pennsylvania Press, 1972), 120.
41. Robin Queen, "I Don't Speak Spritch: Locating Lesbian Language," in *Queerly Phrased: Language, Gender, and Sexuality*, ed. Anna Livia and Kira Hall (Oxford: Oxford University Press, 1997), 233–256.
42. Rusty Barrett, "The Homo-genious Speech Community," in *Queerly Phrased: Language, Gender, and Sexuality*, ed. Anna Livia and Kira Hall (Oxford: Oxford University Press, 1997), 181–201.
43. Pratt, "Linguistic Utopias," 60.
44. This has happened, for example, for kindergartens, many of which are no longer public but operated by cooperatives funded in part by the Ministry of Education and the city council, and in part by the families. Other areas affected have been the construction and cleaning of public facilities.
45. As a social worker noted in an interview, there is much money to be made by charging immigrants for services that help them deal with bureaucracies.
46. Baumann, *Contesting Culture*.
47. Raymond Williams, *Keywords: A Vocabulary of Culture and Society* (New York: Oxford University Press, 1983), 76.
48. Michael Ignatieff, "Why 'Community' Is a Dishonest Word," *Observer*, May 3, 1992.
49. A pseudonym.
50. The soccer teams included only males. Soccer is perceived as a masculine activity in Italy. When I asked about parallel sport events for women, he said none were done and then, in an interesting twist, put the fault for it on "Muslim culture."
51. In Italy fans of opposite soccer teams are hostile to each other to the point of violence and even killings.
52. In my opinion, to foster cooperation and 'getting to know each other' mixed teams with Italians and immigrants working together would have made more sense.
53. The Italian state is divided into regions, which are divided into provinces (*province*) and commons (*comuni*). Each province has a *prefettura* that represents the central government locally. In Tuscany many commons and provinces have centers to help immigrants navigate the system. The region similarly has some services.
54. The rift and at times hostility between the central government and the local governments have historical roots; see Carl Levy, ed., *Italian Regionalism: History, Identity and Politics* (Oxford: Berg, 1996).
55. Common people cannot speak in the council unless expressly authorized. Presence during council meetings is also restricted.
56. They were still the same after four years, when I did my fieldwork.

4 Legislated Isomorphism of Immigrant Religions

Lessons from Sweden

Gwendolyn Yvonne Alexis

LESSONS FROM SWEDEN

> The [Burial] Law allows other denominations to have their own grave-yards—but, then one has to come to an agreement with The Church's Lutheran parish in the area. This is not always easy. We Catholics and the Muslims can attest to that. (Swedish Catholic priest Åke Göransson)[1]

Göransson made this comment at the dawn of this millennium; he was addressing religious pluralism in a Sweden that had changed dramatically as a result of immigration. Sweden was no longer a religiously homogeneous land of Nordic Lutherans; it had become a multireligious, multicultural society. This was a historic time for the Church of Sweden (Evangelical-Lutheran); effective January 1, 2000, the mandatory church tax that had supported it for five centuries was abolished. Voluntary church dues replaced the tax and these dues, collected through payroll deduction, were paid to the religious denomination designated by the taxpayer. Nevertheless, as indicated by Göransson's statement, dethroning 'the Church' did not serve to put all religions on an equal footing. For one thing, Sweden's Burial Law designates the Church as national trustee (*Huvudmannen*) of the public cemeteries. And, under this authority, the Church administers all of Sweden's public grave-yards save those in Stockholm and the small town of Tranås.

All Swedish taxpayers (regardless of religious affiliation) pay a manda-tory burial tax that entitles them to burial under the National Burial Plan. The Church annually informs the National Tax Authority of its budgetary needs to administer the public cemeteries for the coming year; and that figure is used to establish the burial tax level for all of Sweden. Because there are virtually no private graveyards in Sweden, the Church wields an enormous amount of power with respect to one of the most sacred of reli-gious rituals, the rite of burial. The Swedish National Burial Plan covers the following:

- "Basic burial" with right to a grave for twenty-five years
- Grave opening and closing

- Cremation
- Locale for preserving and viewing body
- Use of funeral chapel without religious symbols
- Transport for body from the time the cemetery authority takes charge of the body until burial

The Church alone has the prerogative to determine whether new cemeteries need to be built to accommodate minority religious faiths in Sweden such as Islam, Catholicism and Judaism. The growth of Sweden's Muslim population has been exponential—from only one thousand Muslim inhabitants in 1970 to a Muslim population of over three hundred thousand by 2001.[2] Today, the number is closer to a half million Muslim inhabitants, which means Muslims now constitute 4.5 percent of Sweden's nine million inhabitants. Eighty percent of these Muslims live in the three largest cities in Sweden—namely, Stockholm, Göteborg and Malmö.[3] Under the Burial Law, the Church has four options for accommodating the burial needs of non-Christian religions:

(1) Construct autonomous public cemeteries for each non-Christian denomination (e.g., a Muslim cemetery, a Jewish Cemetery, a secular-humanist cemetery, etc.);
(2) Construct one cemetery to accommodate all non-Christians;
(3) Construct a separate section in an existing public cemetery for burial of non-Christians; or
(4) Arrange for burial of non-Christians in existing public cemeteries that can accommodate the burial needs of the decedent.

Of course, any denomination—whether Christian or non-Christian—with an eschatology that does not comport with recycling graves after twenty-five years prefers the first option as this allows each denomination to have separate cemeteries, which they administer as autonomous 'keepers of the graves' who are not bound by the administrative guidelines of the Church as national trustee. Although the Burial Law anticipates the possibility of an autonomous graveyard for non-Christian denominations only, the Catholics have succeeded in having a number of Catholic cemeteries built. Nonetheless, constructing autonomous cemeteries for each different religious tradition is an expensive proposition, and as noted by Göransson in the opening quote, Catholics and Muslims are forced to negotiate with the Lutheran parish authorities in order to get their own graveyards built.

NEGOTIATING RELIGIOUS SPACE IN THE US

The burial situation in Sweden came to mind while I was watching an evening news report about a zoning battle being waged in Connecticut by the

Al-Madany Islamic Center of Norwalk to get zoning board approval to build a mosque and community center for the Muslim religious community in the Greater Norwalk area. Since 2010, the Al-Madany Islamic Center has been trying to overcome the objections of would-be neighbors to the proposed mosque. The Islamic center is also trying to overcome the objections of Norwalk residents who do not live in the immediate vicinity of the prospective site of the mosque but who are nonetheless opposed to its construction.[4] The three main reasons given for opposing construction of a mosque on the particular site are concern over (a) plans for a 2,700-square-foot structure on a 1.5-acre lot in a residential neighborhood—here, it is noted that such a large complex will 'dwarf' the existing homes in the neighborhood; (b) plans that provide only eighty-nine parking spaces—here, it is noted that an Islamic center in another Connecticut town with a prayer hall of the same size as that anticipated by the Al-Madany Islamic Center generates 271 vehicle trips for Friday afternoon prayer services; and (c) plans that include construction of a 91-foot minaret—here, little credence is being given to the Al-Madany Islamic Center's statement that the minaret will not contain a horn to sound the traditional five-times-daily call to worship.

The foregoing objections to the siting of the mosque neatly sidestep the issue of the 'foreignness' of the religion that will be practiced in the proposed house of worship. However, the vast majority of zoning and board of adjustment disputes that arise in the US involve minority religions such as Jehovah's Witnesses, Evangelical Christian faiths, Hinduism, Islamism and other religious traditions with religious practices that 'stand out' as different from those of the dominant religion in the area. And so, anticipated traffic problems or overuse of the proposed site due to large membership numbers for the nonconforming religious congregation are just convenient 'red herrings' to raise. These complaints are often expressed in the following way. *Oh, we have nothing against* [fill in the name of the religious minority]. *They can pray to whomever they want; however, our property values will deteriorate and so will our quality of life due to the traffic congestion, and the unsightly building they want to construct in our family-oriented neighborhood.* As will be discussed in more detail ahead, raising these kinds of objections is facilitated in countries with an abundance of 'universal norm legislation' (UNL). UNL allows for the cloak of *universality* (i.e., these same rules apply to everybody), thus serving to divert attention away from the underlying prejudices that are fueling the objections.

Islam is a newly arrived 'immigrant religion' in Connecticut—one of the thirteen original American colonies and a state that, during the early days of the Republic, imposed a mandatory church tax on its residents to support the Congregational Churches of the Standing Order of New England.[5] Thus, Islam in Connecticut suffers from the same stigma of 'foreignness' that burdens Catholicism and Islam in predominantly Lutheran Sweden. Although in one case the issue is securing religious space for the living, whereas in the other the issue is setting aside religious space for the departed, the disadvantage that must be surmounted is the same in both situations. Namely, before immigrant religions can stake a claim to their share of the religious landscape, they must first forge an agreement with the dominant religion in their newly adopted homeland. And yet there is an additional challenge to these new arrivals—namely, in becoming part of the religious rainbow of multicultural societies, immigrant religions must fight against having their distinctive colors muted. Religion is a bearer of culture, making it important for migrant peoples to strive to transmit intact their distinct religio-cultural heritage to the next generation. This will serve to instill immigrant youth with the values that were held dear by those who came before them and, moreover, will give them a valuable sense of self-worth and pride in their particularized identities as hyphenated Americans, Frenchmen, Canadians, Swedes, etc.

However, maintaining religious orthodoxy in the diaspora is not a simple matter. For example, studies have shown that regardless of how a religion is practiced in its country of origin, it takes on a congregational form in the US:

> That Hindu temple may resist calling itself a congregation, but the forces of "institutional isomorphism" still push them to have a leader and a board, an ad in the Yellow Pages "churches" section, and an increasingly predictable range of worship, fellowship and educational activities.[6]

In the foregoing quote, noted sociologist of religion Nancy Ammerman describes how "institutional isomorphism" comes about in the US, a country with an embedded Christian culture and therefore a country with laws rooted in Christian norms and values. America's deeply rooted Christian heritage means *institutional isomorphism* should not be viewed as a harmless sociological phenomenon. The potential for a diminution of the First Amendment right of religious freedom is at risk, especially where religious orthodoxy for adherents to a minority religion entails engaging in rituals (e.g., animal sacrifice) or practices (e.g., smoking peyote) that are either frowned upon or actually illegal under US law. As with UNL, the type of legislation that serves to protect religious liberty is predictive of the problems that will be experienced by those adhering to nontraditional religious faiths in the predominantly Christian West. All Western democracies have laws protecting religious liberty as one of the most fundamental individual rights in a free society. These laws are generally found in a nation's constitution—the overriding general law that establishes the relationship of the government to the citizenry. Broad and vague language of a paraenetic, premonitory and aspirational nature is common in this type of 'de minimus legislation' (DML), which, having anthem-like qualities, sounds more like hope than law.

DML is thus easily circumvented by more directed legislation on the order of UNL. However, an even greater threat to DML is found in 'religion-friendly legislation' (RFL). It is hard for minority religious groups to resist the temptation to shed nonconforming religious practices that might impede their ability to qualify for tax benefits under the law. For instance, in the US, RFL provides for benefits such as exemption from property taxes for real estate used for religious purposes and for the deductibility of donations (on the donor's income tax return or estate tax return) made to religious groups qualifying as eleemosynary organizations under Internal Revenue Code Section 501(c)(3).

Ninety-five percent of the revenue of American religious organizations comes from charitable contributions.[7] The deductibility of a charitable donation is determined by Section 170(c) of the Internal Revenue Code. Because this section provides only for the deductibility of donations to 501(c)(3) organizations, it is crucial for organizations whose main source of revenue is donations to maintain 501(c)(3) status. A factor that the Internal Revenue Service (the regulatory agency in charge of administering the US tax code) takes into consideration in making the determination as to whether a given religious organization is entitled to tax-exempt status is whether the organization resembles other religious organizations that have qualified for Section 501(c)(3) tax-exempt status.[8] Becoming a corporate entity is the first step in achieving Section 501(c)(3) status; this involves incorporating under the laws of the state where the religious group maintains a house of worship.

For religious groups that are not organized as denominations, congregations, presbyteries, parishes or the like, there is no naturally occurring hierarchy upon which to base the formation of an incorporated entity. Hinduism immediately comes to mind as an example of a religion with no inherent structure to utilize for purposes of identifying persons to register with the appropriate secretary of state as the governing body/board of trustees, clergy and membership of the religious group for purposes of incorporation under state law.[9] In fact, Hindus generally worship at home with portable altars and deities that easily fit into the same cabinets or closets where incense is kept on hand for burning during the at-home prayer services. The Hindu 'temple and cultural center' that has increasingly become a part of the religious landscape in US cities is mainly a site for celebrating important Indian festivals and holidays as well as serving as a community center to facilitate the transmission of Hindu culture, Indian values and languages to the next generation in the diaspora.

The actual use of the prototypical Pan-Hindu 'temple' in the US is reflected in the similar architectural plans that have been used for construction of these religious monuments in the US—plans for a small, unassuming second-floor chamber to house four or five of the most popular deities and a capacious ground floor of the structure to contain an auditorium, banquet area, meeting rooms, several small classrooms, an industrial kitchen and an adjacent annex that houses the 'cultural center'. Nonetheless, the 'temple' qualifies as religious space in the 501(c)(3) sense, albeit religious space that has come at a cost of authenticity.

How to 'fit in' but still maintain one's cultural and personal integrity is the challenge that most immigrants in the United States face in their transition from immigrants to ethnics. Indian immigrants from a Hindu background have achieved this end by using Hinduism, albeit a Hinduism that has been recast and reformulated to make this transition possible.[10] Hence, RFL such as 501(c)(3) contributes to *institutional isomorphism* as immigrant religions scramble to adopt the outer manifestations of organized religion in the US by forming congregations, and in some cases even including Sunday worship and Sunday school as part of the mix.[11]

In a book such as this, devoted to 'migrant marginality', it would be remiss not to examine the extent to which homogenization of religious practices in highly administrative immigrant host nations such as the US and Sweden contributes to the marginalization of immigrants by denying them the distinctive voice of particularized religion. The tripartite theoretical model (TTM), which utilizes the DML, UNL and RFL taxonomy discussed earlier, is a useful theoretical tool for assessing the quality of religious liberty accorded to religious minorities in highly administrative states that have in place a large body of legislative enactments as well as administrative law that has been created by regulatory agencies. The remainder of this chapter is devoted to a more thorough discussion of the three components of TTM and to demonstrating the effectiveness of TTM in taking the pulse of religious liberty where laws are embedded with the values and norms of a particular religious tradition, as is generally the case.

> Laws may be neutral in the sense that they do not choose between competing religions, but they are not neutral in the sense that they are not based on values. Those values must come from somewhere and they require evaluation.[12]

THE TRIPARTITE THEORETICAL MODEL (TTM)

De Minimus Legislation (DML)

TTM classifies the types of laws and regulations found in Western secular states on the basis of their impact on religious liberty. It assumes that all Western democracies will have in place legislation protecting fundamental civil rights—for example, freedom of conscience, religion, speech, association and assembly and the right to privacy. Hence, under TTM, this type of legislation is classified as *de minimus* legislation (DML). The First Amendment to the US Constitution, dealing with religious freedom, is an example of DML. Here is the First Amendment with its Swedish counterpart:

> Congress shall make no law respecting an establishment of religion, or prohibiting the free exercise thereof. (US Constitution, First Amendment)

Each citizen shall have the right to . . . alone, or together with others, practice his religion. (Swedish Constitution, SFS 1974:152, chap. 2, sec. 1)

DML allows an individual to adopt either a secular or a religious worldview in accordance with her own personal conscience. It does this by creating an enforceable right that the individual can exercise to hold the state at bay in matters that do not directly affect the community at large. Because DML protects *individual* rights, one does not have to belong to a group to seek redress in the judicial system of a democratic state for protection of rights secured by law.

Nonetheless, because DML is general, broad legislation, it is vague. Hence, it is easily circumvented by more directed legislation, legislation that serves a specific purpose. Under TTM, there are two categories of directed legislation: (1) religion-friendly legislation (RFL) like Internal Revenue Code Section 501(c)(3) discussed earlier and (2) universal norm legislation (UNL) such as the zoning laws discussed earlier in connection with the opposition to the Muslim mosque in Norwalk, Connecticut. Yet the fact that RFL and UNL tend to emasculate DML does not make DML superfluous. Quite to the contrary, in terms of empowerment of religious minorities, DML has the distinct advantage of vesting in the individual the right to file a lawsuit to protest denial of her civil rights, thereby enabling her to have the 'cooler heads' of the judiciary settle the dispute.

> And who should be the bearers of rights in matters of religious freedom—individuals, and/or faith communities? Should the state in any way support individuals—for instance women, or homosexuals—against their faith communities (the Norwegian state has indirectly done so, by appointing liberal bishops)? Or should religious pluralism only be dealt with in a liberal "politics of recognition" which limits itself to protect and support the freedom of faith communities to choose their particular ways?[13]

Religion-Friendly Legislation (RFL)

Engaging in religious advocacy is an integral part of governing for the liberal Western state. Despite its purported secularity, the democratic state puts RFL in place to ensure that the religious sector never ceases to occupy a commanding role in the private sector. In democratic nations, the government lacks authority to command its citizenry to be upstanding and principled. However, the democratic state can facilitate the establishment of those societal institutions that advance norms and values that contribute to societal uplift and that are conducive to the development of a moral citizenry.[14]

Because RFL is directed legislation, it usually contains a preamble that sets forth the public purpose to be achieved by the legislation. Thus, unlike

DML, which sounds more like paraenesis than law, RFL is not susceptible to diverse interpretations. Indeed, RFL is generally administered by a department or agency ensconced within the national government that is charged with interpreting the legislation and adopting regulations that ensure that the governmental purposes for which the legislation was enacted are achieved.

Under RFL, religious groups can qualify for free state services, public funds and tax incentives. As is typical for RFL, only groups—not individuals—can qualify for the benefits. RFL is crafted using the religious practices of the predominant religious group in the state of enactment as the norm. Hence, RFL sanctions the prevalent societal notion of what constitutes religion and what qualifies as a religious practice by offering benefits to religious groups that conform to the norms embedded in the legislation. That there are embedded Christian norms in the RFL enacted in the immigrant host nations of the West is today more evident. As newly arrived, non-Christian, non-Western religions reach a critical mass within the borders of these predominantly Christian lands, the Christian presumption in laws such as Sunday closing laws emerges as a bone of contention, especially among Friday worshippers (which is often the case with adherents to Eastern religions such as Islam).

RFL as Legislated Isomorphism

> [O]ne is not a member of a mosque. All Muslims are one large denomination expanding the globe. . . . But the initiative to help in collection of church dues shows that it is the perspective of the Church of Sweden that guides the laws.(HüseyinAyata, IKUS, Islamic Culture Center in Sweden)[15]

Swedish law provides for the National Tax Authority to collect church dues for all of the minority religious groups in Sweden through payroll deduction.[16] However, as the imam Ayata notes, Islam does not have church members. This is because Islam is not a congregational religion. Nonetheless, the Swedish government had good intentions when it enacted legislation to put non-Lutheran denominations on an equal footing with the Church. And the Catholic Church in Sweden (the second largest minority religion after Islam) was thrilled with the legislation and the collection service.[17] Having a steady and predictable income stream makes it more certain that nonprofit organizations like churches will continue to exist. This is exactly what the Swedish Parliament intended—namely, to provide minority religious groups with the same steady income stream that the Church enjoys.

However, a certain organizational structure was assumed for those religious organizations desiring to partake of the government's largesse. This meant that even noncongregational religions like Islam and Hinduism would have to become congregational in order to have the state's payroll deduction bureaucracy at their disposal. Additionally, religious groups wanting to take advantage of the church dues collection service are required to become incorporated entities under Swedish law. However, as noted earlier, for religions that are noncongregational, no easily incorporated unit of worshippers exists. Moreover, the need to adopt a formal hierarchical structure with a governing body can actually undermine the theological teachings of a particular religious tradition. This is the case with Islam, in which there is no professional clergy given that Islamic theology admonishes that there is no need for a mediator between the believer and Allah.

In short, nontraditional religious groups have a difficult time qualifying for benefits under RFL (and for their rightful share of the tax revenues that are used to pay for these benefits) unless they are willing to 'repackage' themselves so as to more closely resemble the predominant religio-cultural group. Hence, in Sweden, as is the case in the US, RFL provides an incentive for organizational remolding of new immigrant religions and eventually results in institutional isomorphism, and, in the worst case scenario, a homogenization of religious practices in countries that, with presumably good intentions, have enacted substantial RFL. The following are additional examples of RFL currently in effect in Sweden:

- SFS 1999:932 Subsidization of Religious Groups
- SFS 1999:974, §4 Subsidization of Theological Education
- SFS 1999:974, §12 Subsidization of Acquisition and Maintenance of Sites for Religious Activities

RFL and Civil Society

It is important to emphasize that only *groups* can benefit from RFL. Individuals benefit from RFL only indirectly; they do this by belonging to a *religious* group. Thus, RFL entails a financial incentive for group formation on the basis of religious identity. Although it is no doubt advantageous in terms of social control for immigrants to be colonized under the religious sector, it is worth pondering whether the interests of non-Christian immigrants in a predominantly Christian society would be better advanced by networking with the politically aggressive rather than with the religiously sanguine. Hence RFL can be viewed as merely self-interested behavior on the part of a state bent on steering marginalized minorities away from formation of groups that will focus a critical lens on systemic sources of inequality in the current governmental administration.[18]

It is important to keep in mind that religious institutions serve both secular and sacred functions. When religious institutions function as mediating structures to help immigrants connect with the greater society in their newly adopted homelands, they are performing a secular function; the religious institution is being used as social space, rather than as sacred space. As social space, the 'church' provides a link to the secular world that lies outside of the sacred canopy[19]—a world occupied by those with different worldviews from the believers inside the sacred tent.

On the other hand, sacred space is meant to symbolically shut out the profane world, to provide refuge from the cares of the day. Hence, the social interaction taking place in sacred space is exclusive rather than inclusive. Here social interaction involves participating in religious rites and rituals in fellowship with like-minded believers. RFL is meant to draw on the sacred role of religious institutions, to enable the state to benefit from religion as a source of moral uplift. In enacting RFL, the bureaucratic state is generally not attempting to bolster the role of religious institutions as either mediating structures or agents of civil society.

In 2005, the Swedish government issued *The Blue-Yellow Glass House: Structural Discrimination in Sweden*, a report on an expansive research project that investigated discriminatory treatment of ethnic and religious minorities in Sweden—discrimination that is caused by Swedish laws, structures and institutions (all three being lumped under "structural discrimination" in the report).[20] The investigation included a review of the existing literature on *structural discrimination* in Sweden and a survey of the laws and institutions that are in place in Canada, the UK and the US to deal with *structural discrimination* or 'institutionalized racism'—as it is called in the US. The survey included a thorough coverage of US civil rights laws.

The Blue-Yellow Glass House report concludes that a disturbing inequality exists between the overall welfare of indigenous Swedes and the immigrant population, with the immigrants doing considerably worse—although immigrants from other European countries are not as bad off as the ethnic and religious minorities that were the main focus of the study.[21] Specific areas examined to determine the welfare of the research subjects included their health, housing, education, economics and employment. The report leaves no doubt that racism is a major contributing factor to the inequality.[22]

Among the recommendations made in the report to counteract the pervasive structural discrimination that exists in Sweden is one that is particularly apropos to this discussion of RFL. The recommendation is made that the Swedish state allocate funds to strengthen civil society so that ethnic and religious minorities are empowered to better their own situation by participating in the political process. The report notes that mobilization of civil rights groups in the UK, Canada and the US has helped to combat discriminatory treatment of minorities in these countries.[23]

An interesting finding of *The Blue-Yellow Glass House* report was that Swedish exceptionalism is a myth; the fact that Sweden had never been a colonial power and even its heroic resistance to the Nazis did not make Sweden immune from the same xenophobia and racism against Africans and Asians that arose and spread in other European countries.[24] Indeed, the report attributes the difficulties Sweden has had in banning ethnic discrimination in the workplace to the steadfast denial that discrimination is a problem—a denial that can now be seen "as a thread that runs through Sweden's immigrant policy and later integration policy."[25] In light of these findings, the report notes the similarities between the plight of ethnic and religious minorities in Sweden and the marginalized racial and ethnic minorities in the US, Canada and the UK. Given that the situation of the latter groups improved when they became advocates for their own cause, the report recommends enhancing the mobilization skills of ethnic and religious minorities in Sweden as a way of empowering them to be their own advocates:

> The development of various measures for counteracting discrimination in the USA, Canada and Great Britain has been stimulated by organisations in civil society. They have succeeded in mobilizing those affected, in developing the necessary knowledge base and making demands.
>
> The most prominent tools in these countries for counteracting discrimination, including structural discrimination, have been developed in a process that combined political leadership, strong civil society organisations that gathered those affected, and a focus on changing behavior. The process resulted in stronger laws, institutions and policies—such as anti-discrimination clauses in public contracts (contract compliance).[26]

Certainly, the recognition of the Swedish state that only a mobilized civil society will bring an end to the discriminatory treatment being experienced by Sweden's ethnic and religious minorities has important implications in terms of evaluating RFL and its real effect on religious liberty. With Muslims, in particular, RFL results in encouraging the formation of a collective identity that actually results in a loss of social and cultural capital due to the pariah status of Islam in Sweden. In a 2004 study by the Swedish Board of Integration (*Integrationsverket*)—involving 2,557 respondents—two-thirds of those responding felt that "Islamic values are not compatible with the fundamental values of Swedish society."[27] Since the attack on the World Trade Center, Muslims or people believed to be Muslims have felt the brunt of the terrorist hysteria that has gripped the Western world. The prejudicial stereotyping that befalls Muslims in predominantly Christian lands has attracted a good deal of scholarly attention and research funding. The Open Society Institute (OSI), a nonprofit organization dedicated to "protecting and improving the lives of people in marginalized communities," has commissioned major research projects focusing on Muslims in Sweden, Denmark, Belgium, France, Germany, the Netherlands and the UK.[28] As might be expected in a post–9/11 era, Arab Americans have become frequent targets of harassment, racial bias and discrimination in the US.[29]

Universal Norm Legislation (UNL)

The remaining category of directed legislation is universal norm legislation (UNL), which is a conglomeration of laws, regulations and bureaucratic procedures adopted by various levels of the governmental hierarchy to carry out the social and public policy agendas of the state. UNL enforces what are deemed to be universally valid standards for human behavior in the enacting state. In other words, UNL embodies social engineering based upon the predilections of a particular culture. Hence, even where the standards do not reflect a universal consensus on moral mandates and the UNL is embedded with norms rooted in a country's religio-cultural heritage, UNL will be upheld and requests for exemptions from adhering to the standards will be denied. In Western liberal democracies, a common subject of UNL is the environment, with ecological sustainability being promoted as a moral obligation upon which there is universal agreement. As a matter of fact, the idea of man as shepherd of the earth is rooted in the Christian Bible, which means that many countries lacking a Christian cultural heritage are not yet on board the environmental sustainability bandwagon. As noted, UNL has public policy implications, and carrying out a state's public policy agenda will often outweigh preserving individual rights protected by DML.

As a Scandinavian welfare state, Sweden has a penchant for social engineering. This is reflected in the abundance of UNL in Sweden—UNL that greatly circumscribes the areas in which individuals are allowed to exercise personal choice. Examples of this type of UNL are the Swedish law declaring circumcision to be a medical procedure rather than a religious ritual and the law prohibiting the slaughter of meat in accordance with the theological dictates of Islamism and Judaism. More important in terms of this chapter are the limitations that UNL places upon the ability of Muslims to make burial choices on the basis of religious conviction; I turn to that next.

BURIAL IN SWEDEN

> The Church of Sweden shall by computerized medium inform the Government, or other authority designated by the Government, of the level of the [Burial] Fee assessment rates that it recommends for the following fiscal period. . . . In the same manner, the Church of Sweden shall provide the National Tax Authority with the additional information that it needs to calculate, assess, validate, and collect the Fees. (Burial Law, chap. 9, §14)[30]

Vintage UNL, the Burial Law bans the operation of cemeteries for profit.[31] Moreover, nonprofit entities (e.g., religious groups and foundations) seeking to establish private cemeteries must go through a number of hoops. First, they must establish to the satisfaction of the Swedish government that there is a special need for a private cemetery, and then they must document that they have the financial wherewithal to maintain a private cemetery in accordance with the 'Good Burial Culture' (*God Gravkultur*) mandate contained in Sweden's Burial Law.

A Pragmatic Approach to Burial

Along with birth, coming of age and marriage, death is a rite of passage that is typically observed by engaging in theologically dictated ceremonies or rituals. This means non-Lutherans are likely to have different burial rituals from Lutherans; and these particularized rituals will, more often than not, be better accommodated in cemeteries that are exclusively devoted to the burial of those adhering to the particular religious tradition. In Sweden, an additional factor is that the high degree of secularity among the indigenous Swedes is reflected in the prevalence of a pragmatic attitude toward burial. For instance, in 2008, 75.4 percent of all decedents in Sweden were cremated, up from 74 percent of all decedents in 2007. Additional evidence of a pragmatic approach to burial is the apparent ease with which the Swedes have accepted a National Burial Plan that covers use of a grave site for a limited period of twenty-five years, at which time the grave is recycled.[32]

The theologically dictated Muslim burial ritual stands in stark contrast to Swedish pragmatism in matters of burial.[33] According to the eschatology of Islam, the body shall rise from the grave and be judged at the end of time. Therefore, cremation is prohibited. Other specific requirements of the Islamic burial ritual are that the corpse be washed in a simple ceremony (with male cadavers being washed by males and female cadavers by females). The washing generally occurs at the place of death or in a special room of a mosque. It is important that the washing not be done by funeral home personnel. The body is then wrapped in sheets of unstitched white cloth with three cloths for male decedents and five cloths for females. The body is interred without a casket and is placed on its right side and facing Mecca. The grave is to be mounded or framed to make sure that it will not be walked on by accident. In fact, nothing can be placed on top of a Muslim grave as it is believed that this would delay exiting the grave on the Day of Resurrection.

Additionally, Muslims wish not to be buried in the vicinity of Christian symbolisms, therefore making burial in Swedish churchyards (cemeteries next to a Swedish church) undesirable. Nevertheless, it is conceivable that Muslim burial needs can be accommodated in a cemetery devoted to the burial of all non-Christians, which is one of the burial alternatives available to the Church for handling non-Christian burials under the Burial Law. However, allocating space in an existing public cemetery for Muslim burial cannot be recommended in light of what occurred with the construction of a new section of Furets Woodland Cemetery (Furetsskogskyrkogård) in Mark. The town of Mark is not far from Gothenburg, and the cemetery was being subdivided to build a Muslim cemetery. Happy at the prospect of no longer having to travel to a more distant Muslim cemetery, the Muslims were willing to negotiate with the Church's local parish authority in order to get their section of the Furets cemetery built. After securing a promise from the Furets Parish authority that the new cemetery section would be located on the easternmost portion of the property up against a forest so that there would be no

Christian symbolisms in eyesight when they turn toward Mecca, the Muslims agreed to bury their dead in caskets, rather than merely enshrouding the cadavers in accordance with their religious tradition.[34]

This type of coerced conformity to a Christian burial norm is a violation of the right of Muslims to freely practice Islamism in Sweden.[35] And, although there are fifty Muslim cemeteries in Sweden today compared to fewer than ten Muslim graveyards when the Furets 'horse-trading' occurred, there is still pressure on Muslims to 'rehabilitate' their burial practices by bringing them in line with the Christian burial norm:

> Most of our cemeteries have been in existence for centuries. They are often from the middle ages and are adjacent to the parish church. Over the passage of time, the cemeteries have changed in different respects in accordance with the preferences of the day and local changes in burial practices. Thus, the way the cemeteries appear today reflects in many respects society's development over a long period of time, both in terms of grave monuments and in terms of overall graveyard architecture. Hence the cemeteries are an important part of the cultural heritage and the cemetery authorities have a large responsibility to protect this cultural heritage. The responsibility is based upon regulations contained in the Cultural Monuments Law and the Burial Law, but strong local involvement in the preservation effort is also required if it is to be successful. (Emphasis added)[36]

In protecting the cultural heritage of Swedish cemeteries, the cemetery authorities are aided by the 'Good Burial Culture' (*God Gravkultur*) mandate in the Burial Law,[37] which provides for the cemetery authority to override the personal choices of individual grave owners when necessary to preserve a uniformity of appearance and good taste in the graveyards. As an example of the type of adornment that might be considered in poor taste, while engaged in field research in Lund, Sweden, in 2001, I read newspaper accounts of toys being removed from the graves of young children and of limits being set (in Catholic graveyards) for the height of monuments on the graves of Roma (gypsies). The Burial Law also has a provision that allows the local cemetery authority to make changes to a grave "where the authority deems it necessary in order to protect the environment, the health and safety of cemetery employees, and the visiting public."[38] As an example of the exercise of this prerogative, plastic items (such as plastic flowers) are not allowed as grave adornments in Sweden.

I have chosen to give extended attention to Sweden's Burial Law as an example of UNL because the Burial Law embodies the very element of Swedish culture that puts it on a collision course with not-easily secularized religions such as Islam. This is because a law that rationalizes the processing of the dead (as the Burial Law does) is more easily countenanced in a secular society in which burial is deemed a rite of passage rather than a religious ritual.

There is clearly a need for Muslims to become politically active in Sweden in order to stake their claim to a part of the religious landscape in Sweden. At present, the Burial Law constitutes the most direct assault on their religious liberty. It is UNL versus DML, and for the Muslims this battle must be fought in the political arena. Although they may 'negotiate' with the Church as was done with respect to the Furets cemetery, they cannot influence the policies that the Church implements at the public cemeteries because Muslims do not have a right to vote in the election of officers of the Church because they are not members of the Church. Nonetheless, under the Burial Law it is the Church through the action of its forty thousand elected representatives (the majority of whom are politicians and all of whom are Lutherans) that determines which burial rites and rights are to be honored in Sweden.[39]

CONCLUSION

The fact that UNL and RFL can undercut DML has important implications for policy makers and immigration scholars with an interest in the role that religion plays in the integration of non-Christian immigrants into predominantly Christian societies.[40] Because of UNL and RFL, proclamations that a country has laws protecting 'religious freedom' or that it is a 'secular state' ring hollow. Such labels do not address the real issue for non-Christian religious groups—namely, the legal categorizations that will be applied to their nonconforming religious practices in an overwhelmingly Christian culture. TTM is useful in assessing the likelihood that religious newcomers will be accorded the religious freedom that DML promises.

The immigrant can be likened to Georg Simmel's "stranger"—a person with no vested interest in the *status quo*, someone who has yet to become "committed to the unique ingredients and peculiar tendencies of the group, and therefore approaches them with the specific attitude of 'objectivity'."[41] Whether it is the arrival of Catholicism and Islamism in Lutheran Sweden or the assemblage of a critical mass of non-Christians in the covertly Christian US, having nonconforming religious groups in their midst will serve as a litmus test for the claimed secularity of these pedigreed democracies. Western immigrant host nations have flown the banner of religious neutrality while enjoying largely religiously homogeneous populations. However, they are now experiencing *deep* diversity for the first time as a result of having 'strangers' in their midst. The presence of these strangers with their dissimilar beliefs, cultures and complexions challenges the prevailing paradigm that church-state separation *per se* results in a religiously neutral state.

> The stranger, like the poor and like sundry 'inner enemies', is an element of the group itself. His position as a full-fledged member involves both being outside it and confronting it.[42]

NOTES

1. Original in Swedish; translated by author. As quoted by Ivan Garcia in "Sverigeblirmångreligiöst: Sammareglerför all trossamfundnärkyrkanskiljsfrånstaten" [Religious pluralism in Sweden: The same rules for all faiths when church and state separate], *Sesam* 26, July 7, 1999.
2. Göran Larsson, "Sweden," in *Muslims in the EU: Cities Report*, 2ⁿᵈ Edition (New York: Open Society Institute Publishers, 2010).<http://www.opensocietyfoundations.org/sites/default/files/a-muslims-europe-20110214_0.pdf>Error! Hyperlink reference not valid.
3. Catholics are the second largest religious minority in Sweden after Muslims. In 2010, it was estimated that there were approximately 140,000 Catholics in Sweden. "AntaletKatolikeriSverigeÖkar," StockholmsKatolskaStift, Mar. 31, 2010, accessed Apr. 21, 2010, http://www.katolskakyrkan.se/1/1.0.1.0/103/1/?item=art_art-s1/274.
4. Because crowds of four hundred to five hundred protestors have shown up at the zoning board hearings on the proposed mosque, it is obvious that not all of those expressing an interest are neighbors living in the immediate vicinity of the site for the proposed mosque. Robert Koch, "Neighbors Oppose Proposed Mosque," *The Hour*, posted April19, 2003, accessed April 12, 2003, http://www.thehour.com/newds/norwalk/neighbors-oppose-proposed-mosque/article709e8
5. Unfortunately, in the early days of the republic, the American dream of religious freedom was greater than the reality. Throughout New England, mandatory church taxes supported Protestantism, granting a virtual religious monopoly to the Congregational churches of the Standing Order of New England. Akhil Reed Amar, *The Bill of Rights: Creation and Construction* 64 (New Haven: Yale University Press,1998).
6. Nancy Tatom Ammerman, *Pillars of Faith: American Congregations and Their Partners* (Berkeley: University of California Press, 2005), 257.
7. Woodrow Powel and Richard Steinberg, eds. *The Non Profit Sector: A Reseach Handbook (*New Haven: Yale University Press, 2002), accessed April 12, 2003, http://www.bc.edu/content/dam/files/research_sites/cwp/pdf/Charitable.pdf>
8. One of the most high-profile denials of Section 501(c)(3) status was that involving the Church of Scientology. The US Supreme Court upheld a determination by the commissioner of internal revenue that the Church of Scientology is organized mainly for commercial purposes. Hence, although it is a religion, people making donations to it are not entitled to a tax deduction under IRC §170(c) for their contributions. Hernandez v. Commissioner, 490 U.S. 680, 109 S.Ct. 2136, 104 L.Ed.2d 766 (1989).
9. "Hinduism as a term of reference to a 'faith' is something of an external creation. The name was introduced by the Persians to describe all beliefs in India—across the River Indus. Hindus themselves see what they believe as being how they live. There is no sense of one set of beliefs for everyday life and another for religious life." Joanne O'Brien and Martin Palmer, *The State of Religion Atlas* (New York: Simon & Shuster, 1993), 96.
10. PremaKurien, "Becoming American by Becoming Hindu: Indian Americans Take Their Place at the Multicultural Table," in *Gatherings in Diaspora: Religious Communities and the New Immigration*, ed. R. Stephen Warner and Judith Wittner (Philadelphia: Temple University Press, 1998), 37.
11. "The Mission has made significant changes to common mosque practices in order to adapt to the North American environment. By far the most significant of these has been to accept a professionalized clergy in the form of a hired

imam. Other changes include developing a sense of membership in the mosque, creating Sunday events such as Sunday school, and adopting nonprofit organizational structure in order to have a body to own and govern the mosque." Rogaia Mustafa Abusharaf, "Structural Adaptations in an Immigrant Muslim Congregation in New York," in *Gatherings in Diaspora: Religious Communities and the New Immigration*, ed. R. Stephen Warner and Judith Wittner (Philadelphia: Temple University Press, 1998), 251. See also R. Stephen Warner, "Religion and New (Post-1965) Immigrants: Some Principles Drawn from Field Research," *American Studies* 41, no. 2–3 (2000): 279.

12. Timothy Fort, *Law and Religion* (Jefferson: McFarland, 1987), 115.

13. OddbjørnLeirvik, "Christian-Muslim Relations in a State Church Situation: Lessons from Norway" (paper presented at Muslim Minority Workshop, University of Erfurt, Mar. 2–3, 2001), accessed Apr. 12, 2013 http://folk.uio.no/leirvik/. In 2001, an 'honor killing' of a twenty-six-year-old Kurdish immigrant in Sweden (by her father because she refused to enter into an arranged marriage) sparked public outrage throughout Scandinavia over government policies that prioritized group rights over individual rights, leaving immigrant religious groups functioning as autonomous colonies within the greater Scandinavian societies of Sweden, Denmark and Norway. This government complacency, it was felt, had allowed the father to murder his daughter (who had made several pleas for help that were televised on Swedish TV prior to her murder). Leirvik is making the point that such complacency is not respecting religious freedom; rather it is governments playing 'identity politics'.

14. "Civil Government therefore, availing itself only of its own powers, is extremely defective; and unless it can derive assistance from some superior power, whose laws extend to the temper and disposition of the human heart, and before whom no offense is secret, wretched indeed would be the state of man under a civil condition of any form. This most manifest truth has been felt by Legislators in all ages, and as man is born, not only a social, but a religious being, so in the Pagan world false and absurd systems of religion were adopted and patronized by the magistrate, to remedy the effects necessarily existing in a Government merely civil." Thomas Banes v.The Inhabitants of the First Parish in Falmouth, 6 Mass. 401 (1810).

15. Original in Swedish; translated by author. Garcia, "Sverigeblirmångreligiöst."

16. SFS 1998:1593, §16.

17. "The new method of collecting Church Dues will give our Church greater possibilities to be active in society and to give a public voice to religion." Archbishop Anders Arborelius, "Kyrkoavgiften," KatolskaKyrkan I Sverige, 2000, accessed Oct. 19, 2000, http://www.catholic.se/se/stiftet/kyrkoavgift/info2.html (original in Swedish; translated by author).

18. In this vein, political activity is a grounds for loss of 501(c)(3) status in the US, where there is no doubt that activism on the part of religious groups is frowned upon by the US government. This is ironic in light of the iconic role that black churches played in the civil rights movement.

19. Peter Berger, *The Sacred Canopy: Elements of a Sociological Theory of Religion* (Garden City: Doubleday, 1967).

20. Statens Offentliga Utredningar (SOU), *Det Blågula Glashuset—Strukturell Diskriminering I Sverige* [The blue-yellow glass house: Structural discrimination in Sweden], (Stockholm: SOU, 2005), 56 accessed Aug. 31, 2009, http://www.regeringen.se/sb/d/108/a/46188.

21. Thirteen percent of Sweden's population is foreign-born. According to statistics gathered by the ILO in 2005, almost one-fourth of the foreign-born are from Nordic countries (principally Finland), with another one-fourth of the foreign-born originating in European countries that are not part of

the European Union (e.g., Serbia, Montenegro and Bosnia-Herzegovina); and about one-third of the foreign-born come from Asia and the Middle East.Karin Attström, *Discrimination against Native Swedes of Immigrant Origin in Access to Employment* (Geneva: International Labor Office, 2007),accessed Sept. 3, 2009, http://www.ilo.org/public/english/protection/migrant/download/imp/imp86e.pdf.

22. SOU (Statens offentliga utredningar), *Blue-Yellow Glass House*, 42–43.
23. Ibid, 53.
24. Ibid., 42.
25. Ibid., 42.
26. Ibid., 51.
27. Swedish Board of Integration, *Integrationsbarometer*[Integration barometer](Stockholm: SBI, 2004), 12.
28. "About Us," Open Society Foundations, accessed May 31, 2009, http://www.opensocietyfoundations.org/about.
29. The American-Arab Anti-discrimination Committee (ADC) is the largest Arab American civil rights organization in the US. It was founded in 1980 to protect the civil rights of people of Arab descent in the US and to promote Arab cultural heritage. The ADC has reported that "Arab-Americans continue to face higher rates of employment discrimination than in the pre-9/11 period, in both public and private sectors . . . Arab-American students continue to face significant problems with discrimination and harassment in schools around the country." ADC Research Institute, *Hate Crimes Report 2003–2007: A Report on Racially Motivated Crimes and Civil Rights Violations That Occurred during the Years 2003–2007*(Washington, DC: ADC,2008).
30. Original in Swedish; translated by author.SFS 1990:1144 Begravningslag [Burial law], chap. 9, 14§, revised through 2008, 208.
31. This means Sweden is unlikely to encounter cases in which cemetery operators have dug up bodies and tossed them in heaps in order to resell the plots, as has occurred in Los Angeles, California, with the Lincoln Memorial Park and Paradise Memorial Cemetery (the latter being where the author's parents, a sister and a brother were buried—at least for a while). "Cemetery Owners Are Accused of Dumping Bodies to Resell Graves," *Sunday Star-Ledger*, Aug. 20, 1995, 43. Similar desecration of graves (for crass commercial purposes) in a historically black cemetery occurred in Noble, Georgia, in 2002 at the Tri State Crematory. "Six Bodies Found at Crematory Operators Home," CNN.com, Feb. 20, 2002 accessed Apr 12, 2013, http://archives.cnn.com/2002/US/02/16/crematory.bodies/index.html. And most recently, at Burr Oak cemetery, one of Chicago's oldest predominantly African American cemeteries (where Emmett Till, the young martyr of the civil rights movement, blues legend Dinah Washington and boxing champ Ezzard Charles are buried), detectives found more than 1,100 human bones that had been scattered around the premises in order to accommodate a grave reselling scheme. Don Babwin, "Authorities Stop Getting Evidence at Ill. Cemetery," Yahoo!News, Aug. 7, 2009, accessed Sept. 4, 2009, http://news.yahoo.com/s/ap/us_cemetery_desecration/.
32. Swedish law provides for graves that predate 1850 to be preserved as an exception to the twenty-five-year recycling rule because they are "handmade products that predate the Industrial Revolution." "Kulturminneslagen" [Cultural monuments statute], SFS 1988, 950. There is also the possibility of a surviving relative paying a grave renewal fee for extended rental of the grave site.
33. Group graves containing the cremated remains of several decedents have gained headway in Sweden as an environmentally sensitive approach to

burial. The 'memorial grove' (*minneslund*)—as group graves are called—is usually sited in the most picturesque section of a cemetery and is beautifully landscaped with attractive stone and water elements. Gwendolyn Yvonne Alexis, "Legislative Terrorism: A Primer for the Non-Islamic State; Secularism and Different Believers" (PhD diss., New School for Social Research, 2003), 31.

34. "Muslimsk begravningsplats I Mark" [The Muslim graveyard in Mark], *Kyrkogården* January, 17, 2003.

35. It should be noted that the Furets Cemetery administration offered "consideration of graveyard employees" as a reason for negotiating to have the cadavers placed in caskets before burial.

36. Original in Swedish; translated by author. Central Grave Care Committee, *Gravvårdar: Allmänna råd för bevarande och återanvändning*[Grave care: General advice for preserving and recycling],3rd ed. (Stockholm: CGK, 1998), 1.

37. SFS 1990:114, 7 kap. 26§, Begravningslag [Burial law].

38. SFS 1990:114, 7 kap. 30§, Begravningslag [Burial law].

39. With $4.7 billion in assets, the Church is big business. SvenskaKyrkan [Church of Sweden Homepage], accessed Aug. 31, 2009, http://www.svenskakyrkan.se/.

40. The Pew Charitable Trusts sponsored the 'Gateway Cities Projects' to examine the role of religion in the incorporation of the post-1965 immigrants into US society. The Social Science Research Council has called for immigration scholars to give more attention to the role of religion in immigrant enculturation in the US. Social Science Research Council, "Migration and Religion," accessed Aug. 20, 2012, http://www.ssrc.org/programs/migration-and-religion.

41. Georg Simmel, *The Sociology of Georg Simmel* (New York: Free Press, 1950), 404.

42. Ibid., 402.

Part II

Manufacturing Exclusion

Anti-immigrant Politics and Policies

5 Constructing Otherness
Media and Parliamentary Discourse on Immigration in Slovenia[1]

Ana Kralj

Whenever one discusses the issue of borders and mobility within the context of European enlargement processes, one immediately notices that migration policies are taking shape, above all, as border policies that are transforming the European Union into 'Fortress Europe'.[2] The sharp edges of Eastern Europe, once made of iron and concrete, have been replaced by fabrics that are more refined: electronic communication and paper. In a word, new borders are above all bureaucratic. Pushing immigrants off and beyond the external protected borders of the European Union is simply a partial and inadequate response to migration processes that are becoming more and more dynamic and diversified. " . . . immigrants, beginning with foreigners in irregular situations or who can easily be rendered illegal, are deprived of fundamental social rights (such as employment insurance, health care, familial allocations, housing, and schooling) and can be expelled as a function of 'thresholds of tolerance' or 'capacities of reception and integration' that are arbitrarily established according to criteria of 'cultural distance'— that is, race in the sense the notion has taken on today."[3]

The aim of this chapter is to examine the construction and stigmatization of immigrants in Slovenia, one of the seven countries formed after the dissolution of Yugoslavia. Through a discursive analysis approach we would like to elucidate how the press and the political representatives in the Slovenian parliament reacted to the arrival of foreigners ('illegal' immigrants) in the period of the so-called immigrant crisis in 2000 and 2001. The public discourse of the time established a series of discriminatory discursive practices, in which the dominant thesis was that Slovenianhood was threatened. The research shows that this construction and stigmatization of foreigners was repeated in time and consolidated into a pattern. The reluctant attitude toward to foreign immigration in Slovenia thus presents a general context—a process, rather than a single act that took place over a limited period of time (i.e., during a 'crisis period').

Furthermore, I will try to demonstrate that the construction and stigmatization of foreigners has characteristics of a nationalistic discourse: it hegemonizes certain formulations of the nation against others, thereby blurring the fractures and differences of opinion within the nation and dominates other discourses or alternative political languages, by 'nationalizing' narrative and interpretative frames and ways of perceiving, evaluating, thinking and feeling.[4]

Xenophobia is not only an ethical or a moral problem of a certain society but also a latent scene of action for political conflicts. Prejudices and stereotypes, which support the nationalistic and xenophobic attitude toward 'immigrant others', are more than merely oversimplified judgments arising from narrow-sightedness or limited knowledge. Prejudices and stereotypes are also political measures; ideological tales that are the driving force of existing social and economic relations. They can exist only by incorporating all of the crucial material carriers of ideologies; like the family, school, media and politics, and they require discursive networks of signs, systems of symbols and manners of discourse and coding. Of course they also require the 'living power' of people to start up the material and symbolic machinery and to keep it in motion. Prejudices and stereotypes based on ethnic/racial appurtenance are nothing but alibis for displays of power. Ethnic/racial discrimination and xenophobia—whether insulting remarks and attitudes or the perfidious violence of ignorance—that are based on the alibi of prejudices are therefore never 'an event', but rather a process, nesting within relations of power.

ATTITUDE TOWARD IMMIGRANTS IN SLOVENIA

The politics of exclusion and rejection, institutionalized at (trans)national levels in the form of restrictive migration policies, also resounds at local levels. Different 'civil society' initiatives and movements opposed to 'foreign' migration in the name of 'our autochthony' are increasingly being formed. Slovenia already began witnessing such reactions in the 1970s, with the arrival of workers from the then Yugoslav republics, and again after Slovenia's independence, in the beginning of the 1990s, in the period of the so-called refugee crisis, when refugees from Bosnia and Herzegovina sought shelter in Slovenia. In the years 2000–2001, the so-called immigrant crisis culminated, which was marked by the problematics of 'illegal immigrants' and asylum seekers. Lastly, Slovenia recently witnessed the resistance of several Slovenian local communities that strongly opposed the settlement of a Roma family in "their local environment," expressing their disapproval even by way of forming neighborhood watches.

Research on the opinion of majority populations in Slovenia toward foreign immigration reveal that the predominant attitude is a negative one (see Table 5.1). It is particularly strong in the case of immigrants from ex-Yugoslav countries, who at the same time compose the majority of the immigrant population in Slovenia. Immigration from non-European countries is also unwanted but with an important difference: immigrants from the global South (Africa) and East (Asia, Russia and former countries of the

Table 5.1 Should Slovenia Limit, Encourage or Maintain the Existing Scope of Migration from the Following Parts of the World? (Percentage)

	Limit	Encourage	Maintain at the existing level
From old EU members (EU 15)	35.3	11.9	52.8
From new EU members (2004 enlargement)	48.2	8.4	43.4
From new EU members (Romania and Bulgaria)	61.4	5.3	33.3
From countries of former Soviet Union	64.3	4.2	31.4
From countries of former Yugoslavia	51.2	7.1	41.6
From North America (US, Canada)	47.0	11.3	41.7
From Asia	65.7	3.5	30.8
From South and Central America	57.5	5.7	36.8
From Africa	60.9	5.0	34.1
From Australia	48.9	11.5	39.6

Source: Simona Zavratnik Zimic, Ana Kralj, Zorana Medarič and Blaž Simčič, *Migracije, integracija in multikulturnost—kontekstualizacije sodobnih migracij skozi javno mnenje: Zaključno poročilo ciljno-raziskovalnega projekta Integracijske politike—vzpostavitev evalvacijskega modela in instrumentov longitudinalnega monitoring* (Koper: Univerza na Primorskem, Znanstveno-raziskovalno središče, 2008), 22–23.

Soviet Union) are significantly more undesirable than immigrants from the 'pan-European world' (both Americas and Australia).

Researchers have observed that, in many contemporary societies a qualitative shift is occurring in the expression of prejudicial attitudes. Whereas people used to express their prejudice through direct contact with members of other (stigmatized) social groups, today, prejudice is often expressed through avoidance of contact with these groups.[5] The survey of the Slovenian public opinion, which from 1992 on also measures social distance, can be interpreted along these lines. When the public was asked, "Which of the mentioned groups you would not want to have as your neighbor?" immigrants and foreign workers were chosen as answers. The percentage of people who view immigrants and foreign workers as unwanted neighbors has fluctuated considerably during the years. (It was highest in the years immediately after independence, which coincides with the wars in the area of Croatia and Bosnia and Herzegovina, when a larger number of immigrants moved to Slovenia. A similar trend can be discerned in the year 2000, in the period of the so-called immigrant crisis.) However, according to the latest available data, over one-fifth of survey participants do not want immigrants as their neighbors (see Table 5.2).

Table 5.2   People Who Do Not Want Immigrants as Neighbors

Year	1992	1993	1994	1995	1998	1999	2000	2001	2002	2005	2008
Percentage	39.6	55.6	40.5	18.1	28.3	16.0	28.5	20.6	22.6	17.6	28.4

Source: Social Science Data Archives, http://www.adp.fdv.uni-lj.si/en/, accessed April 12, 2013.

At the level of everyday life, societal integration of immigrants largely depends on majority attitudes—namely, on the 'autochthonous' population. Table 5.3 reviews some of these attitudes, focusing on criteria for immigrant admission that are decisive for whether a person, who was born outside Slovenia, can be granted admission to Slovenia. Besides the results obtained in Slovenia, the table also includes survey results from twelve other European countries.

The results clearly show that in all thirteen countries the following three criteria are of greatest importance: readiness to adopt the country's way of life, knowledge of the official language and possessing professional skills perceived as beneficent for the country. A closely related fourth criterion is (a good) education and qualifications. The most important characteristics of immigrant admission are thus readiness for acculturation (first two indicators) and economic advantage for the target country (latter two indicators). This primarily holds true for the countries of Central and Eastern Europe (Hungary, Poland, Slovenia and Czech Republic), but much less so for the countries of the West and North (the Netherlands, Norway and Sweden). Further, the two groups of countries display basic differences in opinion when it comes to the socioeconomic independence of potential immigrants. It is precisely the possibility of immigrants becoming a burden for the social transfers of the receiving country that is publically presented as a fundamental argument against foreign immigration. However, the successful integration of immigrants into economic, familial and other social networks, as well as financial independence could diminish this fear. The financial situation of immigrants and connections with their family members who already live in the receiving country are considered much more important in the countries of the first group. Looking at indicators of discrimination on the basis of religion and race, we can again discern a discrepancy between the countries of Central and Eastern Europe and the countries of Western and Northern Europe. Discrimination on a religious and racial basis is much more prominent in the countries of the former group.

We can conclude from the results of the comparative table that citizens of Central and Eastern Europe—that is, of the so-called transition countries (Hungary, Poland, Czech Republic and Slovenia)—attribute considerably greater importance to the aforementioned criteria for immigrant admission than other European countries. Here, the significance of race should perhaps be underlined because the criterion that an immigrant person is white

Table 5.3 Criteria for Immigrant Admission—Percentage of Interviewees Who Think That the Stated Criteria Are Very Important (ESS 2002/2003)

	Accepts the country's way of life	Speaks the country's official language	Has professional skills that may benefit the country	Has a good education and qualifications	Close relatives residents of the country	Has a Christian background	Is well situated	Is white
Hungary	86.0	63.9	71.3	48.7	35.4	26.1	13.2	22.9
Poland	44.3	48.8	48.7	39.5	42.8	29.0	17.0	12.3
Slovenia	70.1	58.2	58.2	41.6	28.5	25.6	13.4	14.9
Czech Republic	74.4	60.6	60.6	40.5	41.7	13.4	12.7	14.7
Italy	52.0	28.6	38.5	26.8	18.3	19.8	44.5	6.7
G. Britain	57.4	56.4	45.5	36.3	28.5	10.6	7.8	6.3
Spain	53.8	34.1	44.0	35.6	25.9	14.0	9.0	7.9
Austria	52.9	61.5	47.8	43.2	22.1	14.0	6.5	6.4
Ireland	45.5	43.3	47.7	34.7	25.7	13.2	6.6	7.8
Germany	66.3	65.1	51.5	44.5	25.1	7.8	5.5	4.0
The Netherlands	66.2	64.6	33.3	25.6	17.2	5.1	2.5	3.1
Norway	46.5	49.3	31.8	16.6	17.6	9.3	2.7	4.6
Sweden	65.4	28.8	28.5	19.8	16.7	6.5	4.0	2.8

Source: Mitja Hafner-Fink, "Državljanstvo, (nacionalna) identiteta in odnos do tujcev," in *S Slovenkami in Slovenci na štiri oči,* ed. Brina Malnar and Ivan Bernik (Ljubljana: Fakulteta za družbene vede, IDV-CJMMK, 2004), 55–80.

is twice as important in these transition countries compared to the other European countries included in the research. Hafner-Fink also points out that, in the so-called transition countries, ethnic distance between immigrants and the majority population is more salient. He connects this phenomena to the transition from socialism, which gave full swing to national sentiments, along with the public perception that risk and uncertainty had increased; which can be gathered from negative attitudes toward foreign immigration and increased xenophobia.[6] The results of various public opinion surveys may thus indicate that the resistance to foreign immigration in Slovenia presents a general context, which may in times of pronounced politicization of 'immigrant questions' (in the sense of anti-immigration mobilization provoked by political actors or the media) bring about public expressions of more extreme positions.

ATTITUDE TOWARD IMMIGRATION IN PUBLIC DISCOURSE

Both in the commonsense perception as well as in public discourse, the term *immigrant* usually refers to a specific group of people. Almost as a rule, this group does not include people from the pan-European world or foreign businessmen, representatives of international organizations, diplomatic representatives and other professionals with expert knowledge. These people usually have no difficulties crossing state borders: their destinations are globalized—however, the number of this privileged group is not increasing. This privilege is reserved for a small number of rich countries and a scant number of rich elites from many countries.[7] Typically, these people are not subjected to social exclusion mechanisms. The term *immigrant* thus predominantly refers to those who came to Slovenia from the 'wrong places', for the 'wrong reasons' or simply in the 'wrong way': refugees, asylum seekers and so-called 'illegal immigrants'.

The animated public discussion on the immigrant issue in Slovenia was stirred in the fall of 2000, when the number of 'illegal immigrants' and asylum applicants reached the highest level ever.[8] In the mass media, with rare exceptions, a distinctly stigmatic and discriminative discourse was formed, which presented a new dimension of the immigration problem to the Slovenian public: the so-called immigrant crisis was invented. Ahead, we will attempt to define the fundamental traits of the discourse on ('illegal') immigration in certain Slovenian newspapers.[9] This will be done by way of a brief discourse analysis of the writings. Four national newspapers were included in this analysis: *Delo, Dnevnik, Slovenske novice* and *Večer*. In the first month (December 2000) of the analyzed period, the majority of articles on the subject of immigration appeared in the pages of the crime section in all four newspapers, though in some cases, these articles appeared on the front page or under the 'domestic politics' section. In the case of *Slovenske novice* and *Dnevnik*, however, all immigration-themed articles appeared in the crime section. These articles mainly involved brief reports on 'police actions', 'hunts', 'catches', 'persecutions' or 'deportations' of 'illegals' and the number of 'caught' or 'captured' immigrants. Moreover, several articles also reported on crimes (break-ins and thefts) supposedly committed by the immigrants. At the same time, *Delo* and *Večer* published few articles about preparations for the adoption of new asylum legislation, which emphasized the urgency of, and wide-spread support for, the implementation of more restrictive measures in the asylum granting area. In the second half of January 2001 and beginning of February, more elaborate news items began to appear in the newspapers, which uncritically reiterated statements of anonymous residents of local communities and their mayors. Thusly, the role of journalism was largely reduced to that of producing a connective text, incorporating an array of intolerant or even overtly hostile accounts. In the second half of February, the emotional intensity of reports on the 'immigrant threat' gradually decreased, and for a brief period of time, news reports predominantly focused on the number of captured 'illegal immigrants'. Eventually, reports on appeals for a tolerant discussion about 'immigrants', made by different NGOs, associations and certain representatives of the political elite, began to be published. Statements by individuals were also published, that disapproved of the criminalization of 'immigrants' and which tried to tackle 'immigration problematics' in a more reflective way. Then several months of media silence followed, when it seemed as if the 'immigrant crisis' had never taken place. The number of asylum applicants and 'illegal immigrants' temporarily decreased because of amendments to the Asylum Act, which made the asylum granting procedure even stricter—a development that was accompanied by stricter control at the state borders.

As already pointed out by Roman Kuhar, one of the fundamental traits of media discourse on immigration is that it often merely recapitulates statements of the 'autochthonous' population living near the asylum center or centers for foreigners, be this in Ljubljana or in other parts of Slovenia.[10] Similarly, Breda Luthar argues that these *external voices* "present a putative authentic empirical proof, confirming the authenticity of institutional interpretations. Reference to the 'voice from the street' as an outside voice (so-called vox pop interviews) is the most ideological use of an outside voice as a citation, because it is most arbitrary, thus opening the widest space for 'manipulation.'"[11]

Let us look at some examples:

So far, the immigrants have *broken into* apartments and weekend houses *already eighty times*; several automobiles are missing. The locals *say they live in fear because of the increased violence of immigrants*. They lock themselves in their houses already early in the afternoons, they even neglected the cleaning of the forests. In early morning hours, *husbands accompany their wives on their way to work* to the Prosenjakovci textile factory. *They say the immigrants even started to extort money from kindergarten and school children.* (Emphasis added)[12]

Undoubtedly, the concerns of the people of Prekmurje region *are justified.* They feel *very threatened* and particularly *concerned* for their assets. There are more and more *break-ins and thefts committed by the illegals and asylum seekers.* Many justifiably wonder how long before they turn violent on the locals. (Emphasis added)[13]

We can discern in the foregoing excerpts a tendency for news reports to criminalize immigrants, especially in the sense of stealing (breaking into houses, stealing money and cars and, ultimately, 'stealing' women) and extortion. These criminogenic 'traits' are generalized and attributed to all immigrants.

Another important feature of media coverage is the assumption that the 'autochthonous' Slovenian population is under threat—be it in a security, social, cultural or medical sense. Descriptions of immigrants are commonly infused with rich metaphoric language. The following verbs are commonly employed: to throng, stray, storm, to pressure, siege, flood. In general, metaphors of natural disasters are very popular:[14]

The immigrant flood is washing over the Medjimurje flatland . . . now, even bigger *hordes are swarming* toward the West as in the migration period, with all our Slavic ancestors included. (Emphasis added)[15]

A discourse on 'crisology' provokes the sensation of a state of siege, unmanageable conditions, even moral panic:

The local women feared for their chastity, the fear kept them awake. . . . During summer, others stalked the local women in the gardens. They did not dare to bend to pick the salad, let alone to sunbathe a little in the backyard. . . . The immigrants, pardon the expression, *enjoyed molesting the women* and so on, they are reluctant to speak of actual experiences and *bitter humiliations.* (Emphasis added)[16]

Fear of an outbreak of Ebola or some other epidemic is of course most common among the medically weaker citizens. . . . If one travels to the countries from where the immigrants come, he cannot go there without vaccination. *But, who is checking up on the immigrants?* (Emphasis added)[17]

Xenophobic irrational fears in the foregoing statements are compressed in a very telling way. Proximity of 'illegals' is bad for business and spoils little children who are exposed to contact with foreigners and can thus get ill. Foreigners threaten 'our girls'. References to the 'medical status' of immigrants hint not only toward reproaches about their poor personal hygiene but also toward the need for a 'hygienic' riddance of immigrants from the 'healthy local social body'. Victimization of the 'autochthonous' Slovenian population is clearly noticeable, particularly of the weaker and more vulnerable parts of the population ('helpless women', girls, children and the elderly). However, it is not only those 'natives' who supposedly did have 'unpleasant personal experiences' with the foreigners that were pushed into the role of victims in media discourse: the entire Slovenian nation—the taxpayers, to be exact—is considered a victim. Here, the media discourse pursues a simplifying causal logic: if the 'illegals' left their original countries, they must have had money to pay for the 'illegal' crossing of the border; and if they have money, why should the Slovenian taxpayers pay for their accommodation and otherwise support them? In this context, we often come across statements about the 'poverty' of Slovenian workers, who already hardly manage and are now additionally economically burdened by supporting the immigrants:

> *Foreigners* are becoming *too big a burden* for the state . . . all expenses are paid by the *impoverished citizens*, who already live on the brink of poverty . . . *every tenth Slovenian is hungry*. (Emphasis added)[18]

Nevertheless, the state, which is sometimes identified with the taxpayers, is not only a victim of immigration but also (in this case only as an administrative apparatus, separated from the taxpaying citizens) commonly presented as the one responsible for the situation. The state should take care of the welfare and (social) security of 'its own' people, but fails to do so. Even more, the state acts against or, at best, past its citizens, when it accommodates the immigrants in their environment without 'local' consent:

> Since locals have *extremely bad experience with refugees*, who lived in the refugee center for full eight years, and also with the state . . . On Saturday evening, the locals, indignant because of the mayor's silence about the immigrants' accommodation, gathered in the center's backyard. Many *crisp remarks at the expense of the municipality and the state* were heard. People think that the state is trying to remove *all that is bad and troublesome for the people* out of the capital to other towns. (Emphasis added)[19]

During that time, the xenophobic discourse pervading the 'voice of the people' was also exercised by certain representatives of various expert professions. In an interview, a renowned demographer from the Faculty of Economics at Ljubljana was asked the following question. "Natural growth of the population could be compensated for by the immigrants. In the middle of the 70s, we witnessed a rise of migrants from the republics of ex-Yugoslavia. From which countries will people come in the future?" He answered, "To compensate for the great decrease in birth rates with migrations, the number of actual migrations would need to increase as we speak. Only thus can the number of Slovenian population be kept at the same level. I am not talking about several hundreds of people, but thousands. In ten years' time, we will be dealing with ten thousand and more immigrants per year. *Imagine* more than ten thousand people moving to Slovenia each year. *How* would that *affect life in Slovenia? Surely*, they would *not come from the neighboring countries*. It *is expected*, as anywhere in Europe, that they will *come from the underdeveloped countries*. If we opened the borders, there would *really be a lot, a lot of them coming*" (emphasis added).[20]

We can gather from the foregoing example that there exists a fear of unrestricted admission of foreigners from distant, "underdeveloped places", which might—according to the author—drastically affect the Slovenian way of life and encroach upon Slovenian (cultural) space.

When the decisive factor for racial discrimination is not skin color or bodily shape but rather cultural attributes—for example, customs, traditions, language, music, and the like—we are dealing with cultural racism. In an interview for the newspaper *Dnevnik*, Kuzmanić says that cultural racism "is limited to cultures that are not part of the Western world. All non-Westerners, all non-Slovenians—which doesn't mean the Swedes, Austrians, Australians . . . and so on—are potential objects of such cultural racism."[21]

> We are *besieged with the illegals* and I think that we, the people of Prekmurje are not obliged to keep up with all this quietly and calmly. . . . I am afraid that we might—despite *the trumps in our natural and cultural heritage*—become a kind of *a dump yard* or *a small-scale Balkan*. (Emphasis added)[22]

The media discourse was really only a summary of other discourses: the so-called voice of the people, which was presented by the initiatives of some locals who opposed the settlement of immigrants in their communities, and the institutional discourse, which was displayed in public statements of state officials. In the period of the 'immigrant crisis' from December 2000 to February 2001, the Slovenian parliament discussed the Act Amending the Asylum Act, adopted in 1999. During this time, distinctly restrictive measures were added to amend Slovenian (im)migration policies. Ahead, we will attempt to identify characteristic elements of political discourse during the preparations for the adoption of the Act Amending the Asylum Act,[23] and compare the findings with characteristics of the media discourse on immigration. The analysis will draw upon magnetograms—that is, full transcriptions of two sessions of the working bodies of the Slovenian Parliament (Committee on Domestic Policy) and Parliament's discussion of the issue.[24]

The then minister of the interior presented the Act Amending the Asylum Act as follows:

With regard to the actual law: its *basic idea* is, as you know, *to amend it with a third additional reason for asylum-seekers detention.* Besides the procedure of establishing the identity of asylum-applicants and *prevention of the spread of transmissible diseases*, another factor awaits to be adopted, namely, the *suspicion of misleading or abuse of the asylum procedure.* That there is *a huge amount of such abuses* can be seen from the data, presented in the beginning: over 10 thousand people apply for asylum. However, it is determined in the procedure that only 11 of them are entitled to be granted the asylum status. (Emphasis added)[25]

Again, we can detect a tendency for the 'criminalization' of immigrants. The arguments of the minister of the interior about the abuse of asylum procedures are simplifying and misleading. The fact that in the year 2000 the Republic of Slovenia granted eleven asylum applications from altogether 9,420 applications (in other words, asylum was granted to 0.1 percent of applicants) does not mean that all asylum applicants who were not granted the status abused the procedure or misled the government.

Nevertheless, this particular argument about misleading government workers and abusing asylum procedure turned out to be the decisive factor for the introduction of more restrictive migration and asylum policies. The minister's thesis on the criminogenity of immigrants is not explicit in his presentation, because he was focusing on the abuse of asylum procedure. However, the discourse on criminalization was more prominent in the subsequent discussion.

The second set of measures relates to the prevention of *criminality* of this kind. I cannot emphasize enough how *this kind of criminality is increasing* in Slovenia. We are dealing with two kinds of such *criminality.* One is *criminal offences committed by foreigners*—we keep special statistics on this—and on the other hand, *a great increase of crimes committed by the foreigners.* Basically, these are *criminal offenses*, such as *thefts, break-ins, violation of the untouchability of dwellings*, and so on. (Emphasis added)[26]

Interestingly, only a week before the minister made these allegations, a representative of the Slovenian Police disclosed two pieces of information at a press conference that clearly negate the foregoing statements. First, the police keep no special records of crimes committed by foreigners, and second, the police estimate that the percentage of crimes committed by foreigners is negligible.[27] In this context, the minister's statement can be understood as a political and not an expert statement, for it ignores information from its own specialist services.

Even if the members of the Committee on Domestic Policy were aware of this discrepancy, this cannot be gathered from the actual discussion. Quite the contrary, in spite of statistical data, they particularly stressed the issue of security: " . . . no one is considering *the security of citizens. The citizens are twice threatened.* First, directly *by the immigrants,* and second, *by the crime* connected with this . . ." (emphasis added).[28]

It is clear from the foregoing examples that both discourses—the media and the parliamentary one—are intimately related because they feed off and support each other in creating a presumed public consensus about the 'immigrant problem' and how to deal with it. Through a reciprocal complementarity of both discourses, an active public and political agenda was being created that delineated the grounds, main points and legitimacy for the implementation of national and local policies.

The analysis of the media and parliamentary discourse on immigrants outlines the following characteristics: 1) homogenization (sudden abolition of social differences in the domicile population; creation of 'Us' versus 'Them'); 2) emotionalization (use of highly emotionalized language in relation to 'Them'); 3) victimization of the 'autochthonous' inhabitants ('our' way of life is endangered, 'we' are the real victims); 4) culpabilization of immigrants and the Slovenian state ('They' are threatening 'us'; the state should protect 'us', instead of giving excessive rights to immigrants); 5) hygienization (immigrants are filthy; they are carriers of infectious diseases); and 6) criminalization of immigrants ('They lie, cheat, steal our jobs and our women').[29]

However, a new element appears in the political discourse—namely, referring to European practices and directives which, in the view of the deputies', allows for the adoption of more restrictive measures:

> *We want to join the European Union and to adopt, harmonize our legislation with theirs,* they *would certainly not reproach us if our border authorities were more effective and restrictive* because *they have done it.* Meaning that *they cannot reproach us with something they are doing themselves.* We should therefore orient this law also along these lines, and everything should be aimed at prevention. I welcome and agree with what the European Union has done because this is the only way it works. *What's going on at our borders is intolerable. The more this Asylum Act is restrictive the gladder I will be to support it; if it's restrictive I'll support it with both my arms if necessary.* We should see things from this perspective—protecting our own interests. (Emphasis added)[30]

Another important characteristic of public discourse and political rhetoric in Slovenia is a low level of reflection and analytical thinking. The latter holds particularly true for journalistic texts but also for the public standpoints of professional politicians, who most often claim—as can be seen in the foregoing statement—that Slovenian legislation and practice are in accordance with European standards, without posing the relevant question of whether European standards and grounds for immigration politics are adequate. Here again, the appeal to 'Europe' acts as a conspiracy formula that puts an end to critical thinking.

The foregoing statements from parliamentary sessions were uttered in the time of the so-called immigrant crisis. Regardless of their party provenance, nearly all the speakers in parliamentary discussions displayed a characteristically similar type of discourse.

In 2006, the Slovenian Parliament returned to the issue of migration while amending the Asylum Act, which significantly derogated asylum seekers' rights (it introduced the preliminary police procedure, limited immigrants' right to a free lawyer, etc.). The comparison of media articles and parliamentary debates in 2000 and in 2006 demonstrates that the foregoing characteristics of public discourse on immigrants are a continuous phenomenon, a process, rather than a single act carried out during a 'crisis' period.

BACK TO THE FUTURE?

In the recent past, we have seen a similar type of discourse at work, especially in the mass media or in the public statements of politicians. I will single out three cases.

The first case occurred in the period of the so-called refugee crisis in the beginning of the 1990s, when people fled Croatia and Bosnia and Herzegovina because of the war and sought refuge in Slovenia.

The second case is that of 'the erased'.[31] Erased residents of Slovenia are a group of 25,671 people (over 1 percent of the Slovenian population), originating from the republics of former Yugoslavia (Croatia, Bosnia and Herzegovina, Serbia, Montenegro and Macedonia), whose personal data were unlawfully transferred in 1992 from a register of people with permanent residence to a register of people with no legal status in Slovenia. This measure later became known as the 'erasure' and its victims 'the erased'. The measure was implemented by local administrative units in a secret way and far from the public eye. The action had no basis in the law—it was carried out only on the basis of a classified administrative circular of the Ministry of Interior. The victims were not informed about the measure in advance, no written decision on the measure was issued and served to them, and they had no right to appeal. The erasure seriously affected the situation of its victims. By losing their legal status, the erased lost their jobs and could not get employment, enroll in secondary schools and universities or access free health care and other social benefits. They were evicted and lost housing rights. They were subjected to deportation by the state, detention in alien centers and, in some cases, even police torture and mistreatment. It is also evident that the erasure was an act of discrimination. It was carried out only toward people from republics of ex-Yugoslavia and not toward people from other European countries. Discrimination was carried out on the grounds of ethnicity. All of the erased were of Croatian, Bosnian, Serbian, Montenegrin, Macedonian, Albanian and Roma descent.

The third and most recent case was the case of the Strojan family—an extended family of thirty-one Roma, fourteen of them children, who were forced to abandon their land when a mob from the local village and other nearby villages surrounded their homes and demanded their eviction (on the presumption that 'their way of life is unacceptable' because 'their culture is not civilized enough'). While the police kept the crowd back, Slovenian government officials negotiated the family's removal to a former army barracks thirty miles away. Shortly, the Strojan family was evicted from their land and experienced cultural racism and deportation—another way to put it would be apartheid.

It is evident from the foregoing cases that the construction and stigmatization of foreigners is repeated in time and consolidated into a pattern. What gives this pattern its legitimacy and persuasive power? Our thesis is that this pattern has characteristics of a nationalist discourse, as already pointed out by Umut Özkırımlı.[32] We can distinguish four different dimensions in which nationalist discourse operates.

First, the nationalist discourse divides the world into 'us' and 'them', positing a homogenous and fixed identity on either side. The discourse of nationalism is exclusive and tends to simplify and reduce the world in a dualistic manner to distinguish between the good ones and the bad ones. In nationalist discourse, this simplified mental structure seems constitutive: 'Our' national movements are understood as emancipatory, and 'our' nationalism is benign, introverted and meant to reinforce our sense of national belonging and patriotism, whereas the nationalism of 'others' is malign, extroversive, aggressive and oppressive.

Second, the nationalist discourse exerts its hegemony by affirming a homogenous national-cultural identity. Like other discourses, nationalist discourse is about power and domination as it legitimates and produces hierarchy among actors. A nationalist emphasis on common blood, which allegedly ties the members of a national community into a supposedly homogenous unity, represents an exceptionally strong mechanism of internal unification. At the same time, it can cause devastating consequences for all the others. Those who cannot (or do not want to) recognize themselves in the nationalist-interpretative framework of 'us' are forced into marginalization and/or exclusion.

Third, the nationalist discourse naturalizes itself. Nationalism treats national identity as a system of absolute values. National values are no longer seen as social values but appear as facts of nature: they become taken for granted, commonsense and hegemonic. This ultimately turns the language of national identity into a language of morality and renders nationalism the very horizon of political discourse.

Fourth, the nationalist discourse operates through institutions. The nationalist discourse does not exist in a social vacuum—national identities are produced and reproduced daily through the functioning of various institutions in everyday life. The key role is played by the nation-state, which uses formal and informal techniques to 'nationalize' every domain it feels should be under its sovereign power.

CONCLUSION

The end of the 1980s and the beginning of the 1990s were marked by the disintegration of the Eastern bloc and the evolution of the socialist-egalitarian social order toward liberal, market economies. Within a period of just a few years, serious geopolitical, social, economic and even class divisions previously alien to these societies emerged. It is precisely the phenomenon of inequality that provides a fertile ground for the emergence of intolerance, radical distinction and even exclusion of 'others' and those who are different. Perhaps the main factor that could elucidate the emergence of nationalist extremism and xenophobia in Slovenia is a concept that was shaped at the turn of the 1990s.

The transition from a socialist to a democratic pluralistic system brought a shift in emphasis—at least on an ideological ground—from class to national identity, especially if we understand identity as an ideological instrument aimed at ensuring the legitimacy of the ruling national elite. In the making of a nation-state, or amid the changing of the sovereign scope of a nation-state, there is often a tendency to create ethnically uniform ('pure') communities, to emphasize ethnic identity and to demand loyalty within a national community. "The moment Slovenia became a sovereign state, the ostensibly 'new' (although, in reality, very old) concept of 'citizenship' became formed. In fact, its main features are domesticity and patriotism, based on 'ethnos', or rather, blood and homeland."[33] The 'new' Slovenian identity was affirmed by stressing the distinction between 'us' and 'others' (people from the East and the South, people from the Balkans, etc.). Hafner-Fink argues that the classic concept of nationality, founded primarily on principles of exclusion and delimitation, is more characteristic of those European states that were going through deeper structural changes—especially postsocialist or "transition countries", newly formed states and those joining the European Union. Slovenia was marked by all three characteristics.[34]

The public sentiment, marked as the 'immigrant crisis' in 2000 and 2001, resembled the situation in Slovenia in 1992–1993, when attention was focused on the 'refugee crisis'. Studies dealing with both episodes[35] point to a series of elements that establish discriminatory discursive practices in the media and political institutions. In particular, the following was revealed. At a certain point, different elements of nationalist discourse homogenize and produce a problem or a 'crisis', which is then supported by public media activity, and legitimates deviations from certain core principles that have been accepted as self-evident (e.g., basic human rights and freedoms). Such deviations then prevail as entirely acceptable special measures. As a rule, they are attained through emotionalization of public discourse. During the 'immigrant crisis' of 2000–2001, the markedly restrictive. measures of Slovenian immigration policy from the early 1990s were intensified and further legitimated.

Compared with the 'refugee crisis' of 1992–1993, the period of 2000–2001 saw an even more radical, internal separation of national identity from 'the others,' which continued the logic of a victim identity, which further legitimatized restrictive policies and changes in legislation, strengthening the thesis of a threatened Slovenian nationality. Within everyday public discourse, a prejudiced and hostile attitude toward ' the others' was spread. This discourse was not only xenophobic in character, with elements of racism, but also encouraged joint action against immigration and immigrants' integration. It led to explicit threats and certain players' attempts to act on their own, and outside the legal and institutional framework of the state. Recent developments connected with the eviction of the Roma people can be placed within the same matrix. What seems like an excessive treatment of Slovenian citizens (of Roma origin) is just a current manifestation of a series of developments that stem from the 'refugee and immigrant crisis' of the early 1990s.

Localized rejections are fueled by phantasmatic images that depict immigrants as enemies who undermine/endanger the naturalized autochthony of the majority society. This autochthonous identity is naturalized because it can never be fully or sufficiently explained, and because its naturalization is enmeshed in a constant process of (re)making. The exclusion and marginalization of the Roma family could not be justified by the usual exploitation of metaphors about foreigners 'on our own land'. In this case, the discriminatory discourse was forced to confront its own nucleus, without appealing to 'autochthony', 'one's native soil', etc. The nationalistic discourse was forced to speak a pure form of cultural racism. This flagrant abuse of culture does not end with the identification of a distinction between 'us' and 'them'. The actual variety of immigrants and their personal itineraries are reduced to a phantasmatic homogeneity with one common denominator—cultural difference. This difference is perceived as threatening and the rejection of all of these threatening individuals is carried out in the name of culture. Culture is used as an excuse or legitimization for verbal and sometimes even physical violence.

NOTES

1. First published as Ana Kralj, "Nezazeleni? Medijske in politicne konstrukcije tujcev v Sloveniji," *Dve domovini/Two homelands* 27 (2008): 169–190.
2. The term 'Fortress Europe' is frequently used by immigration scholars to refer to European immigration policies that are becoming more and more restrictive. See, Klaus Bade, "Legal and illegal immigration into Europe:

experiences and challenges,î European Review, 12, no. 3 (2004), 339ñ375; Andrew Geddes, *Immigration and European Integration: Beyond Fortress Europe?* (Manchester: Manchester University Press, 2008).

3. Etienne Balibar, *We, the People of Europe? Reflections on Transnational Citizenship* (Princeton, NJ: Princeton University Press, 2004), 37, and Pierre-André Taguieff, *La France du préjugé: Essai sur le racisme et ses doubles* (Paris: La Découverte, 1988).

4. Rogers Brubaker, *Nationalism Reframed: Nationhood and the National Question in the New Europe* (Cambridge: Cambridge University Press, 1996), 20–21.

5. Mirjana Ule, *Predsodki in diskriminacije* (Ljubljana: Znanstveno in publicistično središče, 1999).

6. Mitja Hafner-Fink, "Državljanstvo, (nacionalna) identiteta in odnos do tujcev," in *S Slovenkami in Slovenci na štiri oči*, ed. B. Malnar, I. Bernik (Ljubljana: Fakulteta za družbene vede, IDV-CJMMK, 2004), 55–80.

7. Rainer Bauböck, "The Crossing and Blurring of Boundaries in International Migration: Challenges for Social and Political Theory," in *Blurred Boundaries: Migration, Ethnicity, Citizenship*, ed. R. Bauböck and J. Rundell (Aldershot: Ashgate, 1999), 17–53; Zygmunt Bauman, *Globalization: The Human Consequences* (Cambridge: Polity, 1998); and idem, *Wasted Lives: Modernity and Its Outcasts* (Cambridge: Polity, 2004).

8. The so-called immigrant crisis, which was marked mainly by 'illegal immigrants' and asylum seekers, originated in 1999, when the police registered 18,695 illegal border crossings, whereas 744 people submitted applications for political asylum (until then the average number of applications per year was 110 people). In 2000, the police registered the largest number of illegal border crossings (35,892). Further, the number of political asylum seekers also increased substantially (9,244), and only thirteen applications were granted. In the following year, the police adjusted its protection of the state border to the 'state of threat' level and immediately began to perform additional actions to prevent illegal migrations; consequently, the number of 'illegal immigrants' decreased by almost 50 percent in comparison to the previous year (20,871).

9. The discourse analysis included 197 articles, published in four leading Slovenian daily printed media (*Delo, Dnevnik, Slovenske novice* and *Večer*) in the period between December 1, 2000, and February 28, 2001—namely, the period when the anti-immigration attitude reached its peak in the Slovenian public space.

10. Roman Kuhar, "Seized and Expelled," in *Intolerance Monitor Report 01*, ed. B. Petković (Ljubljana: Mirovni inštitut, 2001), 45–55.

11. Breda Luthar, *Poetika in politika tabloidne kulture* (Ljubljana: Znanstveno in publicistično središče, 1998), 235.

12. "Prosenjakovčani rekli ne" [The Prosenjakovci Community Said No], *Delo*, Jan. 30, 2001.

13. "Ilegalci kradejo" [Illegals Steal], *Slovenske novice*, Jan. 26, 2001.

14. Charteris-Black speaks about characteristic metaphors of natural disasters, which appear in the speeches of British right-wing and conservative parties in discussions on 'immigration problematics'. "Mio (1997) identifies the major functions of metaphor in politics as to simplify and make issues intelligible, to resonate with underlying symbolic representations, to stir emotions and bridge the gap between the logical and the emotional." Mio, J.S. (1997) 'Metaphor & Politics', *Metaphor & Symbol* 12(2): 113–33, quoted in: Jonathan Charteris-Black, "Britain as a Container: Immigration Metaphors in the 2005 election campaign," *Discourse and Society* 17, no. 5 (2006): 565.

15. "Vodnik zbežal, begunec obležal" [Guide Ran, Immigrant Went Down], *Slovenske novice*, Dec. 20, 2000.
16. "Bodo Bloke spet ječale v grozi?" [Will Bloke Sob in Terror Again?], *Slovenske novice*, Jan. 23, 2001.
17. "Epidemije ebole še ni, jebola pa kar vsak dan" [No Ebola Epidemic Nevertheless Immigrants Spell Trouble], *Slovenske novice*, Jan. 9, 2001.
18. Reader's comment, *Nedeljski dnevnik*, Jan. 14, 2001.
19. "Stenice 'preselile' prebežnike na Goričko" [Bugs 'Moved' Immigrants to Goričko], *Delo*, Jan. 22, 2001.
20. "Število Slovencev se skokovito zmanjšuje" [Number of Slovenians Sharply Decreasing], *Delo*, Nov. 21, 2001.
21. Interview with Tonči Kuzmanić, *Dnevnik*, Mar. 14, 2006.
22. "Bojazen krajanov pred 'Balkanom v malem'" [People Fear Becoming Small-Scale Balkan], *Večer*, Jan. 31, 2001.
23. The basic aim of the amendments was the introduction of more restrictive conditions for granting the asylum status. Namely, the Asylum Act from 1999 grounded the reasons for detention and restrictions on movement of asylum seekers in asylum-applicant identification and prevention of transmissible diseases. The proposed (and later adopted) amendments to the act included another reason—namely, the suspicion of misleading and abuse of the asylum procedure, which at the same time presented sufficient grounds for the authorities to immediately decide upon the application and deny it as unfounded.
24. Transcripts of the Committee on Domestic Policy sessions and Parliament's sessions are available in the archive records of the National Assembly of Slovenia, accessed April 12, 2013, http://www.dz-rs.si/wps/portal/en/Home,
25. Minister of the Interior, Committee on Domestic Policy, Dec. 15, 2000, accessed April 12, 2013, http://www.dzrs.si/wps/portal/Home/deloDZ/seje/evidenca?mandat=III&type=magdt&uid=702BE6135A0A1A75C12569B60 03F74F1, accessed Apr. 12, 2013
26. Minister of the Interior, Committee on Domestic Policy, Feb. 16, 2001, accessed April 12, 2013, http://www.dzrs.si/wps/portal/Home/deloDZ/seje/evidenca?mandat=III&type=magdt&uid=C94C5904101E1F1BC12569F50 04935B6, accessed Apr. 12, 2013
27. "Vlada nad težave bolj sistematično" [Government Will Overcome Difficulties Systematically], *Delo*, Feb. 7, 2001.
28. Deputy of the Liberal Democrats of Slovenia, Committee on Domestic Policy, Dec. 15, 2000, accessed April 12, 2013, http://www.dzrs.si/wps/portal/Home/deloDZ/seje/evidenca?mandat=III&type=magdt&uid=702BE6135A0 A1A75C12569B6003F74F1, accessed Apr. 12, 2013.
29. Similar characteristics of media discourse on immigrants have been investigated by Vlasta Jalušič: emotionalization, culpabilization of immigrants and the state, victimization of the autochthonous population, exaggerated hatred toward the state, legitimization of possible defense measures, and normalization and socialization of xenophobia and racism. See Valsta Jalušič, "Xenophobia or Self-Protection? On the Development of New Citizen Identity in Slovenia," in *Intolerance Monitor Report 01*, ed. B. Petković (Ljubljana: Mirovni inštitut, 2001), 40.
30. Deputy of Slovenian Democratic Party, Committee on Domestic Policy, Dec. 15, 2000, accessed April 12, 2013, http://www.dzrs.si/wps/portal/Home/deloDZ/seje/evidenca?mandat=III&type=magdt&uid=702BE6135A0A1A75 C12569B6003F74F1, accessed Apr. 12, 2013
31. For more on the 'erased', see Neža Kogovšek, Brankica Petković, Jelka Zorn, Sara Pistotnik, Uršula Lipovec Čebron, Veronika Bajt and Lana Zdravković,

The Scars of the Erasure: A Contribution to the Critical Understanding of the Erasure of People from the Register of Permanent Residents of the Republic of Slovenia (Ljubljana: Peace Institute, 2010).

32. Umut Özkırımlı, *Contemporary Debates on Nationalism: A Critical Engagement* (Basingstoke, UK: Palgrave Macmillan, 2005), 32–33.
33. Tonči Kuzmanić, "Xenophobia in Former Yugoslavia and Post-Socialist Slovenia," in *Intolerance Monitor Report 02*, ed. R. Kuhar and T. Trplan (Ljubljana: Mirovni inštitut, 2003), 18.
34. Hafner-Fink, "Državljanstvo."
35. M. Doupona-Horvat, J. Verschueren and I. Žagar, *The Rhetoric of Refugee Policies in Slovenia* (Ljubljana: MediaWatch, 1998), and Petković, ed., *Intolerance Monitor Report 01* (Ljubljana: Peace Institute, 2001).

6 Designed to Punish
Immigrant Detention and Deportation in the US[1]

Mark Dow

In a poem called "Botpipèl" (Boat People), Félix Morisseau-Leroy (1912–1998) of Haiti wrote:

> *Nou tap kouri pou Fò Dimanch*
> *Nou vin echwe nan Kwòm Avni*

which means

> *We were running from Ft. Dimanche*
> *We washed ashore on Krome Avenue.*[2]

Morisseau assumed his audience would recognize not only the first line's reference to the notorious prison and torture center in Port-au-Prince, but also the name of the US immigration detention center in Miami where so many Haitians and others have ended up. Morisseau wrote those lines in the 1980s: at about the same time Amnesty International sued on behalf of a group of Haitian trade union activists allegedly tortured at Ft. Dimanche; and, in a court battle over 2,100 Haitian asylum seekers locked up at the Krome Avenue detention camp and elsewhere, then-Associate Attorney General Rudolph Giuliani claimed that there was "no political repression" in Haiti and that dictator Jean Claude 'Baby Doc' Duvalier had "personally assured him that Haitians returning home from the United States were not persecuted."[3] Giuliani also explained, in a panel discussion on public television, that confining the Haitians "is not punishment . . . it is detention for the purpose of adjudicating someone's right to be here . . . We need an orderly process, and detention aids the orderly process." His point seems reasonable enough when taken at face value. But Giuliani went further, denying the reality of incarceration. When even a top immigration official admitted that the Haitian asylum seekers were "in jail," Giuliani countered that although the facilities look like jails, they are not jails. He continued: "If [the Haitians] attempt to leave, they are stopped from leaving . . . There is usually [sic] perimeter security, [but] they are not held behind bars, they are not locked behind bars at night."[4]

In fact, the Haitians were held not only at Krome but also at the Ft. Allen detention center in Puerto Rico, as well as "Federal correction facilities in Kentucky, New York, Texas and West Virginia."[5] On the TV panel, federal judge Marvin Shoob was the voice of common sense: "We have people who have been incarcerated for *three years*, and Mr. Giuliani says this is not punishment. . . . Cuban detainees have been incarcerated in a maximum security prison in Atlanta, the toughest prison in the United States, and the government says this is not punishment."[6]

The semantics matter. Giuliani's lies about persecution and his distortions about incarceration were integral to detention policy, and they have remained so. The Haitians must be economic, not political refugees, or else the US incurs legal obligations to offer them protection (from regimes we've happened to be supporting). And although the administration uses detention as a deterrent to other potential asylum seekers, in violation of international refugee norms—and uses detention more generally to coerce a range of noncitizens to drop any legal claims they might have—this cannot be 'punishment' because, if it were, the detainees would have certain due process rights.

Many people first heard about immigration detention after September 11, 2001. But on September 10, the Immigration and Naturalization Service (INS), an agency of the Justice Department, already held about twenty-three thousand detainees in its custody. Since March 2003, the Department of Homeland Security's Bureau of Immigration and Customs Enforcement (ICE) has run immigration detention. The people in custody are called 'detainees' but they are, in fact, prisoners, held in federal penitentiaries, private prisons, local jails and 'service processing centers' while awaiting deportation or during legal proceedings. These varied detention facilities can be found in most states as well as in Puerto Rico, the US Virgin Islands, Guam, and the Commonwealth of Northern Mariana Islands.[7]

Between 1995 and 2007, the average daily population of US immigration detainees increased from about six thousand to more than twenty-seven thousand. Although recent enforcement has driven the numbers up rapidly, the major reason for the increase is the anti-immigrant laws of 1996. The Illegal Immigration Reform and Immigrant Responsibility Act (IIRIRA) and the Antiterrorism and Effective Death Penalty Acts (AEDPA), signed into law by Bill Clinton, led to increased immigrant detention in two major ways. First, the new laws drastically expanded the range of crimes for which a *legal* resident is subject to 'mandatory detention' and deportation. Second, the new laws stripped such immigrants of the right even to ask for a so-called waiver of deportation from an immigration judge. Before the new laws, such waivers were granted in about half the relevant cases. Mitigating circumstances (though this is not the term used) might include decades of lawful living, military service, business ownership, years of paying income taxes, and having US citizen spouses or children. And although ICE and Congress work to reinforce the impression that 'illegal alien' is synonymous with 'criminal', the *Denver Post* reports that "a growing share of those deported committed no crimes while in the United States—53 percent this year, up from 37 percent in 2001."[8] In any case, if someone is in ICE custody, then regardless of prior criminal history, she or he is by definition an administration detainee with no release date. These 'detainees' are held for days, weeks, months and years, and have even been held for decades. In FY 2010, ICE budgeted $2.5 billion for Detention and Removal Operations.[9]

In the nineteenth century, 'undocumented' Chinese were regularly forced to work for a year before they were deported. In *Wong Wing* (1896), the Supreme Court ruled that such forced labor constituted punishment and therefore could not be imposed without judicial process—that is, simply as an administrative action. The court also noted, however, that administrative custody for the purpose of deportation was a different matter: "Detention . . . is not imprisonment in a legal sense."[10] About a hundred years later, an INS spokesperson in Newark, New Jersey, told a journalist that INS detainees physically held in a New Jersey county jail were not "'in jail.'"[11] Justice Anthony Kennedy put it more delicately: "Where detention is incident to removal, the detention cannot be justified as punishment nor can the confinement or its conditions be designed in order to punish." (It's telling that in the same opinion, Kennedy revealed a basic misunderstanding of the physical realities of the ICE detention system.[12]) Justice Stephen Breyer was even more careful: "The proceedings at issue here are civil, not criminal, and we assume that they are non-punitive in purpose and effect."[13] *We assume.*

When ICE Public Affairs responded to this writer's critique of the detention system by saying that it failed to understand that the (sole) purpose of detention is deportation, the spokespersons had a point.[14] One is bound to "misunderstand" in this way after seeing that immigration detention *punishes* the prisoner, and that immigration officials use this fact as an instrument of policy. It's certainly arguable that INS/ICE detention was not originally designed to punish, because for the most part it was not designed at all. It has developed in response to bureaucratic imperative and political expediency. But now that it has utilized the penal system's jail cells, prison uniforms, restraint chairs and shackles for twenty-five years, immigration detention is undoubtedly punitive "in purpose and effect." If ICE detention were a straightforward, fair and humane means to deportation, the ICE spokespersons would be right. But because detention is often unnecessary and even illegal,[15] and because the immigration enforcement culture is brutal and racist, they are wrong.

Immigrant advocates have often argued that immigration detainees 'should not be treated like criminals'. This is a well-meaning slogan with an unintended and dangerous implication: How *should* a criminal inmate be treated? Worse than an administrative detainee? The premises of our prison system—stigma, isolation, humiliation, dehumanization—demand reexamination. Meanwhile, the premise that immigration violators should be prisoners at all must be revised. So-called alternatives to detention should not be the exception. Incredibly, and with no public debate, we have taken it as a given that a visa violator, or an asylum seeker, or a thirty-year lawful resident who has paid taxes but committed a nonviolent misdemeanor decades ago, should be strip-searched, dressed in a prison jumpsuit, incarcerated and denied contact with her children. Immigration officials and correctional officers have explained to me at length that mistreatment—punishment—is the inevitable result of imprisoning people who are only subject to 'administrative detention' for the express purpose of deportation. After twenty-five years—taking the Reagan administration's revival of large-scale detention as a starting point—the punishment inherent in this system cannot be dismissed as an unintended side effect. On Krome Avenue in Miami, the guards were instruments of a national policy when they forced Haitian women to clean toilets with their hands, telling them that they all had AIDS anyway. A Krome detention officer who did time in a federal prison for beating a Haitian detainee said that if the authorities had really wanted to punish him, they would have locked him up at Krome.[16]

There is another basic semantic problem here. Immigration detention and deportation are, of course, considered to be 'immigration' issues. Courts often stay away from these issues because of a tradition of giving the executive wide latitude in matters of immigration, which is easily and conveniently elided with matters of national security, and of giving prison administrators latitude in managing their prisons. But the laws responsible for the skyrocketing numbers of those detained and deported are not so much aspects of an immigration policy regime as they are a parallel criminal justice system for noncitizens.

Consider Barbara P., who was sentenced to three years in a Florida prison for shoplifting, and then held by the Immigration Service for another two and a half years. "Two years and a half for the INS," she said, referring to ICE's predecessor, the Immigration and Naturalization Service.[17] She might have been released sooner—the arbitrariness of the system makes it impossible to know—but she had been written up for disciplinary infractions in a Louisiana parish jail contracted to hold her for the federal government (for a fee, of course). Her mistakes lay in trying to escape the jail's filth. One of her 'write-ups' was for trying to stay in the shower beyond the five-minute limit. Another was for possession of contraband in her cell in New Iberia. She had a traveler's size shampoo bottle filled with Windex, which she used to clean the toilet seat in the collective bathroom because she feared germs from women arrested and placed into general population without proper medical screening.

At the time (August 2002), INS was authorized to hold someone like P. until she was dead: she had entered the US *legally* and been taken into immigration custody after completing a criminal sentence, but her country of origin would not take her back. She was in the same category as those Cubans to whom Judge Shoob had referred. P. had no way of knowing when she might be released from her un-sentenced time, a situation that a young Somali man detained in Minnesota referred to as "dead time."[18] So she was taken by surprise when someone interrupted her during a church service at the Calcasieu Parish Jail in Lake Charles to tell her she was getting out immediately. She had assumed INS would first send her to a halfway house "so I could learn my lesson."[19] What lesson? I didn't think to ask. It hadn't been more than a couple of hours since a plainclothes immigration agent walked her out the front door of the jail and drove her to the Greyhound station. (I happened to be visiting someone else at the jail that day, and a friendly correctional officer told me P. was getting out.) In another couple of hours she'd be headed for Miami, where she would see the six-year-old daughter she had been away from for years.

Immigration detainees are regularly transferred from jail to jail without warning, usually in the middle of the night. Transfers are used to punish detainees who seek media attention, to break up peaceful hunger strikes, to isolate detainees from legal help and, more generally, as part of a nation-wide system of intergovernmental service agreements (IGSAs), private con-tracts, available bedspace and *ad hoc* human warehousing. In the course of transfers and processing into new jails, detainees' essential legal paperwork commonly disappears, their personal property is stolen, and families lose track of their loved ones because the immigration agency explicitly dis-claims responsibility for informing family of the unannounced moves.[20] So it is unclear what happened to a care package P.'s mother had sent from Miami, except that P. never got it, and now probably never would. She seemed frustrated, but she wasn't mad. On the contrary: "I took it as part of the punishment," she told me. But her court-ordered punishment had ended two and a half years before she was released. "The punishment ended," she explained. "But them people say I'm illegal in this country, [so] I'm illegal. Even though I come in here legally."[21]

By this time, P. had been here for twenty years. A citizen would have returned to the street after completing the sentenced time. One of ICE's self-proclaimed 'milestones' in 2006 was the creation of its National Center to Coordinate Deportation of Aliens upon Release from Prison,[22] an expan-sion of related programs ongoing since the 1980s. Legally speaking, 'alien' simply means noncitizen, and 'citizen', in many people's minds, is a line in the sand. It *is* a line in the sand; it can be redrawn. Jurists have mused on the category of *de facto citizen*, lying somewhere *alien* and *native*.[23] But in the current immigration detention regime, where the noncitizen prisoner is denied even the dignity of being acknowledged as a prisoner, the *non* status ensures that anything goes. Government officials have even strategized to justify the mistreatment of detainees by using their status as noncitizens. As one Justice Department attorney put it: "an alien's status in this coun-try may also dictate the degree of constitutional protections he or she may be afforded. Perhaps some of these same constitutional principles can be applied to aliens challenging their treatment while in INS detention."[24]

Even when ICE confines a detainee illegally, there is essentially nothing the detainee can do about it. Three years after a Supreme Court decision in *Zadvydas v. Davis*, the General Accounting Office reported that ICE was detaining hundreds of persons who should have been released under that ruling. But the GAO only recommended that ICE itself remedy the problem. In other words, someone who is being illegally incarcerated by ICE has no options other than—if possible—filing a habeas petition in district court to demand justice from an agency already violating a Supreme Court ruling on the matter.[25]

The citizen/noncitizen divide plays out in other ways, too. Despite ICE's claims to the contrary, ICE detainees are commonly held together with prisoners doing time. Citizen inmates from California, Louisiana and Alabama have made articulate pleas on behalf of the noncitizen administrative detainees they've met in the system. On the other hand, at the Orleans Parish Prison (OPP) in New Orleans in the late 1990s, guards provided US citizen inmates with weapons and sent them to beat down a group of nonviolent, noncitizen, Cambodian and Vietnamese immigration detainees. Despite plenty of reports of brutality at OPP—or perhaps because of the brutality and despite the reports—INS had a continuing contract with the jail. Attorney Salvador Longoria made an interesting discovery when he deposed OPP jailers in a lawsuit about the incident. The jailers, he said,

> consider the [immigration] detainees to be criminals. . . . In their mind, there's no distinction. . . . You can argue with them left and right: "They got out of jail in Tennessee in 1997 and finished their whole sentence. Or they didn't even get a criminal sentence, they got probation in Washington State and successfully completed that. They're now under administrative detention." That concept does not enter [the guards'] minds. [As far as they're concerned, the detainees] are criminals doing criminal time.[26]

Justice Kennedy said: "the detention cannot be justified as punishment nor can the confinement or its conditions be designed in order to punish." A central Louisiana warden, discussing the inevitable tensions and conflicts that result from incarcerating immigration detainees with prisoners doing time, told me that the ICE detainees sympathize with his managerial challenges. "They understand that this is a penal institution," he said.[27]

ICE and Department of Homeland Security officials have tried to evade criticism of the detention system by arguing that the detainees can get out any time simply by agreeing to deportation—once again, not true. Over the years, there have been many protests by INS and ICE detainees demanding to be deported. Detainees at one Corrections Corporation of America contract detention center speculated that the delays are intended to generate shareholder profit. In 2005, a West African asylum-seeker wrote from the Hardin County Jail in Iowa: "Many of the detainees, due to the poor conditions of the food, are asking to be deported."[28] In 2006, Krome inmates sent an open letter "to whoever is willing to help" that included complaints about overcrowding, filth, beatings, predatory phone prices and this:

> Some of the prisoners, who have already signed their deportation documents, are still being held by ICE . . . Some prisoners are here for years awaiting deportation. One has been here for over three years.[29]

Several years earlier, detainees from Honduras, Nicaragua and El Salvador organized one of the many hunger strikes that Krome has seen. Participants were "asking to be deported to our countries."[30] One of them, Ismael F., twenty-nine years old, had been in the US for eleven years, nine of those in the Florida Department of Corrections on a homicide conviction. He had the letters 'USA' tattooed on the back of his hand. After only four months at Krome, he told me in Spanish that detention was much worse than doing time for the state. In civil 'detention' there were fewer family visits, and the recreation facilities were inadequate. He said:

> Rights are not respected here. In this system, I am a detainee. I stopped being a criminal after the court sentence. Yes, I was a criminal, but I paid for my crime. Now I must be a person—free. I no longer owe anything to justice.[31]

In 2009, the Obama administration and ICE announced plans to reform the immigration detention system. In what was perhaps the most surprising element of the proposed reforms, ICE acknowledged that the prisons and jails holding most of its detainees are "largely designed for penal, not civil, detention."[32] The agency proposed holding more detainees in ICE-run facilities. One year after the proposals, human rights groups reported that "with only a few exceptions, noncitizens continue to be held in penal detention facilities."[33]

A more fundamental redesign is necessary. After all, consistent with its predecessors, the Obama administration has refused to codify detention standards into regulations, ensuring that even these minimum standards remain legally unenforceable. The proposals for reform rely on ICE itself to continue as police, prosecutor, judge and jailer, and to oversee its own detention system despite overwhelming evidence that it cannot do so humanely or competently. As a law enforcement agency, ICE cannot operate a nonpenal housing system. More fundamentally, proposals for 'reform' fail to address the laws responsible for the rising number of noncitizens subject to detention and deportation/removal in the first place.[34]

And like detention, deportation is not a punishment, even when it is. In 1950, the US Supreme Court ruled in *Wong Yang Sung v. McGrath* "that deportation proceedings were of a judicial character requiring a fair hearing."[35] Hearings were instituted, Mae Ngai explains, and in one year, the number of deportations of Mexicans (the main group being apprehended and deported at the time) dropped from 16,903 to 3,319. "But Congress acted quickly to nullify *Sung* and to restore the INS's ability to deport efficiently."[36] In 1992, INS officials reminded Congress that due process is a problem because it delays deportation.[37] The trend reached another milestone with the 1996 laws when Congress stripped long-term, lawful residents of the right to make claims for deportation waivers before an immigration judge. In 2013, Congressman Steve King of Iowa told the ICE Director that he should find ways "to accelerate their [the detainees'] removal."[38]

'Removal' is the current bureaucratic parlance for deportation, and in the words of another government mouthpiece, "Removal is not punishment or regulation of past conduct. It is a determination of who should be permitted to stay in the United States in the future."[39] Of course one is being punished for past conduct when, because of a particular crime, one is expelled from a place she has lived in and paid taxes for decades, where she has family, perhaps a business—all characteristic of thousands of the permanent residents in ICE detention who are waiting to be 'removed'. One justice has written, "It needs no citation of authorities to support the proposition that deportation is punishment," and this from someone who referred to the victims as "obnoxious Chinese" but was concerned the practice might spread to other "classes."[40] More recently, a majority Supreme Court opinion reminds us that "even when deportation is sought because of some act the alien has committed, *in principle* the alien is not being punished for that act."[41]

What even today remains largely invisible to so many of us has long been a fact of life in immigrant communities around the country. That's why, in the melodramatic logic of the movie *Babel* (2006), Mexican director Alejandro González Iñárritu can equate a rich person's gunshot wound with a Mexican worker's deportation. In the lesser-known *Deportation* (2001), by Haitian director Patrick Jerome, as integral to the plot as sex and romance are the esoteric and impenetrable immigration laws that turn one character into a 'criminal deportee' after a wrongful drug conviction. In other words, the two-tiered criminal justice system to which immigrants are subjected has been defining, and often destroying, immigrant lives all around 'us'.

Detained immigrants awaiting deportation after criminal convictions have often complained that they are being subjected to double jeopardy because they've already served their sentences. But their treatment does not even rise to that level: double jeopardy implies being tried twice for the same crime. The immigrants have been tried only once—and punished twice. The US deports people to countries where they do not speak the language, having left as young children. And back in Portugal, or Nigeria, or Haiti, or El Salvador, they are often stigmatized as 'criminal deportees'—sometimes, as in Jamaica, publicly and within days of their arrival.[42] Or the deportee's 'alien file' is literally handed by the accompanying ICE agent to, for example, the security agent at the Lagos airport.

Penal and *punishment* have etymological roots in *pain* and in *fine*; these are meant to be the *ending* ('fin') of an obligation. For asylum seekers and established US residents, however, deportation is often not an end, but is the start of a new and ongoing punishment.

NOTES

1. First published as Mark Dow, "Designed to Punish: Immigration Detention and Deportation," *Social Research: An International Quarterly* 74, no. 2 (2007): 533–546.
2. Félix Morisseau-Leroy, "Botpipèl," *Dyakout 1, 2, 3, 4* (Jamaica, NY: Haïtiana Publications, 1990), 137; my translation. For the complete poem in English, see Morisseau-Leroy, *Haitiad and Oddities*, translated by Jeffrey Knapp et al. (Miami, Fl.: Pantaléon Guilbaud, 1991), 57–58.
3. UPI, "US Official Finds No Repression in Haiti," *New York Times*, Apr. 3, 1982.
4. *The Constitution: That Delicate Balance*, Program 11: "Immigration Reform," Annenberg/Canadian Public Broadcasting Project, 1984. http://www.learner.org/vod/vod_window.html?pid=545. The program was recorded in June 1983. Guests included Doris Meissner, Executive Associate Commissioner, US Immigration and Naturalization Service, Department of Justice; Rudolph Giuliani, US Attorney, Southern District of NY and former Associate Attorney General, Department of Justice; and Marvin Shoob, Judge, US District Court, Northern District of Georgia.
5. Gregory Jaynes, "US Announces New Policy for Parole of Some Haitians," *New York Times*, June 15, 1982.
6. *The Constitution: That Delicate Balance.*
7. See *Haidee V. Eugenio*, "ICE pulls out its detainees, " *Saipan Tribune*, March 19, 2013.
8. Bruce Finley, "Migrant Cases Burden System," *Denver Post*, Oct. 2, 2006.
9. US Immigration and Customs Enforcement, "Fact Sheet: ICE Fiscal Year 2010 Enacted Budget." www.ice.gov/doclib/news/library/factsheets/doc/2010budgetfactsheet.doc
10. *Wong Wing v. United States*, 163 US 228 (1896).
11. Email correspondence with anonymous reporter, c. 2002.
12. There used to be a procedure for reviewing the custody of long-term detainees in which the paperwork would go to a 'post-order custody review unit' at INS headquarters in Washington, DC. Justice Anthony Kennedy's dissent in *Zadvydas v. Davis* (2001) indicates that he thought the detainee, not the paperwork, was moved to Washington; in other words, he didn't know how the immigration prison system works.
13. *Zadvydas v. Davis*, 533 US 678 (2001).
14. US Immigration and Customs Enforcement Office of Public Affairs, "Statement by US Immigration and Customs Enforcement (ICE) on Mark Dow's 'American Gulag,'" Press Release, (n.d. [2004]). On file with author.
15. American Civil Liberties Union, "ACLU Challenges Indefinite Detention in Southern California Facilities," Oct. 9, 2006.
16. Mark Dow, *American Gulag: Inside US Immigration Prisons* (Berkeley: University of California Press, 2004), 67.
17. Barbara P., interview by author, Lake Charles, La., 2003.
18. Dow, *American Gulag*, 264.
19. Barbara P., interview by author, Lake Charles, La., 2003.

20. US Immigration and Customs Enforcement, *Operations Manual: ICE Performance Based National Detention Standards* (Washington: Department of Homeland Security, 2008). See Part 7, Section 41, "Transfer of Detainees", 3. http://www.ice.gov/doclib/dro/detention-standards/pdf/staff_training.pdf

21. Barbara P., interview by author, Lake Charles, La., 2003.

22. US Department of Homeland Security, "Fact Sheet: ICE Accomplishments in Fiscal Year 2006," Oct. 30, 2006. http://immigration.procon.org/source-files/ice2006achievements.pdf

23. *Fong Yue Ting v. United States*, 149 US 698 (1893). Justice David Brewer's dissent.

24. Paul Kovac, "Force Feeding of Detained Aliens," *Immigration Litigation Bulletin 5*, no. 1 (2001).

25. US General Accounting Office, "Immigration Enforcement: Better Data and Controls Are Needed to Assure Consistency with the Supreme Court Decision on Long-Term Alien Detention," May 27, 2004. http://www.gao.gov/products/GAO-04-434

26. Salvador Longoria, interview by author, New Orleans, La., 2001.

27. Dow, *American Gulag*, 183.

28. Dow, "Guest Commentary: Detained in Eldora," *Cityview* (Des Moines), July 10, 2008. http://www.dmcityview.com/archives/2008/07jul/07-10-08/guest.shtml

29. Unpublished letter from Krome detainees, Miami, Fl., 2006. On file with author.

30. Anonymous detainee, interview by author, Miami, Fl., 1999.

31. Ibid.

32. US Immigration and Customs Enforcement, "2009 Immigration Detention Reforms," Aug. 6, 2009. http://www.aila.org/content/default.aspx?bc=1016|6715|12053|26286|31038|29726

33. Heartland Alliance National Immigrant Justice Center et al., "Year One Report Card: Human Rights and the Obama Administration's Immigration Detention Reforms," Oct. 6, 2010, 9. http://blog.lib.umn.edu/hrp/main/ICE%20report%20card%20FULL%20FINAL%202010%2010%2006.pdf.

34. See Dow, "What the Immigration Reformers are Missing," *The Hill*, December 21, 2012. http://thehill.com/blogs/congress-blog/homeland-security/274061-what-the-immigration-reformers-are-missing

35. Mae Ngai, "The Strange Career of the Illegal Alien: Immigration Restriction and Deportation Policy in the United States, 1921–1965," *Law and History Review* 21, no. 1 (2003): 69–107.

36. Ibid.

37. Dow, *American Gulag*, 350n10.

38. Hearing before the US House of Representatives Committee on Appropriations, Subcommittee on Homeland Security, March 14, 2013.

39. Edwin S. Kneedler, US Department of Justice, Oral Argument, *INS v. St. Cyr*, 533 US 289 (2001).

40. *Fong Yue Ting v. United States*, 149 US 698 (1893). Justice David Brewer's dissent.

41. *Zadvydas v. Davis*, 533 US 678 (2001). Emphasis added.

42. Bernard Headley, Michael Gordon and Andew MacIntosh, *Deported: Volume I: Entry and Exit Findings—Jamaicans Returned Home from the US Between 1997 and 2003* (Jamaica: Stephensons Litho Press, 2005).

7 'We Are Not Racists, but We Do Not Want Immigrants'

How Italy Uses Immigration Law to Marginalize Immigrants and Create a (New) National Identity

Barbara Faedda

This chapter analyzes Italian immigration policy and immigration law, giving special attention to the political discourse that keeps forcing immigration to the top of the institutional policy agenda. In this body of discourse, immigration is criminalized and foreign-ness becomes synonymous with criminality. Italian political parties have reinforced this association between crime and immigration to keep a firm grip on the electorate in a climate of political instability. This chapter examines several aspects of this political strategy. It also observes that institutional approaches to immigration have not changed substantially over the past three decades. Most governments, whether conservative or progressive, have governed immigration through an axiomatic that relegates immigration policy to a constant state of emergency that associates immigration with criminality.

All of these elements, along with the Italian uneasiness about its colonial history, and the chronic slowness of the Italian judicial system, form the basis for a new and more punitive kind of Italian immigration regime. Excessive bureaucracy, a confused *corpus* of law and harsh security-oriented policies leave immigrants unprotected and vulnerable, especially in prisons and detention centers.

This chapter also contributes some new information to the existing scholarship on Italian immigration policy through its analysis of the legal and political discourse of Italian immigration attorneys. The data for this analysis was gathered through structured interviews with immigration attorneys and legal practitioners, who were all members of the Association for Legal Studies on Immigration (ASGI), which is one of the largest and most well-organized immigration attorney organizations in Italy. This interview data supplements the analysis of legislative acts, statistics, newspapers, websites, videos and posters that were used to document the other aspects of Italian immigration discourse that were described earlier.

A flexible approach to the research process was needed to integrate these diverse sources of data. It was also necessary to take a flexible approach in constructing the sample of immigration attorney interviewees. This is because: 1) in Italy, the immigration attorney is still a rather new legal-professional figure; 2) Italian immigration attorneys' organizations are few and very new (ASGI was founded only in 1990); and 3) even though ASGI has approximately 270 members, only one-fifth of them practice immigration law exclusively. I was permitted access to this association and many individual lawyers because of my experience collaborating with two immigration attorneys for more than a decade. I also gained access to penitentiary personnel because of a contact I established with a police officer who had worked in a pretrial detention center for many years.

From the very beginning of the research process it was evident that both the immigration attorneys and the penitentiary officers shared very similar opinions about Italian immigration law and policies. Some main themes that surfaced in all of these interviews include: 1) critical observations about the disjuncture between the goals of Italian immigration laws and the recommendations of immigration experts; 2) the complicated language of the laws; 3) the lack of governmental attention toward integration policy and exaggerated attention toward repressive measures; and 4) the racist inclination of some politicians, which can be seen in the most recent Italian legislation on immigration.

The next several sections describe these conditions in more depth, by reviewing key features of the historical, legal and political context for Italian immigration law and policy. The closing segments of the chapter focus on the interview data that was just described, explaining how Italian immigration attorneys have interpreted and responded to these conditions.

CONTEMPORARY EUROPE AND IMMIGRATION

Faced with a very low birth rate and an aging population, Europe needs immigrants to keep the labor market alive and to maintain an expensive welfare system, but the general attitude toward immigration seems to be hostile. Immigration is viewed as a constant emergency; it is a problem that no country in Europe has been able to solve, although it is a common assumption that immigration is an integral part of European (and global) history.[1]

Because it is so closely tied to the sovereignty and identity of the nation-state, immigration has been deeply politicized and manipulated as a crucial tool of control and coercion. Although northern European countries have been dealing with immigration for several decades in the twentieth century, they are still trying to create a homogeneous policy, whereas the southern European countries strive to take full control of the problem. Immigration policies vary widely from country to country, and Europe is still trying to pursue a sort of general equilibrium.[2] An obstacle to this goal is the opposition between countries that are considered the fulcrum of Fortress Europe and countries with weaker borders that are considered an open door to Europe.

Moreover, throughout Europe there is a worrying phenomenon of right-wing xenophobia and anti-immigration parties, which are gaining higher and higher percentages of the popular vote. There are well-organized groups of nationalists, fascists and neo-Nazis in France, Denmark, Germany, Austria, England, the Netherlands and Italy. The increasing use of racism and xenophobic and anti-immigration discourse affects not only the right-wing parties but also the mainstream political parties.[3]

In the last few decades the EU produced many declarations, directives and official statements against racism, anti-Semitism and xenophobia. Some documents are directly based on Article 13 of the Treaty of Amsterdam,[4] and 1997 was even declared the 'European Year of Equal Opportunities for All'.[5] Although the EU legislation against discrimination is considered among the most extensive in the world, racism in Europe still is very pervasive. Laws, statements and declarations are not enough to ensure equal opportunities and civil rights.

With the Resolution Res (2002), the Council of Europe created the European Commission against Racism and Intolerance (ECRI) to "take firm and sustained action at the European level to combat the phenomena of racism, xenophobia, anti-Semitism and intolerance."[6] In 2003, the Parliamentary Assembly of the Council enacted Resolution 1344 (2003) on the "Threat posed to democracy by extremist parties and movements in Europe." With this resolution, the council expressed concerns about the "resurgence of extremist movements and parties in Europe," affirming that "no member state is immune to the intrinsic threats that extremism poses to democracy."[7]

In spite of these legislative efforts, discrimination based on ethnic origin was still the most common form of racism in the EU in 2008, according to the Eurobarometer 296.[8] It has also been observed that the management of borders is still one of the main challenges facing European migration policy.[9]

HISTORICAL ITALIAN BACKGROUND

There are many scholars working on the so-called elite migrations to Italy during the Old Regime and the nineteenth century,[10] but large, sustained immigration flows to Italy first arrived in the late twentieth century. Historically, Italy was a country of emigrants to the US (which, from 1876 to 1976, was the largest recipient of Italian immigrants in the world), Northern Europe and Canada. It also was—and still is—a country of heavy internal migration from Italian southern rural areas to northern industrial centers.

A significant flow of immigration into Italy began to occur in the 1970s. In the last three decades, Italy—which has since become a member of the Group of Eight industrialized nations—has been transformed into a country that can be considered a 'golden door' to Europe. After the oil crisis of 1973–1984, countries such as France, England and Germany began to limit immigration, closing their frontiers to noncitizens.[11] The decolonization of many African countries set the stage for a boom in African immigration to Europe in the 1960s and 1970s (especially from Algeria, Tunisia and Morocco).[12] Until 1973, France and Germany considered these migrant labor flows an important economic resource, and decided to include foreign workers into the national labor market.[13]

When migrants found the door closed in some Western European countries, they began to look at Italy as a new point of entry. At that time, Italy was seen as an open and friendly door, and many immigrants, who initially were planning to migrate to other parts of Europe, eventually decided to stay in Italy. For a long time Italy received immigrants, but did not consider itself a society of immigrants, because of deeply held beliefs in a homogeneous national culture.[14] Even recently, Prime Minister Silvio Berlusconi defined Italy publicly as a "not multicultural country."[15] Moreover, colonialism is not viewed as being as central to Italian history as it has been for other European countries such as France, UK or the Netherlands.[16] Many scholars have complained about this silence on the legacy of Italy's colonial history,[17] and it's likely that this silence has affected Italian attitudes toward immigration in the present day. Even after WWII, during the Italian Trusteeship Administration in Somalia (1950–1960), Italy failed to lead this former colony to independence.[18] Today the National Italian-Somali Association claims that the Italian government is still indifferent to them, despite the fact that they are all children of Italian parents.[19]

ITALIAN IMMIGRATION POLICY AND LEGAL FRAMEWORK

In the 1980s Italy became a more popular alternative to traditional countries of immigration, mostly because of its less restrictive immigration policy and its less complex immigration laws.[20] Due to its location in the Mediterranean and the peculiarity of its borders, Italy offered easy access, especially to those coming from Northern Africa and Eastern Europe. Another important factor is the underground economy. Many immigrants can find jobs only in the underground economy, especially in sectors such as agriculture, family care and construction. Recent reports show that illegal jobs account for more than 20 percent of the employment sector in the south of Italy, reaching as high as 40 percent for some occupations.[21] In 2004, immigrant workers—at that time representing about 8 percent of the Italian labor force—reported an accident rate double that of Italian workers.[22] In the few last decades, the expansion of this sector of domestic and personal services has been exceptionally rapid, and the large number of small industries, factories and businesses seems to have to facilitated the growth of the illegal workforce.

In 2008, the number of documented immigrants in Italy was almost four million (6.7 percent of the total population). They came mostly from

Romania (which joined the EU in 2007[23]), Albania, Morocco, China and Ukraine. Of this number, 52 percent are European, 23 percent are African, 16 percent are Asian and about 9 percent are from the Americas. More than 60 percent of these immigrants live in the northern part of Italy, 25 percent live in the center of Italy and only 10 percent in southern Italy.[24] In the last few years the acquisition of citizenship has doubled, but Italy still has one of the lowest citizenship rates in Europe. In 2005 and 2006, France granted 303,000 new citizenships, whereas Italy gave only 55,032 for the same period.[25]

In the 1990s, Italy began regulating immigration. Besides a regional act in 1988,[26] the first immigration law was the so-called Legge Martelli in 1990.[27] Until then, the only legislative document defining the status of foreigners had been the Act of Public Safety of 1931, the sole aim of which was to maintain public order.[28] The Legge Martelli not only was the first attempt to bring Italy in line with other European countries in the matters of asylum and immigration, but also forced Italy to see itself as a country of immigration. It was made up of 'urgent regulations' and included an ad hoc pardon law. The first systematic Italian Immigration Act, the Testo Unico (or Turco-Napolitano Act) was promulgated in 1998[29]; it also introduced the detention of undocumented immigrants in special temporary detention centers, where they could be identified and where their application for asylum would be evaluated, leading either to admission or instead to repatriation.

The Testo Unico was modified in 2002 by the two right-wing politicians who gave their name to the new law, the Bossi-Fini Act.[30] Enacted after the attacks of September 11, 2001, it reflected the transformed concept of global security, the tightening of sanctions and the hardening of Western countries with regard to immigrants. The Bossi-Fini Act introduced more restrictive norms for undocumented immigrants: their stay in temporary detention centers was raised from thirty to sixty days. Unidentified immigrants had to leave Italy within five days; those identified were immediately repatriated by the police. Before the Act of 2002, only undocumented immigrants were fingerprinted. Today, all non-EU immigrants applying for a stay permit must be fingerprinted.

Since the end of the 1990s, the National Alliance (formed in 1995 by Gianfranco Fini from the Italian Social Movement—an ex-neo-fascist party) and the Northern League (founded in 1991 by Umberto Bossi) found a common interest in immigration as a powerful means to attract a larger electorate. Together they created a correlation between criminality and immigration, which they have constantly reiterated through the years.

The Northern League, which after the most recent elections has become the third most popular party in Italy, is a populist party, which claims Celtic heritage and focuses on political and fiscal federalism, and separation from Rome and southern Italy. With a very conservative stance on social issues, the League uses a racist political discourse and sees immigrants—when not as plain criminals—only as a necessary source of manual labor. Several recommendations have been addressed to Italy from the EU on racism and xenophobia in political discourse.[31] One of the most notable examples is the Legge No. 205 that was enacted in 1993. But these antiracist laws did not inhibit the Northern League from issuing racist proposals for immigration, one of the most sensational coming from Giorgio Bettio—a League councilman in Treviso. During one of the council's sessions, he declared: "With immigrants, we should use the same system the SS used, punishing 10 of them for every slight against one of our citizens."[32] This anti-immigrant rhetoric reinforces the association between immigration and threats to the public safety. Immigrants are generally viewed as illegal or 'outside the law', and therefore inclined to criminal behavior.[33]

IMMIGRATION, SECURITY AND POLITICS

Part of the right-wing success in the Italian elections of April 2008 lies in fostering this general climate of fear.[34] According to a 2007 report by the Italian National Statistics Bureau (ISTAT), the public perception of risk was high and related to the fear of foreigners.[35] According to a 2008 report by Eurispes, Italy's leading independent research institute, 40.7 percent of Italians thought that foreigners were the main perpetrators of crime; 10.6 percent said that the increasing number of immigrants into Italy made crime more widespread; and 19.2 percent would restrict the entry of immigrants into Italy.

The widespread fear is also closely connected to the concept of 'emergency'. Since the 1980s, the term 'emergency' has always been related to immigration, and in 2002 Silvio Berlusconi declared the status of immigration a national emergency.[36] On December 18, 2008, the prime minister enacted another decree (equivalent to an executive order) that he used to extend "the national emergency to keep opposing the unexpected unprecedented arrival of immigrants."[37] These actions illustrate how the governmental agenda on immigration is still dictated, primarily, by the Northern League. The most severe legislative proposals come from the League, with the goal of securing the loyalty of those social groups that are predisposed to fear and racism. Moreover, to secure its local power, the Northern League seeks to give mayors full powers over security matters. According to several legal practitioners, "media—through constant daily attention to criminal facts related to immigrants—are helping the League to portray the image of a weak state, incapable of managing and eradicating crime."[38] In addition, the minister of the interior, Roberto Maroni of the Northern League, proposed a 'security package'—the *pacchetto sicurezza*—that sought to make illegal entry a crime. Remaining in Italy without permission would constitute a criminal offense punishable by imprisonment. The Northern League wanted to make illegal immigration punishable by up to four years in prison, and it also proposed that doctors report to police any patients who are in Italy illegally, as well as the creation of separate class-rooms for immigrant children. One immigration lawyer observed: "Italy currently has an overall criminal view of immigration . . . even landlords are being asked to become policemen. Criminal law fills the deficiencies of the social system."[39]

ITALIAN IMMIGRATION LAWYERS[40]

Italian immigration lawyers are a new, fast-growing pool of younger legal professionals. Among a few professional associations of immigration law-yers, ASGI (Association for Legal Studies on Immigration, instituted in 1990) is the most influential.[41] It is very active and since 1999 has pub-lished, with Magistratura Democratica (an association of left-wing judges), the journal *Diritto, Immigrazione e Cittadinanza*.[42] In 2008, I began to interview a group of thirty-two Italian immigration attorneys who are associated with ASGI (seventeen women and fifteen men).

The average age of lawyers involved in the study was 35.5. With the exception of a small number of lawyers, the average number of years of experience is less than seven. Six out of the thirty-two had written a final thesis on immigration at law school, twenty-two out of thirty-two responded that the lack of a specific course on immigration law in law schools can cause problems during practice, and one-third suggested creating a specific register of immigration lawyers within the Italian Bar Association. Almost everyone claimed to have acquired training and skills through personal efforts, through reading books and journals; surfing the Internet; participating in conferences and workshops; and exchang-ing ideas with colleagues. The most senior Italian immigration lawyers began as criminal lawyers in the 1990s during the immigration boom and decided to become immigration consultants to associations, political par-ties or Catholic volunteer groups.[43]

According to a senior expert on immigration, immigration lawyers in Italy can be divided into three groups: the first is made up of very motivated professionals, who chose to work in the immigration field because of their strong interest in fundamental civil rights; the second is made up of lawyers not specialized in immigration and who decide only occasionally to work on immigration cases; the third is made up of those not really interested in immigration, but attracted by the pro bono activity—particularly in crimi-nal defense work—that can guarantee a basic salary, given the excessive number of lawyers in Italy. This excess of lawyers is a matter for concern within the legal profession and within the Italian Bar Association. In his 2008 report, the chief justice of the Italian Supreme Court[44] revealed trou-bling data: Italy is the only country in Europe where the number of lawyers exceeds two hundred thousand out of a general population of sixty mil-lion.[45] Almost forty-two thousand lawyers have been admitted to practice in the Supreme Court in Italy, compared to just ninety-five in France and forty-four in Germany.[46]

ASGI is one of the biggest critics of the government's proposals regarding immigration. The association states that the biggest problem is the government's investment in preventing illegal immigration and punishing illegal migrants. It insists that the government should adopt more realistic policies to increase legal entries and to integrate immigrants into the social fabric more effectively. In general, ASGI foresees that the disappointment and frustration produced by the current policies could foment more social tension and foster a distorted discourse on cultural identity. In particular, they accuse the *pacchetto sicurezza* of being not only counterproductive but also in some cases illegitimate—even unconstitutional. These criticisms are consistent with comments gathered from several immigration lawyers, who all defined Italian immigration laws as confusing and incomprehensible. An Italian immigration lawyer with ten years of experience in the immigration legal field said: "In Italy the gap between law and its enforcement is huge. Italian immigration laws are really complex, stratified, inconsistent and ever-changing because they are at the mercy of the current government."[47] Another lawyer said: "The worst side of the Italian immigration law is the confusing language of the laws; they are sometimes completely incomprehensible. The lack of training for government officials and employees, the chronic lack of forms to be filled out and the continuous errors in institutional software endure beyond even the different governments and political parties."[48]

A member of the ASGI board of directors stated: "Italian immigration laws are intentionally complicated. They seem to be written to give more and more power to the public administration, . . . broadening the possibility of different interpretations . . . The laws seem to be made to create situations of illegality rather than to regulate the immigration phenomenon and to promote legality."[49] Another lawyer said: "Our immigration law is incoherent; it doesn't reflect the real needs of immigrants. It is often xenophobic and characterized by an irrational fear. The legislation should consult with experts who deal with immigration at the ground roots level and should avoid manipulating immigration law to divert the general attention from bigger social issues, which are not connected to immigration at all."[50]

On February 19, 2009, ASGI, along with the Italian Council for Refugees, Amnesty International, Doctors without Borders and several nongovernmental organizations (NGOs), sent an open letter to the president of the Italian Republic, to the prime minister and to the minister of the interior. They expressed serious concern about the facts that were surfacing concerning the treatment of immigrant detainees in Lampedusa,[51] in the Center for Identification and Expulsion (CIE). Eight hundred people detained there participated in a hunger strike, and a large fire broke out. The center had been recently transformed from a Center of First Assistance to a Center of Identification and Removal. The first removals caused several concerns, at both a national and international level. The Italian government had decided to concentrate all the migrants arriving to the Italian coasts in Lampedusa, whatever their legal status. This decision provoked tension on the island. Many thought that Lampedusa could not be a different destination than that of a first assistance center, from which migrants are transferred briefly to other centers. Those who signed the letter asked: 1) for a prompt transfer of all the migrants to other centers, where paperwork for asylum in particular could be completed immediately; 2) that Lampedusa go back to being a center for first assistance and reception of immigrants; 3) that liability for what happened in the center be verified.

On February 21, ASGI criticized the law decree—enacted by the government just the day before—that would increase the detention of immigrants subject to expulsion or refusal by up to six months. ASGI interpreted the new measure as a clear signal of an authoritarian policy, given that just a few weeks earlier a similar proposal had been rejected by the Senate. Raising the length of detention from two to up to six months changes the nature of detention, enabling it to become a long-term form of confinement. Such a distressing situation could lead to rebellions in the detention centers, with serious consequences for the safety of the centers. ASGI observed that the Italian government has adopted a repressive policy agenda that is based on ideological propaganda. Moreover, the new measures completely ignore the De Mistura Report—prepared during the previous government—which pointed out not only the dilapidated state of the centers but also their inefficiency.[52]

At the end of its work in 2007, the De Mistura Commission reported several serious problems in the Italian centers dedicated to the reception and detention of immigrants. They include: lack of legal information for asylum seekers and absence of psychological assistance; overcrowding of vulnerable people such as women, children and traumatized asylum seekers; the denial of access to organizations providing advice and support to asylum seekers; structures similar to prisons, where detainees are constrained to near immobility; and use of primitive procedures for determining the age of unaccompanied children. The commission recommended several urgent changes, leading toward the overarching goal of eventually eliminating the centers. At the core of these recommendations was the idea that the reception of asylum seekers should be based on a more humane approach.

These recommendations are especially relevant given that the flow of asylum seekers into Italy has continued to increase. In 2008, Italy received 31,200 applications from asylum seekers—more than double the figure of the year before. Thus, Italy has become the fourth most popular destination for asylum seekers in the industrialized world. Only in 1999 did a higher number apply for asylum in Italy (33,400 claims). Nigeria is the main country of origin of applicants in Italy, with 5,300 new claims (+300 percent), followed by Somalia, with 4,500 new claims (+491 percent), Eritrea, with 2,700 new claims (+21 percent), and Afghanistan, with 2,000 new claims (+202 percent).[53]

IMMIGRANTS' CRIMES AND ITALIAN PRISONS

Before discussing the discomfort of immigrants in the Italian penitentiaries, a brief description of the critical situation of Italian state prisons is necessary, because it was also underlined in a report on human rights in criminal justice systems presented at the 9th Asia-Europe Meeting Seminar on Human Rights. Although prison overcrowding is a major problem worldwide, Italy has the highest level of jail occupancy in Europe, with an incarcerated population that is at 131.5 percent of the official capacity.[54] Spain follows with 129.5 percent, and third is the UK with 112.7 percent. In 2006, these conditions became so extreme that the Italian Parliament passed an ad hoc pardon law granting a three-year sentence reduction for some categories of offenders.[55] The reports from recent years on the situation in Italian prisons confirmed a constant overcrowding, which makes it impossible to guarantee the conditions and treatment established by law and prison regulations, starting with the prisoner's right to have enough space.[56]

The director of an Italian district penitentiary in the north of Italy (a pretrial detention center) explained that Italian prisons suffer not only from overcrowding but also from a chronic lack of funds, adequate infrastructure and staff.[57] This critical situation affects all the inmates, but being an immigrant makes this situation even harder to bear.

Judicial and penitentiary statistics demonstrate that crime rates for immigrants and native citizens are very similar (the crime rate of immigrants is slightly higher).[58] Immigrants, however, commit fewer serious crimes than Italians. So even though there has been a recent increase in the number of immigrants in Italian prisons, it is not because they are more inclined to commit crimes.

Social exclusion and privations are only one aspect—although an extremely important one—of the forces driving these higher incarceration rates. Foreign inmates: 1) are often drug-addicted and do not qualify for or cannot afford reintegration programs into social life; 2) are often extremely poor; 3) are often in a state of effective solitude; 4) very often cannot communicate because of linguistic difficulties; and 5) very often do not have a job, housing or social relations.[59]

The other side of the story is that foreigners' experience with the Italian penal system differs from that of Italians.[60] Immigrants, especially if undocumented, are not permitted to await their trial outside prison, as many Italian are allowed to do.[61] There is an important legal consequence to this different treatment: immigrants tend to accept alternative proceedings such as plea bargaining. Moreover, immigrants 1) usually do not appeal adverse judgments; 2) lack a professional defense; and 3) lack access to *pro bono* defense. When immigrants lack a fixed residence, they cannot claim the benefit of house arrest or other alternative measures to detention before sentencing/trial. Therefore, under the same charge or sentence, immigrants stay in prison longer than Italians.

Prison overcrowding can be the result of a specific government's policy on crime prevention, but it can also demonstrate the slowness of the justice system, rather than an increase in the crime rates or an increased interest in prosecuting violators. The percentage of foreign prisoners (proportionate to the entire prison population) is 37.4 percent in Italy, 35.7 percent in Spain, 43.9 percent in Greece, 26.9 percent in Germany and 19.2 percent in France.[62]

Even if Italian laws encourage equal treatment of Italians and immigrants, immigrants receive worse treatment. It also seems that the recent policies and laws have reinforced this inequality. Article 1 of the penitentiary law clearly states the principle of equality among Italians and immigrants.[63] But on comparing sentences received by immigrants and Italians it appears that there is a double standard, especially with regard to alternatives to incarceration. Not only is it very difficult for immigrants to access alternatives to incarceration, but also, even worse, Italian laws tend to use deportation as the only alternative measure that is available for immigrants.[64]

CONCLUSIONS

With a population of sixty million and the lowest birth rate in Europe, Italy is torn between the advantages that immigration brings and the resistance offered by a 'new' racism and a rising xenophobia—both of which are augmented by strategies and propaganda that instill fear in the population. Political parties work behind the scenes, fueling this dilemma and reinforcing the connections between immigration and crime.

The government of Italy is now using the political and legal systems as its primary tool of racialization and associated subordination. A country of strong regionalism, parochialism and north-south divisions, Italy seems to find a renewed unity by rejecting immigrants and forgetting (or pretending to forget) many other social and economic problems that preceded the new immigration, such as the (Italian) mafia, unemployment and widespread corruption. The deep divisions among Italians are seemingly erased in order to (re)create a homogeneous community that is united against the Other.

Since the 1980s, political, social, legal and cultural approaches to immigration have not changed substantially. Most governments have treated immigration as a national emergency that is closely associated with criminality. Despite the egalitarian and antiracist principles contained in the Italian Constitution, and European and international laws, immigrants are treated differently by the Italian administration: even when open racism is not involved. An excessive bureaucracy and a confused *corpus* of laws leave immigrants unprotected and vulnerable, especially in critical contexts such as in prisons or in detention centers.

Today, immigration law could be seen as a sort of 'ritualized form of exorcism'[65] in a country that is clearly obsessed with foreigners. The myth of the 'immigrant invasion'[66] has become increasingly widespread, acquiring a collective credibility based on feelings of insecurity and fear. Some political parties have taken the role of rescuers upon themselves, choosing a hybrid—but clearly conservative—identity that blends the popular image of the Christian crusader with that of the Celtic warrior. As observed throughout this chapter, these identities must also be understood as political strategies; the structure of political alliances in Italian society and the workings of the electoral system have to be taken into account.[67]

NOTES

1. Saskia Sassen, *Guest and Aliens* (New York: New Press, 1999), 157. See also Kalid Koser, *International Migration: A Very Short Introduction* (Oxford: Oxford University Press, 2007), 1, and Natalia Ribas-Mateos, *The Mediterranean in the Age of Globalization* (New Brunswick: Transaction, 2005), 1.
2. Maria Teresa Bia, "Towards an EU Immigration Policy: Between Emerging Supranational Principles and National Concerns," European Diversity and Autonomy Papers, Feb. 2004, accessed October 13, 2005, http://aei.pitt.edu/6159/1/2004_edap02.pdf.
3. "The Use of Racist, Anti-Semitic and Xenophobic Elements in Political Discourse" (meeting on the International Day for the Elimination of Racial Discrimination, European Commission against Racism and Intolerance, Paris, Mar. 21, 2005), Nov. 2005, accessed November 15, 2005, http://www.coe.int/t/dghl/monitoring/ecri/activities/14-public_presentation_paris_2005/Presentation2005_Paris_proceedings_en.pdf.
4. It reads: "the Council, acting unanimously on a proposal from the Commission and after consulting the European Parliament, may take appropriate action to combat discrimination based on sex, racial or ethnic origin, religion or belief, disability, age or sexual orientation." The Treaty of Amsterdam, Oct. 2, 1997.
5. Eurobarometer, *Discrimination in the European Union: Perceptions, Experiences and Attitudes* (European Commission, 2008), accessed August 20, 2008, http://ec.europa.eu/public_opinion/archives/ebs/ebs_296_en.pdf.
6. Council of Europe Committee of Ministers, Resolution Res (2002) 8 on the statute of the European Commission against Racism and Intolerance, adopted by the Committee of Ministers on June 13, 2002, at the 799th meeting of the Ministers' Deputies, accessed March 31, 2007, https://wcd.coe.int/ViewDoc.jsp?id=289019.
7. Assembly debate on Sept. 29, 2003 (26th Sitting) (see Doc. 9890, report of the Political Affairs Committee, rapporteur: Ms. Feric-Vac), accessed January 16, 2008, http://assembly.coe.int/ASP/XRef/X2H-DW-XSL.asp?fileid=17142&lang=EN.
8. Eurobarometer, *Discrimination*.
9. Ricard Zapata-Barrero, "Political Discourses about Borders: On the Emergence of a European Political Community," in *A Right to Inclusion and Exclusion? Normative Fault Lines of the EU's Area of Freedom, Security and Justice*, ed. H. Lindahl (Oxford: Hart, 2009), 15.
10. Daniela Luigia Caglioti, "Elite Migrations in Modern Italy: Patterns of Settlement, Integration and Identity Negotiation," *Journal of Modern Italian Studies* 13, no. 2 (2008): 141–151.
11. Giovanna Zincone, "Italy—Main Features of Italian Immigration Flows," Mediterranean Migration Observatory, accessed Aug. 20, 2012, http://www.

mmo.gr/pdf/library/Italy/Main%20features%20of%20Italian%20immigration%20flows.pdf.

12. Richard Alba and Roxane Silberman, "Decolonization Immigrations and the Social Origins of the Second Generation: The Case of North Africans in France," *International Migration Review* 36, no. 4 (2002): 1169–1193.

13. James Hollifield, "Immigration Policy in France and Germany: Outputs versus Outcomes," *Annals of the American Academy of Political and Social Science* 485 (1986): 113–128.

14. Italy became an autonomous state quite recently, in 1860, and since then Italians not only have maintained the division between north and south, but also have shared a strong regionalism and parochialism, rather than a homogeneous, nationalistic patriotism.

15. "Berlusconi: Si ai rimpatri. Non apriremo le porte a tutti," *Corriere della Sera*, May 9, 2009, and "Berlusconi: Via i clandestini, non siamo un paese multietnico," *La Repubblica*, May 9, 2009.

16. Judith Adler Hellman, "Immigrant 'Space' in Italy: When an Emigrant Sending Becomes an Immigrant Receiving Society," *Modern Italy* 1, no. 3 (1997): 34–51. See also Gian Paolo Calchi Novati, "Italy in the Triangle of the Horn: Too Many Corners for a Half Power," *Journal of Modern African Studies* 32 (1994): 369–385.

17. Pamela Ballinger, "Borders of the Nation, Borders of Citizenship: Italian Repatriation and the Redefinition of National Identity after World War II," *Comparative Studies in Society and History* 49 (2007): 713–741.

18. Paolo Tripodi, "Back to the Horn: Italian Administration and Somalia's Troubled Independence," *International Journal of African Historical Studies* 32 (1999): 359–380.

19. Gianni Mari (president of ANCIS Italian-Somali National Association), "Italo-somali: Una minoranza che l'Italia vuole ignorare. Le tristi conseguenze della politica italiana coloniale e post-coloniale," interview by Barbara Faedda, *Diritto&Diritti*, Dec. 2001, accessed Aug. 20, 2012, http://www.diritto.it/materiali/antropologia/faedda16.html. See also Francesca Caferri, "I bimbi italiani strappati alla Somalia," *La Repubblica*, June 17, 2008, 36.

20. See also A. Triandafyllidou, "The Political Discourse on Immigration in Southern Europe: A Critical Analysis," *Journal of Community & Applied Social Psychology* 10 (2000): 373–389, and Kitty Calavita, *Immigrants at the Margins: Law, Race, and Exclusion in Southern Europe* (Cambridge: Cambridge University Press, 2005).

21. Simone Trinci, "Underground Work, Immigrants and Networks: Preliminary Findings from Italy," *International Journal of Economic Development* 6, no. 3 (2004): 273–305.

22. Mario Giaccone, *Injuries More Frequent among Immigrant Workers*,, (EWCO European Working Conditions Observatory, Oct. 14, 2005), accessed February 15, 2007, http://www.eurofound.europa.eu/ewco/2005/10/IT0510NU01.htm.

23. J. Meletti, "Romania, ventisettesima stella. 'Da oggi noi valiamo doppio'," *La Repubblica*, Jan. 2, 2007.

24. Caritas, *Immigrazione Dossier statistico 2008, XVIII Report on Immigration* (Rome: Centro Studi e Ricerche, 2008). See also ISMU, *XIV Report on Migrations 2008* (Milan: Fondazione ISMU Iniziative e Studi sulla Multietnicità, 2009), and ISTAT, *Report on Immigrants in Italy* (Rome: 2008).

25. Ministero dell'Interno Italian Ministry of the Interior, *Statistiche, 2005–2008* (Rome: Italian Ministry of the Interior, 2009), accessed January 25, 2009, http://www.interno.gov.it/mininterno/export/sites/default/it/temi/cittadinanza/

sottotema008.html; and ISTAT (Italian National Institute of Statistics), "La popolazione straniera residente in Italia al primo gennaio 2008," Rome, Oct. 9, 2008, accessed December 4, 2008, http://www3.istat.it/salastampa/comunicati/non_calendario/20081009_00/.

26. Legge regionale Local regulation, no. 38, July 4, 1988, "Interventi a tutela degli immigrati extracomunitari in Lombardia e delle loro famiglie.", accessed February 4, 2008, http://www.famiglia.regione.lombardia.it/shared/ccurl/728/258/12502lr38-1988,0.pdf.

27. Legge Martelli, no. 39, Feb. 28, 1990, "Norme urgenti in materia di asilo politico, di ingresso e soggiorno dei cittadini extracomunitari e di regolarizzazione dei cittadini extracomunitari ed apolidi già presenti nel territorio dello Stato. Disposizioni in materia di asilo.", accessed December 4, 2007, http://www.cirdi.org/wp/wp-content/uploads/2011/03/L_39_1990__Legge_Martelli.pdf.

28. Testo Unico della Legge di Pubblica Sicurezza, Regio decreto, no. 773, June 18, 1931, "Approvazione del testo unico delle leggi di pubblica sicurezza," published in the Official Gazette, no. 146, June 26, 1931, , accessed June 21, 2007, http://psm.du.edu/media/documents/national_regulations/countries/europe/italy/italy_law_on_public_security_1931-italian.pdf.

29. Legge, no. 40, Mar. 6, 1998, accessed April 23, 2008, http://www.camera.it/parlam/leggi/98040l.htm.

30. Legge, no. 189, July 30, 2002, , accessed April 23, 2008, http://www.camera.it/parlam/leggi/02189l.htm.

31. In 2005, for example, the Third Report on Italy by the European Commission against Racism and Intolerance (ECRI) stated: "ECRI . . . recommends that the Italian authorities take measures against the use of racist and xenophobic discourse in politics." European Commission against Racism and Intolerance, Third Report on Italy, adopted on Dec. 16, 2005, Strasbourg, made public on May 16, 2006, Council of Europe, accessed on March 25, 2007, http://hudoc.ecri.coe.int/XMLEcri/ENGLISH/Cycle_03/03_CbC_eng/ITA-CbC-III-2006-19-ENG.pdf.

32. Corriere della Sera, Dec. 6, 2007, 25; See also La Repubblica, Dec. 5, 2007, 12; and La Stampa, Dec. 4, 2007.

33. Asale Angel-Ajani, "The Racial Economies of Criminalization, Immigration, and Policing in Italy," Social Justice 30, no. 3 (2003): 48–62.

34. "Rome v. Roma: Silvio Berlusconi's New Government Acts against Immigrants to Italy," Economist, May 22, 2008.

35. ISTAT, Annual Report, (Rome: ISTAT, 2007), accessed on January 23, 2008, http://www3.istat.it/dati/catalogo/20071212_00/contenuti.html.

36. This status of immigration as a national emergency was not even interrupted by the leftist government of Romano Prodi. The second Prodi Government started onMay 17, 2006 and ended on May 6, 2008.

37. Decreto del Presidente del Consiglio dei Ministri, Dec. 18, 2008, "Proroga dello stato di emergenza per proseguire le attività di contrasto all'eccezionale afflusso di extracomunitari," accessed on January 31, 2009, http://www.interno.gov.it/mininterno/site/it/sezioni/servizi/legislazione/immigrazione/0969_2008_12_18_DPCM.html?pageIndex=4.

38. Massimiliano V. (immigration attorney), in discussion with the author, Mar. 21, 2009.

39. Francesco D.P. (immigration attorney), in discussion with the author, Apr. 12, 2008, and Oct. 27, 2008.

40. I wish to thank ASGI for helping in circulating my questionnaires, all the lawyers involved in my research and R. Miele, a former deputy police commissioner and founding director of Studio Immigrazione.

41. Composed of 270 members, mostly lawyers, but also professors, social workers, trade unionists and volunteers.
42. Diritto, Immigrazione e Cittadinanza, accessed Aug. 20, 2012, http://www.francoangeli.it/riviste/sommario.asp?IDRivista=89.
43. Within the whole category of immigration lawyers, asylum and refugee lawyers represent an even smaller group. A large majority work as consultants to NGOs or public institutions, whereas others practice exclusively for these institutions as full-time employees.
44. Annual report by the chief justice of the Italian Supreme Court, legal year 2008.
45. CCBE, Council of Bars and Law Societies of Europe, 2008, cited in Annual Report 2008 by the chief justice of the Italian Supreme Court, 2008.
46. In comparison, in terms of the number of judges, Italy is within the European average, with around eight thousand judges.
47. Lara O. (immigration attorney), in discussion with the author, April 12, 2008 and Mar 15, 2009.
48. Massimiliano V. (immigration attorney), in discussion with the author, Mar. 21, 2008, May 15, 2008, Sept. 2, 2008 and Mar. 17, 2009. .
49. Marco P. (immigration attorney), in discussion with the author, Mar. 17, 2009.
50. Mariella C. (immigration attorney), in discussion with the author, Mar. 19, 2009; Lara O. (immigration attorney), in discussion with the author, March 20, 2009.
51. Lampedusa is an Italian isle strategically located south of Sicily, where Italian-bound immigrants from Africa might be intercepted.
52. See the report (in Italian) on the website dedicated to detention in Europe., accessed August 20, 2012, http://www.detention-in-europe.org/images/stories/2007%20il%20rapporto.pdf. See also European Parliament Resolution on Lampedusa, *Official Journal of the European Union*, Apr. 14, 2005, accessed July 3, 2006, http://www.europarl.europa.eu/sides/getDoc.do?pubRef=-//EP//TEXT+TA+P6-TA-2005–0138+0+DOC+XML+V0//EN; and "Italy—Report of the Visit by the GUE-NGL Delegation to the Lampedusa Holding Center for Migrants," accessed Aug. 20, 2012, http://www.statewatch.org/news/2009/mar/eu-gue-lampedusa-report.pdf.
53. UNHCR (The United Nation High Commissioner for Refugees), "Asylum Levels and Trends in Industrialized Countries 2008, Statistical Overview of Asylum Applications Lodged in Europe and Selected Non-European Countries," made public Mar. 24, 2009, accessed May 7, 2009, http://www.unhcr.org/statistics/STATISTICS/49c796572.pdf.
54. Param Cumaraswamy and Manfred Nowak, "Human Rights in Criminal Justice Systems," (paper presented at the 9th Informal Asia-Europe Meeting Seminar on Human Rights, Strasbourg, France, Feb. 18–20, 2009), accessed November 20, 2009, http://www.asef.org/images/docs/9thHRBackgroundPaper.pdf.
55. Evelyn Shea, "Elections and the Fear of Crime: The Case of France and Italy," *European Journal on Criminal Policy and Research* 15, no. 1–2 (2009): 83–102.
56. According to Associazione Antigone, *IV Report on the conditions of the prisons*, (Rome, Carocci Editore, 2006) at the date of July 31, 2006 there were 61,246 inmates in Italian prisons. Due to the 241 Law of 2006 about clemency toward prisoners, 17,449 inmates were freed.
57. Manuela F., in discussion with the author, Mar. 9, 2009.
58. Milo Bianchi, Paolo Buonanno and Paolo Pinotti, "Immigration and Crime: An Empirical Analysis" (Working Paper No. 698, Banca d'Italia Eurosistema, Dec. 2008), accessed Aug. 20, 2012, http://www.bancaditalia.it/pubblicazioni/

econo/temidi/td08/TD698_08/TD_698_08_en/en_tema_698.pdf; Dossier Immigrazione Caritas-Migrantes and Agenzia Redattore Sociale, "La criminalità degli immigrati: Dati, interpretazioni e pregiudizi", accessed Aug. 20, 2012, http://www.redattoresociale.it/RedattoreSocialeSE_files/Speciali_ Documenti/274795.pdf; Emilio Santoro, "L'esecuzione penale nei confronti dei migranti irregolari e il loro 'destino' a fine pena," AltroDiritto Centro di documentazione su carcere, devianza e marginalità, University of Florence, 2004, accessed Aug. 20, 2012, http://www.altrodiritto.unifi.it/adirmigranti/ detenuti/migrdet.htm; and Giovanna Castellana, "La funzione rieducativa della pena e il detenuto straniero: Aspetti sociologici e costituzionalistici," AltroDiritto Centro di documentazione su carcere, devianza e marginalità, University of Florence, July 2003, accessed Aug. 20, 2012, http://www. altrodiritto.unifi.it/ricerche/migrdet/castella/index.htm.

59. Andrea Di Nicola, ed., *Gli stranieri in carcere tra esclusione e inclusione: L'esperienza trentina. Rapporto finale del progetto* (Trento, Transcrime, 2007).

60. Castellana, "La funzione rieducativa."

61. Sixty percent of foreigners versus less than forty percent of Italians.

62. Roy Walmsley, *World Prison Population List (eighth edition)*, International Centre for Prison Studies Kings' College, accessed September 19, 2009, http://www.prisonstudies.org/info/downloads/wppl-8th_41.pdf.

63. Legge, July 26, 1975, no. 354, art. 1, Trattamento e rieducazione, "Il trattamento penitenziario deve essere conforme ad umanità e deve assicurare il rispetto della dignità della persona. Il trattamento è improntato ad assoluta imparzialità, senza discriminazioni in ordine a nazionalità, razza e condizioni economiche e sociali, a opinioni politiche e a credenze religiose, accessed May 4, 2008, http://www.lavoro.gov.it/NR/rdonlyres/FDF48DF0-FB7D-4D75-AD02-E95E2142DDF3/0/34_Legge26luglio1975n354.pdf.

64. Legge, July 30, 2002, no. 189 (Legge Bossi-Fini), art. 15 (Espulsione a titolo di sanzione sostitutiva o alternativa alla detenzione), accessed Aug. 20, 2012, http://www.interno.it/mininterno/export/sites/default/it/sezioni/servizi/ legislazione/immigrazione/legislazione_424.html; Santoro, "L'esecuzione penale"; and "L'espulsione come sostituzione al carcere: Un *indultino* o una condanna supplementare?," Cestim, accessed Aug. 20, 2012, http://www. cestim.it/argomenti/11devianza/carcere/due-palazzi/studi_explorer_%20 1%20-%204/pagine%20web/espulsionecomemisuraalternativa.htm.

65. Raymond Coulon, "The Alien as a Soft Target for Exorcizing Violence," *International Journal for the Semiotics of Law* 10, no. 1 (1997): 37–53.

66. Hein de Haas, *The Myth of Invasion: Irregular Migration from West Africa to the Maghreb and the European Union*, (Oxford, IMI International Migration Institute Research Report, Oct. 2007), accessed January 27, 2008, http:// www.imi.ox.ac.uk/pdfs/Irregular%20migration%20from%20West%20 Africa%20-%20Hein%20de%20Haas.pdf.

67. Ruud Koopmans, Paul Statham, Marco Giugni and Florence Passy, *Contested Citizenship: Immigration and Cultural Diversity in Europe* (Minneapolis: University of Minnesota Press, 2005), 204.

Part III

Gendered Peripheries

Emigrants, Asylum Seekers and the
Feminization of Migrant Marginality

8 Gendered Global Ethnography

Comparing Migration Patterns and Ukrainian Emigration[1]

Cinzia Solari

The US immigration literature clusters around two key questions: why do people migrate and how can we understand their integration into host countries? This reflects a well-established division in migration studies in which scholars tend to *either* study the sending country *or* the receiving country but rarely both.[2] The bulk of migration research occurs in the receiving site where the focus is on economic,[3] occupational[4] and political integration.[5] Studies that engage with the sending site have often done so through abstract models.[6] Recently there is a small but growing ethnographic literature that looks at how sending states 'manage' their populations abroad.[7] I argue that this division between research on sending and receiving sites obscures the different effects that contrasting *migration patterns* can have in the sending country. With the collapse of the iron curtain, capitalist market relations, ideals and moralities have flooded into Ukraine. Ukraine's dominant national project at this historical moment is the construction of Ukraine as an independent nation-state in the global arena.[8] A confluence of gendered processes of economic transformation and nationalism inside Ukraine has encouraged emigration to Italy and California, the two largest receiving sites of post-1991 Ukrainian emigrants. I suggest, however, that these two migration streams are not simply about two different destinations for migrants, but rather they produce two divergent migration patterns that are not equally tied to Ukraine's gendered processes of transformation. I maintain the migration pattern to California—a permanent migration of families—is a drain on Ukraine's resources and is both structurally and discursively peripheral to Ukrainian nation building. In contrast, the migration pattern to Italy—the temporary migration of middle-aged women, mostly grandmothers—has a different set of effects in Ukraine. I argue this migration pattern is a constitutive element in Ukraine's nation building process that, in this post-Soviet context, involves a gendered reorganization of family and work relations.

I use the methods and tools of global ethnography. This shapes both the methods of qualitative researchers and the analysis of the data gathered. I argue the perspective of global ethnography allows migration scholars to overcome the bifurcation between studies on sending and receiving countries and move the literature in productive directions. I will demonstrate this by drawing on my research with Ukrainian domestic workers in Italy and California. First I will show how the perspective of global ethnography led me to expand my research sites in order to study migration from both ends with consequences for theorizing migration and its interactions with other processes of social transformation. Second I will explain how 'reaching for the global' has changed my unit of analysis from comparing receiving sites, the most common example of comparative work in migration studies, to comparing migration patterns. This revealed that migration patterns have differing effects in Ukraine. This is in contrast to studies that often treat emigration as having uniform effects in the sending country. Finally I will draw on my ethnographic data, which compares the migration patterns from Ukraine to Italy and Ukraine to California to illustrate what ethnography can reveal about macro-level processes of globalization. But first, what is 'global ethnography'?

GLOBAL ETHNOGRAPHY: GENDER, METHOD AND ANALYSIS

In his call for a "global ethnography," Michael Burawoy argues that ethnography has become too confined by privileging the micro and has allowed studies of globalization to remain abstract schemas devoid of the experiences of individuals.[9] Globalization is not some *thing* or even a set of processes that float abstractly above us. Rather global processes are necessarily produced in local contexts by specific agencies, institutions and individuals. According to Burawoy, macro-level processes can and must be studied by ethnographers in tangible sites in order to study "globalization from below." He argues that "Globalization is not a cause but an effect of processes in hierarchical chains that span the world" and it is only in locales—the domain of the ethnographer—that one can study the production and concrete effects of globalization.[10]

Winifred Poster has both embraced and critiqued this view, arguing that Burawoy may have coined the term 'global ethnography', but feminist ethnographers have long been practicing aspects of what Burawoy is proposing.[11] She suggests that global ethnography is a useful tool in describing a shift in feminist research from confirming the presence of gender in the global economy to exploring the complexities of gender as a category.[12] Although she agrees that global ethnography is an important perspective, Poster argues that gender has been left out of Burawoy's conceptualization and calls for a "gendered global ethnography." I propose that one way we can achieve this is to follow Joan Scott, who asks us to think about the ways in which gender is constitutive of social relations and apply this to the macro-level processes revealed through the practices of global ethnography.[13]

Expanding Research Sites

This chapter is based on sixteen months of ethnographic work and 158 in-depth interviews conducted between June 2004 and November 2006 in Rome, Italy, L'viv, Ukraine, and San Francisco, California. I did not begin this project expecting to conduct research in three countries. Most studies of migration focus on the receiving country. Following this literature, I set out to conduct a cross-national comparison of Ukrainian domestic workers caring for the elderly in Italy and California. Following feminist studies of domestic work that are interested in the negotiations that occur between women and across racial and economic realities, I planned to focus on the micro-level processes of performing caring labor. However, when I arrived in Rome, my first research site, I discovered that informants did not want to talk about the intricacies of providing care or negotiating with their employers. Instead, Ukrainian spaces in Rome were dominated by themes of post-Soviet nation building. Thinking my findings through the perspective of global ethnography allowed me to see that these migrants were agents in processes of globalization that were as much about what was happening in Ukraine as what was happening in Italy and California.

During six months in Italy, I conducted sixty-one in-depth interviews with women and men from Ukraine providing care to the elderly and many more formal interviews with community leaders, including religious leaders and labor organizers. Although the primary language of communication was my American-accented Russian, as the US-born daughter of Italian immigrants, my fluency in Italian also proved vital to the project, allow-ing me to conduct participant observation in the Italian organizations that represent and service domestic workers as well as the Ukrainian women workers' union and the offices of Rome's Ukrainian- and Russian-language newspaper. I conducted ethnographic work in a Ukrainian Greek Catholic and a Russian Orthodox church, where I attended weekly services, meals and activities. Three months into my fieldwork, a contested presidential election in Ukraine sparked the Orange Revolution.[14] I spent countless hours observing Ukrainians demonstrating in solidarity with the mass protests in Ukraine in addition to attending cultural events and informal gatherings.

These experiences in the field made it clear to me that I had to go to Ukraine. There I conducted interviews with the families of migrants and followed political and media representations of emigration in Ukraine. Italy and Ukraine are physically connected by a fleet of Soviet-era courier vans and buses that carry goods and workers back and forth. I rode the 'migration bus' from Rome to L'viv in Western Ukraine, the region most of my informants are from. I stayed in L'viv for three months and conducted thirty-eight interviews with young adults who had one or both parents working abroad. I then completed the migration circuit by riding the bus back with Ukrainians heading to Italy to work.

I also spent seven months intensively immersed in the San Francisco field sites. I conducted forty-one interviews with Ukrainian home care workers providing in-home cleaning and caring services to the elderly. I attended Russian-language union meetings for home care workers, participated in the parishes of two Ukrainian churches and attended countless community cultural events.

Some might call this a multi-sited ethnography.[15] But the term 'multi-sited', like the concept of 'transnationalism', implies that the sites are discrete entities with people and ideas flowing between them. Global ethnography, however, asks us to look at sending and receiving countries as dynamic sites that are interacting with and shaping each other. Placing gender at the center of global ethnography asks us to consider sending and receiving sites, almost always studied separately in migration studies, as linked through global processes. Gender is a useful idiom for the perspective of global ethnography precisely because gender is central to articulating and maintaining global economic and cultural systems. Ukraine, California and Italy are connected by macro-level processes of migration and global economic transformation, which are, I argue, fundamentally gendered processes. I found myself excavating these large-scale processes on the ground through the experiences of migrant domestic workers and their families, something that is possible only by conducting research in both sending and receiving countries.

Shifting Units of Analysis

The perspective of global ethnography not only led me to expand my research sites to include the sending country, but it also led me to change my unit of analysis. A growing literature on 'contexts of reception' is pushing the immigration literature toward two types of comparison. The first is to look at immigrant groups from many different sending countries to the US. Once scholars control for variables such as age, education and sex, the groups are comparable and their sending countries are no longer important in the analysis. The second type of comparison is to look at a group from the same sending country in two different receiving sites. Here the sending country is considered unimportant in terms of affecting immigrant outcomes because the sending country is being held constant and therefore should have the same effects regardless of the migrants' destination.[16] Therefore, in both types of comparison, variation in immigrant outcomes or practices is attributed to differing contexts of reception with a focus on the unique institutional landscape that 'receives' immigrants in each site, and the sending sites fall out of the analysis.

Expanding my research sites to include the sending country had analytical implications for what exactly was being compared. Certain characteristics of my informants were kept constant. The workers I interviewed in both Italy and California left Ukraine after 1991. All had some higher education as well as professional work histories. The most common professions reported were high school teachers, accountants and engineers. I also controlled for occupation. Italy is experiencing a 'care crisis' for its elderly, and therefore in-home care worker is the predominant job for many immigrant groups, including Ukrainians, in Italy. Whereas the migrants in Italy were overwhelmingly between forty and sixty-five years old, there was more age variation in the migration to California. However, because immigrant-receiving institutions in San Francisco channeled older women into jobs caring for the elderly, my interviewees in San Francisco were also mostly women and some men between forty and sixty-five years old.[17]

Holding on to the site as analytically meaningful meant I was no longer comparing Italy and California as receiving sites but rather two migration patterns: the temporary migration of individual women over forty to Italy on the one hand, and the permanent migration of families, led by these same grandmothers, to California on the other. What I discovered by following these migration streams back to Ukraine is that Ukraine, far from being a variable held constant, had different effects for the lived experiences of migrants in Italy and California and that the reverse was also true; the migration pattern to Italy and California had different effects in Ukraine.

Elsewhere I privilege the effects of these migration patterns for the production of migration subjectivities in the receiving countries, but here I will highlight the effects these two migration patterns have in Ukraine as the sending country.[18] The migration patterns to Italy and California are differentially implicated in Ukraine's nation-building processes through which Ukraine aspires to be 'European' and 'capitalist'. It is through the lens of a gendered global ethnography that we are able to see these complex intersections. Let us now turn to these contrasting migration patterns that I call 'constitutive circularity' and 'resource drain'.[19]

CONSTITUTIVE CIRCULARITY: MIGRATING TO ITALY

The gendered migration pattern to Italy provides both the structural and the discursive basis for Ukraine's post-Soviet nation-building process. In fact, I argue that what my informants call the 'new' Ukraine is actually built on the shoulders of migrant women.[20] In order to understand how this migration pattern, the gendered reorganization of family and work structures, and Ukrainian nationalism intersect, I must place this migration pattern in the context of post-Soviet transformation, Ukraine's attempt to constitute itself as a legitimate nation separate from Russia, and the importance of Ukraine's claim that it is a *European* nation.

The informants I interviewed in Rome and San Francisco grew up in the Soviet Union. The Soviet state required full employment to meet production quotas in a labor-intensive, production-based socialist economy. To facilitate the employment of women and 'liberate' women from the 'triple burden' of housework, mothering and wage work, the Soviet state attempted to socialize domestic labor and provided maternity benefits, state-run child care facilities and even collective dining halls.[21] The state usurped certain patriarchal functions and responsibilities and replaced men as the head of the Soviet family. Men were pushed to the periphery of Soviet families whereas women were 'married to the state'.[22] Women achieved near full participation rates in the labor force. However, although the Soviet state did restructure domestic labor to some extent, women continued to take primary responsibility for the home as well as perform wage work. The Soviet state relied on youthful retirement ages (generally fifty-five for women and sixty for men) to perform unpaid household labor.[23] The Soviet family was an extended family with multiple generations living in one household, often with a grandmother figure who ran the household and was responsible for rearing the grandchildren while young mothers worked in the paid labor force.[24] Therefore a particular gendered understanding of the relationship between men and women and women and the state (underlined by an economic need for women's employment) not only made 'mother-workers' a structural reality but also was accompanied by state discourses that exalted mother-workers as Soviet 'heroes'. In fact, migrants I interviewed in California and Italy expected to continue in this Soviet family structure and retire at fifty-five to raise their grandchildren.

With the collapse of the Soviet Union, the socialist economy was dismantled and with it this Soviet gender order. The radical egalitarianism of Soviet rhetoric was never achieved. Women in the Soviet Union rarely attained top-level jobs, were channeled into sex-segregated occupations and earned lower wages than men. Since Ukrainian independence, these trends have been exacerbated. Top management and executive positions are still dominated by men, sex segregation of the labor market has increased and women currently earn wages 30 percent lower than men.[25] Women face considerable gender discrimination in Ukraine's expanding 'free' market in the form of local hiring practices, such as job advertisements that ask that only young, attractive women apply. and increasing rates of sexual harassment at work.[26] Women also face increased barriers to employment because of their reproductive functions. As the state shifts the economic burden of social entitlements to private industry, women, as potential mothers, become expensive to employ.[27] Additionally, the number of state-subsidized child care facilities has drastically declined due to budget cuts.[28] The transformation of the workplace from state-run to private has forced women who can no longer rely on the state for child rearing support to take substantial time out of the labor market.[29] According to anthropologist Katherine Verdery, with the coming of market capitalism the socialist welfare state, that had once taken on some of women's nurturing and caregiving roles, is now considered too costly, and the free market economy is devolving these responsibilities back onto the shoulders of women.[30] Verdery further argues that the gendered organization of capitalist households cheapens the cost of labor for capital by assigning reproductive labor to women and calling it 'housework', which is unpaid. This cheapening makes postsocialist economies viable in the global marketplace. Given these structural barriers to employment for women since Ukrainian independence, it is not surprising then that "in every age group the level of employment is lower for women than for men."[31] Highly educated women clustered in state-run services and enterprises such as education, health care and scientific research institutes have been hit especially hard by the Ukrainian state's closure of these institutions, reductions in staff or inability to pay state employees.[32]

Compared to the Soviet era, during which the state pursued a policy of full employment, Ukraine's economic transformation has meant high rates of unemployment and underemployment for both women and men. However, market reforms were supposed to raise the economic welfare of families and simultaneously make the one-earner family possible; that 'one-earner' is assumed to be a breadwinner husband who supports a stay-at-home wife.[33] This shift in Ukraine's structural reality is produced, in part, through a reorganization of gendered relations. In post-Soviet discourse, the way to deal with high unemployment rates is to "send women back to the home where they belong."[34] It suggests that Soviets were the 'enemies of nature' by trying to force humans to act contrary to their 'biology', creating 'weak' men and 'masculine' women. Socialist paternalism and women are jointly accused of having destroyed the ethno-nation (almost extinct due to low birthrates), the national character and 'traditional' national values.[35] The natural order between the sexes is now understood as best exemplified by the capitalist, European, nuclear family. In Ukraine, this shift from a Soviet extended family to a traditional patriarchal family is seen as a 'return' to an imagined authentic, pre-Soviet Ukrainian culture that constructs the newly independent Ukraine as separate from all things 'Soviet' or 'Russian'.[36] The rise of neofamilialism is a fundamental part of nationalist discourse and is further tied to a religious resurgence of Catholic, Christian Orthodox and Protestant denominations in Ukraine.[37]

It is not only women who are called to embrace new 'Ukrainian' norms. There are new moral rules for men as well, who must reject the 'weak' and 'effeminate' position of their Soviet fathers, reclaim their masculinity through breadwinning and take back from the state their rightful place as the head of the family. Nevertheless, in this narrative about Ukraine's national identity it is 'our women' that make Ukrainians *Ukrainian* and not Soviet. The new icon of ideal Ukrainian womanhood is *Berehynia*, an ancient pagan goddess who has come to embody the protectress of the family hearth and the Ukrainian nation.[38] Like Ukrainian women, Berehynia is strong but committed to maternal duties, independent but family-oriented and respectful of husbands, and symbolizes a pre-Soviet and distinctly Ukrainian national culture in which Ukrainian men and women had separate responsibilities but were equally respected. It is this respect accorded to women for their 'separate responsibilities' that is understood as one of Ukraine's cultural traits that makes Ukraine 'modern' and 'European'. In the context of development discourse, gender equality is one of the measurable indexes that provide access to such labels. The power of the Berehynia image lies in part in the fact that it is a symbol of an independent Ukraine that all Ukrainian citizens from east to west can embrace.[39] The image is widespread, but it is most prominently displayed in Kyiv's Independence Square, the city's center, where the statue of Lenin has been replaced with the statue of Berehynia atop a 40-foot-tall column, where she reigns as the symbol of the Ukrainian nation.

Being a 'mother-worker', then, has become structurally difficult so that young mothers in Ukraine are increasingly becoming housewives by default if not by choice. If young women become *Berehynia*, what happens to grandmother? Roxalana, a retired school teacher said:

> I taught history and was busy all day with classes. I also had many admin- istrative responsibilities and sat on the board for the whole L'viv region. My mother took care of my daughter, Olha, stood in the breadlines, everything. They used to hold your job for you three years when you had a baby. But now, you lose your job. No one wants to be a mother-worker anymore. I felt useless at home. All I was doing was fighting with my daughter over, you know, what to feed my grandson, how to dress him and how to discipline him. And with just my son-in-law working and my small pension there was not enough money. So I came here to [Rome].

Roxalana, like many other women over forty, has been marginalized from the labor market. She was forced into early retirement because the state could not afford to pay its teachers. She was also marginalized from her expected role as primary caregiver to her grandson because her daughter is now a stay-at-home mom. Roxalana and other women of her generation, *doubly marginalized*, saw migration as the best way to make themselves useful to their families.

This change in Ukraine's gender order is at the root of this migration pattern and explains why it is women over forty who migrate. It also sug- gests that the 'new' Ukraine is being built on the shoulders of these women. This new nuclear family in which mothers are housewives and men are breadwinners is understood as a necessary building block for the creation of capitalist Ukraine. The dilemma is that this nuclear family formation, considered the foundation of the post-Soviet, 'capitalist', and 'European' Ukrainian nation, does not happen spontaneously with capitalism. Men's wages are not high enough to support this family formation. In order to produce *Ukrainian* women as Berehyni and *Ukrainian* men as patriarchs, someone must go abroad and send back remittances.

The 'new' European Ukraine imagined by Ukrainian nationalists is then literally built on the labor power of migrant women. This is not sim- ply about migrants having transnational ties to their homeland. Instead, I am arguing that the very structure of the migration pattern itself is constitutive of a particular reorganization of work and family structures as well as the core understandings of what post-Soviet Ukraine—the 'new' Ukraine—will look like both materially and discursively. This link between the lived experiences of individual migrants and the production of macro-level processes is one of the contributions of a gendered global ethnography to migration studies.

RESOURCE DRAIN: MIGRATING TO CALIFORNIA

Whereas the migration pattern to Italy is deeply implicated in the transformations of nation, work and family in Ukraine, the post-Soviet migration to California or the US more generally is peripheral to these processes. Although it is the same intersections of gender, nation and capitalist transition in the Ukrainian context that encourage emigration in both migration patterns, the migration pattern to California is not constitutive of these processes. Most families who migrate to California do so in stages, slowly collecting their members over time as family members in the US become eligible to sponsor other family members in Ukraine. The migration pattern to California involves naturalization with the intent of following family trees both horizontally and vertically in order to collect extended families in California, a process that often spanned years and even decades. I found that as long as families were separated and family members in the US had not incurred large debts such as a home mortgages, those in the US sent remittances back to Ukraine.[40] However, once families were reconstituted in the US, informants generally stopped sending remittances to Ukraine, explaining that there was "no one left to send money too."

Over the long term, net resources in this post-Soviet migration flow from Ukraine to California. For those who migrated after 1991, there are few formal institutional channels that connect them to Ukraine. The Ukrainian state does little to encourage remittances or facilitate the renovation of schools or the repairing of roads by post-Soviet Ukrainian emigrants abroad, nor does it recognize dual citizenship. This is in sharp contrast to the Mexican state, which also has a permanent migration of families to the US and yet actively seeks to maintain access to the material resources of its emigrants through state-sponsored institutions such as hometown associations. In other words, even when entire families move to the US, the Mexican state makes sure there is 'someone to send money to' in Mexico. The Mexican state also maintains its human resources by extending dual citizenship to Mexican nationals who become naturalized US citizens, supporting the incorporation of emigrants into homeland political parties, and encouraging the formation of a Mexican lobby in Washington.[41] Mexico, emulating other sending states, is able to 'manage' its emigration as part of an economic development strategy and as a way of reinforcing the Mexican state.[42] The processes of post-Soviet transformation have resulted in a weak state in Ukraine.[43] At least for now, the emigration of Ukrainians to California is characterized by a continuous loss of material and human resources. Immigrants continue to arrive to California and sponsor others, and the Ukrainian state simply does not have the ability to manage this process.

COMPARING MIGRATION PATTERNS
AND THE UKRAINIAN STATE

We have seen how constitutive circularity and resource drain have different sets of effects in Ukraine. Let us briefly consider the Ukrainian state's response to these migration patterns. The Ukrainian state is actively pursuing the gendered reorganization of family and work structures discussed earlier with some measure of success. One might assume that the Ukrainian state would view the migration pattern to Italy favorably. After all, it is the physical removal of these women as grandmothers and the monetary remittances earned through their labor power abroad that provide the basis of these 'traditionally Ukrainian' nuclear families and the 'capitalist' reorganization of Ukraine's labor market. The migration pattern to Italy not only supports the Ukrainian state's economic goals, but also reinforces the state's discourse that this restructuring of gendered relations between men and women is an imagined 'return' to an authentic Ukrainian culture that places Ukraine firmly in the European family of nations. Additionally migrants in Italy send back remittances that make up a significant percent of Ukraine's GDP, whereas I discovered that post-Soviet migrants in California send few remittances. And yet, whereas the migration pattern to California is benignly tolerated by the Ukrainian state, those who leave to work in Italy are negatively stigmatized by the Ukrainian state as 'prostitutes' and 'betrayers' of the Ukrainian nation. In fact, although former Ukrainian president Leonid Kuchma famously addressed Ukrainian women inside Ukraine as the "Berehyni of our people," every informant I interviewed in Italy repeated with indignation that he called all Ukrainian women abroad 'prostitutes'. I suggest that these two migration patterns are viewed differently by the Ukrainian state precisely because the emigration of families to the US and the emigration of older women to Italy are differentially implicated in Ukraine's nation-building process.[44]

In nationalism discourse more generally, women are often constructed as the symbolic bearers of the nation, responsible for both its biological and cultural reproduction, and the examples of this range from India to Romania.[45] Emigration policies are as much a product of national identity as economic concerns. This is especially true when the migrants are women. In other words, the kind of emigration policy a state has toward its women, and whether the state is 'protecting their women', is understood as a reflection of the national identity and the values that nation possesses as well as an indicator of where the nation-state lies with respect to the accepted global markers of development: democracy, human rights and gender equality.[46] Not only does the emigration of women violate Ukrainian national identity constructed around a particular idealized conception of an authentic Ukrainian woman as Berehynia, but also it violates the Ukrainian state's most dearly held sociopolitical goal: joining Europe. For the Ukrainian state this means being accepted into the European Union and international recognition of Ukraine as a European nation. It is a signifier of prestige and of a particular historical-cultural heritage as well as affirmation of Ukraine's 'First World' economic trajectory.

Whereas the effects of the migration pattern to the California are linear, the effects of the migration pattern to Italy are circular and contradictory. The Ukrainian state produces this migration pattern through its economic and social policies, and the migration pattern in turn provides the structural basis for the realization of the state's domestic goals of reorganizing the institutions of family and work. At the same time, nothing signals 'Third World' in the international arena like the mass emigration of women to do domestic labor abroad. Ironically, the very migration pattern that allows for the constitution of the social and economic structures within Ukraine that permits the state to make claims to Europe and the 'First World' also makes Ukraine look like it may belong to the 'Third World' instead.

GENDERED GLOBAL ETHNOGRAPHY: IMPLICATIONS FOR MIGRATION AND POST-SOVIET STUDIES

The perspective of global ethnography is good for migration studies. New studies on sending countries risk repeating the paradigm of receiving site studies by studying sending countries in isolation. This approach homogenizes emigration as if it is a singular phenomenon. This comparative ethnographic analysis of two migration patterns from Ukraine reveals that migration patterns, an analytical framing that requires a consideration of both sending and receiving countries, can have differential effects. Whereas the most salient effect in Ukraine of the permanent migration of families to California is a continuous loss of human and economic resources over time, the temporary labor migration of mostly grandmothers to Italy is productive of Ukraine's nation-building project and part of a large-scale reorganization of gendered relations. This gendered reorganization has a structural dimension that consists in a shift from an extended to an increasingly nuclear family, as well as a changing labor market that includes men as breadwinners while excluding more and more women as mothers or potential mothers. It also has a discursive dimension that constructs this particular family formation as modern, capitalist, and European, as well as ethnically and culturally Ukrainian, and promotes it as the building block of a new Ukraine knocking at the door of Europe and the First World. These two migration patterns—resource drain versus constitutive circularity—are visible only through the perspective of global ethnography.

Gendering global ethnography reveals that although gender is always a useful category of analysis, it may not always be the most salient category. Although gendered processes of economic transformation inside Ukraine are important in creating the material basis of both migration patterns, gender is at the center of theorizing constitutive circularity and decentered in resource drain.

Finally, this study shows that gendered global ethnography is an important perspective in understanding the production of 'capitalism' in the post-Soviet world. Most scholars studying the 'transition to capitalism' in the post-Soviet region focus on top-down economic transformations that deploy the abstract schemas of traditional studies of globalization.[47] The approach of gendered global ethnography reveals that Ukraine's economic transformation is constituted by people in their everyday negotiations with nationalisms, markets and the moralities that accompany them. Whereas most scholars of the region wonder if you can have capitalism from above, a gendered global ethnography illustrates that, in the case of Ukraine, economic transformation rests on a particular set of gendered relations that structure the most basic elements of social and economic life from below.

NOTES

1. I thank Michel Burawoy for many years of helpful insights and am also grateful to Raka Ray and Irene Bloemraad. Thanks also to Winifred Poster and Pei-Chia Lan for organizing a productive panel at the American Sociological Association in August 2011, where I originally delivered this chapter. Finally I thank Phil Kretsedemas, Glenn Jacobs and Jorge Capetillo for their attention to this chapter.
2. Barbara Schmitter Heisler, "The Sociology of Immigration: From Assimilation to Segmented Assimilation, from the American Experience to the Global Arena," in *Migration Theory: Talking across Disciplines*, ed. Caroline Brettell and James Frank Hollifield (New York: Routledge, 2008), 83–111.
3. Alejandro Portes and Ruben Rumbaut, *Immigrant America: A Portrait* (Berkeley: University of California Press, 1996).
4. Roger Waldinger and Michael Lichter, *How the Other Half Works: Immigration and the Social Organization of Labor* (Berkeley: University of California Press, 2003).
5. Irene Bloemraad, *Becoming a Citizen: Incorporating Immigrants and Refugees in the United States and Canada* (Berkeley: University of California Press, 2006).
6. Douglas Massey et al., *Worlds in Motion: Understanding International Migration at the End of the Millennium* (Oxford: Clarendon, 1998), and Saskia Sassen, *The Mobility of Labor and Capital: A Study in International Investment and Labor Flow* (New York: Cambridge University Press, 1988).
7. David Fitzgerald, *A Nation of Emigrants: How Mexico Manages Its Migration* (Berkeley: University of California Press, 2009); Robyn Rodriguez, *Migrants for Export: How the Philippine State Brokers Labor to the World* (Minneapolis: University of Minnesota Press, 2010); and Rachel Sherman, "From State Introversion to State Extension in Mexico: Modes of Emigrant Incorporation, 1900–1997," *Theory and Society* 28 (1999): 835–878.

8. I am aware of the debates around 'methodological nationalism' and write about them elsewhere. Nonetheless, in the case of Ukraine, which declared independence from the Soviet Union in 1991 but did not have a popular independence movement until the Orange Revolution of 2003–2004, constructing a coherent nation-state with legitimate claims to independence in the face of perceived internal and external threats, the concept of the 'nation-state' takes on heightened importance.

9. Michael Burawoy, "Introduction: Reaching for the Global," in *Global Ethnography: Forces, Connections, and Imaginations in a Postmodern World*, ed. Michael Burawoy et al. (Berkeley: University of California Press, 2000), 1–40, and idem, "Manufacturing the Global," *Ethnography* 2, no. 2 (2001): 147–159.

10. Burawoy, "Manufacturing the Global," 156, 149.

11. Winifred Poster, "Racialism, Sexuality, and Masculinity: Gendering 'Global Ethnography' of the Workplace," *Social Politics* 9, no. 1 (2002): 126–158.

12. Ibid., 126.

13. Joan Scott, *Gender and the Politics of History* (New York: Columbia University Press, 1988).

14. See Cinzia Solari, "Transnational Politics and Settlement Practices: Post-Soviet Immigrant Churches in Rome," *American Behavioral Scientist* 49, no. 11 (2006): 1528–1553.

15. Sarah Mahler and Patricia Pessar, "Gender Matters: Ethnographers Bring Gender from the Periphery toward the Core of Migration Studies," *International Migration Review* 40, no. 1 (2006): 27–63.

16. Irene Bloemraad, "Becoming a Citizen in the United States and Canada: Structured Mobilization and Immigrant Political Incorporation," *Social Forces* 85, no. 2 (2006): 667–695; Rachel Salazar Parrenas, *Servants of Globalization: Women, Migration and Domestic Work* (Stanford: Stanford University Press, 2001); and Jeffrey Reitz, *Warmth of the Welcome: The Social Causes of Economic Success for Immigrants in Different Nations and Cities* (Boulder: Westview, 1998).

17. See Cinzia Solari, "Professionals and Saints: How Immigrant Careworkers Negotiate Gendered Identities at Work," *Gender & Society* 20, no. 3 (2006): 301–331.

18. See Cinzia Solari, "Exile vs. Exodus: Nationalism and Gendered Migration from Ukraine to Italy and California" (PhD diss., University of California-Berkeley, 2010).

19. For a more detailed look at these two migration patterns see Cinzia Solari, "Resource Drain vs. Constitutive Circularity: Comparing the Gendered Effects of Post-Soviet Migration Patterns in Ukraine," *Anthropology of East Europe Review* 28 (2010): 215–238.

20. Cinzia Solari, "Between 'Europe' and 'Africa': Building the New Ukraine on the Shoulders of Migrant Women," in *Mapping Difference: The Many Faces of Women in Ukraine*, ed. Marian Rubchak (New York: Berghahn Books, 2011), 23–46.

21. Katherine Verdery, "From Parent-State to Family Patriarchs: Gender and Nation in Contemporary Eastern Europe," *East European Politics and Societies* 8, no. 2 (1994): 225–255.

22. Marina Kiblitskaya, "Russia's Female Breadwinners: The Changing Subjective Experience," In *Gender, State and Society in Soviet and Post-Soviet Russia*, ed. Sarah Ashwin (New York: Routledge, 2000), 55–70.

23. Verdery, "From Parent-State to Family Patriarchs."

24. Anna Rotkirch, *The Man Question: Loves and Lives in Late 20th Century Russia* (Helsinki: University of Helsinki-Department of Social Policy Research Reports, 2000).

25. United Nations Development Programme, *Human Development and Ukraine's European Choice* (New York: United Nations, 2008), 29, accessed Jan. 1, 2009, http://hdr.undp.org/en/reports/nationalreports/europethecis/ukraine/name,3244,en.html.

26. United Nations Development Programme, *Gender Issues in Ukraine: Challenges and Opportunities* (New York: United Nations, 2003), 28–30, accessed Mar. 1, 2007, http://www.undp.org.ua/files/en_64099super.pdf.

27. Suzanne LaFont, "One Step Forward, Two Steps Back: Women in Post-Communist Societies," *Communist and Post-Communist Studies* 34 (2001): 203–220.

28. Brienna Perelli-Harris, "Family Formation in Post-Soviet Ukraine: Changing Effects of Education in a Period of Rapid Social Change," *Social Forces* 87, no. 2 (2008): 767–794.

29. Ibid.

30. Verdery, "From Parent-State to Family Patriarchs." Also see Michael Burawoy, Pavel Krotov and Tatyana Lytkina, "Involution and Destitution in Capitalist Russia," *Ethnograph* 1, no. 1 (2000): 43–65.

31. United Nations Development Programme, *Gender Issues in Ukraine*, 29.

32. Ibid.

33. Tatiana Zhurzhenko, "Strong Women, Weak State: Family Politics and Nation Building in Post-Soviet Ukraine," in *Post-Soviet Women Encountering Transition: Nation Building, Economic Survival, and Civic Activism*, ed. Kathleen Kuehnast and Carol Nechemias (Baltimore: Johns Hopkins University Press, 2004), 23–43.

34. LaFont, "One Step Forward, Two Steps Back."

35. Verdery and Gal and Kligman further argue that nationalist policies driving women back to their 'proper' nurturant role, an increasingly visible ethno-nationalism coupled with an antifeminist and pronatalist politicking, are features common to post-Soviet Eastern European countries. They suggest that these processes are tied to the post-Soviet experience. However, the way in which this plays out in individual countries varies. See Verdery, "From Parent-State to Family Patriarchs"; idem, "Nationalism, Postsocialism, and Space in Eastern Europe," *Social Research* 63, no. 1 (1996): 77–95; and Susan Gal and Gail Kligman, *The Politics of Gender after Socialism: A Comparative-Historical Essay* (Princeton, NJ: Princeton University Press, 2000).

36. Although in popular discourse this is seen as a 'return' to a provider-housewife family structure, LaFont reminds us most former bloc countries had agricultural societies in which women worked alongside men in the fields until the communist push for industrialization. Therefore the 'bourgeois family of a man as provider and woman as homemaker' was not the norm and in most cases did not exist in the first place. See LaFont, "One Step Forward, Two Steps Back," 213.

37. Irina Predborska, "The Social Position of Young Women in Present-Day Ukraine," *Journal of Youth Studies* 8, no. 3 (2005): 349–65, and Zhurzhenko, "Strong Women, Weak State."

38. Marian Rubchak, "Christian Virgin or Pagan Goddess: Feminism versus the Eternally Feminine in Ukraine," in *Women in Russia and Ukraine*, ed. Rosalind Marsh (Cambridge: Cambridge University Press, 1996), 315–330.

39. For more regarding the cultural, ethnic and political divisions in Ukraine, see Andrew Wilson, *The Ukrainians: Unexpected Nation* (New Haven: Yale University Press, 2000). For more on how the divisions between eastern and western Ukraine play out on the terrain of nation building and migration, see Cinzia Solari, "'Prostitutes' and 'Defectors': Gendered Migration and the

Ukrainian State" (paper presented at the annual meeting of the American Sociological Association, Atlanta, August 2010).

40. Interestingly, informants in California, even when children or parents were still in Ukraine, reported sending smaller percentages of their total wages than migrants in Italy. Many cited mortgages, car payments or the high cost of living in general that prevented them from sending more money to Ukraine.

41. Fitzgerald, *A Nation of Emigrants*, and Sherman, "From State Introversion to State Extension in Mexico."

42. Ibid.

43. Cinzia Solari, "The Disarticulated Nation-state: Stigma and Transnational Nation-building in Post-Soviet Ukraine, Ukraine" (paper presented at the annual meeting of the American Sociological Association, Denver, CO, August 2012).

44. Solari, "'Prostitutes' and 'Defectors'".

45. Smitha Radhakrishnan, *Appropriately Indian: Gender and Culture in a New Transnational Class* (Durham: Duke University Press, 2011), and Katherine Verdery, "Nationalism and National Sentiment in Post-Socialist Romania," *Slavic Review* 52 (1993): 179–203.

46. Oishi Nana, *Women in Motion: Globalization, State Policies, and Labor Migration in Asia* (Stanford: Stanford University Press, 2005).

47. For notable exceptions see Michael Michael and Katherine Verdery, eds., *Uncertain Transition: Ethnographies of Change in the Postsocialist World* (Oxford: Rowman & Littlefield, 1999), and Caroline Humphrey and Ruth Mandel, eds., *Markets & Moralities: Ethnographies of Postsocialism* (New York: Berg, 2002).

9 Remittances in Provincial Georgia
The Case of Daba Tianeti[1]

Tamar Zurabishivili and Tinatin Zurabishivili

After the dissolution of the Soviet Union, international labor migration became an indispensable feature of everyday life for many families living in the post-Soviet republics, including Georgia. Between 1989 and 2002, the population of Georgia shrank by more than one million people mainly because of decreased fertility rates and increased emigration.[2] However, poor organization of demographic statistics in contemporary Georgia makes it difficult to get reliable information on population movements in general and on the rate of labor migration in particular; hence, it is hard to get precise numbers of Georgian citizens who emigrated in order to work abroad. As various studies suggest, up to 10 percent of Georgian households have at least one emigrant, although this number varies in different regions of Georgia.[3]

In Georgia, existing data suggests that remittances have been increasing both in absolute terms and relative to GDP during the last decade. In 2000, the estimated amount of remittances sent by Georgian labor emigrants to their families through official channels (bank transfers, MTOs) was US$63 million. Already in 2006, officially transferred remittances topped US$553, 250 million, and in 2008 they reached almost US$1 billion. The economic crisis did have a significant impact—the amount of remittances sent to Georgia in 2009 was only US$841,775 million, but quickly recovered and started to increase again. In 2010 the volume of remittances again reached US$1 billion, in 2011 it was US$1.25 billion, and in 2012 it wasUS$1.334 billion.[4] The amount of unofficially transferred remittances is a subject of much speculation, but there is no doubt that remittances are far from being limited to official channels of transmission.

Taking into consideration the increasing amount of remittances sent by Georgian labor emigrants to their families, investigating the role of remittances in the economic development of Georgia becomes even more important. However, until now, studies of Georgian labor emigration have primarily dealt with the demographic characteristics of emigrants, their socioeconomic status abroad, directions of emigration and destination countries.[5] Only recently some scholarly attention has been paid to estimating the volume of remittances sent by Georgian labor emigrants back to their families, and the role of remittances for economic development of Georgia in general.[6] However, the role of remittances for rural communities in particular, which tend to benefit the most from the development impact of remittances,[7] has been largely left unstudied.

This chapter tries to fill this gap, focusing on the economic role of remittances in a small, rural migrant-sending community of Georgia, Daba Tianeti, populated by ethnic Georgians. The population of Daba Tianeti did not have much experience of large-scale international migration prior to the 1990s. Moreover, unlike other migrant-sending communities in Georgia, emigration from Daba Tianeti is overwhelmingly directed toward Western Europe, Israel and North America, which are relatively new migration destinations for Georgian labor emigrants (compared to the traditional flow of these migrants to Russia). The emigration flows of Daba Tianeti are also distinguished by their gender composition, being predominantly composed of women, who are typically employed as low-skilled domestic workers in the receiving countries.[8]

Our research demonstrates that remittances sent to families in Daba Tianeti by these flows of mostly female emigrants constitute a significant and, in some cases, the sole source of income for emigrant household budgets. Furthermore, most of the remittances of Daba Tianeti emigrants are spent on the everyday needs of households along with medical and educational expenses. We explain this through reference to 1) the widespread poverty among the Daba Tianeti population and 2) the existing pessimistic assessment of the current economic situation and investment opportunities by the Daba Tianeti population.

REMITTANCES AND DEVELOPMENT:
THEORETICAL FRAMEWORK

For many developing countries remittances have become one of the main sources of foreign exchange, being more reliable than Foreign Direct Investment (FDI), especially during economic crises.[9] A rich body of scholarship looking at the role of remittances for economic development and growth suggests that although they are an important source of financial flows for remittance-receiving households and communities, remittances have a less significant impact on economic growth. According to Adams and Page, a 10 percent increase in the share of remittances in a country's GDP will contribute to a 1.6 percent decline of the population living on $1 per day.[10]

When assessing the effects that remittances can have on the economies of the receiving countries, along with the positive ones, such as poverty reduction of migrant communities and better nutrition and education, there are some negative ones. Remittances can contribute to the creation of a culture of dependency and a decrease of productivity and labor force participation. Furthermore, an increasing volume of remittances leads to the appreciation of local currencies, which affects the export of local goods, while contributing to the increase in imports.[11] Chimhowu, Piesse and Pinder suggest that remittances can generate inequality among households as well because they are "embedded in the structures that perpetuate poverty in the developing countries and can promote economic stagnation rather than economic growth".[12]

In the case of Daba Tianeti, based on informal observation and interviews with the residents of Daba Tianeti, inflow of remittances does lead to a decrease in productivity when the households receiving remittances start limiting their agricultural production activities. Outflow of the female emigrants creates imbalances in the household composition, with husbands often not able to adapt to changing realities, resulting in increased rates of alcoholism. Moreover, informants noted that in the households where females became head of the household due to emigration of their spouses, remittances are used more efficiently than in the households where males remain in charge after the emigration of their wives.

For many remittance-receiving households, remittances constitute a major source of income. Remittances are also used by the households in the same way as income from other sources.[13] But once the remittances stop, the well-being of the household may be threatened if the household is unable to ensure a stable inflow of income from other sources.

Debate on how remittances can be used to produce more economic growth has resulted in various state-funded programs in several migrant-sending countries, such as Mexico and Philippines. The rate of so-called productive investment of remittances is often affected by the investment climate and opportunities in receiving countries and by the managerial and business skills of migrants or their family members. Migrants also face difficulties accumulating the capital necessary to invest, which further decreases their ability to invest in productive activities. Despite these problems, there is evidence that remittances do indirectly contribute to economic development: "In addition to providing financial resources for poor households, they affect poverty and welfare through indirect multiplier effects and also macroeconomic effects."[14] Remittances spent on everyday needs of the households have a positive impact on the development of local economies through increase in consumption, trade and the establishment and development of service facilities, which could lead to a decrease in unemployment and even to an increase in wages.[15]

In the case of Georgia, existing evidence suggests that only a small fraction of remittances is used for investment purposes, due to limited investment opportunities and lack of managerial and entrepreneurial skills among remitters and their families.[16] However, remittance-receiving households spend quite a significant share of expenses on education and health. By investing in human capital, remittance-receiving households are, in a certain way, improving their future prospects, especially, when taking into consideration investments in education.

METHODOLOGY OF THE STUDY

The present analysis is based both on qualitative and quantitative data collected in Daba Tianeti in April and August–September 2006. Funding for the qualitative fieldwork was provided by a research scholarship from the Heinrich Boell Foundation of the South Caucasus Bureau. The data was collected in April and September 2006. This portion of the research consisted of twenty-three in-depth interviews with Daba Tianeti residents (eighteen women, five men, 22–72 years old): returned migrants, members of the families of current migrants and potential migrants. In some cases, informants were both returned migrants and members of families of current migrants, as well as potential migrants. Informants were located using a snowball sampling method.[17]

Quantitative data was collected during the household census conducted in August through September 2006. This data collection process was supported by a research fellowship granted by the Caucasus Research Resource Center Georgia Office (CRRC). Because there was no reliable information available on the level of emigration from Daba Tianeti, the researchers decided to conduct a census of all Daba Tianeti households to better document the emigration process. According to the 2002 Georgian National Census, there were 1,237 households in Daba Tianeti.[18] We interviewed 1,062 households (210 houses were registered as closed[19] or dilapidated). Thus, we registered a total of 1,272 dwellings. We believe that we have collected data that accurately describes the entire population of Daba Tianeti.

For our qualitative survey, we interviewed the head of the household, a member of the household who was well informed about the conditions of the household, a returned migrant, or a member of the household who was both the head of the household and a returned migrant. Our quantitative survey collected information on the socioeconomic conditions of the households; current, returned and potential emigrants; their migration networks; and remittances and uses of remittances.

RESEARCH SITE AND ECONOMIC CHARACTERISTICS OF THE HOUSEHOLDS

Daba Tianeti is situated in the northeastern part of Georgia (Mtskheta-Mtianeti region). According to the 2002 State Census, its population was 3,598 people.[20] As a 2003 study of poverty in Georgia demonstrated, the Mtskheta-Mtianeti region and the Daba Tianeti district in particular are among the poorest regions and districts of Georgia. In 2003, 63 percent of the population of Daba Tianeti was below the poverty line, compared to 47 percent of the Georgian population.[21] Taking into account the fact that since 2003 until the time of the fieldwork—2006—the economic situation has not improved significantly, we assume that during the fieldwork period Daba Tianeti still was one of the poorest districts in Georgia.[22]

During the Soviet era, Daba Tianeti was a district (*rayon*) center. As the personal communication with Daba Tianeti residents and in-depth interviews revealed, during the Soviet era there were many employment opportunities in the district, with several food processing enterprises and factories, as well as poultry and meat production.[23] A Soviet cultural, medical and educational infrastructure was also developed there. In 2006, Daba Tianeti was still the center of the municipality (which is the contemporary analogue to the Soviet era *rayon*) with two secondary schools, two kindergartens, a vocational school, library, hospital and ethnographic museum. Other state institutions located in Daba Tianeti include the municipality's self-governance office, post office and police station. One of the Georgian banks has an office in Tianeti. There are several private grocery stores and a farmer's market. None of the factories and farms that operated during the Soviet era are working today. At the time of the fieldwork, Daba Tianeti was experiencing shortages in the electricity supply and drinkable water, there was no internet connection and the 60-km drive from Tbilisi, the capital of Georgia, to Daba Tianeti took about two hours due to poor road conditions. Since the fieldwork was conducted, several major infrastructural improvements have been made by the government. In addition to road reconstruction, rehabilitation of municipal buildings, and an improved water and electricity supply, Internet access is available in the settlement, and there are several small enterprises, such as a guest house and an Internet café.

A small part of the population works at state institutions (so-called budget jobs: schools, the hospital, local self-governance office, post office). Traditionally, females occupy teaching jobs in the schools/kindergarten or work in the retail sector, in nursing or in the administration of state organizations. However, females seem to be underrepresented in the self-governing bodies of the municipality, because there was not a single woman in the local council (Sakrebulo) of the municipality as of summer 2012.[24] Income from subsistence farming also contributes to a significant share of budgets of local households. However, Daba Tianeti has a shortage of arable land.[25] In addition, the climate is quite severe and the land is not fertile. Sometimes the population is unable to harvest crops before the winter.

Not surprisingly, during our census, 61 percent of Daba Tianeti households reported having debt at the time of our study. Debt is reported less frequently by households with emigrants that send remittances (53 percent). In contrast, debt is more frequently reported by households without emigrants or with emigrants who do not send remittances (70 percent).

According to our study, the self-reported mean, per capita monthly income of Daba Tianeti's population was GEL 52.[26] By comparison, the subsistence-level, minimum monthly income according to the State Department for Statistics of Georgia for this same period of time was GEL 97.4 (US$55). The income threshold for determining the extreme poverty rate

Table 9.1 'Coefficient of Debt' of Tianeti Households

Type of household	'Coefficient of debt'
All households	1.62
Among these	
Households without emigrants	1.70
Households with emigrants	1.43
Among households with emigrants	
Households receiving remittances	1.16
Households NOT receiving remittances	2.48

Note: Ratio of households having debt and households not having debt, per respective group.

in 2006 (which accounts only for food expenses) was GEL 68.2 per capita. Hence, the mean, per capita income of Daba Tianeti was about the half of the official subsistence minimum, and 1.3 times lower than the extreme poverty line.

Households in all categories were spending more than their reported income, with households receiving remittances demonstrating better economic standing than other types of households. There were only 399 households in Tianeti that did not have debts at the time of the survey, most of them being households receiving remittances.

Subjective assessments of household well-being tend to be very low. Less than 1 percent of households stated that their economic situation was 'very good'. Forty-six percent and sixteen percent of the households believed that

Table 9.2 Reported Per Capita Income and Expenses of Tianeti Households

	Income	Expenses
All households	52	68
Among these:		
Households without emigrants	49	68
Households with emigrants	61	69
Among households with emigrants:		
Households receiving remittances	70	76
Households NOT receiving remittances	40	53
Out of all households:		
Households NOT reporting having debt	67	75
Households reporting having debt	43	64

GEL: mean per respective group.

their situation was, respectively, 'bad' and 'very bad'. The rest believed that the situation of their household was 'average'. Thus, the difficult economic situation, unemployment and underemployment, low quality of life, debts and lack of prospects push many Tianeti dwellers to emigration, which is believed to be one of the most effective ways of escaping poverty.

EMIGRATION FROM DABA TIANETI: AN OVERVIEW

Out of the 1,062 Daba Tianeti households surveyed, 28 percent reported to have at least one emigrant. The number of current emigrants totaled 413, which makes them 13.3 percent of the permanent population[27] of Daba Tianeti (3,097 people, according to our census). But if we take into consideration the fact that the mean age of emigrants from Daba Tianeti is around thirty-five years old—on an everyday level their emigration could be considered an 'exodus' of the labor force.

In the case of migration from Daba Tianeti, we are predominantly dealing with labor emigration: 90 percent of the current and 88 percent of returned emigrants from Tianeti went abroad with one aim—to work and help their families back in Georgia. The rest of them emigrated to study or to travel. Moreover, fifty out of fifty-seven Daba Tianeti residents claiming to be potential emigrants also stated that their primary reason for going abroad was to find a job, work and support their families back in Daba Tianeti.

According to the estimations for Georgia, up to 10 percent of Georgian households have at least one migrant.[28] In the case of Daba Tianeti, this number is almost three times higher. Another striking difference is the gender composition of the emigrants: men constitute the minority of Daba Tianeti emigrants at 32 percent, which, compared to the nationwide data, is considerably low (65 percent of all Georgian emigrants are men[29]). Thus, in the case of Daba Tianeti, we observe the 'feminization of emigration'. This process is partly conditioned by the gender-specific labor demand in the most popular receiving countries among Daba Tianeti emigrants. The majority of emigrants to Greece and Germany are women, whereas the majority of emigrants to Ireland and the US are male. The destination of international migration flows from Daba Tianeti again differs from the general picture of emigration flows from Georgia, with most emigrants going to Western Europe, North America and Israel instead of Russia. By 2006, most migrants from Daba Tianeti were in Greece (59 percent) due to less costly travel arrangements, well-developed migration networks and more chances to legalize their status. The next most popular destinations after Greece were Ireland (9 percent), Germany (8 percent), Israel (5 percent), Russia (4 percent), the US (4 percent) and Italy (4 percent).

Most emigrants from Daba Tianeti perform so-called 3d jobs (dirty, dangerous and demeaning) abroad—more than half of them work as housekeepers, nannies/babysitters and caregivers (see Table 9.3). Men

Table 9.3   Main Occupation of Tianeti Emigrants Abroad[a]

Occupation	n female	N Male	n all
Housekeeper, Nanny/babysitter, Care-giver to elderly	219	2	221
Construction worker	1	55	56
Unqualified manual worker	9	34	43
Student	20	8	28
Unemployed	10	9	19
Other	23	23	46
Total:	282	131	413

2006, n=413
a The question was asked in the following way: "What is the main occupation of the emigrant abroad?"

mostly work as manual laborers in the construction industry, in factories or on farms. Only 7 percent of emigrants—mostly young emigrants to Germany—study abroad.

Emigrants from Tianeti tend to have a rather high level of formal education due to the compulsory secondary education system during the Soviet era, and accessibility of higher education for the wider population. However, their often undocumented status in the receiving countries and lack of language proficiency prevent many of them from being employed in positions commensurate with their educational credentials. As a result, they experience downward mobility and the de-qualification of their educational credentials. For some emigrants, these stressors and inequalities lead to serious psychological problems.

Regardless of the country of destination and of the type of work performed, the majority of emigrants from Daba Tianeti send remittances to their families with certain regularity, although in varying amounts and with varying frequency.

REMITTANCES IN DABA TIANETI

According to our census, 20 percent of all Daba Tianeti households and 71 percent of migrant households receive remittances on a more or less regular basis.[30] Many emigrants from Daba Tianeti regularly send not only money but also food, clothes and even household appliances. Among the 236 emigrants who assist their families, however, an overwhelming majority do send money (Table 9.4).

Table 9.4   What Kind of Support From the Emigrant Did Your Family Receive During the Last 12 Months?

Type of support:	Percent
Money	97
Clothes	45
Food	21
Household appliances	11

If not for some extraordinary expenses, such as investment in real estate/home renovation, health problems of family members or weddings/funerals, Daba Tianeti emigrants usually remit regular amounts of money for everyday needs of their families. Emigrants also try to save part of their income for the time they return to Georgia. Female migrants who work as live-in housekeepers or nannies often manage to remit a bigger share of their incomes compared to male migrants even if their income is generally lower than that of male workers. Of course, to achieve this, they work very hard, often requiring extra hours. The following interview excerpts illustrate further:

My salary was not enough, I had US$800, and then . . . I worked extra hours during the day-offs, to be able to buy an apartment in Tbilisi. And my daughter was studying, and you know, how many things students need, so, I did not have day-offs at all, and I was so tired when I was coming back from the work that I was feeling how the blood was circulating in my body, so tired I was, I could not do anything, not even eat, nothing. (G., female, forty-nine years old)

[From the first salary] I transferred all the money, so that my hungered family could be fed. After that, about US$300–400 [per month]. . . . For example, I sent [package] only twice. A lot of [migrants] were sending [packages] when the families were giving them things, but my children told me they did not need them, so, if I were buying something, like, VCR, DVD, linens, things like that, I was sending things like that. . . . I also bought an apartment in Tbilisi, managed somehow before the prices boomed. (B. female, forty-nine years old)

Of course, look, all those three years that I was there, I provided for my family, besides, I sent my sister to Greece with my money, I sent my sister-in-law to Greece; my mother, my father, my children, I provided for everybody. This year, my daughter graduates from the university, and I paid for her graduation, and besides, I improved elementary living conditions [built a new house next to the old one], here is my daughter-in-law and we live separately, so that we do not quarrel and do not make each other nervous. (L., female, fifty-two years old)

Table 9.5 Frequency of Money Transfers (Percent)[a]

	Percent
Once a month or more frequently	29
Approximately once in every 2-3 months	40
Approximately 3-4 times a year	18
Approximately 1-2 times a year or less frequently	13
Total:	100

Tables 5 and 6 and 11 are based on the responses from the households receiving remittances from labor emigrants (213 households).

Two-thirds of Daba Tianeti emigrants send remittances to their families left behind on a regular basis—either once a month or once every two to three months (Table 9.5).

Daba Tianeti emigrants send money using different channels. In the case of Greece, where most emigrants from Daba Tianeti live and work, an effective bus connection between Daba Tianeti and Athens has been established. Every week a bus takes packages and letters from Daba Tianeti to emigrants, and brings remittances, letters and packages back to Daba Tianeti. The service is rather convenient for Daba Tianeti dwellers, because it's reliable and operates on a regular basis and the fees are much lower than using official money transfer orders (MTOs). With this service, personal letters can be sent and/or received free of charge. Sometimes migrants put small amounts of money—up to €100—in these letters, so that they don't pay any fees at all. As a rule, money does not get lost and everything arrives to addressees securely.

In 2006, a significant amount of remittances received by Daba Tianeti households was sent through unofficial channels (Table 9.6). Again, this process is reliable, more convenient and less expensive. When using official MTOs, recipients had to go to the capital of Georgia, Tbilisi (about two hours' drive from Daba Tianeti), to get money. This is because in Tianeti there was only one operating branch of the Georgian bank, and this branch did not have the necessary equipment to provide MTO services. By 2009 it became possible to receive money transfers made via MTO services directly in Tianeti, and the share of remittances sent via unofficial channels decreased drastically.[31]

Daba Tianeti emigrants remit different amounts depending on their countries of emigration and their gender. Migrants working in Ireland send the highest amount of remittances—€1,995 per year on average, followed by emigrants in Israel and Greece (€1,770 and €1,220, respectively). In absolute terms financial assistance sent by male migrants was higher compared to the assistance sent by females, partly because male emigrants are concentrated in Ireland and in the US, where incomes generally are higher

Table 9.6 During the Last 12 Months, How Has Your Emigrant Household Member Been Sending Remittances?

	Percent
Sent with courier/agent/bus driver	57
MTO	26
Transfers to bank accounts	19
Sent with acquaintances/friends/relatives	12
Brought personally	1

than in Greece (where most women from Daba Tianeti tend to migrate). The mean amount of remittances received by emigrant households in Daba Tianeti between September 2005 and September 2006 was €1,320. Thus, we estimated that in the period between September 2005 and September 2006, the total amount of remittances sent by all Daba Tianeti migrants to their families back home was at least €280,000.

Most remittance-receiving households (74 percent) asserted that their economic situation improved after the emigration of their household member, which, again, serves as an incentive for the local population to pursue the path of migration. Not surprisingly, the improvement of a household's economic situation was linked with the frequency and amount of remittances sent.

Remittances have a definite poverty-mitigating impact on those Daba Tianeti households that receive them. The average monthly income of households receiving remittances from their family members working abroad (GEL 297) is more than twice the average monthly income of households without emigrants (GEL 131) (see Table 9.7). As demonstrated earlier, remittance-receiving households are much less likely to be in debt than other households.

Table 9.7 Mean Monthly Income and Spendings of Tianeti Households

	Income	Spending
All households	165	210
Among these:		
Households without emigrants	131	135
Households with emigrants	256	286
Among households with emigrants:		
Households receiving remittances	297	319
Households NOT receiving remittances	156	203

GEL: mean for the respective group

Remittances constitute a significant part of Daba Tianeti households' budgets. Not surprisingly, salary, pension and income from agricultural production play a lesser role in the incomes of households with emigrants compared to other households.

USES OF REMITTANCES

Migrant households are able to use remittances not only to meet everyday needs but also to invest in real estate and education, and to improve their quality of life in general. Remittances received by Daba Tianeti households are typically spent on what they have been intended for. A major expense category for 98 percent of Daba Tianeti households was the purchase of 'primary necessity' goods, such as food, personal hygiene items and clothes. Fifty-one percent of remittance-receiving households spent these transfers on medical expenses, followed by paying off debts (18 percent) and expenses related to agriculture (17 percent). On the other hand, remittances spent on education and health, which are quite common in Daba Tianeti, can be definitely considered an investment in human capital. Investments in real estate and/or renovation of already existing dwellings are also rather popular in Daba Tianeti. Successful emigrants buy houses and apartments not only in Daba Tianeti but also in Tbilisi. Apartments in Tbilisi are often renovated, rented out and used as an additional source of income. In this respect Daba Tianeti does not differ from the general pattern characteristic of many migrant-sending communities all over the world. Walking through Daba Tianeti, one can easily spot houses of economically successful emigrants by their modern appearance. New standards of comfort are emerging in Daba Tianeti—indoor toilets, washing machines, DVDs, etc.—which are made possible almost entirely thanks to the remittances.

During the census only three households out of all remittance-receiving households stated that their remittances were used for starting a small-scale business in the twelve months preceding the study. Thus, the effect of remittances on the 'productive' economy of Daba Tianeti can be considered rather limited. When comparing expenses of households receiving remittances to expenses of households not receiving remittances, only slight differences can be found in some expense categories (Table 9.8). This indicates that remittances do not necessarily lead to changes in the spending patterns of remittance-receiving households. In both cases the major expense categories remain the same, except for the real estate category. In general, we can assume that remittances increase the amount of funds allocated for staple consumer items, and that the preexisting spending pattern does not change significantly.

A study conducted in 2008 by an International Organization for Migration (IOM) project in Daba Tianeti revealed that the majority of the local population assessed the investment climate and existing investment

Table 9.8   During the Last Month on Which Items Has the Income of Your
Household Mainly Been Spent?

	HHs receiving remittances (n=215)	HHs not receiving remittances (n=847)
Items of primary necessity	98	98
Medical expenses	42	53
Agricultural expenses	15	16
Renovation / construction /purchase of an apartment/house	9	2
Purchase of durable goods	3	1
Purchase of a car	2	–
Apartment rent / land rent	2	1
Educational expenses	2	2
Ceremonies (funerals /marriages)	2	1
Purchase of equipment necessary for agricultural production	1	1
Savings	2	0.4
Purchase of furniture	1	0.2
Start up of entrepreneurial activities	0.5	0.5

opportunities in a rather pessimistic way. Most people believed that it was very difficult to find a job in Daba Tianeti, that there were no good prospects for starting a business and that these emigrants should not return to Daba Tianeti until the local economic situation improves. When asked about the industries that have the potential to be developed in Daba Tianeti, most respondents could not detach themselves from the recent history of their community, naming those industries that had been developed during the Soviet era. Notably, all of these industries have limited potential for success, taking into consideration existing economic realities both within and outside the country. According to this report, another problem hindering the development of small businesses in Tianeti was the lack of necessary skills and financial capital among the local population.[32]

CONCLUDING REMARKS

Although labor emigration from Daba Tianeti started recently, it has already become a widespread phenomenon that affects the lives of a significant part of Daba Tianeti's population. For most remittance-receiving households, remittances constitute a crucial part of their household budgets and are the only source of income for some of them. Remittances received by

Daba Tianeti households exacerbate economic inequalities within the local population. Meanwhile, the relative deprivation of households without emigrants becomes a major stimulus for future emigration flows. Because of the low quality of life in Daba Tianeti, meeting the primary needs of local households is of utmost importance. Besides, the very limited investment opportunities in the region, the lack of business skills among the local population and the insufficient promotion of business opportunities lessen the possibilities of the productive investment of remittances.

When taking this all into account, it is hard to expect that the level of emigration—and, specifically, female emigration—from Daba Tianeti will decrease in the near future. On the contrary, the proliferation of female emigration in the community, the existing demand for a female workforce in Western countries and developed migrant networks[33] will continue to support the established patterns of emigration. Because of international emigration, the lives of residents of this small Georgian community are now dependent on the economies of the receiving countries. Even if the number of emigrants from Daba Tianeti remains about the same and they continue to send remittances at the same pace, remittances could potentially increase inequality in the community, with households with emigrants increasingly improving their economic state, and households without emigrants increasingly falling into poverty.

In the case of Daba Tianeti it becomes evident that the dichotomy of the 'productive' versus 'unproductive' consumption of remittances does not give proper consideration to the investment climate in the remittance-receiving communities—which often does not provide any possibility to 'productively' invest remittances. Moreover, when we consider remittances as a source of private income just like regular incomes/pensions, it becomes even clearer that in the case of emigrant communities like Daba Tianeti, calls for 'productive' investment of remittances have limited validity. For remittance-receiving households, remittances often constitute the only source of income, and as such they are spent on the most pressing needs of the household, just like regular income would be spent.

NOTES

1. Earlier versions of this chapter have been published in: *Migration*, ed. M.Tukhashvili (Tbilisi: Universali, 2007), 92–102, and *International Research: Society, Politics, Economics* no.1 (2) (2010): 110–117.
2. State Department for Statistics of Georgia, *General Population Census of Georgia: 2002* (2003), accessed April 5, 2013, http://geostat.ge/cms/site_images/_files/english/census/2002/01%20Population%20By%20Municipalities%20and%20sex.pdf, and A. G. Vadachkoria, "International Migratory Processes in Georgia, 1989–2002" (PhD diss., Institute of Demography and Sociology, Tbilisi, 2003).
3. Irina Badurashvili, "Illegal Migrants from Georgia: Labor Market Experiences and Remittance Behavior," 2004, accessed April 5, 2013, http://

iussp2005.princeton.edu/papers/51259, and USAID, Save the Children, IPM, *The Status of Households in Georgia, Final Report* by Larry Dershem and Tea Khoperia, (Tbilisi: , 2004).

4. National Bank of Georgia, Money Transfers in Months , accessed April 10, 2013, http://nbg.gov.ge/index.php?m=306&lng=eng.

5. See, for example, N. Chelidze, *Labor Migration from Post-Soviet Georgia* (Tbilisi: Lega, 2006); R. Gachechiladze, *Migration of Population in Georgia and Its Socio-Economic Consequences* (Tbilisi: UN, 2007); T. Gugushvili, *Problems of International Migration and Demography in Georgia, 1990–1998* (Tbilisi: Office-Press, 1998); G. Tsuladze, *Emigration from Georgia according to the 2002 Census Data* (Tbilisi: CRRC, 2005); Vadachkoria, "International Migratory Processes in Georgia"; Badurashvili, "Illegal Migrants from Georgia"; idem, "Determinants and Consequences of Irregular Migration in a Society under Transition: The Case of Georgia, Caucasus," 2004, accessed: April 5, 2013, http://paa2004.princeton.edu/papers/41960; Dershem and Khoperia, *Status of Households in Georgia*; International Organization for Migration (IOM), *Hardship Abroad or Hunger at Home*, Tbilisi: IOM, 2001, accessed April 5, 2013, http://jcp.ge/iom/pdf/hardship.pdf; and International Organization for Migration (IOM), *Labor Migration from Georgia*, Tbilisi: IOM, 2003, accessed April 5, 2013, http://iom.ge/pdf/lab_migr_from_georgia2003.pdf.

6. See, for example, European Bank for Reconstruction and Development (EBRD), "Summary of Findings from National Surveys," accessed Sept. 29, 2011, http://www.ebrd.com/downloads/sector/etc/natsum.pdf; European Bank for Reconstruction and Development (EBRD), "Georgia National Public Opinion Survey on Remittances," accessed Sept. 29, 2011, http://www.ebrd.com/downloads/sector/etc/surge.pdf; Robert Tchaidze and Karine Torosyan, *Georgia on the Move* (Tbilisi: CRRC/ISET, GDN/IPPR, 2009); and International Organization for Migration (IOM), Tianeti Household Census 2008 & Tianeti Emigrants to Greece 2008, Tbilisi: IOM, 2009, accessed Sept. 29, 2011, http://jcp.ge/iom/pdf/tianeti.pdf.

7. Samuel Munzele Maimbo and Dilip Ratha, eds., *Remittances: Development Impact and Future Prospects* (Washington, DC: World Bank, 2005).

8. For a more detailed discussion of the feminization of labor emigration from Daba Tianeti, see Tamar Zurabishvili and Tinatin Zurabisvhili, "Feminization of Labor Emigration from Georgia: Case of Tianeti," *Rethinking the South Caucasus Laboratorium: Russian Review of Social Research* no. 1, (2010): 73–83.

9. Ibrahim Sirkeci, Jeffrey H. Cohen and Dilip Ratha, eds., *Migration and Remittances during the Global Financial Crisis and Beyond* (Washington, DC: World Bank, 2012), 1–15.

10. Richard Adams and John Page, "The Impact of International Migration and Remittances on Poverty," in *Remittances: Development Impact and Future Prospects*, ed. S. Maimbo and D. Ratha (World Bank: Washington, DC, 2005), 290–291.

11. Maimbo and Ratha, *Remittances*.

12. Admos Chimhowu, Jenifer Piesse and Caroline Pinder, "The Socioeconomic Impact of Remittances on Poverty Reduction," in *Remittances: Development Impact and Future Prospects*, ed. S. Maimbo and D. Ratha (Washington, DC: World Bank, 2005), 88.

13. Richard H. Adams Jr., Alfredo Cuecuecha and John Page, *Remittances, Consumption and Investment in Ghana* (Washington, DC: World Bank, 2008).

14. Dilip Ratha, *Leveraging Remittances for Development* (Washington, DC: World Bank, 2007), 4, accessed Aug. 25, 2012, http://siteresources.

worldbank.org/INTPROSPECTS/Resources/334934–1110315015165/
LeveragingRemittancesForDevelopment.pdf.

15. Dilip Ratha, "Worker's Remittances: An Important and Stable Source of External Development Finance," in *Remittances: Development Impact and Future Prospects*, ed. S. Maimbo and D. Ratha (Washington, DC: World Bank, 2005), 19–52.

16. International Organization for Migration (IOM), Tianeti Household Census 2008 & Tianeti Emigrants to Greece 2008 (Tbilisi: IOM, 2009), accessed Sept. 29, 2011, http://jcp.ge/iom/pdf/tianeti.pdf.

17. Giorgi Tavberidze served as a research assistant in the quantitative part of the research. Both the quantitative and the qualitative fieldwork were greatly facilitated by assistance from Tianeti residents Mrs. Natalia Gonjilashvili, Mrs. Nino Chikhradze, Mrs. Tamar Kurshavishvili and Ms. Irma Turkiashvili.

18. Tamar Kurshavishvili (head of Tianeti Branch of State Department of Statistics of Georgia), personal communication, Aug. 25, 2005.

19. Families that left Tianeti and emigrated entirely, or moved to other parts of Georgia, and come to Tianeti only for summer vacation still have their houses in Tianeti, which are closed, and if unattended become dilapidated.

20. State Department for Statistics of Georgia, *General Population Census of Georgia: 2002*, 47.

21. G. Labbate, L. Jamburia and G. Mirzashvili, *Poverty Mapping in Georgia* (Tbilisi: UNDP, 2003), 21.

22. Despite the recent impressive growth rates in the Georgian economy, there has been no decrease in the poverty level. On the contrary: from 2004 to 2005 the level of urban poverty increased from 34.3 percent to 37.1 percent, and the level of rural poverty from 37.1 percent to 41.7 percent. Gini coefficients of income (0.44) and consumption (0.39) are high as well. See Government of Georgia and UNDP, *Country Programme Action Plan: 2006–2010* (Tbilisi: UNDP, 2006), 4.

23. *Georgian Soviet Encyclopedia* (Tbilisi: Georgian Soviet Republic State Committee Printing Department, 1979), v. 4, 678–679.

24. Tianeti Municipality official website, accessed Sept. 11, 2012, http://tianeti.org.ge/?l=E&m=2&sm=0.

25. Labbate, Jamburia and Mirzashvili, *Poverty Mapping in Georgia*, 21.

26. Georgian *lari*; during the study, the rate of GEL:USD was 1.72:1.

27. According to the classification of the State Department for Statistics of Georgia, 'permanent population' means the population that is registered in a given settlement, regardless of their actual place of residence.

28. Badurashvili, "Determinants and Consequences," and Dershem and Khoperia, *Status of Households in Georgia*.

29. Dershem and Khoperia, *Status of Households in Georgia*, 45.

30. Comparable results were received during a study in Khatlon, Tajikistan, conducted in 2005. See Abdul Mughal, *Migration, Remittances, and Living Standards in Tajikistan: A Report Based on Khatlon Remittances and Living Standards Measurement Survey 2005* (Dushanbe: International Organization for Migration, 2007), 107.

31. Results of a study conducted in Tianeti in 2008 revealed that remittances were mostly sent via MTOs (42 percent), bank transfers (28 percent) and informal channels, such as a driver, an agent or a courier (27 percent). Data from International Organization for Migration (IOM), Tianeti Household Census 2008 & Tianeti Emigrants to Greece 2008, 18–20.

32. IOM, Tianeti Household Census 2008 & Tianeti Emigrants to Greece 2008.

33. For a detailed discussion of the migrant networks of labor emigrants from Tianeti, see Tamar Zurabishvili, "*Migratsionnye Seti Trudovykh Emigrantov iz Tianeti* [Migration networks of labor migrants from Tianeti]," *Vestnik Obschestvennogo Mnenia: Dannye, Analiz, Diskussii* 3, no. 89 (2007): 56–65, and idem, "Migration Networks of Emigrants from Tianeti," in *Figuring Out the South Caucasus: Societies and Environment* (Tbilisi: Heinrich Boell Foundation, 2008), 84–106.

10 The Dominican LGBTIQ Movement and Asylum Claims in the US[1]

Jacqueline Jiménez Polanco

This chapter analyzes the LGBTIQ movement in the Dominican Republic and the migratory experiences of Dominican sexual minority refugees seeking asylum in the US. It examines national and international laws pertaining to refugee status and asylum claims and their effects on sexual minorities who apply for asylum. It argues that the lack of a coherent definition of 'social group' in US asylum laws and the Geneva Convention and the difficulties sexual minority applicants have faced in presenting material proof of sexual identity/orientation and associational status hamper the possibility for LGBTIQ refugees to be granted asylum. This is particularly critical for lesbian women because the majority of sexual minority refugees who apply for and are granted asylum are gay men on the basis of their persecution as HIV-positive people.[2]

Sexuality is interpreted in this chapter as a somatic fact created by a cultural effect, and the social organization and expression of human sexuality are considered complex and, therefore, neither timeless nor universal.[3] The abbreviations, terms and social categories used to describe sexual minorities (as well as the dualism woman/man, male/female, masculine/feminine) are considered simplistic and nonexclusive and miss much of the variety of actual human experience.[4] Their use has been adopted for the purpose of analyzing gender and sexual inequality toward sexual minority migrants, refugees and asylum seekers.[5]

This chapter also discusses the fear of persecution suffered by many LGBTIQ refugees, as members of a subordinate nonheterosexual group. The prevailing heteronormativity of the Dominican Republic prompts these asylum seekers to hide their sexual identity/orientation and preference, making their 'associational status', as members of a persecuted minority, harder to prove. This is acutely critical for Dominican gender/sexual minority refugees who seek asylum in the US. Despite the Dominican Republic's long-standing migratory movement to the US and establishment of old settlements, particularly in New York City, many members of the mainstream Dominican American community reject total assimilation to the US's dominant culture and, in turn, exacerbate the Dominican Republic's conservative and homogenizing national identity in discourse and practice. Consequently, many Dominican Americans embrace the traditional homeland's values and beliefs and perpetuate in the host country the Dominican culture's classist, racist, sexist and discriminatory attitudes and behaviors toward sexual minorities. In addition, those Dominican Americans who have assimilated to the US's dominant culture might not find substantial reasons to accept sexual minorities considering their stigmatization and limited legal protection.[6] As a result, many Dominican LGBTIQ immigrants hide their sexual identity/orientation for fear of their family's and society's rejection, and those who eventually come out experience a ghettoization process by being forced out of the conventional Dominican American community.

Difficulty proving associational status has driven some US attorneys to test more than one reason for asylum petitions, so that the category 'membership in a particular social group' overlaps with others, such as the fear of imminent death by criminal actions or by medical negligence in the case of applicants with HIV-AIDS. However, this legal approach may create an ethical conflict because it could damage the international image of the Dominican Republic on human rights issues. For example, with the exception of the increasing number of attacks targeting trans-individuals, Dominican sexual minorities in general are not permanent victims of crime, and admitting this would ignore the advances achieved by the advocacy work of the LGBTIQ community in raising the levels of tolerance toward sexual minorities in the Dominican Republic. Additionally, sustaining the idea that HIV-AIDS patients die in the Dominican Republic's public hospitals due to medical negligence denies the country's improvements in the prevention and treatment of the illness, particularly in the last decade, as recognized by national and international health organizations.

Finally, this chapter argues that police brutality, ostracism and fear of persecution are currently the major causes leading Dominican LGBTIQ individuals to become refugees and seek asylum. In the particular case of male-to-female (M-F) trans-individuals, fear of death by criminal actions is the major cause for asylum seeking. There has been a great increase in the number of murders of M-F trans-individuals since 2006 without further investigation by the police, who in some cases have been incriminated by the community. This lack of further investigation also prevents these criminal actions from being reported as human rights violations. The murder of M-F trans-individuals could be associated with their victimization on the basis of their gender identity as female and the high incidence of women's murders or femicides in the country.

The US deportation policies and their effects on the fast-spreading anti-immigrant movement also limit the success of asylum claims by Dominican LGBTIQ people. Deportation has affected many lawful Dominican permanent residents who have been deported on the basis of past offenses, criminal convictions and misdemeanors that were committed a long time ago and that were not grounds for mandatory deportation before the passage of the 1996 immigration law. Current data indicates that of the top seven immigrant groups deported in 2007, Dominicans have the highest proportion of those deported for criminal convictions.[7]

In essence, the violation of the civil and human rights of LBGTIQ people in the Dominican Republic, the intricacy of the migration and asylum policies and their challenges for sexual minorities to seek asylum may find a sociological explanation in the following assertions: (a) human rights violations occur not only in the public sphere but also in the domestic or private sphere; (b) persecution on account of gender, sexual identity/orientation, ethnicity and family is a category of social experience that shapes and gives meaning to gender and sexuality; and (c) national and international institutions, community-based organizations, policy makers and individual advocates should consider the real existence of barriers that prevent victims from seeking justice both at home and in foreign countries.[8]

REFUGEE AND ASYLUM LAWS: THEIR EFFECTS ON LGBTIQ ASYLUM SEEKERS IN THE US

Thus far, the prevailing definition of an asylum seeker has been a refugee who applies for asylum in a foreign nation due to well-founded fears of being persecuted for reasons of race, religion, nationality, membership in a particular social group or political opinion. The applicant should be outside of his/her national country and unable or unwilling (owing to such fear) to avail him-/herself of the protection of that country or return to it. If the asylum is granted, the person could seek permanent residence. If the asylum is denied, the person would face deportation.

The Geneva Convention Relating the Status of Refugees does not contemplate aspects such as discrimination or persecution for gender and sexual identity, orientation or preference. Therefore, gender and sexual minority refugees who seek asylum need to found their cases on the basis of fear of persecution for membership in a particular social group. They must satisfy three main legal tests: (1) they must demonstrate a well-founded fear of persecution; (2) they must substantiate that the persecution they fear is on account of their membership in a particular social group; and (3) they must demonstrate that the particular social group exists. In addition, refugee protection is conferred only if the claimant succeeds in showing that the country of nationality or habitual residence is unwilling or unable to offer protection.[9]

There is an ongoing discussion among attorneys and scholars about the ambiguity of the definition of 'a particular social group' as a ground for recognition of refugee status. This ambiguity has been magnified by the fact that some receiving countries have laws that make homosexual conduct illegal. Hence, many LGBTIQ individuals seeking asylum often fear persecution for more than one reason, and the definition of their 'social group' often overlaps with other categories, predominantly that of political opinion. Some applications for refugee status on the grounds of sexual identity/orientation are claimed under the category of political opinion despite the fact that many sexual minorities do not consider their sexual identity/orientation to be political. In addition, the increasing number of claims that are made under the social group category has resulted in an expanded definition of the factors defining the associational status. Accordingly, sexual orientation as a basis for membership to a particular social group encompasses three factors: sexual behavior, sexual orientation and sexual identity.

In the US, following the precedent set by the *Matter of Toboso-Alfonso* case in 1994, LGBTIQ asylum applicants fall under the rubric 'membership of a particular group', meaning that immigration judges look for evidence that the petitioner falls within this category. As pointed out by Sridharan of the US Council on Foreign Relations, "this task is not straightforward." The protection has a wide scope and unclear definition. In response, US courts have developed three tests to help determine whether applicants are members of a particular social group: (1) the *immutability* rule (the characteristics defining an applicant's membership in a particular social group cannot be changeable); (2) the *association* rule (courts look for association with other individuals who belong to this social group and share the characteristic that is the basis of the asylum application); and (3) the *recognizability* rule (individuals in the social group in question must possess characteristics recognizable to others). As a result, after 1994 the number of LGBT asylum claims has gradually increased in the US, but seeking asylum is still a hard task. Between 1998 and 2008 annual applications averaged forty-six thousand, but only 62 percent were approved.[10]

Sridharan also explains that, "asylum claims based on persecution related to a lesbian, gay, bisexual, or transgender (LGBT) individual's sexual orientation are particularly difficult to file, argue, and win—even with substantial evidence of persecution and ill-treatment." The success of these claims is limited by the following: (1) the focus on homosexual identity (not homosexual conduct) in US laws; (2) the inapplicability of the usual tests for asylum eligibility in this context; (3) varying definitions of persecution; and (4) inadequate legal precedent and discriminatory attitudes in US courts.[11]

By observing the experiences of asylum seekers from other Latin American nations (i.e., Mexico) as well as the Dominican Republic, in the following sections I will analyze the effect of US immigration court decisions to deny asylum to refugee lesbian women, sexual minorities who conceal their identities in their homeland and the receiving country, and people living with HIV but who have past criminal convictions and are considered eligible for deportation. I will also examine the legal strategies used by some US attorneys to overlap the criterion of association with other criteria for defining group membership, and how this might create ethical problems for the sending nations, the Dominican Republic serving as the main example. Then I will discuss the paradigmatic case of the first Dominican gay male person who has been granted asylum in the US.

LESBIAN WOMEN—LAST IN THE LIST OF LGBTIQ ASYLUM SEEKERS AND GRANTEES

The ambiguous and restrictive nature of asylum laws affects lesbian women by keeping a tight rein on the number of lesbians who seek the refugee status and are granted asylum, leaving them underrepresented among the LGB-TIQ people who apply for and are granted asylum. The European Council on Refugees and Exile states that, although women represent the majority of asylum seekers worldwide, there has been a noticeable absence of refugee status being granted to women and an absence of applications based on sexual orientation made by women. Of the reported asylum claims based on sexual orientation, the majority of them have been made by male applicants under fear of persecution due to their HIV-positive status. This may open a discussion about the long-standing exclusion of lesbian women from public mobilization and research, health care, and financial and technical support for HIV-AIDS, and its effects on their migratory experiences.[12] Argüelles and Rivero, for example, interviewed one hundred immigrant and refugee women from Mexico whom they met while conducting mental health work and AIDS prevention education in Southern California. The authors discuss the difficulties faced by those immigrant and refugee women whose migration motivations and outcomes, as well as their gender definitions and sexualities have been greatly impacted by intimate and public violence. They assert that US immigration authorities have been "reluctant to recognize or respond compassionately to such realities."[13]

In general, the underrepresentation of women in the asylum petitions has been changing, and today they make up the overwhelming majority of asylum seekers worldwide, particularly because they are the main victims of war and murder associated with domestic violence. However, when it comes to sexual minorities, there is still a conspicuous absence of sexual orientation applications by lesbians and the granting of refugee status to women based on their sexual orientation. The majority of claims based on sexual orientation are still made by male applicants.[14]

The international legal vacuum that affects the possibilities for lesbians to be granted asylum also includes Dominicans. I became acquainted with a young, Dominican lesbian who was caught in this dilemma. Her Minneapolis-based attorney contacted me for pro bono consulting about her asylum petition in December 2005. In her email communication with me, the attorney explained that her client had previously filed a claim for asylum in San Francisco, California, and was jailed for failing to appear at a hearing for which she received no notice. Her attorney retained my help after she was detained and jailed in Minnesota, and acknowledged the contribution of my research to the eventual success of her client's case. The attorney also explained that she was able to release her client from detention and get her an asylum hearing for March 2006. To date, I have not heard from this attorney nor have I received further information about the outcome of this case. I recalled that some asylum cases were referred to me by Francisco Lazala, founder and executive director of GALDE (Gay and Lesbian Dominican Empowerment), so I asked him whether among the organization's two thousand members there is any record of this or any other asylum approval and his response was negative. GALDE does not have any record of asylum among its members.[15]

LGBTIQ CONCEALED SEXUAL IDENTITY IN THE RECEIVING COUNTRIES

Because the US still has laws that make homosexual conduct illegal, it becomes difficult for asylum applicants to argue they would receive adequate protection in the US from similar laws in their home countries. Therefore, immigration courts favor claims founded on persecution based on sexual identity and not on homosexual conduct. These legal obstacles are critical for Dominican LGBTIQ petitioners because, although the violation of human and civil rights routinely happens, due to fear of persecution, violence and stigmatization, many sexual minorities may conduct themselves as such but do not necessarily identify as members of this category or group (i.e., Decena's "tacit subject").[16] Hiding their identities in the homeland causes sexual minorities' mental disorientation and panic, pushing many to migrate and seek asylum. However, becoming an immigrant does not represent a real guarantee for LGBTIQ people to come out of the closet, and in many cases they continue to hide their sexual orientation in the receiving nation for fear of persecution, bias and stigmatization.

Francisco Lazala is the director of GALDE, the oldest NGO incorporating Dominican LGBT in the US. He admits that, in the over two decades running the group between 1996 and 2008, the Dominican LGBT Pride celebration in New York City (that hosts between 1,500 and 2,000 people in the annual 'picnic') was being held in a cloak-and-dagger way, in a public park underneath the Washington Bridge near the Dominican neighborhood in Washington Heights. Many of the members felt that they could be themselves in this covert place, because it "gave them a sense of security and freedom." He added that this long-standing practice of hiding their sexual identity/orientation has been changing for gays, bisexuals and transgender persons in the last couple of years toward a more visible and open mobilization. This changing social climate has encouraged GALDE to hold the picnic in a more accessible public space at Inwood Hill Park, another

Dominican neighborhood in the city. These changes, however, are of little consequence for lesbian women, because the majority of them do not participate in community activities, as many of them live in the closet in heterosexual marriages and have children.[17]

The tendency to hide one's sexual orientation in the US is currently aggravated by the increasing rate of new HIV infections among LGBTIQ youth of color, hate crimes, lesbo/bi/trans/homophobic sentiments in communities, the spate of incidents involving bullying and teen suicides, failure to secure marriage equality and many other issues ravaging the sexual minority community.

LIVING WITH THE HIV-AIDS VIRUS AND SEEKING ASYLUM— WHAT WOULD A US LAWYER DO TO WIN THE CASE?

In the last six years, I have become acquainted with other asylum petitioners whose cases also illustrate their victimization in the Dominican Republic. These petitioners have not been granted asylum and have faced deportation. These cases suggest contradictions between the statements used by US immigration attorneys to sustain asylum claims and social and cultural changes in the Dominican Republic that have improved the public health care system. I have sadly observed the despair of young lesbians, gay males and M-F transgender people who have been denied asylum because US courts did not find enough evidence of fear of persecution for social membership.

In 2008, while I was a research associate at the CUNY Dominican Studies Institute at City College, a young Dominican gay man seeking asylum reached out to the DSI and its director, Dr. Ramona Hernández, asking for assistance. He desperately explained that his petition was likely to fail due to an old criminal antecedent involving drug trafficking. He said he was HIV-positive and feared to be deported to a country whose people and culture he was not familiar with any longer due to a long migratory experience that had taken him to Europe and the US. He also feared potential isolation in the Dominican Republic, because he had no family ties as most of his relatives had emigrated as well. His attorney in New York City asked witnesses to attest in a court hearing that, in the Dominican Republic, homosexuals living with the HIV-AIDS virus were denied medical assistance in public hospitals and frequently died of medical negligence.

I rejected that inquiry because I had not witnessed any case of medical negligence causing the death of an LGBTIQ person with HIV-AIDS and had not read any report on such a case. It is well known, however, that the public health care system of the Dominican Republic is highly inefficient and poorly equipped. Service in most public hospitals is deplorable, and the media constantly reports cases of medical negligence. In 2002, the Inter-American Human Rights Commission solicited the Dominican government to adopt preventive measures to preserve the life and physical integrity of ten PVVS (people living with the HIV-AIDS virus), some suffering from a high level of infection. The commission reported that the Dominican government's response was that it had the disposition to provide those patients the requested treatment and antiretroviral medicaments and that it would comply with the request in four months. The commission denounced the indifference and negligence of the Dominican government regarding preventive measures to preserve the life and physical integrity of PVVS patients.[18]

This pattern, however, has been steadily changing since 2006, through the active involvement of the civil society, the government and international organizations. These collective efforts have increased access to diagnostic tests and antiretroviral treatment for HIV-AIDS patients through the National Program of Vertical Distribution (*Programa Nacional de Transmisión Vertical*). Despite these improvements, the program's effectiveness has still been criticized, particularly the service provided to pregnant women, children and Haitian immigrants.[19] Additionally, the transgender organization COTRAVET (Dominican Trans and Transgender Committee/ *Comité de Trans y Transgénero Dominicana*) reports on the participation of its members in the AS I Am (*Tal Cual*) health program sponsored by the nongovernmental organization COIN (Center for Integral Orientation and Investigation/ Centro de Orientación e Investigación Integral). The AS I Am initiative includes a transgender clinic in which STI and HIV patients are integrated within a context of primary care for specific transgender health care needs, such as the use of hormones. COTRAVET's leader, Nairobi Castillo, states that: "We have seen how this builds trust and self-esteem and results in reduced risk taking behavior and greater adherence with anti retroviral medication."[20]

In an interview with Raquel Batista, US attorney at law and expert in immigration and deportation, she explained that US attorneys have been using such statements on a regular basis to win asylum cases that otherwise would be rejected and followed by deportation. She stated, however,that these arguments could be difficult to make nowadays due to the advancements in HIV-AIDS prevention and treatment in the Dominican Republic: a fact that official authorities and attorneys in the US should be aware of.[21]

ASYLUM CLAIM FOR FEAR OF CRIMINAL DEATH: THE PERILOUS LIFE OF M-F TRANSGENDER PEOPLE

In recent years, it has become increasingly common for US attorneys to inquire about murders, and other criminal actions in the Dominican Republic, that target people because they are gay. They have asked witnesses to testify that, if their clients return to the Dominican Republic, they would become the victims of murder. Although some US immigration attorneys might be using these testimonies to substantiate their client's membersip in a category that is difficult to prove (i.e., association), it is just about the only way that M-F transgender people in the Dominican Republic can make a successful petition for asylum.

Dominican independent media outlets report that the murder of sexual minority individuals is a common criminal action in the country, and that the main targets are M-F trans-individuals. The increasing number of crimes has resulted in the murder of ten transgender people between January 2006 and April 2010 (three in 2006, four in 2008, two in 2009 and one in 2010)[22] and eighteen in 2012.[23]

M-F transgender people occupy the lowest gender, sexual, age and socioeconomic strata. They are victimized for being female, nonheterosexual, young and poor. This multivictimization forces them to rely on prostitution as their only means of income. In some cases, unidentified trans-phobic elements perpetrate deliberate criminal actions against transgender groups; randomly shooting them while they are hanging out in the streets or waiting for their clients. In other cases, they have been brutally killed by their clients. The police do not undertake further investigation, and in some cases the community has accused police members of being either the perpetrators or accomplices.

The victimization of M-F trans-individuals and their brutal murders could be correlated to their female identity and the increasing rate of femicides in the country.[24] In a report from the ad hoc procurator for women's affairs, Judge Rosanna Reyes, indicates that two hundred women were murdered in 2010 and twenty only in January and February 2011, which represents an increase of two femicides compared to the same months last year.[25] The National Commission on Human Rights reports that the incidence of femicides was 614 between 2005 and 2011, and over 200 women were assassinated in 2010.[26] Femicides increased in 2011 with 204 women assassinated and barely decreased in 2012 with 198 women murdered by their partners or ex-partners.[27]

The M-F transgender coordinator of the group TRANSSA, Thalía Almendares, explains that surviving as a trans-woman is a hard task. She asserts that for M-F trans-individuals conducting themselves in public automatically excludes them from access to the educational system and labor market, because society does not conceive the presence in public spaces of a person who was born a biological male but dresses up like a female. Ms. Almendares states: "We have no other choice than working as hairdressers, florists, or cosmeticians. Others work as prostitutes, they have no other choice" (No nos queda más que trabajar en una peluquería, una floristería o de maquillistas. Otras recurren a la prostitución, no tienen otra alternativa).[28]

Because migration is mostly a socioeconomic phenomenon and the typical migrants are members of subordinate sectors with more access to economic resources, it is difficult for trans-individuals to contemplate legal migration as a means to eventually liberate themselves from the violence, oppression, discrimination and stigmatization they suffer in their homeland. Many die while young and well before they could have been able to accumulate the economic capital needed to migrate.

THE VILLALONA-PÉREZ CASE:
THE DOMINICAN ASYLUM CLAIM PARADIGM?

Luis Villalona Pérez is the first Dominican gay male who has been granted asylum in the US. Although it was a painful and long process, Villalona-Perez's case could be considered paradigmatic, for no other successful Dominican cases have been either approved or publicized. There is a combination of factors that contributed to his attorney winning this case. Two important factors include the support of a nonidentified local Dominican organization that witnessed his 'fear of persecution for membership in a particular group' and also that his lawyer submitted his petition exactly one year before Dominicans became the main target of the US deportation program. This asylum case was also heard during the same time when advocates and lobbyists were challenging *sexual deviation* as a legal ground for LGBTIQ people to be barred from entering the US.

Villalona Pérez was approved for a permanent residence after an eight-year process that ended in 2003. He filed his asylum request in 1995, and a year later Jarrett Barrios represented him in New England's first gay asylum case to be heard in Boston. Villalona Pérez's request for asylum was denied in 2001, by Immigration and Naturalization Service (INS) Judge Thomas Ragno. Villalona Pérez's next attorney, Bruce Barnett, handled the appeal with the Board of Immigration Appeals (BIA), which reversed Judge Ragno's decision in 2003, and granted Villalona Pérez asylum. The BIA stated that Villalona-Pérez had presented "credible evidence . . . that he had suffered threats, beatings, harassment and humiliation in the Dominican Republic because of his sexuality."[29]

At the time, Villalona-Pérez lived in Boston with family members. He applied for asylum "to escape anti-gay threats and persecution in his homeland." He claimed he feared for his life if he was forced to return to the Dominican Republic, where he had been "violently persecuted since age 13 for being gay." He also claimed that "in high school he was tormented, threatened and physically attacked. He was forced out of college after constant harassment, physical assaults and death threats. When he got a job in a factory, his supervisor attacked him. A gang of youths once chased and stoned him and police twice imprisoned him without charges."[30]

The Human Rights Campaign (HRC) and the Boston law firm Hill and Barlow contributed funds in the case to bring in an expert witness to provide testimony about the persecution of gay people in the Dominican Republic. The witness worked at a "Dominican AIDS and Human Rights organization that was forced to work covertly under the threat of government persecution." He testified that "Dominican police routinely and arbitrarily harass and imprison gay people."[31]

Villalona-Pérez's asylum request was initiated during the early application of the 1990 Immigration and Nationality Act. This act increased the limits on legal immigration to the US, revised all grounds for exclusion and deportation, and limited the Immigration and Naturalization Services (INS) regulations that used *sexual deviation* as a ground for gays and lesbians to be barred from entering the US. The passage of this act can be credited to the efforts of Massachusetts congressman Barney Frank with the support of President Bill Clinton, in conjuction with the HRC lobby to allow asylum claims for men and women persecuted abroad on the basis of their sexual orientation.

When Villalona-Pérez's asylum request was first heard in 1996, roughly thirty-five to forty asylum cases based on sexual orientation had already been granted in the US, because of the standards introduced by the Immigration Act in 1990. Although Villalona-Pérez's asylum case was initially denied, he would also, eventually, benefit from these more progressive legal standards. That same year, however, the Illegal Immigration Reform and Immigrant Responsibility Act (IIRIRA) was enacted into law, and thousands of Dominican individuals who were lawful permanent residents and had spent most of their lives in the US began to face deportation. The deportation crack-down on Dominican migrants may have played a role in the denial of Villalona-Pérez's first asylum petition and that of other Dominican LGBTIQ applicants. By 2003, when the BIA granted him asylum, six hundred individuals had received political asylum based on their sexual orientation (counting from 1990) and Villalona-Pérez's case was the only one from a Dominican petitioner.

At the end of his case, Villalona Pérez asserted that the eight-year struggle to obtain asylum in the US became such an ordeal that he had considered leaving the US and seeking refuge in a third country. He declared: "It was very hard for me because I had to keep recounting all the bad things that happened to me in the Dominican Republic. . . . At times, I wanted to throw in the towel, but I was seeking a better life for myself."[32]

Paradoxically, the maltreatment of Dominican gender/sexual minorities while seeking asylum in the US replicates some of the negative experiences in their homeland that forced them to emigrate. In most cases, deportation forces them to return to a society that had inexcusably expelled them and that at some level will continue to oppress them.

TENSIONS BETWEEN HUMAN RIGHTS AND SECURITY: THEIR EFFECTS ON ASYLUM PETITIONS

Asylum petitions have become a huge ordeal since the end of the Cold War era and the September 11, 2001, terrorist attacks. A major, contributing factor is, the tension between human rights and security in the US government's immigration policies. Because, in recent years, migration is understood as a security 'problem', many countries feel the need to protect against this 'threat'. Immigration and border control strategies have restricted the rights and mobility of nonskilled workers, whereas these same laws and policies allow skilled migrants to circulate quite easily. Consequently, denying nonskilled workers the legal channels to migrate encourages them to present themselves as asylum seekers, which, in turn, casts doubt on all refugees and leads to restrictive measures and unmanageable procedures to 'prove' the existence of persecution.[33]

The application of restrictive policies, which have made it more difficult for asylum seekers to demonstrate their association to a protected category of persons, the US's deportation policies and the intensification of the anti-immigrant movement have greatly affected the possibility for Dominican LGBTIQ people to be granted asylum. These punitive developments have exacerbated the following problems, which further undermine the claims of Dominican, LGBTIQ asylum seekers.

First, since the early 1960s the Dominican migratory movement has been mainly characterized by its economic nature and the nation is recognized as a long-standing political democracy. Second, since 1996 thousands of Dominicans have faced deportation, most of them lawful permanent residents who have spent most of their lives in the US. And, third, the nonconformist and spontaneous nature of the LGBTIQ movement is contrasted by the monopolistic orientation of two well-established nongovernmental organizations, *Amigos Siempre Amigos*/Friends Always Friends (ASA) and *Colectiva Mujer y Salud*/Woman's Collective and Health (*La Colectiva*). The patronizing discourse of ASA and *La Colectiva* hampers the possibilities for LGBTIQ asylum seekers to prove their associational status. I will develop these ideas in the following sections, which will examine the following factors: 1) the relationship between macroeconomic development and political stability in Dominican migration and how it compares to the US, 2) the US deportation of Dominican migrants and its effects on asylum seekers, and 3) the spontaneous nature of the Dominican sexual minority mobilization and its monopolistic control by conventional organizations.

MACROECONOMIC DEVELOPMENT AND POLITICAL STABILITY: PUSH FACTORS IN THE DOMINICAN EMIGRATION TO THE US

In her salient analysis of Dominican workers' migration to the US since 1966, Hernández asserts that, although emigration was originally stimulated by Joaquín Balaguer's expatriation of political dissidents and Leftist revolutionaries who participated in the 1965 civil war (*Revolución de Abril*),[34] it "also had a long-term goal for the Dominican government and the power structure, and it had to do with economic development in the country." On the one hand, emigration was a channel for the country to "systematically eliminate unwanted and unneeded surplus workers whom the new system of production could not absorb." On the other hand, the exodus was conceived as a means to "prevent the eruption of civil disobedience and social unrest caused by an impoverished people who could find no way to make a decent living." During his twelve-year (1966–1978) regime Balaguer imposed an inequitable and autocratic economic and political model that was backed up by the Pentagon and the CIA, so the government could attract US investments by focusing on development and stability.[35] Meanwhile, the 1965 US open-door immigration policy allowed a vast contingent of economically displaced Dominican workers to enter the US with tourist visas that, following their expiration, converted them into unauthorized migrant workers. The Balaguer government launched a dual economic plan that promoted the formation of, on the one side, an urban middle class associated with the expansion of public jobs and the commercial and financial sectors that expanded the level of consumption in the internal market, and on the other a disenfranchised and growing working class, unemployed and underemployed, who could barely afford basic necessities. Thus, in the first half of the 1970s, the Dominican Republic experienced the highest rate of economic growth in the Latin American region, whereas more than half of the work force was underemployed. As a result, in the 1970s the annual average of Dominican immigrants who legally arrived in the US reached sixteen thousand per year, and in the 1980s it rose to more than thirty thousand.[36]

This inequitable socioeconomic model was replicated during the 1980s and 1990s. The Dominican Republic's neoliberal macroeconomic policies prompted the displacement of many skilled workers from public jobs, and the growing technological industry expelled the surplus of nonskilled workers from private companies, forcing many middle- and lower-class Dominicans to emigrate. But the competitiveness of the US globalized high-tech service sector and the decay of the manufacturing sector displaced Dominican immigrants from the mainstream economy and pushed them to work in low-paid jobs. The English-language barrier of middle-class Dominicans and low educational levels of the lower class placed them along with other non-European immigrants and poorly educated American workers from ethnic and gender/sexual minorities. Hernández and Rivera-Batiz assert that in 2000 the Dominican labor force was very young and unskilled and its overall educational attainment was among the lowest in the country.[37]

In the 2000s Leonel Fernández's governmental policies focused on developing the free-market economy and institutionalizing the public sector. The country has experienced macroeconomic growth that has not been accompanied by public policies to reduce poverty and social inequity. The macroeconomic growth that reached 3 percent in 2009 contrasts with high levels of stratification and inequality on the basis of a poor distribution of wealth, in which the poorest 40 percent of households share only 11.5 percent of the wealth and the richest 10 percent of households shares 34.8 percent of the wealth. The majority of poor people are children, women, Haitian immigrants and LGBTIQ individuals. In addition, with the purpose of 'controlling delinquency' the police have enthroned a reign of terror in which youths from poor neighborhoods are their main victims.[38]

The migration of Dominicans to the US has steadily grown in the last decade. By 2010 the Dominican population represented 1.6 million, the third largest Latino group following Cuban and Puerto Ricans, and the fastest growing in New York City.[39] But this accelerating population growth has not been equally proportionate, across all socioeconomic levels. Although the majority of Dominicans are legal residents and over one-third of them are naturalized American citizens, they are still a predominantly low income population. The last decade saw spreading socioeconomic burdens for Dominicans in the US caused by the great recession and deportation policies.

THE US DEPORTATION OF DOMINICANS

Since the IIRIRA was enacted into law in 1996, people of Dominican descent have been a major target for deportations on the East Coast. Official records indicate that by 2008 over thirty-six thousand Dominicans were deported, and unofficial estimates place the total number of deportations above fifty thousand. Many of the individual deportees were lawful permanent residents and had spent most of their lives in the US. A total of 2,990 Dominicans were deported in 2007, of which 2,108 were removed for reasons of 'criminal status'. In 2009, over five thousand Dominicans were deported, almost doubling the rates of the previous years. The combination of overpolicing Dominican neighborhoods, racial profiling, lack of job opportunities and harsh laws has led to a disproportionately high rate of Dominicans being incarcerated. Deportation uproots families and rips communities apart, pushing down owned businesses that drive the local economy.[40]

Among US citizens there is a generalized perception that it is acceptable for developed nations to get rid of undesirable immigrants, particularly in a time of great recession. Therefore, these removals might continue to grow in the following years, reinforced by the general perception that those who are deported are undocumented criminals. The 2009 Angus Reid Strategies poll indicates that 66 percent of US Americans felt that immigration was having a negative effect on their country. They endorsed the deportation of undocumented immigrants, with almost 50 percent of respondents advocating for this course of action.[41]

These trends indicate that refugee and asylum laws, as they have been interpreted in US courts and immigration services, are serving contradictory functions. On the one side, the laws attempt to meet the country's obligations, under international accords, to shelter those persons whose national governments cannot or will not protect them from persecution. And on the other side, the laws attempt to limit the number of successful asylum claims in response to anti-immigrant feelings strongly expressed by the national public.[42]

THE SPONTANEOUS NATURE OF THE LGBTIQ MOBILIZATION AND ITS MONOPOLISTIC CONTROL BY CONVENTIONAL ORGANIZATIONS

Historically, the Dominican gay and lesbian movement has been volatile, nonconformist and nonbureaucratic, mostly composed of youths and led by radical feminist-lesbians. This path has prevailed until today, and the lack of formal and stable organizational structures hampers the access of the LGBTIQ community to international resources that support organizations that do advocacy work for the recognition, respect and protection of the civil and human rights of gender/sexual minorities. Because of the lack of incorporated LGBTIQ organizations, Dominican sexual minority asylum seekers have few legal resources to help them prove that they are recognized as members of LGBTIQ groups in their homeland. Suitable information on legally recognized ties can be utilized in the asylum hearings as a means to prove the immutability, association and recognizability criteria that determine whether asylum applicants are members of a particular social group.

Since the 1990s, the LGBTIQ movement's formal representation has been controlled by two stable, bureaucratic and conformist organizations that receive heavy technical and financial support from international agencies and governmental health care programs. One of those organizations is ASA, a gay men-only NGO that monopolizes the official representation of the sexual minority movement and its national and international funds. ASA receives support for educational and preventive HIV-AIDS initiatives. It is the only sexual minority organization that has been unremittingly operating in the Dominican Republic since 1989. It was founded with the financial support of the state secretary of public health's AIDS and Sexually Transmitted Diseases Control Program to provide emotional and physical support to gay males suffering from HIV-AIDS. Since its legal incorporation, ASA has had the same executive directorship and has not had any top-level hierarchical changes, factionalisms or ruptures—contrary to the general pattern of Dominican sexual minority organizations. ASA's main sources of support are the US Agency for International Development (USAID), COPRESIDA (Presidential Council for HIV-AIDS), GALDE and gay male owners of the entrenched and covert sexual minority nightclubs.

ASA's advocacy work is also endorsed by the patronage of lesbians incorporated in the well-established women's NGO *La Colectiva*, which receives international and national funds for preventive health care programs for women. Although *La Colectiva* is not a lesbian organization, it is led by institutional feminist-lesbians who have attempted to monopolize the official representation of youth lesbian activism through the creation of vertical organizations, such as the short-lived 'Germinando Ideas'.[43] Both ASA and *La Colectiva* maintain a solid and disguised political alliance that aims to preserve an official and conformist LGBTIQ community—protecting the mainstream, status quo gender/sexual minorities and holding down the mobilizations of alternative sexual minority communities.

ASA's institutional control over the Dominican LGBTIQ movement goes back to the HIV-AIDS epidemic in the 1980s and the flow of financial aid for preventive and educational programs. Several years after its foundation ASA enthroned a conventional and nonconfrontational image of the gay community that has given the wrong impression that tolerance toward sexual diversity prevails on Dominican soil and that gay males are the only gender/sexual minorities in need of social assistance, as the main victims of HIV-AIDS. To preserve its monopolistic control over LGBTIQ activism, ASA's leadership in alliance with *La Colectiva*'s leadership has nurtured apparently friendly relations with newly founded organizations. In fact, the two organizations disguise their conspiracy against the growing visibility of new groups and their potential public recognition. Some examples of these machinations took place in the early 2000s. First, the gay male leader of ASA and the institutional feminist-lesbian leaders of *La Colectiva* attacked the radical feminist-lesbian leaders of the newly founded group GAYLESDOM (Dominican Gay and Lesbian Collective), triggering its disintegration. The second instance occurred when the empowerment of youth artists, scholars, professionals and college students through the political advocacy of the group CAP LGBTIR (Political Action Committee for Lesbians, Gays, Bisexuals, Transgender, Transsexuals, Transvestites, and Female & Male Queers) challenged ASA and *La Colectiva*'s passive and nonconfrontational image of the LGBTIQ movement. In this case, ASA's leaders and lesbian leaders from *La Colectiva* joined CAP LGBTIR, tried to co-opt it and then fiercely attacked its autonomous feminist-lesbian leadership, prompting the breakdown of the group one year after its foundation. This happened after CAP LGBTIR had successfully organized the academic event, History of the Dominican LGBTIQ Movement: An Analysis of Sexual Minorities in the Island and the Diaspora. This was the first event of its kind ever held in the country, sponsored by the UNESCO university program Latin American Social Sciences Faculty (FLACSO) and with the participation of scholars, graphic artists, performers and the NGO's leaders from the Dominican Republic and the US. Soon after CAP LGBTIR disappeared, ASA founded a juvenile gay and lesbian group apparently meant to continue CAP LGBTIR's work. The short-lived group The Female and Male Kids from the Rear Table (*L@s Muchach@s de la Mesa de Atrás*) disappeared due to the controlling actions of of ASA's gay male members, that forced the exodus of lesbian leaders from the group. After this group was dismantled, ASA founded the gay male group REVASA.

In the late 2000s, members of the M-F trans-community founded COTRAVET, which gained international recognition in 2009 through its participation in the Caribbean Transgender Health and Human Rights Training and Strategy Consultation, sponsored by the International Gay and Lesbian Human Rights Commission (IGLHRC). Meanwhile, the murders of M-F trans-individuals escalated, and ASA founded the organization TRANSSA, which operates with the financial support of COPRESIDA. Soon after the emergence of TRANSSA a public controversy emerged in which TRANSSA's leadership claimed that it seized the real public representation of the trans-community and accused COTRAVET of fake representation. Following the controversy, TRANSSA has developed an active campaign on the Web denouncing the criminal actions against the trans-community, whereas COTRAVET has developed a good rapport on health care initiatives for trans-individuals. To date, it seems that both organizations are collaborating on advocacy programs, such as the recent event for the HIV-AIDS Forum, Talking from the Heart (*Foro Hablando desde el Corazón*), led by ASA and also integrated by REVASA, Integral Orientation Committee (*Comité de Orientación Integral*), MODEMU and This Love (*Este Amor*).[44] Ironically, there was no lesbian representation in that forum, giving the impression that lesbian women are not a part of the vulnerable communities affected by HIV-AIDS.

CONCLUSION: 'THERE IS NO GUARANTEE NI AQUÍ NI ALLÁ'

This chapter has analyzed the critical contradictions between the defining characteristics of the Dominican LGBTIQ movement and the criteria used under US law, to determine eligibility for asylum, which limit the legal arguments of Dominican sexual minorities. These contradictions have been analyzed in the context of the outrageous increase in the deportation of documented and undocumented Dominican migrants, rampant anti-immigrant sentiment in the US, and the economic nature of Dominican migration.

This chapter has also explored the difficulties faced by Dominican LGBTIQ asylum seekers who need to provide well-founded proof of association with other members of the LGBTIQ community. These difficulties are exacerbated by the lack of a coherent legal definition of the term 'association' and the absence of a progressive, supportive and inclusive organizational representation of sexual minorities in the Dominican Republic. These difficulties have led some US attorneys to test other arguments that indirectly relate to the criterion of association, such as fear of imminent death by the criminal actions of others, or medical negligence in the case of people living with the HIV-AIDS virus. As explained above, fear of death could be applied to M-F trans-individuals due to the fast-growing number of murders of transgender people based on their female gender identity and the prevalence of femicides. Conversely, fear of death for HIV-AIDS patients because of medical negligence is problematic and needs a careful examination due to the advances of the Dominican public health care system in its treatment of HIV-AIDS. It also bears emphasizing that migration to the US does not constitute a guarantee of freedom for LGBTIQ Dominicans, because discrimination based on sexual orientation is not prohibited in most US states. Therefore, many LGBTIQ migrants fear coming out in the receiving country because they could be targets of discrimination, bias, bullying, and family and community ostracism.

NOTES

1. The author would like to express her sincere gratitude to Danielle Prichett (Rutgers University) and Anthony Stevens (CUNY Dominican Studies Institute) for generously reading, commenting and doing editing work on her chapter.
2. As examined in the last section of this chapter, the obstacles for sexual minorities seeking asylum and the major exclusion of lesbian women as petitioners and grantees are critical for Dominican LGBTIQ individuals due to two main reasons. First, there are several features of the Dominican LGBTIQ movement and perceptions about the situation of sexual minorities on the island-nation that clash with the very restrictive nature of asylum laws that bound the petition to fear of being persecuted for 'membership in a particular social group'. The fluid and nonstructural feature of the Dominican LGBTIQ movement, the control of its monopolistic representation by a conformist HIV-AIDS gay male nongovernmental organization, the co-optation of potential lesbian leaders by conservative feminists incorporated in a well-established women's health organization, and the government and mainstream media's false image of the Caribbean nation as a pluralistic gay-friendly paradise create the wrong perception that Dominican LGBTIQ are happy in their homeland and do not need to go anywhere to seek freedom. Second, although lesbians are the leaders of the LGBTIQ spontaneous mobilization, their lack of formal institutional representation makes it harder for lesbian women who seek asylum to prove their fear of persecution due to their association with sexual minority groups.
3. Anne Fausto-Sterling, *Sexing the Body: Gender Politics and the Construction of Sexuality* (New York: Basic Books, 2000); Michel Foucault, *The History of Sexuality*, vol. 1, *The Will to Knowledge* (1976; London: Penguin, 1998); and Judith Lorber, "Beyond the Binaries: Depolarizing the Categories of Sex, Sexuality, and Gender," *Sociological Inquiry* 66, no. 2 (1996): 143–160.
4. Lorber, "Beyond the Binaries."
5. The abbreviation LGBTIQ refers to lesbians, gays, bisexuals, transgender, transsexuals, transvestites, intersex and queer, all of which are also referred to as 'gender/sexual minorities' and relate to gender identity and sexual identity, orientation or preference. The category lesbian woman is used here because the term 'lesbian' alone does not exclusively pertain to biologically born women but also to transgender, transsexual, transvestite and intersex women. The abbreviations 'F-M' and 'M-F' are used for female-to-male and male-to-female transgender individuals, transsexuals or transvestites respectively; 'MSM' means men who have sex with men and do not identify as homosexuals or gays.
6. Although US society has achieved important advances in the protection of human and civil rights of sexual minorities, only seventeen states, including New York, prohibit discrimination based on sexual orientation. Therefore, sexual minorities face discrimination on both personal and legal levels. The inability to marry denies LGBTIQ couples many civil rights that married couples take for granted, such as making decisions for an incapacitated

partner and the right of dependents to receive government benefits such as Social Security payments. A 2007 US national survey of attitudes toward gay marriage shows an almost even split among the public, with 46 percent saying it should be considered valid and 53 percent that it should not be recognized. Gallup, "Homosexual Relations" (www.gallup.com), cited in Richard T. Schaefer, *Sociology: A Brief Introduction* (New York: McGraw-Hill, 2009), 305.

7. Northern Manhattan Coalition for Immigrant Rights (NMCIR), "Dominicano, Deportado y Humano: The Realities of Dominican Deportations and Related Policy Recommendations," 2009, accessed April 7, 2013, http://www.nmcir.org/Deportado%20Dominicano%20y%20Humano.pdf

8. Greg Mullins, "Seeking Asylum: Literary Reflection on Race, Ethnicity, and Human Rights," *MELUS* 28, no. 1 (2003): 145–171, accessed April 7, 2013, http://www.questia.com/googleScholar.qst?docId=5001984532.

9. European Council on Refugees and Exiles, "ELENA Research Paper on Sexual Orientation as a Ground for Recognition of Refugee Status," 2009, accessed April 7, 2013, http://www.ecre.org/files/orient.pdf, and Nichole LaViolette, "The UNHCR'S Guidance Note on Refugee Claims Relating to Sexual Orientation and Gender Identity," *American Society of International Law* 13, no. 10 (2009), accessed April 7, 2013, http://www.asil.org/insights090730.cfm#_edn1.

10. Swetha Sridharan, "The Difficulties of US Asylum Claims Based on Sexual Orientation," Migration Information Source, 2008, accessed April 7, 2013, http://www.migrationinformation.org/Feature/display.cfm?id=700.

11. Ibid.

12. Anne Vassal, John Fisher, Ralf Jürgens and Robert Hughes, *Gay and Lesbian Issues and HIV/AIDS: A Discussion Paper* (Montreal: Canadian HIV/AIDS Legal Network & Canadian AIDS Society, 1997), and Ulrick Boehmer, "Twenty Years of Public Health Research: Inclusion of Lesbian, Gay, Bisexual and Transgender Populations," *Public Health* 92, no. 7 (2002): 1125–1130.

13. Lourdes Argüelles and Anne M. Rivero, "Gender/Sexual Orientation Violence and Transnational Migration: Conversations with Some Latinas We Think We Know," *Urban Anthropology* 22, no. 3–4 (1993): 259–275 at 271.

14. European Council on Refugees and Exiles, "ELENA Research Paper."

15. Francisco Lazala, personal communication, Mar. 4, 2011.

16. Carlos Ulises Decena, "Tacit Subjects," *GLQ: A Journal of Lesbian and Gay Studies* 14, no. 2–3 (2008): 339–359.

17. Lazala, personal communication.

18. Agua Buena Asociación de Derechos Humanos, "Boletines Informativos: Acceso Centroamérica—República Dominicana," 2002, accessed April 7, 2013, http://www.aguabuena.org/boletines/setiembre152002.html.

19. COPRESIDA y ONUSIDA, "Medición del Gasto en Sida en la República Dominicana," 2008, accessed April 7, 2013, http://www.unaids.org/en/media/unaids/contentassets/dataimport/pub/report/2008/NASA_Republica_Dominicana_2008_es.pdf. and United Nations Programme on HIV/AIDS, "Custom Analysis Extract of UNGASS National Composite Policy Index, Dominican Republic," 2008, accessed April 7 2013, http://data.unaids.org/pub/Report/2008/dominicanrepublic_2008_ncpi_en.pdf.

20. "Dominican Republic (Nairobi Castillo)," Caribbean Vulnerable Communities, accessed April 7, 2013, http://www.cvccoalition.org/pages/News/2009/WAD.php.

21. Raquel Batista (Northern Manhattan Coalition for Immigrant Rights), in discussion with the author, June 20, 2008.

22. José Rafael Sosa, "En RD han asesinado ya a 10 transexuales.accessed April 7, 2013, http://josersosa.blogspot.com/2010/04/nueve-de-los-diez-transexuales.html.

23. "Han matado dieciocho travestis en el 2012 en Dominicana por crímenes de odio". Alternativas Noticiosas.com, accessed April 13, 2013, http://www.alternativasnoticiosas.com/2012/12/han-matdo-en-el-2012–18-travestis-en.html.

24. Comparative research shows that there were 167 femicides in the Dominican Republic in 2003, which represents an increment of 69.09 percent between 2000 and 2003 and a prevalence rate of 37.25 per million, higher than Puerto Rico (29.75) and Mexico (24.50). There were 99 femicides in 2006, equivalent to 66.99 percent between 2000 and 2006. The Dominican Republic reached the highest ratio in the region, equivalent to 21.47 femicides per million, followed by Panama (14.75) and Puerto Rico (11.75). José San Martín et al., 3rd International Report on Partner Violence against Women: Statistics and Legislation, Serie Documentos 16, Centro Reina Sofía, accessed April 7, 2013,http://www.fundacionluisvives.org/upload/88/18/informe.pdf.

25. "Determinan han asesinado 20 mujeres en dos meses." Senda en Las Noticias, accessed April 7, 2013, http://sendaenlasnoticias1680am.blogspot.com/2011/03/determinan-han-asesinado-20-mujeres.html

26. Noticias Sin, "DD.HH. asegura es preocupante la cantidad de asesinatos de mujeres," accessed April 7, 2013, http://www.noticiassin.com/2011/03/dd-hh-asegura-es-preocupante-la-cantidad-de-asesinatos-de-mujeres/

27. "Disminuye 15% número de mujeres asesinadas en R. Dominicana". Spanish.people.com.cn, accessed April 13, 2013, http://spanish.peopledaily.com.cn/31614/8076781.html

28. TRANSSA (Trans Siempre Amigas), "Hieren una transgenera en República Dominicana y asesinan otra en ciudad de Guatemala," accessed April 7, 2013, http://transsadominicana1.blogspot.com/2009/10.

29. Monica Rhor,"US Grants Asylum to Gay Man: Rules Dominican Faced Threat at Home," *Boston Globe*, Sept. 5, 2003, accessed April 7, 2013, http://www.highbeam.com/doc/1P2–7801683.html.

30. Loren King, "Gay Man Living in Boston Seeks Political Asylum: Hearing Slated for August 19," *Bay Windows*, Aug. 15, 1996, 3, accessed April 7, 2013, http://www.asylumlaw.org/docs/sexualminorities/Dominican%20Republic%202_36683E.pdf.

31. Human Rights Campaign, *Human Rights Campaign News*, Aug. 20, 1996.

32. Rhor, "US Grants Asylum to Gay Man," accessed April 7, 2013, http://www.asylumlaw.org/docs/sexualminorities/Dominican%20Republic%202_36683E.pdf

33. Antoine Pécoud and Paul de Guchteneire, "International Migration, Border Controls and Human Rights: Assessing the Relevance of a Right to Mobility," *Journal of Borderlands Studies* 21, no. 1 (2006): 69–86.

34. Balaguer's authoritarian regime began in 1966 following his triumph over Juan Bosch in the 1966 noncompetitive elections sponsored by the US and the Organization of American States (OAS), led at the time by Latin American military regimes. These elections put an end to the 1963–1965 political turmoil and US military occupation triggered by the assassination of General Rafael Trujillo and the military coup that broke down Bosch's brief presidency, following the demise of Trujillo's bloody and long-standing dictatorship (1930–1961).

35. Ramona Hernández, *The Mobility of Workers under Advanced Capitalism: Dominican Migration to the United States* (New York: Columbia University Press, 2002), 8–9.

36. Ibid., 12.
37. Ramona Hernández and Francisco L. Rivera-Batiz, *Dominicans in the United States: A Socieconomic Profile, 2000* (New York: CUNY Dominican Studies Institute, 2003).
38. Jacqueline Jiménez Polanco, "República Dominicana: Crecimiento macro-económico y estabilidad Política versus desigualdad social e insatisfacción popular," *Revista de Ciencia Política*, 14, no. 2 (2010): 479–498.
39. Ibid.
40. Northern Manhattan Coalition for Immigrant Rights (NMCIR), "Domini-cano, Deportado y Humano . . .", 6, 8, 12, accessed April 7, 2013, http://www.nmcir.org/Deportado%20Dominicano%20y%20Humano.pdf.
41. Mario Conseco, "Anti-immigrant Sentiment Rising in Britain: Community of Interest," *Vancouver Sun*, accessed April 7, 2013, http://blogs.vancouver-sun.com/category/community/politics-community/community-of-interest/page/33/
42. Mullins, "Seeking Asylum."
43. *La Colectiva*'s leadership boycotted 'Germinando Ideas' as soon as it noticed that the group was getting out of its absolute control due to the independent scope of the young, radical feminist-lesbian leaders.
44. José Rafael Sosa, "Grupos sociales de RD reclaman sus derechos," *El Nacional*, accessed April 9, 2013, http://www.elnacional.com.do/nacional/2010/2/3/38750/Grupos-sociales-de-RD-reclaman-sus-derechos.

11 Becoming Legible and 'Legitimized'

Subjectivation and Governmentality among Asylum Seekers in Ireland

Deirdre Conlon

The Republic of Ireland's long history as a sending country for migrants is a familiar story, and the country's designation as an "emigrant nursery"[1] was apt when migrant outflows exceeded inflows and natural population growth for most of the nineteenth and twentieth centuries. Recently, there was a dramatic—albeit short-lived—change in this familiar account. Coinciding with an unprecedented period of economic growth, as well as political and social transformations, Ireland experienced a momentous shift in migration trends. Beginning in the mid-1990s and for roughly a decade, the number of immigrant arrivals to Ireland consistently exceeded emigration from the country. Although the rate of emigration has picked up again in association with the current global economic slowdown,[2] the impact of inward migration in Irish society and, more specifically, the ways in which asylum seekers become legible and 'legitimized' in this context are worthy of attention.

Asylum seekers and refugees—for whom migration is often spurred by violence, conflict and unrest, as well as natural and manmade disasters[3]—have been a dominant focus as migration studies has burgeoned in Ireland. Labor migration has garnered attention comparatively recently, with scholarship examining the experiences of migrant workers from European Union (EU) accession states, including Poland, Latvia and Lithuania,[4] analyses of remittance practices[5] and comparisons with broader EU labor issues.[6] The early and dominant emphasis on asylum seekers and refugees reflects the rhythm of migration flows in Ireland. Initially, inward migration was marked by growth in the asylum seeker population; an upswing in labor migration occurred later and was spurred by EU expansions in 2004 and 2007. In addition, for several years, asylum seekers and refugees—in Ireland and throughout Europe—have been subjected to intense scrutiny as national and international spheres have grown increasingly inhospitable to asylum seeker and refugee flows.[7] In Ireland, this sentiment coalesced around citizenship rights. As is still the case in the US, until 2004 Ireland was among a handful of states to grant birthright citizenship. Coinciding with this, Ireland's Supreme Court also granted residency rights to noncitizen parents whose children, having been born in Ireland, were automatically Irish citizens. As the number of foreign-born residents arriving in Ireland grew, these constitutionally enshrined provisions became flash points for anti-immigration platforms in political and popular cultural spheres. In 2003, the Irish Supreme Court removed guarantees of parental residency rights for noncitizens. Subsequently, in 2004, a constitutional referendum was held wherein 79 percent of the electorate voted to do away with birthright citizenship, instead replacing it with the *jus sanguinis* doctrine, in which citizenship rights are determined by familial descent or in association with establishing a legal right to belong.[8] The highly charged nature of these issues has led asylum seekers and refugees to become a focal point for popular cultural and social science discourse and research on migration issues.

This chapter furthers the discussion of immigration within this context with a focus on asylum seekers and refugees in particular. My interest lies in presenting a nuanced analysis of asylum seekers' encounters with Irish society and governance therein. Specifically, I examine how asylum seekers are called upon to present themselves in ways that make them legible to members of the receiving country in the hope that they will be granted status as a 'legitimate refugee'. The chapter draws on a qualitative study that included examination of discourses and experiences encountered routinely by asylum seekers and interview narratives from women asylum seekers who participated in the study. The analysis engages Michel Foucault's writings on discourses of confession, micropractices and the ways in which pastoral power and governmental mechanisms intersect while shaping the subjectivation or construction of the asylum seeker subject.

I begin with an overview of historical trends and shifts toward immigration in Irish society. I then situate global trends with regard to asylum seekers as the backdrop to discussing how legibility and legitimacy have come to assume great importance within European societies, where, of late, those seeking refugee status are met with increasingly restrictive migration policies. Following a brief account of Foucault's discussion of governmentality, I turn to the experiences of asylum seeker women in contemporary Ireland in order to illustrate how becoming legible is linked with pastoral power and practices of governmentality. Becoming legible and being understood as a 'legitimate' refugee require that these individuals understand themselves as 'asylum seeker' subjects.[9] Using interviewees' accounts as well as observations about discourses that circulate amid asylum seekers' routine exchanges, I highlight how micropractices are connected to subjectivation and self-management through governmental means.

FROM 'EMIGRANT NURSERY' TO IMMIGRANT SOCIETY: AN OVERVIEW

As previously noted, Ireland has a well-established relationship to migration. Until recently much scholarship on Irish migration called attention to the dominance of emigration, and its impact in Irish society.[10] Several accounts also detail the experiences of Irish emigrants abroad, particularly in the US and UK, and contribute to understanding processes of migrant integration.[11] Emigration trends have endured throughout most of the twentieth century and up to the present time; thus Irish society is commonly understood as one of the emigrant nurseries for the modern world. Although net migration was positive for a brief period in the 1970s, the slow pace of economic growth and correspondingly high levels of unemployment meant that mass emigration returned in the 1980s. As recently as the period between 1988 and 1989, approximately 2 percent of the Irish population left the country.[12] As a consequence of sustained emigration there are almost three million Irish citizens living overseas today; 1.2 million of these individuals were born in Ireland.[13]

In 1996, however, there was a remarkable shift in this state of affairs. That year, the number of people entering the country as immigrants exceeded emigrant outflow. With this, a net migration figure of 8,000 people was recorded; this figure jumped to 22,800 in 1998, with additional marked increases through 2006.[14] Recently, inward migration has dwindled considerably, and in 2009 the rate of emigration exceeded immigration for the first time since the mid-1990s.[15] Nonetheless, the rapid shift in migration trends continues to exert profound effects within Irish society. Among the several factors that account for this shift, perhaps the single most important was a period of successful, and now enviable, economic growth. This phenomenon—dubbed the 'Celtic Tiger'—helped transform Ireland's standing as one of Europe's consistently underperforming economies into a place that offered attractive investment and employment opportunities, a relatively high standard of living and the promise of a cosmopolitan lifestyle.[16]

Against this backdrop, immigration to Ireland became a viable and attractive option for significant numbers of people, so much so that over a span of roughly a decade, the proportion of foreign-born residents grew to 10 percent of the overall population and now surpasses countries with much longer immigration histories, such as the UK and France.[17] Ireland's immigrant population includes returning Irish migrants, labor migrants, asylum seekers and those who have been granted refugee status. Table 11.1 presents a broad overview of in-migration classified by region of origin. Although these data do not disaggregate distinct migrant categories, they provide an indication of the shifting rhythm of migration flows, with significant increases in migration from areas other than Europe and the US giving way to recent waves made up largely of migrants from within the European Union.

Among the groups arriving in Ireland, former emigrants returning to live in Ireland made up a substantial number initially; Ní Laoire observes that from 1996 to 2006 return migrants made up between 20 percent and 50 percent of net migration flows to Ireland.[18] Concurrent with recent expansions of the European Union, more recent waves of immigrants to Ireland, as elsewhere in Europe, are largely made up of labor migrants from Central and Eastern Europe, with significant numbers coming from Poland, Lithuania and Latvia, as well as from Slovakia and the Czech Republic. Between 1997 and 2007 the percentage of migrants from all regions working in the Irish labor force increased from 3 to 16 percent.[19]

Table 11.1   Immigration to Ireland Classified by Region of Origin

Immigration to Ireland (000)	1996	1998	2000	2002	2004	2006	Total
Irish	17.7	24.3	24.8	27.0	16.7	18.9	129.4
UK	8.3	8.6	8.4	7.4	7.4	9.9	50.0
EU	5.0	6.1	8.2	8.1	13.3	62.6 *	103.3
US	4.0	2.3	2.5	2.7	2.3	1.7	15.5
Rest of world	4.0	4.7	8.6	21.7	18.8	14.7	72.5
Total	39.0	46.0	52.5	66.9	58.5	107.8	370.7

* Includes immigration after EU enlargement on May 1, 2004, to include Cyprus, Czech Republic, Estonia, Hungary, Latvia, Lithuania, Malta, Poland, Slovakia and Slovenia. For 1996–2004 these countries are included with 'Rest of world'.
Source: Central Statistics Office (CSO), "Population and Migration Estimates 2003–2009" accessed August 2009, http://www.cso.ie.

Asylum seekers and refugees are another category of migrants in Ireland. The designation of asylum seeker refers to individuals who have been forced to leave their usual place of residence on account of disaster, conflict or fear of persecution, whereas the classification of 'refugee' is reserved for individuals whose requests to reside in a given host country have been granted in accordance with UN Convention and UNHCR guidelines—in effect, 'legitimacy' as a refugee has been attained.[20] As a proportion of the overall population, asylum seekers make up approximately 10 percent of recent in-migration to Ireland.[21] Table 11.2 shows notable increases in the number of individuals seeking asylum between 1996 and 2002, which was the year asylum applications peaked at 11,634. By 2006, however, the number of applications declined to 4,314.[22] Several factors contributed to this dramatic decrease; Ireland's changing economic fortune and persistent antagonism toward asylum seekers played a role, but perhaps the most significant factor was the outcome of the 2004 citizenship referendum.[23] As previously mentioned, the referendum replaced birthright citizenship with citizenship via familial lineage or legal mechanisms. Although it is beyond the scope of this chapter to give a detailed account of this process, it will suffice to note that through the referendum autonomous voters 'reterritorialized'[24] the nation-state, which served to 'secure' Ireland's population by thwarting and curtailing the entry of asylum seekers.[25] Recently arrived asylum seekers in Ireland have come from states including China, Sudan, Georgia and Iraq.[26] At the time of this study in 2004, Nigeria and Romania were the largest single source countries for individuals seeking refugee status in Ireland.[27]

The absence of a comprehensive comparative framework with regard to race and ethnicity, or even where migrant categories are disaggregated, complicates assessments of stratification.[28] However, it seems that recent

Table 11.2　Applications for Asylum in the Republic of Ireland, 1992–2006

Year	No. of asylum applications
1992	39
1993	91
1994	362
1995	424
1996	1,179
1997	3,883
1998	4,626
1999	7,724
2000	10,938
2001	10,325
2002	11,634
2003	7 900
2004	4,766
2005	4,323
2006	4,314

rapid demographic shifts have merely exacerbated existing patterns of stratification and exclusion in Ireland. For example, in 2004, among arrivals from outside the EU, unemployment was almost three times higher than among Irish nationals and higher than the rate for EU migrants.[29] In addition, ethnic and racial minorities and foreign-born groups report a higher frequency of occurrences of discrimination—on measures such as using public transportation, accessing health services and in the workplace—than other groups.[30] In general, it appears that all immigrants, but especially those from areas outside the EU, are subject to patterns of exclusion and discrimination that have been long-standing practices in Irish society. In this chapter, I suggest that these patterns are bolstered by policies and practices that affect asylum seekers in Ireland in particular ways. Before examining these practices and their impact in detail, an overview of global and EU policy trends will help to further contextualize Irish society within current migration and asylum regimes.

COMPELLING 'LEGIBILITY': SEEKING ASYLUM AMID INCREASINGLY RESTRICTIVE MIGRATION REGIMES

The flow of asylum seekers, numeric trends, and policy and practices for this population follow a pattern reflecting the development of increasingly restrictive migration regimes across Europe and globally. An overview of these trends thus proves instructive in understanding the circumstances that compel these individuals to become 'legible' as asylum seekers. Globally, in 2006, the UN High Commissioner for Refugees reported an estimated population of 744,000 asylum seekers.[31] Of this group, almost 38 percent applied for refugee status in industrialized countries including North America, Australia and European Union (EU) states. Of these 290,000 people, just under one-quarter, or approximately 69,000 individuals, were granted refugee status in accordance with UN Convention guidelines.[32] From this, it is reasonable to deduce that the stakes are rather high when it comes to possibilities for 'success' in being granted refugee status.

In recent years, the number of individuals applying for asylum, or refugee status, in industrialized countries has declined markedly. When data on asylum seekers in industrialized countries are compared over the five-year period prior to 2006, we find that applications for asylum in these countries have halved. In 2006, throughout Europe, applications for asylum were the lowest in twenty years; in the same year, Ireland reported the smallest number of applications for refugee status since 1997.[33] The UNHCR identifies several factors that may influence these downward trends. These include declining threats to security associated with the end of conflict and improvements in living conditions in a number of regions that have been source countries for asylum seekers in recent years. Declines in arrivals to industrialized countries are also attributed to increasingly stringent border control measures and ever more restrictive policies for asylum seekers.[34] Among these are policies such as the Schengen Treaty, 1985, Dublin Convention, 1990, and Dublin II Regulation, 2003, which harmonize EU regulations on immigration and asylum, stipulating where and when an application for refugee status must be filed, as well as laying out conditions allowing for the immediate discharge of asylum seekers to another country. In effect, EU borders have become increasingly fortified, and there is little doubt that these immigration policies have been instrumental in the declining number of asylum seekers arriving in Ireland and elsewhere in Europe in recent years.

The remainder of the chapter focuses on the way these trends and policies impact the subjectivation of asylum seekers. I take Foucault's perspectives on governmentality as a lens for examining this process. Following a brief introduction to Foucault's work in this area, the discussion turns to experiences recounted during interviews with several women asylum seekers in Ireland. By homing in on one account, which was as compelling as it was disturbing and telling, I illustrate how individuals seeking refuge in states like Ireland come to apprehend themselves as part of a process that demands that they fashion, construct and govern themselves in ways that legitimize the asylum seeker subject. Being confronted with tighter controls, ever more intricate regulations and greater 'competition' for the 'coveted' yet increasingly inaccessible status of refugee helps to produce a set of circumstances in which the exacting and transparent presentation of the 'asylum seeker' self garners considerable weight in the desire to be understood, legible and ultimately 'legitimized' as an authentic refugee.

GOVERNMENTALITY AND SUBJECTIVATION

Numerous scholars have detailed the significance of Michel Foucault's *oeuvre* in seeking to understand and critically examine society and culture.[35] One enduring theme that has been put to productive use in the social sciences is Foucault's attention to the historical emergence, interconnectedness and dynamic forms of power and knowledge in society.[36] In numerous of his writings this interest is articulated in a concern with government and governmentality. Foucault traces the history and continuity of different formations of power and knowledge, including territorial controls executed by sovereign states; government by disciplinary mechanisms that work to order, prohibit and occlude; pastoral power focused on the salvation of an individuated population; and finally the analysis of neoliberal techniques in which free, or liberal, individuals govern themselves by actively participating in processes of their own production.[37] Interest in neoliberal forms of government has increased with the translation into English of *Security, Territory, Population* as well as *The Birth of Biopolitics*.[38] Among the issues these works highlight is the imbrication of pastoral power with the workings of modern mechanisms of governmental power.

Central to Foucault's perspective is an understanding of government beyond its political form as the domain of states or elected bodies. For Foucault, government refers to perceptions, conduct and actions at the individual and social level; it is the form "by which, in our culture, human beings are made subjects."[39] According to Huxley, studying governmentality therefore involves attending to the processes and practices by which individuals and society "fashion and guide the bodily comportment and inward states of others and of the self."[40] This conception of government invites a focus on some of the ways in which individuals who are given the designation 'asylum seeker' come to apprehend, represent and conduct themselves as subjects. I contend that these processes are acutely significant in efforts to secure the legibility and legitimacy of asylum claims, and hence the possibility of being granted refugee status.

I draw on observational data and one-to-one interviews focused on accounts of everyday life and routine encounters with twenty-five women who self-identified as 'asylum seeker' or 'refugee' when presented with a range of possible migrant categories.[41] These women had arrived in Ireland from countries including Nigeria, Uzbekistan, Iraq and the Democratic Republic of Congo. They ranged in age between nineteen and forty-three years, with an average age of thirty-two years. At the time they were interviewed participants had resided in Ireland between six months and six years; average length of residency was 2.4 years. In conversations with these women one of the questions asked was, "What was it that brought you to Ireland?" Responses to this question were frequently disturbing and quite difficult for interview participants to recount. Despite this, I suggest this distressing process is necessary because it enacts a confessional, which comes to be understood as crucial to asylum seekers' subjectivation, to the manner in which they govern—or conduct—themselves and thus to the general process and practices of governing asylum.

LESSONS IN CONFESSING

Among many compelling and disturbing accounts provided by the women I interviewed was that of Ana, who had come to Ireland from Nigeria.[42] In the discussion that follows, I focus on her narrative to highlight the role that learning to 'confess' plays in asylum seekers' subjectivation. When I asked Ana to explain what had brought her to Ireland, she noted that she had been forced to leave the oil-rich Rivers State region of Nigeria, where she and her husband had been business owners. Ana explained that several years earlier her husband had gone into hiding because his life and family members' lives had been threatened in association with his involvement in political and social justice activism focused on indigenous oil rights in the region. While authorities searched for her husband, Ana was subjected to excruciating circumstances that, for many people, seem unimaginable. Her phones were tapped, her mail was intercepted and eventually military authorities detained her for a period of five months. Ana's captors wanted to know her husband's whereabouts. In the attempt to garner this information, Ana was tortured and traumatized even further by being forced to witness the torture of others; on one of these occasions she was forced to watch a woman being buried alive.

Ana was not alone in recounting such distressing circumstances. Another woman, also from Nigeria, explained that prior to arrival in Ireland she had been a medical doctor living in the capital city of Abuja. She explained that when she left her home and a successful professional career, she did so without her husband and with only four of her five children. The reason was her eldest daughter had been murdered in retaliation for her husband's involvement in political activities. Another young woman from Ghana reported that she had been enslaved in a forced labor camp for eight years. In her case, she had been brought to Ireland with assistance from a priest who helped her escape and facilitated her passage to Ireland. Yet another described her family's experience as indentured laborers who had lived on a plot of land provided by her father's 'employer'. She explained that her family had lost everything, including their home and piece of land, because of a feud between tribal groups. Three other women recounted how they were ostracized by family members or harassed, hounded and ultimately expelled from their communities because they had married across ethnic or religious lines. Still others detailed how they had been forced to leave their homes when their families' lives had been threatened because of political views or involvement with organizations that opposed dominant political views.

Almost half of the participants in this qualitative study were eager to give an account of their lives and the conflicts and unrest that had spurred them to leave their homes prior to becoming asylum seekers in Ireland. This was the case in spite of becoming upset in the process of recounting these—often—harrowing circumstances. Furthermore, these 'confessions' ran counter to forewarnings I was given at the outset of my project. As is common in social science research, at the outset of the study I met with representatives from organizations working with asylum seekers and refugees.[43] They offered insights on key migration issues and assistance in recruiting participants and scheduling interviews; these gatekeepers also advised me on the need for sensitivity in interviewing asylum seekers. They warned against probing too deeply into personal histories, particularly prior to arriving in Ireland, noting that to do so might open up troubling traumas, interfere with the integrity of the research relationship or matters of confidentiality and expose the dilemmas and delicate politics of asylum.[44] In spite of this, interviewees' narratives indicate that many women felt compelled to 'confess' the circumstances surrounding departure from their home country. The eagerness of these disclosures is indicative of the powerful and productive effects of confession for asylum seekers. It also highlights the intersections between pastoral power and the micropractices associated with governmentality.

In *The History of Sexuality* Foucault traces the significance of confession in the emergence of sex as a discourse to the Middle Ages. From this period onward, and increasingly pried from religious spheres, confession has become a mechanism for the production of truth, and thus a means of establishing acceptable forms of knowledge. As Foucault notes:

> The confession became one of the West's most highly valued techniques for producing truth. We have since become a singularly confessing society. The confession has spread its effects far and wide. It plays a part in justice, medicine, education, family relationships, and love relations, in the most ordinary affairs of everyday life, and in the most solemn rites: one confesses one's crimes, one's sins, one's thoughts and desires, one's illnesses and troubles; one goes about telling, with the greatest precision, what is most difficult to tell.[45]

Over time, confession has become deeply ingrained in all facets of individual life as well as throughout society. For asylum seekers the apparent compulsion to 'confess' highlights this process and also reveals one of the ways pastoral power suffuses governmental power and the practices of the modern state. For individuals who are seeking asylum, recounting the traumas and conflicts they have experienced enacts techniques such as vigilant self-examination and the discursive rendition of daily life, which originated in monasteries, spilled over into Christian society and now infuse secular society. These scrutinizing practices are not merely a way to produce one's own truth, one's subjectivity as an asylum seeker; in addition, they become a benchmark against which others' asylum claims are measured and thereby work to establish the legitimacy of asylum seekers as a population in a more general way. In this sense, the mechanisms that govern asylum make confession a requirement. In conjunction with the ever-increasing restrictions associated with European Union policies related to asylum, compulsions to confess take on even greater importance. As the number of places where asylum seekers may seek refuge diminishes and the probability of successfully achieving refugee status shrinks, the need for an account that adequately authenticates the individual as an asylum seeker subject gains even greater weight. Because these accounts have such grave consequences, acts of confession must be practiced well. Beyond their implications for individual subjectivity and the asylum seeker population as a whole, these lessons in confessing reveal what Golder identifies as "the theological basis of modern state power."[46] To better appreciate these connections, I turn attention to some of the overlaps between confession, pastoral power and micropractices of governmentality.

LEARNING TO BE LEGIBLE: PASTORAL POWER AND MICROPRACTICES OF GOVERNMENTALITY

It might be tempting to view asylum seekers' accounts of conflict and trauma somewhat skeptically as consciously managed or manipulated performances, as described by Erving Goffman, rather than performative in the sense that Judith Butler—drawing on Foucault's work—suggests.[47] For both Butler and Foucault, to manage one's subjectivation in some preconceived way is implausible because individuals are produced through what Foucault describes as the "art of government".[48] For individuals who hope to be granted refugee status, this 'art' and corresponding practices of subjectivation are enacted through a range of mechanisms including myriad discourses and ongoing micropractices in which asylum seekers must 'reveal' themselves repeatedly in hopes that the circumstances they have endured will confirm that they are worthy of salvation. Asylum seekers confront these situations from the time they arrive in Ireland to the moment a decision on the viability of their claim is delivered. To highlight some of these practices and the ways they are tied to asylum seeker subjectivation, Ana's experience is, once again, illustrative.

When she first arrived in Ireland with her two children, Ana noted she "wasn't aware of this idea of asylum"; for her, asylum was a foreign concept.[49] What had brought her to Ireland specifically was news that her

husband was alive and staying in Dublin. With that, and through a complicated journey, Ana managed to leave Nigeria in an effort to find and reunite
with her husband. Within a few hours of her arrival, and following several
misadventures, Ana learned that her husband was no longer at the address
she had been given. As she became more distraught a taxi driver suggested
the best place to go with her predicament was the office of the Department
of Justice, Equality and Law Reform, the state organization responsible
for handling applications for refugee status in Ireland. Ana took the taxi
driver's advice. Once there she was placed in a reception center and subsequently 'dispersed' to an accommodation center with other asylum seekers
in accordance with the Irish government's policies for asylum seekers.

Ana recounted that her initial meetings with Department of Justice
officials and social support staff were a source of frustration because of
a question she was constantly being asked. The question, "What was
the basis for her asylum claim," was one Ana did not understand; as
a result she invariably explained that she was simply "there to find her
husband."[50] It was only when she laid out details of her detention and
persecution in Nigeria, Ana realized, that she began to make sense to
the people around her in Ireland. In other words, it was only when she
recounted a particular presentation of asylum seeker subjectivity that she
became legible and comprehensible.

This encounter illustrates several interrelated points. First, asylum seekers do not arrive in Ireland with an implicit sense of themselves as subjects
of asylum. Instead, through a continuous assortment of mundane encounters—or micropractices of government—these individuals come to realize
that becoming legible and potentially legitimized necessitates their subjuga-
tion as asylum seekers. Ordinary encounters reinforce particular constellations of conduct for the entire asylum seeker population as it becomes
evident that persistent self-examination, self-disclosure and obedience are
mechanisms through which the legitimacy of refugee claims is established.
As Foucault suggests, these ongoing practices require that "one confesses—
or is forced to confess."[51] These processes also instantiate pastoral care as
a way to govern the asylum seeker population as a whole. Furthermore,
through this legitimizing process, salvation—being granted refugee status—is possible. In this way pastoral power suffuses governmental power
while also affirming micropolitical mechanisms of government.

BECOMING LEGITIMATE THROUGH
NEOLIBERAL GOVERNMENTALITY

These everyday encounters are bolstered by agencies that provide advice
to asylum seekers in advance of interviews and hearings related to their
asylum claims. The processing of asylum claims involves what is referred
to as a 'substantive interview' with officials from the Department of Justice

and Refugee Applications Commissioner's Office, the state body responsible for assessing the viability of applicants' requests for refugee status. In Ireland, several organizations provide guidelines—primarily in the form of pamphlets and web-based guides—to asylum seekers, to help familiarize them with the refugee claim process and to prepare them for what will be the ultimate act of confession. A typical example of the advice that is distributed in leaflets and websites is outlined in Table 11.3.

These guides advise asylum seekers to "explain in detail why they fear returning to their country of origin", offer reminders to do so "clearly and precisely" and issue warnings of possible negative consequences if the asylum seeker does not fulfill his or her duty "to co-operate fully and to be completely truthful." These discourses resound elements of pastoral power by emphasizing obedience and an obligation to 'the truth'. Simultaneously, they reflect neoliberal formations of power and government that place the burden of establishing authenticity on asylum seekers themselves; in this sense, asylum seekers are produced as individuated, autonomous subjects. Overall, these discourses reinforce particular instantiations of asylum seekers as individuated subjects and as a population that is compelled—again and again—to obediently produce cogent accounts of the circumstances leading to their forced migration.

This emphasis on an individuated population alongside notions of beneficence further highlights how pastoral power girds governmentality in the management of asylum. The distinctions between government via disciplinary mechanisms and Foucault's later work on biopower and related neoliberal forms of government are well known.[52] Disciplinary mechanisms focus on the individual and are associated with processes and institutions that monitor, segment and isolate individuals. Neoliberal government, infused with pastoral power, targets a flock or a group of people. Foucault describes

Table 11.3   Example of 'Substantive Interview' Advice Guidelines

Substantive interview process	*Advice to asylum seekers*
Purpose	"to establish full details of your claim"
What asylum seekers should do	"explain clearly and precisely your fears"
Asylum seekers' responsibilities	"your opportunity to explain in detail why you fear returning to your country of origin" "co-operate fully and be completely truthful"

Source: Citizens Advice Bureau, "Investigation of applications for refugee status in Ireland by the Refugee Applications Commissioner," last updated June 25, 2009, accessed April 16, 2013, http://www.citizensinformation.ie/en/moving_country/asylum_seekers_and_refugees/the_asylum_process_in_ireland/how_refugee_applications_commissioner_deals_with_applications.html.

pastoral power as an individualizing power that requires "care for each and every member of the flock."[53] This form of power combines with neoliberal governmentality marked, as Rouse suggests, by an "avalanche of printed numbers."[54] In this process, masses of data are gathered that permit the categorization, sorting and incorporation of particular population groups, while obedient, truth-telling, enterprising and self-directed individuals are simultaneously produced.

For asylum seekers, the substantive interview becomes a significant site where these processes culminate. There, responsible confessing asylum seekers are called upon to make themselves legible, and thus to authenticate and legitimate themselves. As this process is repeated over and over, a mass of data accumulates; the resulting evidence works to normalize an individuated population and to exclude those who are 'illegible' or 'illegitimate' in some way. The process enacts a form of charity for those whose claims are deemed truthful by awarding legitimized asylum seekers the right to remain. The interview also serves to 'weed out' those whose confessions are not sound, thereby guaranteeing the security of the population as a whole by differentiating those who can from those who cannot, or who ought not, be saved. Overall, these micropractices, which emanate from sources including institutions and discourses, as well as day-to-day encounters, mutually reinforce each other, producing legible asylum seekers, sorting legitimate and apparently illegitimate subjects, and ultimately, managing this population through governmental means.

We can extract a number of concluding points from this study of individual asylum seekers' narratives and experiences in Ireland. As is the case in other Western industrialized societies, there have been substantial declines in numbers of individuals seeking asylum in recent years. Several observers identify the enactment of increasingly restrictive immigration policies, often in the name of border security, as a significant contributor to this downward trend. In this chapter, I have suggested that Foucault's analysis of governmentality offers an important adjunct in understanding the effects of such policies and trends at the individual and social level. Immigration policies work in tandem with a range of spaces and mechanisms of government, including state institutions, nongovernmental organizations, discourses and practices of pastoral power and micropractices that characterize the neoliberal everyday. These mechanisms compel individuals who are seeking refugee status to articulate their lives in accordance with particular regimes of knowledge, truth and power. In turn, this autonomously enacted presentation of the self reinforces a regime of truth, and institutes a sorting mechanism, whereby asylum seekers whose requests for sanctuary are seen to be more unreliable or, apparently, untrue can be 'weeded out' from those whose requests are deemed intelligible and worthy. Through these governmental processes of subjectivation, forced migrants, in Ireland and elsewhere, become legible and—on occasion—'legitimized' asylum seeker subjects.

NOTES

1. Jim MacLaughlin, *Ireland: The Emigrant Nursery and the World Economy* (Cork: Cork University Press, 1994).
2. Central Statistics Office (CSO), *Population and Migration Estimates* (Dublin: Stationers Office, 2009), accessed Sept. 8, 2009http://www.cso.ie/releasespublications/documents/population/current/popmig.pdf.
3. Stephen Castles, "Towards a Sociology of Forced Migration and Social Transformation," *Sociology: A Journal of the British Sociological Association* 37 (2003): 13–34.
4. Brian McCormick, "Analysis of the Irish Labour Market and Immigration since EU Enlargement," *Translocations Migration and Social Change* 3, no. 1 (2008): 142–152.
5. Moira McCarthy, "The Study of Migrant Remittances from Ireland," *Translocations Migration and Social Change* 4, no. 1 (2009): 144–152.
6. Ian Shuttleworth, "Reconceptualising Local Labour Markets in the Context of Cross-Border and Transnational Labour Flows: The Irish Example," *Political Geography* 26, no. 8 (2007): 968–981.
7. For discussion see: Lisa Schuster, "A Sledgehammer to Crack a Nut: Deportation, Detention and Dispersal in Europe," *Social Policy & Administration* 39 (2005): 606–621, and S. Collinson, "Visa Requirements, Carrier Sanctions, 'Safe Third Countries' and 'Readmission': The Development of an Asylum 'Buffer Zone' in Europe," *Transactions of the Institute of British Geographers* 21, no. 1 (1996): 76–90.
8. For discussion see: Deirdre Conlon, "Ties that Bind: Governmentality, the state and asylum in contemporary Ireland" *Environment and Planning D: Society and Space* 28, no. 1 (2010): 95–111, and Mary Gilmartin and Alan White, "Revisiting Contemporary Irish Migration: New Geographies of Mobility and Belonging," *Irish Geography* 41 (2008): 143–149.
9. The larger study focused on women's migration—both historical and recent—in social and cultural productions of the Irish nation-state; see Deirdre Conlon, "The Nation as Embodied Practice: Women, Migration and the Social Production of Nationhood in Ireland" (PhD diss., City University of New York, 2007).
10. Joseph Lee, *Ireland 1912–1985: Politics and Society* (Cambridge: Cambridge University Press, 1989), and Michael O'Connell, *Changed Utterly: Ireland and the New Irish Psyche* (Dublin: Liffey Press, 2001).
11. For example: Kerby Miller, *Emigrants and Exiles: Ireland and the Irish Exodus to North America* (Oxford: Oxford University Press, 1988); Noel Ignatiev, *How the Irish Became White* (New York: Routledge, 1996); Bronwen White, *Outsiders Inside: Whiteness, Place and Irish Women* (London: Routledge, 2001); and Breda Gray, *Women and the Irish Diaspora* (London: Routledge, 2004).
12. P. MacÉinrí, "Immigration: Labour Migrants, Asylum Seekers and Refugees," in *Understanding Contemporary Ireland*, ed. B. Bartley and R. Kitchin (London: Pluto, 2007), 237.
13. Martin Ruhs, *Ireland: A Crash Course in Immigration Policy* (Washington, DC: Migration Policy Institute, 2004).
14. Central Statistics Office (CSO), *Measuring Ireland's Progress—Indicators Report Volume 1* (Dublin: Stationery Office, 2003), accessed July 14, 2008, http://www.cso.ie/en/releasesandpublications/othercsopublications/measuringirelandsprogressvolumes1and2/.
15. Central Statistics Office (CSO), *Population and Migration Estimates* (Dublin: Stationery Office, 2009), accessed Sept. 20, 2009, http://www.cso.ie/releasespublications/documents/population/current/popmig.pdf.

16. Deirdre Conlon, "Fascinatin' Rhythm(s): Polyrhythmia and the Syncopated Echoes of the Everyday," in *Geographies of Rhythm*, ed. T. Edensor (Aldershot: Ashgate, 2010), 71–83.

17. Office of Economic Cooperation and Development, *OECD Economic Surveys: Ireland 2008* (Paris: OECD, 2008).

18. Caitriona Ní Laoire, "'Settling Back'? A Biographical and Life-Course Perspective on Ireland's Recent Return Migration," *Irish Geography* 1 (2008): 195–210.

19. This a dynamic figure; with rising unemployment significant numbers of EU-migrants have left Ireland. The data indicate, among those emigrating in 2009, EU-migrants make up the largest single group at 30.1 percent of the total; see notes 10 and 22.

20. James Hathaway, *Reconceiving International Refugee Law* (The Hague: Klewer Law International, 1997).

21. Ronit Lentin and Robbie McVeigh, *Racism and Anti-racism in Ireland* (Belfast: Beyond the Pale, 2002), and idem, *After Optimism? Ireland, Racism and Globalization* (Dublin: Metro Éireann, 2006).

22. Office of the Refugee Applications Commissioner, *Annual Report and Statistics* (Dublin: ORAC, 2007), accessed Aug. 14, 2008, http://www.orac.ie.

23. For insights on migrants' experiences of racism and antagonism in Ireland, see Steve Garner, *Racism in the Irish Experience* (London: Pluto, 2004), and Patricia Kelleher and Carmel Kelleher, *Voices of Immigrants: The Challenges of Inclusion* (Dublin: Immigrant Council of Ireland, 2004).

24. Jeremy Crampton and Stuart Elden, *Space, Knowledge and Power: Foucault and Geography* (Ashgate: Aldershot, 2007), 683.

25. For a detailed discussion of governmentality and the citizenship referendum, see Deirdre Conlon, "Ties That Bind: Governmentality, the State and Asylum in Contemporary Ireland," *Environment and Planning D: Society and Space* 28, no. 1 (2010): 95–111.

26. Office of the Refugee Applications Commissioner, *Annual Report and Statistics*.

27. Migrants arriving from Romania were categorized as asylum seekers prior to this country joining the European Union in January 2007.

28. Jane Pillinger, *The Feminisation of Migration: Experiences and Opportunities in Ireland* (Dublin: Immigrant Council of Ireland, 2007).

29. 2004 unemployment rates were as follows: Irish 4.8 percent, EU 7.9 percent and other areas 12.7 percent. See, Office of the Refugee Applications Commissioner (ORAC), *2007 Annual Report* (Dublin: ORAC, 2007), accessed April 16, 2013, http://www.orac.ie/website/orac/oracwebsite.nsf/page/publications-main-en

30. Lentin and McVeigh, *Racism and Anti-racism in Ireland*; *After Optimism?*.

31. At time of writing, this was the most complete annual set of figures available. Asylum seekers are a subset of the overall population of concern to the UNHCR, estimated at 32.9 million persons in 2006. See UNHCR, *Statistical Yearbook 2006: Trends in Displacement, Protection and Solutions* (Geneva: UNHCR, 2006).

32. This includes Convention status granted in the first instance and on appeal. An additional thirty-eight thousand were granted the status of 'leave to remain' on humanitarian grounds; see note 34.

33. Irish Refugee Council, "20-Year Low for Asylum Applications," press release, 2007, accessed Mar. 4, 2009, http://www.irishrefugeecouncil.ie/press07/unhcr.html.

34. UNHCR, *Statistical Yearbook 2006*.

35. For example: Hubert Dreyfus and Paul Rabinow, *Michel Foucault: Beyond Structuralism and Hermeneutics* (London: Harvester Wheatsheaf, 1982); Gary Gutting, *The Cambridge Companion to Foucault* (Cambridge: Cambridge University Press, 2005); and Clare O'Farrell, *Michel Foucault* (Thousand Oaks: SAGE, 2005).
36. Joseph Rouse, "Power/Knowledge," in *The Cambridge Companion to Foucault*, ed. G. Gutting (Cambridge: Cambridge University Press, 2005), 95–122.
37. See Michel Foucault, *Discipline and Punish: The Birth of the Prison* (New York: Vintage Books, 1979); idem, *The History of Sexuality*, vol. 1, *An Introduction* (New York: Random, 1981); idem, *The History of Sexuality*, vol. 3, *The Care of the Self:* (London: Penguin, 1990); idem, "Governmentality," in *The Foucault Effect: Studies in Governmentality*, ed. C. Gordon, G. Burchel and P. Miller (Chicago: Chicago University Press, 2001), 87–104; and idem, *Society Must Be Defended: Lectures at the Collège de France 1975–1976* (New York: Picador, 2003).
38. Michel Foucault, *Security, Territory, Population: Lectures at the Collège de France 1977–78* (New York: Palgrave Macmillan, 2007), and idem, *The Birth of Biopolitics: Lectures at the Collège de France 1978–1979* (New York: Palgrave Macmillan, 2008).
39. Michel Foucault, "The Subject and Power, Afterward," in *Michel Foucault: Beyond Structuralism and Hermeneutics*, ed. H. Dreyfus and P. Rabinow (London: Harvester Wheatsheaf, 1982), 221.
40. Margo Huxley, "Geographies of Governmentality," in *Space, Knowledge and Power: Foucault and Geography*, ed. J. Crampton and S. Elden (Aldershot: Ashgate, 2007), 187.
41. In total, forty women were interviewed; participants were recruited through migrant advice centers, service organizations and ads in a multicultural newspaper and an online community bulletin board. Categories were: 'asylum seeker', 'refugee', 'EU-immigrant', 'work permit holder', 'return migrant' and 'other'.
42. Participants' names have been changed at their request in order to protect their privacy.
43. Representatives included program directors/coordinators, social workers and community liaison staff. I wish to thank these organizations for their assistance throughout this research.
44. Heeding the advice I was given, the interview protocol involved conveying to participants that they were not obliged to respond to any of the questions that made them feel ill at ease or overexposed.
45. Foucault, *History of Sexuality*, 59.
46. Ben Golder, "Foucault and the Genealogy of Pastoral Power," *Radical Philosophy Review* 10, no. 2 (2007): 159.
47. Erving Goffman, *The Presentation of Self in Everyday Life* (New York: Doubleday, 1959), and Judith Butler, *Gender Trouble: Feminism and the Subversion of Identity* (New York: Routledge, 1990).
48. Foucault, *Birth of Biopolitics*, 2.
49. Ana, in discussion with the author, Oct. 28, 2004.
50. Ibid.
51. Foucault, *History of Sexuality*, 59.
52. See Foucault, *Society Must Be Defended*; idem, *Birth of Biopolitics*; and Stephen Legg, "Foucault's Population Geographies: Classifications, Biopolitics and Governmental Spaces," *Population, Space and Place* 11, no. 3 (2005): 137–156.
53. Foucault, *Security, Territory, Population*, 125.
54. Rouse, "Power/Knowledge," 10.

Part IV

Immigrant Identities and the Politics of Race and Nativity

12 Immigration and Identity in the US Virgin Islands[1]

Jorge Capetillo-Ponce and Luis Galanes

In this chapter we document the experience of migration into the US Virgin Islands (USVI) during the period 1917 to the present, as well as the social processes and friction that derived from the experience of massive labor migration to supply the tourism industry. We then compare those experiences of migration in the USVI to global trends in migration patterns, as documented by migration scholars like Stephen Castles, Michael Douglass, Aihwa Ong and Ronald Skeldon.[2] This comparison is done in an attempt to argue that neoliberal strategies for controlling labor migration were present in the Caribbean long before it started to become 'global'. The Caribbean was the place where many of these neoliberal practices where first put to the test, before they were exported elsewhere. In fact, we propose that we view contemporary patterns of migration as part of a broader process that we could call, metaphorically at least, a process of the 'Caribbeanization of the world'.

We therefore argue, with Sidney Mintz, that many of the global phenomena under study today are not new to the world, and that in many ways "the world has now become a macrocosm of what the Caribbean region was in the 16th century."[3]

A BRIEF HISTORY OF IMMIGRATION TO THE USVI

The USVI, formerly Danish possessions in the Caribbean, were purchased by the US from the Danish government for $25 million in 1917. But it was not until the 1960s, after the Cuban revolution had closed that island to American tourists, that the island of St. Thomas was developed as a tourist destination, and immigration to the island became massive. The native population, which in 1917 amounted to 26,051, actually decreased during the period 1917–1940, due to the poor economic conditions of the newly acquired territory. A series of unfortunate events that took place in the years following the acquisition, beginning with the outbreak of World War I only weeks after Transfer Day (March 31, 1917), followed by the prohibition of alcohol in the US in the 1920s (which was detrimental to the local rum industry), the decrease in the price of sugar in world markets, and the Great Depression in the 1930s, all contributed to turn the USVI into what President Herbert

Table 12.1   USVI Population Increase and Decrease, 1917–2005

Year	Population	Increase/(decrease) as percentage
1917	26,051	
1930	22,012	(15.5)
1940	24,889	13.1
1950	26,665	7.1
1960	32,099	20.4
1970	63,200	96.9
2005	111,470	56.7

Source: Isaac Dookhan, History of the U.S. Virgin Islands of the United States (Jamaica: Canoe Press, 2002), 289.

Hoover once characterized as "the effective poorhouse" of the US.[4] During this period, a good portion of the native population immigrated to Puerto Rico, mainland US, Cuba or Panama in search of better job opportunities.

The USVI registered an increase in population of 96.9 percent during the period 1960–1970, and an additional increase of 56.7 percent during the period 1970–2005. The total increase in population during the period 1950–2005 was 318 percent (from 26,665 to 111,470).

The development of the islands (particularly St. Thomas and St. John) as a tourist destination during the same period is not unrelated to the increase in population, because most immigrants who have historically come to the USVI have come to work for that industry. Tourism in the USVI increased from 16,000 tourists in the year 1949 to 164,000 in 1959, 1,122,317 in 1967, and over two million in the present day. St. Thomas is today the most visited cruise ship's port in all the Caribbean, with as many as ten cruise ships visiting the island in one single day. It is probably, in fact, the most visited island in the world if measured in amount of tourists per square mile (approximately 64,520 tourists per square mile per year).[5] On top of that, St. Thomas and St. John have a significant population of 'residential tourists', or foreigners (mainly North Americans) who buy a property on the island and use it as a vacationing residence part of the year, or who actually move to live on the islands.

The reported place of birth of participants in the USVI 2005 Community Survey gives a broad idea of the origins of this immigrant population. Whereas a little over 18 percent of those who reported not being born in the USVI came from mainland US (9,902 out of 54,268), the remaining 82 percent comes mainly from at least eleven other Caribbean islands: Puerto Rico, Anguilla, Antigua and Barbuda, British Virgin Islands, Dominica, Dominican Republic, Haiti, Montserrat, St. Kitts and Nevis, St. Lucia, and Trinidad and Tobago (see Table 12.2).

Table 12.2   Place of Birth by Island and Race

Place of birth	Total	Black	White	Other races
All persons	111,470	90,758	9,995	10,718
US Virgin Islands	57,202	47,851	3,061	6,290
US (other)	9,903	4,496	4,774	634
Puerto Rico	4,134	2,262	498	1,374
Other Caribbean	38,177	35,751	1,072	1,353
Anguilla	658	536	122	–
Antigua and Barbuda	6,576	6,214	36	327
British Virgin Islands	3,439	3,439	–	–
Dominica	5,053	4,849	204	–
Dominican Republic	4,869	4,006	158	705
Haiti	954	918	–	36
Monserrat	949	949	–	–
St. Kitts and Nevis	8,458	8,075	383	–
St. Lucia	2,712	2,569	36	107
Trinidad & Tobago	1,798	1,583	72	143
Elsewhere	2,055	398	590	1,067

Source: University of the Virgin Islands, *United States Virgin Islands Community Survey* (King-shill: University of the Virgin Islands, 2005), 6.

Moreover, whereas a little over 51 percent (57,202 of 111,470) of the participants reported being born in the USVI, a good portion of these people are themselves children of immigrants. In the 2005 Community Survey, only 25 percent of the present-day population (28,928 of 111,470) declared USVI as their "Father's birthplace" and only 30 percent declared USVI as their "Mother's birthplace."[6] Thus, the immigrant or nonnative population of the island is well over the 49 percent that reported being born elsewhere, and a conservative estimate would indicate that they amount to at least 70 percent of the total population.

It must be clarified that this 70 percent figure includes people who, technically speaking, are not immigrants: they are US residents living in a US territory. But in the USVI the notion of 'immigrant' is closely related to the concept of 'native', and in the local-specific scheme of things US citizens who came to live on the islands after 1917 (known locally as 'Yankees'), although technically speaking not immigrants, are considered as such in discourses about nativism. In this context, natives are broadly defined as those who resided on the island before Transfer Day (March 31, 1917), and their descendants.

IMMIGRATION AND SOCIAL FRICTION

The presence of this massive immigrant population in the USVI is a source of social friction in the community. This friction is significantly evident in debates about two major issues: access of natives to working positions in the tourism industry and control over land.

Regarding the first issue, there is among natives the typical claim that immigrants 'steal' their jobs. But beyond the fact that the native population would be insufficient to supply the labor force needed by the tourism industry, and that immigration is therefore an economic necessity, there is also an apparent preference in the tourism industry for 'imported' employees (including Yankees) over and above native workers, particularly for the best-paying positions. Our interviews with people with links to the tourism industry (some 'Yankees' among them) revealed that such preference for nonlocals is often justified as resulting from the poor social abilities of the natives, particularly in their treatment of tourists.

According to some of our informants, this preference for imported workers has existed for a long time but is never spoken about publicly. It nevertheless became public in December 2007, when the influential publication *National Geographic Traveler* rated St. Thomas as the worst island destiny in the world, and made explicit reference, among other things, to precisely this "unfriendly" behavior of natives. The survey, conducted by a panel of 522 experts, rated 111 islands worldwide, and St. Thomas was rated the worst of all 111 islands. Some panelist had harsh words to describe the island: "totally spoiled, low-quality high-volume destination"; "a mess—with too many cruise ships disgorging their passengers into the small town"; or "Must have been a lovely place before it became the shopping mall for cruise ships." Charlotte Amalie was described as "one big, ugly jewelry store" where "the native population is unfriendly, with a coldness that borders into outright hostility."[7] Thus, local employers now point to the *National Geographic Traveler* article as a confirmation by a neutral and impersonal viewer of something they had known for years but were not able to say publicly for reasons of political correctness.

Now, beyond the employment discrimination issue, there is also the more important issue of control over land resources. The development of the tourist industry after the 1960s had as one of its major effects the increase in demand for land, and therefore the increase in the price of land. Therefore, it has been mainly the land issue that makes natives feel like, to use Dookhan's words, "foreigners in their own land." Dookhan summarizes the history of how the natives lost access or control of land in their own island:

> A survey in 1950 revealed that approximately .5 percent of the population owned 80 percent of the land. Much of this land was sold to wealthy outsiders who could afford to pay the high prices demanded . . . The great majority of native Virgin Islanders saw little hope of coming

Table 12.3 USVI House and Condominium Prices, 1970–1981

Year	Average price for house	Average price for condominium
1970	$34,971	$46,873
1975	$42,224	$47,028
1977	$51,345	$51,216
1978	$63,105	$47,735
1979	$80.825	$60,932
1980	$97,420	$92,006
1981	$99,133	$98,139

Source: U.S. Virgin Islands Growth Statistics Office of Policy, Planning and Research, U.S. Virgin Islands Department of Commerce, as cited in Harold Willocks, *The Umbilical Chord: The History of United States Virgin Islands from the Pre-Columbian Era to the Present* (St. Croix: Harold Willocks, 1995), 390–391.

into independent possession of land which they could later bequeath to their children . . . This factor, together with being outnumbered population-wise on the one hand, and being faced with difficulties in the acquisition of property on the other, has made Virgin Islanders fearful of becoming *foreigners in their own land*. (Emphasis added)[8]

Even those natives who had land and sold it could not afford to repurchase a house or a condominium due to the great increase in the price of property during the 1970s and 1980s (as shown in Table 12.3), and were forced to seek public housing.

It was then the development of the tourism industry, the waves of immigration, the alleged discrimination toward natives in employment practices and the struggle over land that gave way to the emergence of this feeling of becoming foreigners in their own land among natives, and the consequent emergence of a nationalist/nativist discourse. This wave of massive immigration, moreover, took place in a political context in which natives had no control over immigration policies because, as a US possession, these functions were centralized at a federal government level. In fact, it took place without any consideration whatsoever of natives' wishes or desires.

THE EMERGENCE OF A NATIVIST DISCOURSE:
THE WRITING OF A CONSTITUTION

In the summer of 2008, US Virgin Islanders were getting ready, for the fifth time in their history as a US possession, to write a constitution that would override what many in the USVI consider the 'colonial' arrangement of 1954 (the Organic Act of 1954). If this convention fails, it will be the fifth time in the past forty-three years that Virgin Islanders have failed at writing a constitution for themselves. Four prior attempts, in 1965, 1971, 1977 and 1980, also failed. The 1965 convention went as far as submitting a draft of the constitution to the US Congress for approval, but because it called for presidential voting rights, Congress never took action. All three future attempts made the draft more attractive to Congress by strategically eliminating the request for presidential voting rights. In the 1971 convention, a draft was voted in referendum, but the whole process was declared void because it failed to entice the required 51 percent of the electorate. Both the 1977 and 1980 conventions reduced the required participation turnout to two-thirds of the electorate, but in both cases the drafts were rejected by a majority of voters, with a poor voter turnout as well. A status plebiscite held in 1993 was also declared void again for the same reason. If there are cases in which the decision to not vote is seen by the electorate as the most legitimate and productive for their interests, even *within the framework of democratic politics*, this certainly would be one.

Since its inception, the nativist discourse in the USVI has been historically tied to the struggle for the creation of this local constitution for the semiautonomous territory, and it is perhaps within this context that the debates between natives and nonnatives more prominently come afloat. The controversy, more specifically, centers heavily on the inclusion of the following paragraph in the draft of the constitution, under the heading of "Definition of a Native Virgin Islander":

> All former Danish citizens who, on January 17, 1917, resided in the Virgin Islands of the United States, and were residing in those islands or in the United States or Puerto Rico on February 25, 1927, and who did not make the declaration required to preserve their Danish citizenship by Article 6 of the treaty entered into on August 4, 1916, between the United States and Denmark, or who, having made such a declaration have heretofore renounced or may hereafter renounce it by a declaration before a court of records. [9]

The constitutional definition of a native, if approved, could later open the way for preferential political and economic rights for natives, including preferential access to land.

To be sure, the idea of privileged political rights for natives is not new to the region. In fact, special voting rights were in place during a great part of the 1917–1936 period, when colonial councils were composed and elected exclusively by natives who shared some degree of political power under US Naval rule. During this period, voting rights were extended only to 'qualified' Virgin Islanders. Qualification, in turn, was determined based on place of birth, ownership of land and level of income. Thus, the percentage of people residing on the Virgin Islands who actually had voting rights during the 1917–1936 period amounted to approximately 5.5

percent of the total population,[10] and it was not until the US Congress passed the Organic Act of 1936 that all birth, property and income qualifications were eliminated.

The ratification of the Organic Act of 1936 was, thus, the event that brought real democratic change to the territory. It had the effect, as Highfield puts it, of breaking the "minority rule of the merchant and the planter class . . . after 264 years of slavery, servitude and peonage."[11] Highfield is here referring to the 264 years that run from 1672, the year when the first African slaves were brought to the Danish West Indies, to 1936, when the Organic Act went into effect. The only voting qualification that remained in the Organic Act of 1936 was the English-language proficiency qualification, and this was eventually eliminated too with the Revised Organic Act of 1954.

Since 1936, then, natives have been devoid of preferential rights, and the inclusion of a definition of a native Virgin Islander in the draft of the new constitution reveals the desire to reacquire those rights, and to perpetuate them into the future by stamping them in the constitution. Although the full list of these preferential native rights remains to be determined in an official manner, the issue over land rights dominates with force in the debates.

Thus, after four failed attempts, the Fifth Constitutional Convention was working on a draft during the summer of 2008, which was due on July 27, 2008. The July 27 convention never convened, however, because of a legal dispute over a confusing legislative directive specifying the appointment of delegates to the convention between St. Thomas and St. John that gave rise to litigation in the courts by delegate candidate Harry Daniels. Judge James Carol III of the USVI Superior Court granted mandamus relief to Daniels under the argument that the delegates "will be known to future generations as the Founding Fathers of the Virgin Islands." Yet it took Judge Carol until September 29, 2008, to resolve the issue and open the way for the resuming of the convention. The convention never resumed, however, and as of April 2009, the calendar of events that appears on the convention's web page has a big red message written on top that says: "All canceled due to lack of funds."[12]

The Fifth Constitutional Convention was finally able to convene on May 26, 2009, and it approved on that day a revised draft of the Constitution. Under this revised version, a new differentiation was introduced, this time between "Native Virgin Islanders," on the one hand, and "Ancestral Native Virgin Islanders," on the other. They were defined in Article 3, Sections 1 and 2, as follows:[13]

An Ancestral Native Virgin Islander is:
(a) a person born or domiciled in the Virgin Islands prior to and including June 28, 1932 and not a citizen of a foreign country pursuant to 8 U.S.C. 1406 in its pertinent part, and his/her descendants, and
(b) descendants of an Ancestral Native Virgin Islander residing outside of the U.S., its territories and possessions between January 17,

1917 and June 28, 1932, not subject to the jurisdiction of the U.S. and who are not a citizens or a subjects of any foreign country.

A Native Virgin Islander is:
(a) a person born in the Virgin Islands after June 28, 1932, and
(b) descendants of a person born in the Virgin Islands after June 28, 1932

The revised Constitution, moreover, required candidates for governor and lieutenant governor to fall into either of these two categories (Article VI, Section 3 (d)); and grants ancestral native Virgin Islanders exemption from payment of property taxes on their primary residence or undeveloped land (Article XI, Section 5 (8)).

The document was forwarded on May 31, 2009, to the elected governor of the territory, Hon. John P. de Jongh, who expressed opposition to a number of aspects contained in the text and declined to transmit the proposed constitution to the US Congress. He was later ordered by the territory's court in December 2009 to forward the text to the president and Congress of the US.

Upon receipt of the document, President Barack Obama asked the Department of Justice, in consultation with the Department of the Interior, to review the document. The Department of Justice, after reviewing the document, concluded that some of the provisions were inconsistent with the applicability of the US Constitution. It pointed in particular to nine problematic aspects of the document and its possible consequences: namely, "(1) the absence of an express recognition of United States sovereignty and the supremacy of Federal law; (2) provisions for a special election on the territorial status of the United States Virgin Islands; (3) provisions conferring legal advantages on certain groups defined by place and timing of birth, timing of residency, or ancestry; (4) residence requirements for certain offices; (5) provisions guaranteeing legislative representation of certain geographic areas; (6) provisions addressing territorial waters and marine resources; (7) imprecise language in certain provisions of the bill of rights of the proposed constitution; (8) the possible need to repeal certain Federal laws if the proposed constitution of the United States Virgin Islands is adopted; and (9) the effect of congressional action or inaction on the proposed constitution."[14]

Moreover, regarding the specific issue of granting native rights, the Department of Justice expressed its belief that the special designation of opportunities afforded to native and ancestral native Virgin Islanders is not "rationally" based, and in violation of the Equal Protection Clause of the US Constitution. In its memorandum, the Department of Justice states: "Because we find it difficult to discern a legitimate governmental purpose that would be rationally advanced by the provisions conferring legal advantages on certain groups defined by place and timing of birth, timing of residency, or ancestry, we recommend that those provisions be removed from the proposed constitution."[15]

The Fifth Constitutional Convention, in reaction to the Department of Justice's report, issued a Response Memorandum on May 12, 2010.[16] It first points to the fact that the idea of a native Virgin Islander was a notion first devised by US Congress in its naturalization act of 1932, and therefore it is a population whose existence has been previously recognized by Congress in the past. Moreover, it points to the existence of special rights granted to other "native" communities in the US. "In this regards," the response reads:

> Congress has continued to accept responsibility for the welfare of natives. Congress has established special programs in areas of healthcare, education, employment and loans. Rice at 496. It has enacted laws providing for special and different treatment of Native Hawaiians, Native Alaskans, Aleutians and Native Indians. The special treatment laws have allowed for special voting privileges, special taxation, segregated property ownership and other benefits as the United States has sought to fulfill its obligations to Native people . . . The United States is on record accepting the responsibility for the welfare of native people. In its brief in the case of Rice v Cayento, 528 U.S. 495, the Government of the United States declared that a special right to vote should be bestowed on "native" people to the exclusion of non-natives.

Regarding the tax exemption for Ancestral Natives, the response memorandum adds:

> Since 1992, the Supreme Court has recognized that a property tax exemption based on longevity of ownership can have a legitimate government purpose if the government has an interest in local neighborhood preservation, continuity and stability of life and family. See Nordlinger v. Hahn, 505 U.S. 1, 13 (1992), 112 S.Ct. 2326.

The Response Memorandum, unfortunately for natives, was not able to produce the desired effect. The US House of Representatives, squarely siding with the Department of Justice, unanimously adopted Senate Joint Resolution 33 on June 29, 2010, which calls on the Fifth Constitutional Convention of the US Virgin Islands to reconvene to consider the Justice Department's objections.[17] No doubt, nonnatives see this decision of the Department of Justice and US Congress as representative of their position. A comment posted on the Internet by nonnative Verdel L. Petersen points to this fact:

> Will the convention delegates persist in their obstinate refusal to accept the U.S. Constitution as the supreme law of the land? It is

incredible that educated, intelligent people do not understand their role as delegate and that any constitution drafted must be consistent with Federal Laws and the US Constitution. I pray they come to their senses and correct the mess that they created. The ball is now in their court. It is an opportunity to demonstrate that they are true diplomats and humanitarians.[18]

The measure is now on the desk of an African American US president, Barack Obama, waiting for his signature. It seems like natives' last hope rests on his sensitivity for a people who, presumably like him, are the descendants of slaves who were brought unwillingly, and who have been forced to forge identities based on this past experience. Stuart Hall is right when he says that events like the ones taking place in the USVI are part of "the history of all enforced diasporas."[19] But even if Virgin Islanders were able to get congressional and presidential approval for their constitution, the ultimate *litmus test* for its final adoption is the general plebiscite, and nonnatives are well aware of the fact. The plebiscite would need a voter turnout of 51 percent for it to be considered valid, and 51 percent of votes, in order to become effective. It had been tentatively scheduled for November 2011, although it cannot take place without the US congressional and presidential approval.

It should be noted that reliable estimates about the numerical proportion of 'real' natives (that is, those who actually have the qualifications to be recognized as such according to the draft's definition) within the total population are nonexistent, but most informants estimate it at 5 percent of the population at the most. The estimates are based on the fact that only 5.5 percent of the population had voting rights during the period 1917–1954, when 'place of birth' was a required qualification for voting. But we also know that: (a) the total USVI population in 1917 was 26,051; (b) according to the UVI 2005 Community Survey, only 51 percent of the present-day population (57,202 of 111,470) reported being born in the USVI; and (c) only 25 percent of the present-day population (28,928 of 111,470) declared USVI as their "Father's birthplace" and only 30 percent declared USVI as their "Mother's birthplace."[20]

So it perhaps would be fair to conservatively estimate the native population at somewhere between 5 and 30 percent. Although the true figure is probably closer to 5 than to 30 percent, voting results in elections for constitutional delegates of the Fifth Constitutional Convention do seem to indicate a popular support for nativist candidates well above the 5 percent figure. In either case our argument would still be valid, because the point is that if privileged voting rights were granted only to natives, which is the action that nonnatives fear the most, the action could be perceived as a *de facto* disenfranchisement of an absolute majority of the population.

The reasons for the rejection (or for the poor voter turnout) of the 1971, 1977 and 1980 drafts by a majority of the population are multiple, to be sure, but most observers agree that the most polemical and emotionally charged issue leading to the rejections was the definition of 'native' Virgin Islander through genealogical categories, which could have the effect of placing a large percentage of the USVI population in the category of second-class citizens. Arnold Highfield, for example, has referred to the native issue as the "quandary that has bedeviled every attempt to write and pass a constitution for our islands," and as the single most important issue leading to "a standoff of sorts that has muddied the waters of present attempts at dialogue and discussion."[21] It is not clear if this fifth attempt at agreeing on a draft for the constitution will be able to overcome this "standoff of sorts," but the inclusion once again of the definition of a native almost certainly condemns it to failure in a general referendum.

THE CONTROL OVER IMMIGRATION POLICIES

The fact that natives have had absolutely no control over immigration laws plays a central role in their claims, simply because it is tantamount to saying that they have become a numerical minority in their own land *unwillingly*. Highfield has summed up the views of natives regarding this issue in the following terms:

> The U.S. government has allowed a flood of immigrant laborers to pour into the Territory . . . This upsets the political balance of power . . . , thereby making it impossible to write a constitution today that would reflect the political will of [native] Virgin Islanders.[22]

Some have gone as far as equating the situation of natives as a contemporary form of 'slavery'. Edward Brown, a native delegate of the Fifth Constitutional Convention and a local political activist—who actually went on a twelve-day hunger strike in 2007 to protest the absence of a US presidential vote for Virgin Islanders—stated the following when addressing the convention in June 23, 2008:

> Anyone born before March 31, 1917 is a slave. You have to emancipate them . . . The U.S. never emancipated them or Denmark . . . If you are able to get this done, we would have emancipated our own people.[23]

Despite the abolition of the slave trade by Denmark in 1806, and despite the emancipation of the slaves in 1848, says Brown, the actual date "when the last slaves were bought" (by the US government in this case) is, properly speaking, March 31, 1917 (Transfer Day).

It should also be noted that the idea of special privileged rights that natives could potentially claim for themselves does have precedent in the context of US politics, as in the case of Indian reservations. But the model that is closer to native Virgin Islanders is that of their close neighbors, the British Virgin Islands, and this is particularly true when related to land rights. In any case, such special privileged rights are only possible if island-ers are able to agree on a constitution that includes the definition of a native Virgin Islander, given that such a constitution can become effective only once it is approved by a majority of residents in a general referendum. The past four decades show how delicate and polemical the approval of such a constitution could be.

CONCLUDING REMARKS

The globalization of neoliberalism has implied, among other things, the free flow of commodities and of capital through sovereign borders. Yet deregulation of the flow of individuals has not received the same treatment, and the free flow of people has not been 'globalized' in the same way as that of commodities and capital. This differential treatment is evidenced in, among other places, the absence of global institutions to regulate the movement of people. As Castles argues, "there are no global governance institutions for migration, comparable to the IMF and the World Bank for finance, or the WTO for trade."[24] Nonetheless, migrant workers have increasingly become a necessity for most developed countries, and the flow of people is taking place in a *de facto* deregulated context, with no controls other than those imposed by the states involved, particularly those of the reception state. In 2009, 214 million people lived outside their country of birth, which represents 3.1 percent of the world population. And in the US, there are nearly twelve million irregular residents.

The causes of this need for migrant workers in developed countries are all too well known: a mixture of population aging and low fertility rates. The causes of low fertility rates, in turn, are the drastic changes in the reproductive and family values of these modern nations, which are also becoming 'global'.

> Currently, more than fifty countries are experiencing below replace-ment fertility, with some already experiencing absolute population decline. High divorce rates, late marriages without children, the insti-tutional warehousing of the elderly, and the phenomenal increase in single resident housing units (more than 50 percent in major cities in the North [US]) are all indicators of retrenchment of the household.[25]

To be sure, immigration policies in many developed countries have been managed ambivalently and irregularly, and 'hypocritically', to use Cas-tles's characterization. That is, many states prohibit illegal immigra-tion but derive an undeniable economic benefit from the presence of the undocumented population. As Castles says: "A widespread approach of governments is to crack down on irregular migrants, while tacitly accepting their major contribution to the economy. The US . . . is the world's leader in this hypocrisy."[26]

Some experts on migration trends have argued that the future of migration patterns will be determined by an inevitable shortage in the global surplus of migrant laborers. Castles, for example, argues that:

> There are signs that things may change. As economic and demographic transitions take place, the global surplus of labor may soon disappear. The highly developed countries will find it increasingly difficult to meet their economic needs and to alleviate the effects of population age-ing. Cooperation with origin countries may prove essential, and this is likely to lead to measures to ensure that migration can take place in safety and dignity.[27]

Skeldon also points to the changing scenario that is increasingly taking place in terms of immigration policies in highly developed countries, due also to increasing shortage of migrant laborers. It has come to a point, says Skeldon, where receiving countries need to rethink their migration policies, and enter into negotiation with the origin states. Skeldon explains:

> Migration policy has long been considered a prerogative of the receiving state, and that state alone is responsible for selecting who comes within its borders . . . Today, a more nuanced approach to migration policy has emerged: the idea that population migration can be managed, not just for the benefit of the destination state, but also for the origin states and the migrants themselves. Such an approach brings immigration and development policy into an uneasy dialogue . . . Migration no longer remains a unilateral matter but emergence as a matter of foreign policy through bilateral and multilateral negotiation among states.[28]

Aihwa Ong has explored the existence of a grading system in contemporary migration policies in the US. It is a grading system based mostly on the cultural attitudes exhibited by individual immigrant groups toward work and dependence on welfare aid, as well as family values. But economic globalization here has meant that states are beginning to develop new immigration policies informed and shaped by the work ethic and entrepreneurial attitudes of different cultural groups.

In her "Cultural Citizenship as Subject-Making," based on ethnographic work among Asian immigrants on the West Coast of the US (i.e., Cambodians, Vietnamese, Japanese, Chinese, Koreans), Ong evidences the existence of a system for evaluating immigrants—part of a process she will later call "mutations of citizenship"—which rests on a continuum between the two polarities of black and white, on what she calls "the white and black poles of American citizenship."[29] It is a process of "racialization of class"[30] by which racist ideas of the differences that divide black and white populations coming from "the history of European-American imperialism" are reproduced in an unproblematic manner. Ong says:

> I maintain that the white-black polarities emerging out of the history of European-American imperialism continue to shape attitudes and encode discourses directed at immigrants from the rest of the world that are associated with racial and cultural inferiority.[31]

This black-and-white polarity is then extended, Ong explains, to judge and grade nonwhite immigrants who enter the US, in an "attempt to discriminate among them, separating out the desirable from the undesirable citizens according to some racial or cultural calculus."[32] In the neoliberal world, this "racial and cultural calculus," which helps to separate the desirable from the undesirable, is based on cultural attitudes toward work and patterns of dependence on welfare aid. As Ong explains:

> There is . . . a regulatory aspect to neoliberalism whereby economics is extended to cover all aspects of human behavior pertaining to citizenship . . . In the postwar era, such thinking has given rise to a human capital assessment of citizens . . . , weighing those who can pull themselves up by their bootstraps against those who make claims on the welfare state. Increasingly, citizenship is defined as the civic duty of individuals to reduce their burden on society and build up their own human capital—to be "entrepreneurs" of themselves . . . Indeed, by the 1960s liberal economies had come to evaluate non-white groups according to their claims on or independence of the state. [33]

Based on her comparison between different Asian immigrant groups, Ong describes the perception of Cambodian immigrants as "blackened," or transformed into "black Asians." The idea of black Asians comes from the cultural similarities exhibited by both Cambodian and African American populations, in terms of welfare dependency and attitudes toward work, as well as many other indicators traditionally associated with poverty, like teenage pregnancy rates:

> Once [Asiatic] immigrants arrive in the country, whatever their national origin or race, they were ideologically positioned within the hegemonic bipolar white-black model of American society. The racialization of Southeast Asian refugees depended on differential economic and cultural assessment of their potential as good citizens . . . Cambodians . . . were often compared to their inner-city African American neighbors in terms of low-wage employment, high rates of teenage pregnancy, and welfare-dependent families . . . Immigrants situated closer to the black pole are seen as at the bottom of the cultural and economic ranking . . .

This positioning of Cambodians as black Asians is in sharp contrast to the model-minority image of Chinese, Koreans, and Vietnamese [including Sino-Vietnamese], who are celebrated for their "Confucian values" and family businesses.[34]

Now, what we wish to argue is that the processes described by Ong for the US in the 1990s were similar in many ways to the processes of migration experienced by the USVI in the 1960s and 1970s. Moreover, we would like to point to the similarities between these two latter experiences, and the experience of slavery: mainly, that there also existed in the Caribbean multiple systems of grading African slaves based on their tribes of origin, and according to the working capacity of each group. We therefore maintain that the policies that were used to control immigration into the USVI during the 1960s onward were based on the same type of cultural calculus that Ong describes for Asian immigrants in the US at the present, and that therefore what we are witnessing is the globalization of practices that were put into effect in the Caribbean long before they were exported elsewhere.

In fact, what we maintain is that the globalization of neoliberal policies is yet another example of a broader process of what we could call 'the Caribbeanization of the world'. Sidney Mintz reminds us that many of the global phenomena under study today are not new, and that the Caribbean is the place where many of these practices were first put to the test, before they were exported and started to become 'global'. Mintz asks rhetorically:

> Is one entitled to wonder whether this means that the world has now become a macrocosm of what the Caribbean region was in the 16th century? If so, should we not ask what took the world so long to catch up—especially since what is happening now is supposed to be qualitatively so different from the recent past? Or is it rather that the Caribbean experience was merely one chapter of a book being written, before the name of the book—world capitalism—became known to its authors?[35]

NOTES

1. Fieldwork for this chapter was supported by the UMASS-UPRC Caribbean Summer Institute, a collaborative project between the University of Massachusetts-Boston and the University of Puerto Rico at Cayey.
2. Stephen Castles, "Foreword," *Whitehead Journal of Diplomacy and International Relations* 10, no. 1 (2010): 11–12; Michael Douglass, "Globalizing the Household in East Asia," *Whitehead Journal of Diplomacy and International Relations* 11, no. 1 (2010): 63–77; Aihwa Ong, *Spirits of Resistance and Capitalist Discipline: Factory Women in Malaysia* (Albany: State University of New York Press, 1987); idem, "Cultural Citizenship as Subject-Making: Immigrants Negotiate Racial and Cultural Boundaries in the United States," *Current Anthropology* 37, no. 5 (1996): 737–761; idem, "Mutations in Citizenship," *Theory, Culture and Society* 23, no. 2–3 (1996):

499–531; and Ronald Skeldon, "Managing Migration for Development: Is Circular Migration an Answer?," *Whitehead Journal of Diplomacy and International Relations* 11, no. 1 (2010): 21–33.

3. Sidney Mintz, "The Localization of Anthropological Practice: From Area Studies to Transnationalism," *Critique of Anthropology* 2 (1997): 270.

4. Isaac Dookhan, *A History of the Virgin Islands of the United States* (Jamaica: Canoe Press, 2002), 271.

5. The island of St. Thomas is 31 square miles. The amount of tourists per year is approximately two million. This produces a figure of 54,268 tourists per square mile per year or 148.7 per day.

6. University of the Virgin Islands, *USVI Community Survey* (Kingshill: University of the Virgin Islands, 2005), 6.

7. See "Places Rated, The World's Best Islands," in *National Geographic Traveler*, Nov./Dec. 2007. See also www.nationalgeographic.com/traveler/features/islandsrated0711.

8. Dookhan, *History of the Virgin Islands*, 307.

9. The definition makes reference to the ten-year phase-out period agreed to in the transfer, at the end of which period all former Danish citizens would have to decide whether they wanted to become North American citizens or remain Danish citizens. Excerpted from, The Constitution of the Virgin Islands of the United States, Fifth Annual Convention (May 31, 2009), accessed April 15, 2013, http://www.google.com/url?sa=t&rct=j&q=&esrc=s&frm=1&source=web&cd=2&ved=0CDsQFjAB&url=http%3A%2F%2Fwww.main-justice.com%2Fwp-admin%2Fdocuments-databases%2F16-1-Proposed-Virgin-Islands-Constitution.pdf&ei=SShsUb-FG6bG0wH92IDQDw&usg=AFQjCNFjtMPqTETDCyxZ0TqhTDMKsNXfpA&sig2=4nFGdSmpYVEF5lqROJlIEA&bvm=bv.45175338,d.dmQ.

10. See Dookhan, *History of the Virgin Islands*, 276.

11. Arnold Highfield, "A Constitution for the Virgin Islands?" *Crucian Trader* 1, no. 10 (2007): 1–3.

12. Constitution of the Virgin Islands of the United States, Fifth Annual Convention (May 31, 2009).

13. Ibid,

14. Ibid.

15. US Department of Justice, "Department of Justice Views on the Proposed Constitution Drafted by the Fifth Constitutional Convention of the United States Virgin Islands," (February 23, 2010), accessed April 15, 2013, www.justice.gov/olc/2010/usvi-doj-view-ltr100223.pdf.

16. Overseas Territories Review, "US Virgin Islands Constitutional Convention Replies to US Concerns: Reply of US Virgin Islands Constitutional Convention to the Memorandum of the US Department of Justice Regarding the Proposed Constitution for the US Virgin Islands, Marcy 29, 2010," (May 11, 2010), accessed, April 15. 2013, http://overseasreview.blogspot.com/2010/05/us-virgin-islands-constitutional.html.

17. A copy of this resolution is available at Overseas Territories Review, "US House Mandates US Virgin Islands Constitutional Convention to Reconsider Autonomous Proposals," (June 29, 2010), accessed April 15, 2013, http://overseasreview.blogspot.com/2010/06/us-house-mandates-us-virgin-islands.html.

18. Comment posted in response to Overseas Territories Review, "US House Mandates US Virgin Islands Constitutional Convention to Reconsider Autonomous Proposals."

19. Stuart Hall, "Cultural Identity and Diaspora," *Framework* 36 (1989): 222–237 at 235 20. University of the Virgin Islands, *USVI Community Survey*, 6.

21. Highfield, "Constitution for the Virgin Islands?," 3.
22. Ibid.
23. Brown, cited in Tom Eader, "Delegates Debate Definition of Slavery," *St. Croix Abis*, 2008, 1–5.
24. Castles, "Foreword," 12.
25. Douglass, "Globalizing the Household in East Asia," 63.
26. Castles, "Foreword," 11.
27. Ibid., 12.
28. Skeldon, "Managing Migration for Development," 21.
29. Ong, "Cultural Citizenship as Subject-Making," 743.
30. Ibid., 739.
31. Ibid., 751.
32. Ibid., 741.
33. Ibid., 739.
34. Ibid., 749.
35. Mintz, "Localization of Anthropological Practice," 120.

13 What Rises from the Ashes
Nation and Race in the African American Enclave of Samaná

Ryan Mann-Hamilton

On the 13ᵗʰ of October 1946, flames engulfed the town of Samaná located on the northeastern portion of the Dominican Republic (DR). The flames spread from warehouse to warehouse, consuming the mahogany and cedar planks culled from the hillsides of Samaná. The townspeople watched as the fire devoured ninety-four of their homes.[1] The flames slowly spread beyond the commercial sector of town as the people scrambled, trying to find empty containers to fill with water to douse the flames. One of the few structures that remained—whether by celestial protection or its fortuitous hillside location—was the African Methodist Episcopal (AME) Saint Peters Church, locally known as 'La Churcha'. The materials for the church had been donated to the descendants of African Americans who lived in the region and had been brought from England in 1901.[2] In addition to all the structures, the 'Great Fire of Samaná', destroyed most of the documents related to land tenure, debt, mercantile exchanges, and records pertaining to the history of the community and its unique ethnic and cultural population.

Accounts differ as to where the fire started, but the communal memory points to a macabre story that traverses the realms of jealousy, and domination, and attributes the fire to the artifices of General Rafael Leonidas Trujillo. What rose from the ashes of this devastating incident was a disjointed community that no longer had control over its political, religious and educational institutions. They were at the mercy of the ideologies transmitted through the powerful military and political structure in Santo Domingo. This was just one in a series of efforts that were aimed at coercing the Afro Caribbean community of Samaná to succumb and consent to the nation-building pressures of the Dominican state.

The peninsula of Samaná has been one of the main regions of the Dominican Republic (DR) where projects of rule have focused their gaze and where attempts to control the space have produced local transformations. Control of the peninsula of Samaná has been a central aspect of the region's history, where populations have served as markers, like flags of convenience, to locate a national allegiance and to claim political power over the landmass. The various designs and trajectories of these projects of rule provide an understanding of the practices and processes that lead to Dominican Nation State formation and reveal the continual forced encounters between self-governed peoples and the nascent democratic state. Among these projects was the 1824 invitation extended by President Jean Pierre Boyer to free African Americans, which brought an estimated seven thousand of them to the region. At the time, Haiti controlled the entire island, and Boyer's intentions were part of a larger racial project to create a black republic and establish commercial interests with other Western nations. With this invitation, he hoped to gain a population that would be in solidarity with his efforts and through this relationship gain recognition as a nation from the US.[3] For Dominican historian José Gabriel García, "the motive behind Boyer's immigration scheme was not so much to provide the country with able laborers and artisans, but rather to change the social physiognomy of the Spanish part of the island and to awaken racial preoccupations in the immigrants' minds which would tend to create their identification with the Haitians."[4] In 1844 the Haitians lost control of the eastern portion of the island, retreating to the western portion. After a series of dictatorships and constant fluctuations in the caudillo power structure, the Dominican nation, recently recuperating from US intervention, elected General Trujillo to power in 1930.

Under Trujillo's leadership, residents experienced the first concerted efforts to unite the country under a vision of 'Dominicanidad'. Through Trujillo and his ideologues, a national identity was forged and espoused, and institutions were created to support these endeavors. A new form of sociocultural hegemony was constructed through direct efforts of coercion and consent of the population. The consolidation of power in the urban realm challenged the regional autonomy that had reigned in the island sphere and marked the beginning of increased government intervention. In Samaná, the African American emigrants had imagined a transnational space not bounded by language, religion or race. Trujillo was required to dismantle this space as a prerequisite of inclusion within the Dominican nation.

Between 1930 and 1950, Trujillo initiated his visionary construction of the Dominican 'nation'. During these early years the support of rural populations, the church and many other sectors of Dominican society gave Trujillo ample latitude to embark on his nation-making endeavors. In the Dominican Republic, the intertwining of race and nation has been at the center of the nation-building process. Focusing a lens on Samaná, one can see how these processes played out. It was perhaps the 'otherness' of the community of Samaná that in the eyes of the regime demanded a transformation to fit it within the Dominican national imaginary. The Samaná residents' blackness was a challenge and therefore needed to be subsumed within Dominican identity. What follows is an analysis of the various government interventions made at the rural level to create a notion of a homogenous Dominican experience. I then measure the impact of these national policies as they impinged upon the rural African American descendants in Samaná who had previously succeeded in defying the national narrative of language, race, religion and education.

(THEIR) STORY

The idea of transporting African Americans to Haiti had been expounded by the early 1800s, and interest had been expressed by both the US and Haitian governments.[5] It was under the leadership of Haitian president Jean Pierre Boyer that actual attempts were made to fulfill these ideas. Boyer enlisted Jonathas Granville as his representative in the US, to gain support for the migration of African Americans to Haiti and take charge of making the travel arrangements for those accepting the invitation. Boyer had supplied Granville with fifty thousand pounds of coffee to be sold in order to finance the migration.[6] For Granville, the first stop in the US was Philadelphia, where he met with the Reverend Richard Allen, later traveling along the eastern seaboard, meeting with other African American political and religious leaders.[7] As part of his efforts toward disseminating Boyer's proposal, announcements were printed in many of the local newspapers. Among those was an article published on July 1, 1824, in the *Niles Weekly Register* in Baltimore, promising "a free country to Africans and their descendants."[8]

The majority of those who arrived in Samaná were members of the Mother Bethel African Methodist Episcopal Church (AME) founded in Philadelphia by Reverend Richard Allen in 1794.[9] The AME was one of the few churches at the time that allowed blacks to preach to their own communities. It rejected "the negative theological interpretations which rendered persons of African descent second class citizens."[10] Its members thus migrated to Hispaniola with their own religious practices and culture. These established their difference from the existing local population even as the church provided a solid spiritual, familial and historical base. In the face of a constant influx of other English-speaking emigrants from neighboring Caribbean islands, the AME provided the arrivals from the north with resources for the continuance of their identities and the use of English within a Spanish-speaking region.

The African Americans who accepted Boyer's invitation departed between 1824 and 1825 from various ports in the eastern US.[11] The first ship of emigrants arrived on November 29, 1824, in Port au Prince, and they were assigned to different areas around the island of Haiti.[12] Boyer was specifically anxious to receive agricultural laborers and artisans to fulfill the needs of the country. His "plan was to send 3,600 emigrants to traditionally Haitian areas and 2,400 to traditionally Spanish areas", desiring to populate specific areas of the island with black families who would be receptive and supportive of the newly created Haitian nation.[13]

Upon arrival some families chose to stay in the Haitian capital, whereas others were scattered to the communities of Puerto Plata, Samaná, Santo Domingo and La Romana. It is unclear why these areas were selected over others, but the strategic location, abundance of land and scarce population in the Samaná peninsula may have influenced the decision. The Bay of Samaná had also been used as a point of entry for the French forces led by General Leclerc intent on stifling the events of the Haitian Revolution. In responding to this threat, Boyer may have presumed that the relationship between the African Americans and the US would interrupt further attempts by the French to meddle in Haitian affairs.

The emigrants escaped a racially divided US society and attempted to assert their own ideals in forming the community of Samaná. Reverend Narcissus Miller went to Samaná along with twenty families with thirty-three different surnames; most of them could read and write in English. They immediately focused on forming their own institutions to facilitate their transition to the island. They established their own English-speaking schools, an AME affiliated church and cultural organizations that were to be the backbone of the community. These structures were their attempt to establish agency in the place they now called home and provide adequate resources for the growth of the community. The weekly church services in English and yearly celebrations such as the Harvest Festival held in October helped to maintain the English language and customs. "Of the five to six hundred colonists in 1870 there were two hundred members of the Methodist church . . . the average attendance at public worship being three to four hundred."[14] Isolated by land, there was little contact with the conflicts that prevailed on the island. Throughout the constant changes in governments and alliances, the African American community continually aligned themselves with those who meddled in their political and religious affairs the least.[15]

The geographic location of the African American community of Samaná, and its relative economic prosperity after 1870, allowed it to escape the sway of caudillo interests in the region. During this period in Samaná, there existed a library, theater, baseball teams, a printing press and various newspapers. There was also lighting for many of the public areas, which was not available in the rest of the country. Its prized location and strategic importance to foreign and national trade brought an influx of products and services from the exterior and the establishment of consulates for the French, Italian, British, Dutch and US governments. Ship logs indicate that the ports of embarkation to Samaná were predominantly in the US, but also in Italy, Norway, Spain, France and Britain.[16]

The Samaná peninsula held economic primacy over many of the other regions because of its port and because of the construction of the railroad bringing products from El Cibao to Sanchez. 'Jabonerias Unidas del Cibao', the largest soap factory in the country, brought a number of jobs and economic resources to the community.[17] As infrastructure projects linked Samaná by road to the rest of the nation, it was less feasible to maintain its autonomy.

Trujillo's many visits to Samaná provided him a familiarity with the different racial, cultural and linguistic makeup of the community, which did not support the unification of the Dominican nation. It is these details that many older Samanenses describe in terms of imagining Trujillo as having had a hand in the burning of the town. "He watched as a policeman hit a man who tried to put out the fire. The man didn't get up. The police prevented people from putting the fire out. At one time the governor asked men to help put it out, but he himself refused to participate . . . He said that Trujillo set the fire because he was envious of the prosperous site of affairs in Samaná."[18]

For many of the residents of Samaná, the fire was the final manifestation of Trujillo's will to transform and conform the region and its population within his vision. It created a moment of uncertainty, in which the community's rebirth would be under the watchful eyes of the state and the 'father' of the nation. In an interview conducted in 2004, Papito Coplin (Copeland) repeated the claim that Trujillo had burned down the town as he was jealous of the prosperity its inhabitants enjoyed at the time.[19] Additional eyewitness testimony describes how many of the police attempted to keep the residents of the town from fighting the fire, in many cases striking the men who were attempting to run toward the fire to help.[20] The attributing of jealousy as the inspiration for the fire could be linked to the decline in the economic sphere in the port of Samaná and the increasing accumulation of wealth in the urban areas.

TRUJILLO: "FATHER OF THE NATION"

The 1916 intervention of the United States into Dominican affairs provided an opening for the rise of the dictator Rafael Leonidas Trujillo. Rising through the ranks of the US-established military force, Trujillo "served under the infamous Captain Merckle, notorious for his persecution and oppression of Dominican nationals".[21] Once he gained power in 1930 Trujillo embarked on a series of educational, infrastructure, sanitary, land redistribution and economic and commercial programs to move the island into the modern world. The subsequent rise to power and nation building efforts of the Trujillo regime beginning in 1930, closed off Samaná from its maritime connections and brought an increase in the suppression of local educational and social institutions and the establishment of state based institutions.

Through these policies Trujillo attempted to bring unity to a nation that had been in disarray. "In 1930 there did not exist here a Nation enjoying its just attributes. Instead there was a group of humanity—a group tormented by unrest, insecurity, compromise, injustice and servitude."[22] This unity came at the expense of those who had a more fluid vision of the nation, as his was very rigid. In his autobiography Trujillo wrote, "A nation is a clearly delineated territory united by a series of cohesive elements: inhabitants, production, tradition, culture, historic vicissitudes, customs . . . if one of them is lacking, the Nation dwindles in primacy and is reduced to a fragile, inert entity."[23] The regime needed to effect change on the rural population and transform their image of complacent, malnourished and uneducated people into an image of people for whom labor was their principal input toward the nation.

Trujillo believed his dreams for the DR could come to fruition only by controlling the powers of dissent and by paying attention to the needs of the rural population, who until then had been ignored by previous governments. He demanded obedience from the population and violently repressed any dissent. The state "infiltrated every day peasant life not only with vagrancy ordinances, compulsory community labor, political rallies, and local meetings, but also with sanitary inspections, vice regulations, paternity laws, health clinics, day and night schools and literacy campaigns."[24] All of these efforts were watched over by the military forces dispersed throughout the country, which both enforced and subjected the rural population to Trujillo's whims.

Race played a pivotal role in Trujillo's vision of 'Dominicanidad'. Race and nation in the context of the DR must be viewed as interdependent processes that are continually contested, reworked and transformed to allow subjects to enter into the national imaginary. In *Imagined Communities*, Benedict Anderson attributes the social construction and rise of the nation and nationalism in the Americas to a new spatial organization of the world transformed by the confluence of capitalism and colonialism. This new form of nationalism was to be built on personal sacrifice, and a relinquishing of religion as central in the political process.[25] Rather than an ideology, Anderson sees the nation as a tool for shaping subjects and the rise of nationalism as a way of linking horizontally "fraternity, power and time," bringing large groups of people to relate to each other in a common language.

One's position within a particular society dictates the degree of sacrifice, which may lead to dependence on the nation to supplant that which has been relinquished. Anderson's suggestion that nation-building processes were easily transplanted to different spaces glosses over the historical and social particularities that have helped each nation to become what it is. In his analysis, absent are the struggles of gender and race that were integral in the construction and the imagination of national identities. In spite of actual social inequalities, Anderson makes the claim that the nation is "imagined" as horizontal and shared, thus failing to acknowledge that power shapes specific populations within structures of inequality and ignoring the possibility that this deep horizontal comradery could be achieved through coercive circumstances. [26]

Many authors have commented on the power that Trujillo held in the DR, describing it as absolute and tyrannical.[27] Richard Turits in *Foundations of Despotism* takes a detour from this vision of totality to emphasize the hegemonic processes and the forces of coercion and consent that allowed Trujillo to stay in power for thirty years. "Peasants recalled the policies of development and state intervention under the Trujillo regime as eviscerating certain traditional freedoms, but also offering desirable benefits."[28] The power and legitimacy of the Trujillo regime came from the integration and disciplining of the rural peasantry as they became participants in the political and social processes of Dominican nation building.

Gramsci's conception of hegemony as a class-structured dominance led by the bourgeois class is integral in understanding the Trujillo regime. Hegemony is established by controlling both political and social realms whereby the state and civil society are ideologically linked and power is exerted over the population through a balance of coercion and consent. Hegemony is enforced by economic, social and educational means and is conceived through the state. "The state is the entire complex of practical and theoretical activities with which the ruling class justifies and maintains its dominance, but manages to win the active consent of those over whom it rules."[29]

RACE AND NATION

One way to understand race and racialization in Latin America is to look at it as a progression that is formed through the mediation of different imaginings by different populations.[30] Racialization is not restricted to national borders, but projected in spatial terms, between, within and outside of nations. Race played a pivotal role in Trujillo's vision of 'Dominicanidad'. Race and nation in the context of the DR must be viewed as interdependent processes that are continually contested, reworked, and transformed to allow subjects to enter into the national imaginary. Much of his vision of the Dominican nation was constructed in juxtaposition to neighboring Haiti.

In continuation of the US discourse of division between Haiti and DR and so as to secure his hold on power, Trujillo manipulated Dominican nationalism to serve his interests and create a clear distinction between Dominicans and Haitians that continues to manifest itself today. This conflict would figure prominently in Trujillo and his ideological construction of the Dominican nation. Haitian historian and politician Jean Price Mars, and Dominican intellectual and political figure Juan Bosch both wrote about the worsening conflict between Haiti and the DR as a consequence of US policies and military interventions in both countries starting in 1916.

In his book *Race and Politics in the Dominican Republic* Ernesto Sagas produces a detailed analysis of the design, development and use of Anti-Haitianismo by the political establishment during the regime and beyond. He traces the socio cultural and historical implications and forms of socialization that deny and subjugate Blackness in the DR. As described by Sagas, "Anti-Haitianismo ideology combines a legacy of racist Spanish colonial mentality, nineteenth century racial theories, and twentieth century cultural neoracism into a web of anti-Haitian attitudes, racial stereotypes and historical distortion."[31] This ideology consolidated national emotions in order to otherize Haitian blacks, equating blackness with Haitian populations,

and assigning blackness negative traits. The construction of the Dominican nation in opposition to Haiti was based on a revisionist history that
excluded the multiple moments of collaboration between the two countries
and the historical ties that bound them in similar pasts and futures.

The national identity cards (*cedulas*) established in 1932 became a major
generator of capital for the government and helped to further its ideology
of '*mestizaje*' by identifying black Dominicans as 'Indian'.[32] The *cedulas*
were required to be carried by all Dominican citizens and was another way
to recondition and strip a black identity. Thus the 'African Americans',
'Cocolos'[33] and black Dominicans were forced to adhere to an 'Indio' classification and acquiesce to the national and political vision.[34] "Ethnically,
Indians represented a category typified by non-whiteness as well as non-
blackness, which would easily accommodate the racial in-betweeness of
the Dominican mulatto."[35] 'Indio' thus became an ethnic category that was
used to classify any of the dark-skinned populations of the island vis à vis
the blacks (Haitians) who lived next door.

Anti-Haitianismo ideologies were constructed by Trujillo and supported
by the elites of the nation in order to consolidate and maintain their power
under the threat of the Haitian desires to unite the island. Lil Despradel
argues that it was Dominican historians who maintained and created
revised versions of anti-Haitianismo while exalting the Hispanic heritage
to influence nationalist feelings. Previous governments, beginning with the
Spanish colonial authorities, had used this rhetoric to drive the national
image, but it had not been made into a state-sponsored ideology until Trujillo. This anti-Haitianismo began to be enforced in regions with larger
Haitian and black populations following the massacre of Haitians and
black Dominicans along the Dominican border in 1937.

Alongside the government and the elites the local branch of the Catholic Church also promoted anti-Haitianismo, by promoting and helping to
instill "white Hispanic values in the colonist."[36] In the Dominican Republic
and much of Latin America, unlike Anderson's assertion of secularity, the
church and the state were linked in structuring the nation. In the Trujillo
regime's initial years the Catholic Church and the government had a strong
relationship. 'Dominicanidad' was built upon the tenets of Catholicism that
were linked to the European motherland. Several letters published in Saez's
work point to the various levels of relationship, including the incorporation
of religious doctrine such as Catholic morals into the Dominican educational system.[37] The church and the state engendered a symbiotic relationship in which they mutually supported and benefitted from the advances of
the nation. This relationship had its tensions as the Church was the only
organization that Trujillo could manipulate but not control. Their relationship waned toward the end of the regime as the violence and repression in
the country escalated, affecting representatives of the Church.[38]

The power Trujillo needed to fulfill his vision required the domination of
both the state and civil society. Civil society then became the material base

for hegemony whereby coercion was exerted by the state, legally enforcing these behaviors for non-consenting groups. For the rural population, prosperity could be reached through acquiescing to the desires of the nation and leaving behind their individual identities. Communities not willing to succumb to these powers were forced to comply through direct action and violence. In the case of the African American enclave in Samaná these eviscerations were far more pronounced than those of other communities because of their linguistic, racial, educational and religious differences.

By redefining the Dominican nation through anti Haitianismo, the regime demanded that the black and mulatto population within the DR 'lighten' themselves by assuming the 'Indio' identity and Hispanic culture, or to be "ostracized and excluded from the national mainstream."[39] Anti-Haitianismo in the context of Samaná provided the basis for the identity shift that occurred in the town from the 1930s onward as a "manifestation of the long term evolution of racial prejudices, the selective interpretation of historical facts, and the creation of a Nationalist Dominican false consciousness."[40]

The indoctrination that occurred through education, history, politics and popular culture was too intense to navigate for some families. Interviews with various descendants of the African American immigrants reveal a serious disconnect between the past and present.[41] In one family of descendants, all seven children married white men and women, as a way to improve their phenotype. Most of the younger generations remain unaware of the story of their ancestors and do not speak English. Dora Vanderhorst, one of the descendants, explains:

No, that [referring to the population of Haitians in the area] was cut out. My mother what saw that. Ay they had cut that out for years . . . all the different presidents cut that out . . . 'Cause they run out the Haitians from here twice. So then some of the presidents didn't want to know about them Haitians. Especially Trujillo.[42]

OLD-TIME RELIGION AND COMMUNITY EDUCATION

The AME Church was a space of collective praxis to shape thinking and create an organic intellectual class that differed from the rest of the population. The Church assumed a space of contention against national ideologies, and it became a space of collectivity, education and organization of a mass element. The Church became a beacon of resistance, a place of expression and collaboration and a place to maintain the language and identity of the community. Because the state was conflated with the Catholic Church, the two saw the need to intervene in the religious practices of the AME Church in Samaná. These interventions caused the religious and educational systems to change.

The Church "had traditionally provided and continues to provide the sources for role models and mate selection."[43] Various travelers' accounts of the nineteenth century mention that the community rarely intermarried, which could account for their ability to maintain English in a Spanish-speaking land.

> Well, here we use to have several little English schools . . . There was a minister from Jamaica called Elijah Mear. He had a college in the mission house an' they taught English, Spanish and French. So when I come to have knowledge, they had different little small English schools here and there about. My father was one. There was lady from Turks Islands named Ruth James. She know a lot of English and she always had a little school . . . Am' here too the AME church, they taught English because Jacob James wife was from Turks Islands. An' you know on Turks Islands they very intelligent. Not only intelligent, but they educated. They use to teach English an' in Norwe' up in Los Algarrobos, the AME had ah . . . Mr. Fade. He was an English man, an English teacher called Mr. Fade . . . He uses to teach in English in Los Algarrobos. Georgie Ray use to teach English in the Northwes'. Ruth James use to teach English in Honduras. An in Clara, they had another lady from Turks Island use to teach English—Miss Rhodie.[44]

Religion became a further space of contention. The churches within the island attempted to exert control over the community. Many of the pastors of Samaná's AME church were from outside of the island. There was also a major struggle over the growing number of protestant congregations as the Catholic Church attempted to attract more followers. "After the 1931 integration of the AME into the Iglesia Evangelica, the pastors were Puerto Rican until in 1957, the first Dominican minister was appointed."[45] The education of the community was an important function supported by the AME Church.[46] "Of my congregation about one quarter can read the hymn books . . . We once had a schoolhouse and a mission house and did much in the way of scattering books and teaching the people; but all was destroyed and burned up during the wars."[47]

> An' the pastors that preached here before came from Jamaica, an when came from England, but, this bein' independent country and the language of the country Spanish, well they preach in Spanish to win the natives from here. Well then the work was transferred to the Board of Christian Work in Santo Domingo, An' they prepared young men, they had sent them to seminary to Puerto Rico. An when they graduated they come back to Santo Domingo and they'r preachin Spanish. But we still preach in English for the ol' people who don't understand or didn't learn Spanish language.[48]

Every relationship of "hegemony is necessarily an educational relationship . . . because it implies both coercion and consent."[49] Trujillo knew that he had to create "a specific situation to justify change in popular psychology"; if he were to realize his dreams of "restoring and consolidating" his country, it would be vital to "stimulate all positive factors and to strip away the negative and inert."[50]

Understanding this, the regime invested in various educational initiatives. The schools were seen as the "vehicles for Trujillista indoctrination."[51] Within them, a new curriculum was established that highlighted the benefactors of the nation, rewriting stories of conflict and creating a new identity of the 'Indio' versus the black neighbors who were a threat to their existence. Starting in the 1940s many of the educational textbooks began to emphasize the Spanish and Indian backgrounds of the population, excluded the Afro-diasporic peoples and demonized its Haitian neighbors. Dominican children "grow up, first, despising and discriminating against Haitians for their past atrocities, second, perceiving themselves as light skinned Hispanics vis a vis the Haitian black, and third, rejecting blackness as alien and barbaric."[52] By establishing schools in all parts of the country and providing a government-sponsored curriculum to be taught, Trujillo ensured that his ideas would be promoted, inculcated and absorbed by the vast majority of Dominicans.[53] His team of historians rewrote the history of the new republic, making sure to center Trujillo as the father of the nation. This indoctrination was pervasive throughout all levels of education.

WHO SPEAKS?

With Trujillo in power Spanish was designated the national language and the church- and community-run schools were closed or abandoned or had to resort to using Spanish as the means of instruction. Martha Ellen Davis argues that language competence is the key to assimilation, and that is what the government of Trujillo achieved by disbanding the English-speaking schools. Dominican scholars have repeatedly lamented the linguistic differences in the region, which indicated the abhorred non-Hispanic influence. For the emigrant community, language was always an integral aspect of their identity and provided a space to maintain a very tight-knit community.

> My mother didn't allow them to speak Spanish in the home. She didn't want them to . . ."Don't you marry with them natives" "Don't you speak that here! Stop with that, don't speak that here." They were living in a country, well, they didn't understand, they didn't understand. They didn't know anything in Spanish. So she didn't want to hear them speak that at all. And less they didn't want their children to mix up with them natives, less with them Haitians . . . They say that was going

to bring down the religion. And it's true because look two sisters of mine have children with the natives, with the Spanish people, as we call them the Spanish people. An they don' go to church.[54]

ERASURE AND REBIRTH

Many historians and writers during the Trujillo era wrote briefly about Samaná and the historical and linguistic backgrounds of its inhabitants, pointing to the differences with the rest of the nation.[55] Some describe it as an aberration to the nation both linguistically and racially. In the introduction to his novel *Macabon Estampas de Samaná*, Bourget in his introduction paints an exotic image of Samaná, quoting Dr. Manuel de Jesus Troncoso de la Concha speaking at a historical conference. "If in Samaná Spanish has become the normal language used, it has been because of the service of obligatory instruction and because of the continuous efforts of the established schools in that region of the country, especially since the year 1930."[56]

Published in 1998, Gregorio Elias Penzo Devers wrote the first volume of his *Compendio histórico de Samaná, 1493–1930* which ended his narrative in 1930; therefore a full historiography of the community of Samaná has yet to be produced. The book does not incorporate Trujillo's modernizing project and its effects on Samaná.[57] Dominican historian Rodriguez Demorizi in his book *Samaná, Pasado y Porvenir* covers the initial period of the foundation and growth of the community until its expansion and the creation of the town of Sanchez. Throughout the book he emphasizes the Hispanic history of the peninsula. Similar to other historians of the time, there was an erasure of the contributions and history of the African Americans and other Afro-diasporic populations.

CONCLUSION

"Anti-Haitianismo ideology is the manifestation of the long term evolution of racial prejudices, the selective interpretation of historical facts, and the creation of a Nationalist Dominican 'false consciousness'."[58] The Afro descendant population in Samaná has continually challenged the dominant racial, linguistic and religious tropes of the Dominican nation. Dominicans "have not escaped the mental scars inflicted by generations of official vilification of Haitians. Anti-Haitianism(o) persists as a viable political instrument for conservatives."[59] Nearly 90 percent of the Dominican Republic is made up of Black and mulatto populations, "yet, no other country in the hemisphere exhibits greater indeterminacy regarding the populations sense of racial identity."[60] The historical narratives and elite visions of the country still maintain and support ideological processes of whiteness that were taught in the schools and reinforced through media images from outside as well as within the country. Managed by the state, these processes have transformed the ethnic and historical landscape of Samaná.

An analysis of the community of Samaná provides the opportunity to explore state spatial configurations and interventions in issues of identity and processes of socialization. The local inhabitants have both resisted and acquiesced to the multiple strategic and global interests that have historically swept through the region. The differing backgrounds of people and experiences with structures of governance led to the formation of a decentralized form of governance that could be equated with autonomy. This autonomy was constantly at threat through the multiple projects of rule that the region encountered. In the context of Samaná, power exerted through these projects of rule have managed to rewrite the historical narrative to leave out the experience of those who do not fit within its construction. With the consolidation of the Dominican state and the transition to capitalism escalating, there were pronounced transformations in the spatial configuration and concerted efforts to dismantle the perceived autonomy of the community. These changes had direct impacts on how the community organized and subsisted, and affected their racial, religious and linguistic identities.

The town of Samaná is currently going through a process of foreign gentrification and environmental degradation and already shows signs of extreme cultural and social change. This process has now reached its height with the entry of Spanish multinationals that have purchased and built new hotels in the area and have been important in the establishment of an international airport near the town. Those willing and wanting to develop the region are undecided on the effects of tourism and whether the benefits will actually reach the people. Because of the increased amount of tourism there has been a resurgence of English language in Samaná, but its importance for the community "has shifted from performing a highly symbolic and affective function to strategic commercial functions."[61]

The community is rapidly being taken over by foreigners and other affluent members of Dominican society, devouring the lands for sale to construct yacht clubs and limited access facilities. These changes to Samaná society and the African American community have had dire effects on the young within the community, who are no longer taught their history within the educational system. The contemporary descendants of the Samaná community are bombarded by foreign images of capital and consumed by increasing rates of drug abuse and AIDS. They observe the mostly white tourists who seasonally invade their coasts, spending lavishly and effortlessly. They watch as the beaches they grew up on are now set aside for hotel guests.[62] Influenced by the educational indoctrination received throughout various generations, many seek partners of lighter complexion to 'improve the race'.

Focusing a lens on Samaná, showcases the 'otherness' of the community that in the eyes of the regime demanded a transformation to fit it within the Dominican national imaginary. The Samaná residents' Blackness challenged the interests of the Dominican regime. The generational transformation orchestrated by the Dominican state, led many Samaná descendants to not learn the language, and to become enmeshed in the notion of 'improving the race'. In building a national identity their language needed to be set aside for the creation of the new nation. The indoctrination that occurred through education, history, politics and popular culture were too intense to navigate for some. Interviews with various descendants have shown a large disconnect between the past and present. Many of the youth do not know the story of their ancestors, and have come to identify as Dominicans in the image of Trujillo, a country where blackness can no longer reside. To reclaim Black identity is now a revolutionary act. Too many local youth grow up without knowing the history of their families and their surnames, and would greatly benefit from perceiving their ancestors as participants in the shaping of the region of Samaná and the Dominican nation.

Family was at the forefront of the identities of the African Americans of Samaná, and with the familial breakdown and flight to the cities this became less important. The everyday identities of the descendants in Samaná are rooted in deeply historical processes. They have been able to rework the meanings and memories that have been mutually influenced by power and geography. Although the printed historical narrative points to the isolation of the community as the reason why they maintained these historical links, it is a false claim. My initial research suggests a different story, a story of the articulation of global and local forces. Tracing the story of Samaná is a methodological enterprise that uses individual family life to observe the Caribbean entanglements that scholars have avoided. These entanglements suggest the power of individuals in deciding their own identities based on needs and desires rather than impositions from afar. This is a continuing concern in a community that fled the US and was contemplated later by authorities as a North American foothold on a potential US territory. Through the maintenance of their religious and ethnic identities, the African American descendants of Samaná defy simplifying, dominant narratives of nation and race.

The increasing dependence on the state by the rural population gave the Trujillo regime the power to exert its pressures and maintain its hegemony throughout the countryside. For Turits, the "Trujillo regime may be unique amongst dictatorships of the twentieth century Latin America for the extent to which elderly peasants have nostalgically recalled its support of the peasantry."[63] Aside from these memories, there also exist memories of destruction and disagreement, of resistance and claims of agency. These are the memories that permeate the community of Samaná. Of course, memories are selective visions of moments, but the coinciding narrative behind these memories is consistent with attribution of the burning of the town to the jealousy of a man who, for many, had already brutalized the community in more ways than simply physical. In its rebirth, the control would no longer rest in the hands of the community, but in the rural planners and state-induced development strategies for interests beyond the local.

NOTES

1. Unless otherwise noted, all accounts of the destruction of Samaná provided in this chapter are derived from oral histories that I collected as part of my Masters thesis and as preliminary work for my doctoral degree. During the period of 2004–2009 I conducted 29 interviews with elderly residents in the town of Samaná who shared the surnames of the original African American settlers in Samana

2. To fund their religious endeavors, the African American descendants contacted the Wesleyan Church of England who offered them support in the form of a pre-built church and a Reverend to lead their services. This account is derived from the oral histories described in n1. Interviews by author, Samaná, Dominican Republic, 2004–2009.

3. The US did not recognize Haiti as a sovereign nation until 1862.

4. Harry Hoetink, "Americans in Samaná," *Caribbean Quarterly* 2, no. 3 (1962): 6.

5. Julie Winch, "To Reunite the Great Family: Free Blacks and Haitian Emigration" (paper presented at the annual meeting of the Organization of American Historians, Apr. 6–9, St. Louis, MO), 3.

6. Hoetink, "Americans in Samaná," 6.

7. Winch, "To Reunite the Great Family," 8.

8. Ibid,. 12.

9. Hoetink, "Americans in Samaná,", 10. and Jean Stephens, "La Emigracion de Negros Libertos Norteamericanos a Haiti en 1824–25," *Estudios Dominicanos* 3, no. 14 (1974).

10. Richard Newman, *Freedoms Prophet: Bishop Richard Allen, the AME Church and the Black Founding Fathers* (New York: New York University Press, 2008), 72.

11. To attract many of the emigrants Boyer offered incentives to the African Americans. They would receive full political and civil rights, freedom of worship, free passage, paid sustenance for four months and an allocation of thirty-six acres for every twelve farmers. Boyer was also seeking support for his black nation by seeking solidarity with other blacks in the hemisphere.

12. Stephens, "La Emigracion de Negros Libertos Norteamericanos," 40.

13. Hoetink, "Americans in Samaná," 6.

14. Ibid., 10.

15. As the generations passed they began to participate in the politics of the area and became involved in several of the Dominican revolutionary movements.

16. For a ten-year period there existed a direct steamer line that connected New York, Samaná, Santo Domingo and New Orleans, whereby information and people moved unrestricted through these spaces.

17. Gregorio Penzo Devers, *Compendio Historico de Samaná* (Santo Domingo, RD: Editora Buho, 1991), 121.

18. Jose Vigo, *Language and Society in Samaná* (New York: Schomburg Center for Research on Black Culture, 1987), 44.

19. Papito Coplin, in discussion with the author, 2004.

20. Ciriaco Stubbs, in discussion with the author, 2012.

21. Howard J. Wiarda, *Dictatorship and Development: The methods of control in Trujillo's Dominican Republic* (University of Florida Press, 1968), 28.

22. Rafael Molina Trujillo, *The Basic Policies of a Regime* (Santo Domingo: Editora del Caribe, 1960), 13.

23. Ibid., 11.

24. Richard Turits, *Foundations of Despotism* (California: Stanford University Press, 2003), 218.

25. Benedict Anderson, *Imagined Communities*, (New York: Verso Press, 1983), 75.

26. Ibid,. 89.

27. Juan Bosch, *Trujillo, Causas de una Tirania sin ejemplo* (Santo Domingo: Editora Alfa y Omega, 1961); Wiarda, *Dictatorship and Development.*

28. Turits, *Foundations of Despotism*, 13.

29. Antonio Gramsci, *Selections from the Prison Notebooks: Antonio Gramsci*, ed. Quintin Hoare and Geoffrey Nowell Smith (New York: International Publishers, 1971), 244.

30. Nancy Applebaum and Karin Rosenblatt, *Race and Nation in Latin America*, (Durham: North Carolina Press, 2007).

31. Ernesto Sagas, *Race and Politics in the Dominican Republic*, (Gainesville: University of Florida Press, 2000), 21.

32. Turits, *Foundations of Despotism*, 87.

33. Cocolos was the name given to the English-speaking emigrants from the British Virgin Islands into the region. Many of the 'Cocolos' married with African American descendants and participated in the same spaces for religious ceremonies and schooling.

34. On a personal note, in 2007 I applied for my first cedula in Samaná. After receiving it I saw that, on the identification portion of the cedula, I had been categorized as "I", indicating 'Indio'. I was never asked—it was assumed.

35. Silvio Torres-Saillant, "The Tribulations of Blackness: Stages in Dominican Racial Identity," *Latin American Perspectives* 25, no. 3 (1998): 139.

36. Jose Luis Saez, *La sumision bien pagada: La iglesia Dominicana bajo la era de Trujillo (1930–1961) Tomo 1* (Santo Domingo: Archivo General de la Nación, 2008), 88.

37. Letter by Can. Armando Lamarche to Dr. Pedro Henriquez Urena, superintendent of teaching, requesting the incorporation of religion into the national schools. Saez, *La sumision bien pagada*, 123.

38. Trujillo went as far as signing a concordat in 1954 giving the church additional rights within the state; in return he received a papal blessing for his family and an official annulment of his second marriage. Wiarda, *Dictatorship and Development*, 143; Saez, *La sumisión bien pagada*, 91.

39. Sagas, *Race and Politics in the Dominican Republic*, 66.

40. Ibid., 122.

41. Many of the younger generations of African American descendants were unaware of their ancestor's historical migration. Interviews by author, Samaná, Dominican Republic, 2008.

42. Dora Vanderhorst, interview by Jose Vigo, Samaná, Dominican Republic, 1982. This interview was conducted by Linguistic Anthropologist Jose Vigo in 1982, who passed away before he was able to publish his work. It is part of the Jose Vigo Collection at the Schomburg Center of the New York Public Library System.

43. Valerie Smith, "A Merging of Two Cultures: The Afro Hispanic Immigrants of Samaná, Dominican Republic," *Afro-Hispanic Review* Vol. 8 No. 1/2 (Jan./May 1989): 9.

44. Vanderhorst, in discussion.

45. Hoetink, "Americans in Samaná," 19.

46. Once the church services began to be conducted in Spanish, English was relegated to the home environment, where many of the youths could understand the language but did not speak it.

47. Hoetink, "Americans in Samaná," 15.

48. Sam James, interview by Jose Vigo, Samaná, Dominican Republic, 1982. This interview was conducted by Linguistic Anthropologist Jose Vigo in

1982, who passed away before he was able to publish his work. It is part of the Jose Vigo Collection at the Schomburg Center of the New York Public Library System.

49. Gramsci, *Selections from the Prison Notebooks*, 350.
50. Trujillo, *Basic Policies of a Regime*, 30.
51. Wiarda, *Dictatorship and Development*, 129.
52. Sagas, *Race and Politics in the Dominican Republic*, 76.
53. The textbooks used in the schools carried the name of Trujillo as the author, making him an educator as well as a statesman.
54. Vanderhorst, in discussion.
55. What prevails in the novel is the alienation of linguistic differences and the mocking of the heavy accents used by the characters in the book purported to be those of African American descent. The constant images constructed throughout the novel are of inadequacy, foreignness and difference that somehow must be subdued. Luis Eduardo Bourget, *Macabon estampas de Samana* Santo Domingo: La Trinitaria (1961), 9.
56. Bourget, *Macabon estampas de Samaná*, 9.
57. His plans were to create a second volume that incorporated the later years, but he passed away before this work was ever completed. We are left with what was published and the conspicuous date of 1930.
58. Sagas, *Race and Politics in the Dominican Republic*, 76.
59. Torres-Saillant, "The Tribulationsof Blackness, 139.
60. Ibid,. 126.
61. Vigo, *Language and Society in Samaná*, 42.
62. When purchasing a cell phone in the summer of 2009, I was asked for a foreign passport and was told that if I had one the price of the phone and the service would be one hundred pesos, the equivalent of three dollars cheaper than it would be for residents. There was no explanation given when questioned as to why, only that it was company policy.
63. Turits, *Foundations of Despotism*, 206.

14 Redrawing the Lines

Understanding Race and Citizenship through the Lens of Afro-Mexican Migrants in Winston-Salem, NC[1]

Jennifer A. Jones

In this chapter, I examine empirical data from a case study on immigration and race relations in Winston-Salem, North Carolina. Winston-Salem has experienced a dramatic increase in the number of Afro-Mexican, Mestizo Mexican and other Latino migrants since the 1990s. Recent migration estimates indicate that about half of persons who moved to North Carolina over the last two decades are Latino, and over three-quarters of Latinos in the state are Mexicans. Using sixteen months of ethnographic fieldwork and in-depth interviews with Afro-Mexicans, Mestizo Mexicans and community members in Mexico and North Carolina, I explore both contexts to explain the racialization and assimilation outcomes of Afro-Mexicans and Mestizo Mexicans in Winston-Salem.

Existing theory has generally explained assimilation in two ways. First, assimilation is described using a straight-line model,[2] in which cultural assimilation and economic mobility operate in tandem, and increase with each generation. This model was derived from the experiences of early twentieth-century European migrants and their descendants. The second is a segmented assimilation model,[3] in which ethnic background serves as a resource for mobility. This model was developed in response to the different patterns of mobility among the ethnically diverse post-1965 migrant waves and highlights two paths—an ethnic-identified path that leads to upward mobility, and a race-identified path that leads to downward mobility and assimilation among US minority groups. Like other non-European migrants in the segmented model, immigrant Mexicans experience both state and interpersonal discrimination, and arrive with little access to capital.

However, over the last decade, the legal regime around ethnic identity has shifted, leaving Mexican immigrants unable to capitalize on their ethnic identities. Moreover, in North Carolina, unlike Mexicans in traditional receiving contexts such as Texas, California and Arizona, there are no capital-holding ethnic communities from which they can draw support. As a result, the ethnic path to mobility is cut off. Instead, Mexican migrants see their fates not through the prism of the American Dream, but through the lens of the African American experience of discrimination. Mexicans in Winston-Salem and across the South experience pervasive institutional discrimination, are focused on the struggle of survival and are living in a context in which the Latino population arrived less than two decades ago.

Building on the framework of obstacles presented by segmented assimilation theorists, I find that certain contexts deny mobility through both traditional means, as well as offer an alternative pathway to mobility through race-based solidarity. My data suggests that migration to new economically robust urban and suburban regions in the South, migration from new sending areas and increasingly repressive immigration policies at the state and municipal level can produce the conditions to develop a sense of closeness and shared status with African Americans, allowing them to lay claim to resources as racialized minorities rather than as coethnics.

Contemporary immigration paradigms contribute to a popular discourse about immigration that marks (often incorrectly) all Latinos as noncitizens.[4] Formal legislation such as CAPS, Secure Communities, 287(g) and other anti-immigrant state-based policies such as Alabama's HB56 reinforces the idea of Latinos, particularly Mexicans, as illegal, as not belonging, and as 'Others'. Scholars of Latino identity and citizenship suggest that these policy and discursive shifts, as Young notes, "uniquely positioned Latinos as permanently foreign immigrants in the imagination of Anglo Americans."[5]

For Latinos, particularly Mexicans, discriminatory practices predicated on the assumption of noncitizenship and the risk of deportation make racial and ethnic associations an important aspect not only of mobility but also of daily survival. This new context thus calls into question the applicability of traditional and segmented assimilation models[6] in describing the experiences of contemporary Mexican migrants to new immigrant destinations in the Midwest and South.

Specifically, contrary to previous studies,[7] I find that a significant number of Mexicans express closeness to African Americans as a result of the specific and relatively neutral meanings they attach to blackness before they migrate, as well as the increasing anti-Mexican sentiment in new immigrant destinations throughout the US. Due to these constraints, both Afro- and Mestizo Mexicans recognize their new contexts as one in which mobility is blocked. As a result, they assert a sense of shared minority status and interests, framing African Americans as their coethnics who both share their racialized experience and provide tangible support. These findings contradict much of the race and immigration literature, which tends to gloss over racial variation among Latinos, as well as the shifting local context within the arrival country, in determining racial and ethnic identities.[8]

In analyzing these conditions I argue that the specific racial imaginaries that Afro- and Mestizo Mexicans bring with them, combined with conditions of high levels of surveillance, perceived threat and new structural constraints, produced an assimilation paradigm of blocked mobility, in which the termination of access to social, political and economic capital racializes rather than ethnicizes Mexicans. In doing so, I challenge current assimilation paradigms and highlight the ways in which racialization can paradoxically both close off avenues to mobility and integration and create alternative avenues for accessing resources through a shared minority identity.

RACIAL DISTANCING

As highlighted earlier, the origins of the literature on immigration and incorporation is the concept of straight-line assimilation, theorized initially by Park, and then more notably by Gordon, as well as Glazer and Moynihan.[9] In an effort to theorize the incorporation of Eastern European immigrants in the 1920s and 1930s into the white majority, Gordon and others elaborated a theory of assimilation in which Europeans lost their ethnic distinctiveness over time through extended contact, adaptation, intermarriage and reproduction. This process of becoming white Americans was viewed as more or less inevitable, as well as necessary to achieve socioeconomic mobility. Even when taking into account later waves of non-European immigrants, the literature continues to highlight incorporation and assimilation as a function of avoiding native-born minorities, particularly African Americans, if upward mobility is to be achieved.[10] In this articulation, the more time poor, nonwhite immigrants spend in the US, and therefore presumably become acculturated into the minority underclass, the more negative the structural assimilation trajectory. Thus, to be associated with African Americans is to lose one's access to opportunity.

More recently, historians and sociologists of the early European migration waves expand on this proposition by highlighting the process of both being accepted by mainstream whites and actively seeking out such acceptance. Whiteness scholars argue that acquiring a white identity had everything to do with facilitating structural assimilation, arguing that a key piece of this process was to distance oneself from being identified with blacks, as many European groups, including Hungarians, Italians and Irish, initially were.[11] In this framework, whiteness was perceived by new immigrants as a key asset in accessing economic mobility. As a result, distancing oneself from blackness was a necessary strategy in acquiring access to the privileges that whiteness afforded. This linking of racial identity, distancing and upward mobility is an essential frame, many scholars argue, through which immigrant incorporation is achieved and understood.

In the post-1965 era of immigration in which the vast majority of migrants to the US (regardless of status) are non-European, new paradigms for understanding the prospects for assimilation have become necessary for contemporary immigration scholarship. In taking on contemporary immigrant incorporation, scholars of nonwhite immigration have sought to uncover how migrants assimilate when phenotype makes the strategy of achieving whiteness difficult, if not impossible.[12] Because African Americans are situated in this paradigm as the prototypical 'underclass', most immigration scholarship has taken a prescriptive view of the whiteness theory of immigrant incorporation, arguing that non-European immigrants who seek a slice of the pie are best served by avoiding blackness and aspiring toward whiteness and mobility through racial distancing.

Although some scholars maintain that straight-line assimilation processes continue to dominate, even among Latino, Asian, African and other nonwhite immigrants, segmented assimilation has become the dominant paradigm of contemporary immigration theory. This framework modifies the straight-line assimilation model with attention to racial differences and the relative difficulty immigrants may experience being accepted into the mainstream and achieving structural mobility, as well as avoiding downward mobility into the minority underclass.[13] Even in the case of black migrants, association with African Americans is found to be problematic. Among black immigrants, who presumably face discrimination due to skin color, upward mobility is achieved through distancing themselves from African Americans.[14] As a result, the vast majority of the literature on Afro-Caribbeans highlights their efforts to maintain ethnic ties in order to practice what immigrants, regardless of era, seem to already know—it is a strategy to make them appear preferable for hiring and allows them to tap into ethnic networks, and therefore, upward mobility.[15] As Rogers notes, "Waters has argued this tendency is most pronounced among middle-class Afro-Caribbeans eager to shore up their status and guard themselves and their children against socioeconomic backsliding."[16]

This framing in which mobility and access to resources is obtained by distancing from African Americans is prevalent throughout the immigration and whiteness literatures, but it has not gone unchallenged. Scholars such as Portes and Rumbaut, Portes and Stepick, and Rogers find distancing practices to be untenable over time.[17] They maintain prevailing racial inequalities in American life ultimately compel the immigrants to identify with African Americans around a shared racial group identity.[18] Rogers in particular finds that those Caribbean blacks with collectivist beliefs were more likely to routinely interact with blacks in civil and social networks. They in turn adopted black group consciousness as a source of identification. It is worth noting that this form of identity had an empowering effect on those Afro-Caribbean respondents, with none of the demoralizing consequences typically associated with race-based oppositional consciousness among immigrants in other studies.[19]

Moreover, as Stepick and Stepick argue,[20] there is growing evidence that associating with native minorities as collective nonwhites can produce positive outcomes, such as access to diversity programs in which employers and universities seek out applicants who will increase institutional diversity.[21] Moreover, there is reason to believe that the advantages or disadvantages of identifying and developing close social relations with native-born minorities, particularly blacks, vary depending on the conditions of minorities in local context. Neckerman, Carter and Lee address this criticism concretely, arguing that the segmented assimilation paradigm largely ignores the cultural and class heterogeneity of minority communities, and thus does not consider the range of possibilities that acculturation into minority populations can mean.[22] In particular, they highlight that acculturation into middle-class minority communities that have been able to overcome structural barriers and discrimination to achieve economic and social mobility. They propose attention to a "minority culture of mobility" that "draws on available symbols, idioms and practices to respond to distinctive problems of being middle class and minority".[23] Indeed, Perlmann and Waldinger note that the problem of the incorporation of newcomers that results in downward assimilation (a situation that scholars argue is best achieved in part by avoiding relations with native-born minorities) is that immigrants are incorporated into highly segregated inner city structures where both resources and attitudes toward mobility are poor.[24]

Their findings indicate that the issue of mobility and intergroup relations between new immigrant groups and native-born minorities is not determined by race, but instead is shaped by class status, access to the labor market and community-level resources, in which some minority communities may indeed hold mainstream norms and significant resources. Therefore, despite an overwhelming emphasis on racial distancing as a key mechanism through which strategic racial and ethnic identities are produced, this smaller body of emerging scholarship indicates that minority racial affinities can be more productive than a strategy of avoidance. In what follows, I explain how the structural conditions of both the sending and receiving context contribute to productive racial affinities among Mexicans and blacks in Winston-Salem.

RACE IN MEXICO

In Mexico, it is estimated that Afro-Mexicans make up between 1 and 10 percent of the 105 million Mexican nationals. Unlike many indigenous ethnic groups in Mexico, the historical and contemporary presence of Afro-Mexicans is relatively unknown to Mexicans at large. Despite this rich history of Afro-Mexicans over the early centuries of modern Mexico, Afro-Mexicans have been erased from the national imaginary. Spurred by the abolition of slavery and the end of the War of Independence in 1821, Mexico shifted to a more nationalist frame built around an ideology of mestizaje,[25] rather than the specific racial caste ordering of the colonial period.[26] Although some cultural vestiges remain, it is assumed that Afro-Mexicans have fully assimilated, if not disappeared, into mainstream Mexico.

In many cases, however, particularly along the rural Pacific coastal areas of Guerrero and Oaxaca and the small towns of central Veracruz, Afro-Mexican towns are abundant. Afro-Mexicans were virtually isolated from the rest of Mexico until the late 1980s and 1990s. Although there has always been a trickle of migrants to the US from these areas, few of these towns were connected to highways or had local phone lines until recently. This isolation created a strong sense of local community, but also a general disconnect from the nation for most of Mexico's history.[27] As a result, identity formation processes within these towns are varied, involving complex myths and ideas about blackness that define Afro-Mexican origins through Caribbean migration, a largely historical framing that places Afro-Mexicans outside the national consciousness.

In Mexico, the rise of mestizaje as a national racial identity defined as the union of European and indigenous backgrounds has come to represent a multiethnic but distinctively nonblack national identity. This has resulted in a situation in which blackness has relatively little social meaning in terms of national, political, social or cultural identity. This social erasure distinguishes Afro-Mexicans from the racialization of other Afro-Latinos who come to the US in significant numbers (i.e., Puerto Ricans, Dominicans and Cubans)[28] and arrive from sending nations with significant, if marginalized, black populations. Although many migrants from these regions are also poor, Latino, foreign and noncitizens in the US,[29] blackness is a part of their national mythology (such as antiblack or racial democracy ideologies) in ways that simply do not exist for Mexicans.

As a result, although their identities are understood and made meaningful within the context of their own towns, because Afro-Mexicans' Mexicanness is largely rendered invisible outside of their regional homes, Afro-Mexicans traveling outside of their regional contexts are frequently perceived as immigrants. They are often requested to show proof of citizenship or residency. In some cases, they are requested to prove their national allegiance by singing the national anthem at checkpoints because it is assumed they are Caribbean nationals, most often Cubans. This social erasure of their identity as Mexicans undoubtedly has consequences for the identities they assume in Mexico and carry with them upon arrival in the US.

In many Afro-Mexican towns, since the early 1990s, migration has increasingly become a way of life. In these regions, the influx of cheap agricultural goods from the US due to NAFTA, increased prices for farming goods and food, and the low value of the peso resulted in massive job loss in small-scale farming,[30] creating a massive incentive to migrate. As a result, whereas migrants to Winston-Salem, North Carolina, are coming from all over, migrants from the Costa Chica make up a significant proportion of the local Mexican population.

MIGRATION AND SHIFTING CONTEXTS

This growth of Afro-Mexican migration is a hugely significant change, because, whereas Mexicans immigrating to the US have been arriving steadily since the mid-1800s, the 1990s marked a huge uptick in migrants coming from regions other than the traditional sending areas of western and northern Mexico. Moreover, there has been a massive increase in migrants settling in the Midwest and the South.[31] Coastal states (including Veracruz) have rarely accounted for more than 2 percent of migrants prior to 1990, and migrants from the central states (including the Costa Chica) accounted for fewer than 20 percent until the late 1980s.[32] My fieldwork in Mexico suggests that migration patterns have expanded largely because of the economic and political shifts in both countries. In turn, remittances now serve as an essential form of supplementary income where local economies are dominated by small-scale agriculture.

Hoppenjans and Richardson suggest that Afro-Mexican migration to Winston-Salem can be traced to a single man in 1978 by the name of Biterbo Calleja-Garcia, whose *coyote* persuaded him to settle in North Carolina instead of Texas.[33] Shortly after, Calleja-Garcia persuaded family members to leave Santa Ana, California, a prominent settling region for Mexican migrants from the Costa Chica in the 1980s and early 1990s. Like Calleja-Garcia, Mexican migrants trickled into North Carolina throughout the 1980s and 1990s. By the end of the 1990s, however, North Carolina was firmly embedded in an economic shift from a primarily agricultural and manufacturing economy to a diversified model that attracted finance, medical centers and other large corporate plants. As economic expansion continued, the demand for labor increased.

Scholars argue that in the 1990s the US South drew such a significant proportion of migrants in part because of a general reluctance in the region by employers and their allies to engage in immigration enforcement, as well as the low cost of living and abundant work.[34] Census data, as well as respondents, indicate that not only were Latinos coming from the Mexican states of Guerrero, Oaxaca and Veracruz in large numbers, but also they were leaving traditional receiving states, such as California and Arizona, and resettling in the Southeast and Midwest.

In 2008, I attended a meeting for immigrants at the Winston-Salem public library's Hispanic Resource Center. When discussing migration patterns in a community meeting for immigrants, the facilitator, Sara, asked why people were coming from other states. A young woman answered, saying she had a friend from Arizona, and she told her they moved because the law was 'fuerte' (strong) there, and they couldn't do anything, so they left. Sara nodded, saying that she's heard "that people are coming from the border states [of the US] because it's less violent here, it's calmer here, better weather, it's cheaper, and there's more work." Sara also noted that NAFTA was important in stimulating migration because lots of corporations and factories have left for Mexico. She indicated that it made things too cheap so other people lost their jobs. She emphasized that migrants have no choice—they come out of necessity. This pattern of movement was echoed by many of my respondents, who recounted again and again how family members and friends already living and working in Winston-Salem beckoned them to come to North Carolina from Mexico and California, and to make a better life for themselves.

From 1990 to 2000, the North Carolina population of immigrants increased fourfold, by about three hundred thousand new Latinos. Moreover, only 24 percent of Latinos born outside of the US and living in North Carolina at the time were authorized.[35] This huge increase in Latino arrivals did not go unnoticed, prompting a backlash to Latino population growth through a rise in local immigration enforcement. As of 2004, North Carolina was one of ten states that issued driver's licenses to applicants without verification of citizenship status. In 2005, however, the governor signed the Technical Corrections Act, which determined that social security numbers would be the only acceptable documentation for driver's licenses. Then, beginning in 2006, several North Carolina counties signed on to a previously unused provision of the Illegal Immigration Reform and Immigrant Responsibility Act (IIRIRA), 287(g).[36] This provision created agreements between local governments and the Immigration and Customs Enforcement (ICE) to deputize local law enforcement as ICE agents. Although this program was intended to seek out and deport violent felons, 287(g) was a key mechanism through which deportations occurred.[37]

As a result, local officials under 287(g) began to use this voluntary agreement to turn over minor offenders, such as those driving without a license, to ICE.[38] Although this program was activated in twenty-four states, North Carolina was one of the most enthusiastic states in its involvement, with eight active county agreements.[39] Despite recent hearings in the Congressional Judiciary Committee regarding complaints of effectiveness and violations of the rights of undocumented and citizen Latinos alike, rumors of new agreements being signed throughout the state were common, as sheriffs from all over made inquiries regarding requests. In fact, North Carolina counties represented one-fourth of all 287(g) requests as of 2008.[40] Although many sheriffs denied that 287(g) is intended to rid the state of undocumented migrants, a report by the North Carolina ACLU and the Immigration and Human Rights Policy Clinic at UNC Chapel Hill found that:

> Unfortunately, undocumented residence itself is increasingly identified as the predicate crime meriting police attention and resources. Section 287(g) is consequently utilized to purge a town of an 'unwelcome' immigrant presence. In first seven months since implementation of its MOA, Mecklenburg County [Charlotte] processed over one thousand undocumented residents for deportation. Alamance County, although operating with a smaller population and fewer enforcement resources, boasts of deporting over four hundred individuals over the first nine months of participation in the program.[41]

Moreover, the report argues that a majority of individuals arrested by 287(g) officers in the North Carolina counties of Gaston, Mecklenburg and

Alamance were arrested for traffic offenses.[42] The program is credited with deputizing 1,300 officers nationally, as well as identifying 304,678 removable immigrants. A significant proportion of this activity has taken place in North Carolina and neighboring states in the Southeast.[43] The dismantling of rights and privileges included a mix of national, state and local laws that produced particularly dire consequences for undocumented migrants in North Carolina. This included: the requirement of social security numbers to receive state-issued identification, drivers' licenses and plates; the implementation of 287(g) programs; the requirement that all state employees be screened for documentation; reduced social services eligibility; and the barring of undocumented persons from community colleges. Moreover, the assumption that all Latinos in the state are potentially undocumented created a host of opportunities for widespread discriminatory practices regardless of status. Thus, a shift in policy and attitude had very real consequences for North Carolinian Latinos, changing their assimilation prospects dramatically. Indeed, as Sara noted, "the panic around 287(g) is a new fear, it's been sudden, because it's just now being used to control the flow of people who come and go."

RACE AND WINSTON-SALEM

In Forsyth County, where Winston-Salem is located, the Hispanic population reached 12.2 percent of the population by 2008, representing a rise in the Latino population since 1990 of over 1000 percent since 1990.[44] This change was startling for Winston-Salem, a medium-sized but prosperous town built by the oligarchs of RJ Reynolds Tobacco and Hanes Company, long segregated by Highway 52 with blacks on one side and whites on the other. Split with about 40 percent blacks and 60 percent whites for much of the twentieth century, demographic and political change has always come slow to Winston-Salem. The sudden influx of Latinos has in many ways forced Winston-Salem to deal with issues around race, identity and community at a pace to which it was entirely unaccustomed, making it a ripe context for experimental enforcement policies. Although Forsyth County does not participate in the 287(g) program,[45] it has considered entering an agreement with ICE,[46] and experienced similar levels of anti-immigrant rhetoric as was found throughout the state.

My study suggests there have been so few Latinos in the state prior to the 1990s that the primary racial cues available to make sense of the shifting circumstances of the state are the leadership, struggles and conflicts of the African American community. Unlike traditional migrant-receiving destinations, race in North Carolina has been understood almost exclusively through black and white relationships. Moreover, Latinos, particularly Mexican immigrants, felt they were being shunted to the bottom of the racial hierarchy alongside blacks due to the actions of whites who were both feared and mistrusted by many. This was in part because many Latinos have little to no contact with whites, and because they saw whites as the power structure that deprived undocumented migrants of the various rights and privileges they needed to work and live in North Carolina.

Afro-Mexican migrant Juan, in his mid-forties, who has been living and working in Winston-Salem for over ten years, described the position of Latinos this way:

> In my opinion, Latinos are at the bottom. The political climate is bad, and people have no rights. . . . For Latinos, the other problems [that African Americans have] don't matter, because they have no rights . . . You know, the President [Bush] is always saying that it's a country of laws, of family values. I don't see that. The impact of immigration is that the idea of human rights doesn't mean anything. The UN can say we are human beings, the church can talk about that, and our voices, but it doesn't matter if we don't have any rights. But it's not the heart of the problem, the bottom line as they say. If we can't speak as equals, then we can't really change anything . . . We have no rights in this country, under this government. For Afro-Americans, it's true that many times their rights are violated. But they can't send them away.

To Juan, both African Americans and Latinos were discriminated against and oppressed, and perhaps Latinos more so. As a result of these state and institutional shifts, I propose that immigrants became acutely aware of the US history of racism, of which they now perceived themselves to be targets. Symbolically, Mexicans pointed to: whites' consistently higher position in the social structure; their own experiences of discrimination; stereotyping and harassment; the use of laws and political institutions to instill fear and take away rights; the need for political change and a 'civil rights movement'; figures from Martin Luther King to President Obama in situating themselves as persons of color linked to African Americans; and their relative physical proximity to blacks (they live in the same neighborhoods, attend the same schools) in making this analysis.

In many ways, the gradual dismantling of rights and services available to immigrants also created a general sense of distrust and distance among Mexicans when referring to whites that did not occur with blacks. One Mestiza woman told me that Anglos learn Spanish so that they can use it against Latinos. She continued, "You have to be careful. They say they are friends, but they are really racist." Few Mexicans in this study, by 2008, viewed the US as an egalitarian state in which everyone succeeds with hard work. Instead, they saw that African Americans were treated as second-class citizens, and that they as Latinos had no rights at all.

Ramon, a young Mestizo construction worker, described his understanding of relations between blacks and whites this way:

Here we get along . . . I get along with blacks, yes, because they've gone through what we are going through. You know the problems that they've had for years, from slavery and all that. The Americans have treated the blacks badly to this day. They have the same problem that we have: racism. And because of this, we get along better. At least, I do with them. Yes. Because we know what it's about. And there are times that, at work, we are there playing, and between the blacks and I, we say the evil things that Americans do.

Thus, rather than enacting a strategy of achieving mobility by distinguishing themselves from the perceived social and cultural defects of African Americans and/or viewing themselves in economic, political and social competition with blacks, many Mexican migrants saw themselves as close to blackness, both as a way to make sense of their experiences of discrimination and exclusion, and to establish relations with blacks.

Although the Latino community was embedded within black neighborhoods and schools, and thus the level of contact was higher than with whites, there was another layer of segregation within these institutions. Churches are divided into English and Spanish services, large employers often segregate their teams by race, immigrant students are funneled into ESL classes and service providers create special teams or hours for Hispanic clients. As a result, prolonged interaction between blacks and Latinos was often limited, at least among first-generation migrants.[47]

Because immigrants moved to Winston-Salem only in the last two decades, this was not necessarily surprising. Nonetheless, many of my respondents spoke of social, political and cultural similarities to blacks, suggesting a symbolic sense of closeness despite a relative lack of a material one. Moreover, in the cases in which contact does exist, it seems to be highest among Afro-Mexicans, who report the greatest cultural and social similarities with African Americans, and sometimes refer to themselves as black. Indeed, some of my respondents reported what they describe as a familial connection to African Americans. As Jorge, a young Afro-Mexican, noted: "I've got a lot of black friends. We listen to the same music, we have the same outlook you know, we are the same, like family . . . black people here, they treat you like a friend, like a brother. White people here, they just treat you like another guy." For many, this included viewing African Americans as natural allies, rather than adversaries, in the pursuit of mobility and equality.

Like Jorge, those who did have experiences with African Americans highlighted those encounters pointing to the relative openness of African Americans to socialize with Mexicans compared to whites. Many of my respondents reported that blacks were friendlier people, more likely to greet them or talk to them than whites, and that they were more likely to know and talk to their African American neighbors than whites.

This is not to say that conflicts between African Americans and Mexicans did not occur. However, when they did, Mexicans were less likely to view these conflicts as systematic prejudice. Instead, they attributed those problems to individual failings, often defining a person as angry, with bad manners or uneducated, but not representative of the norm. Indeed, my respondents' views fit what Kaufmann terms the 'discrimination hypothesis', which suggests that "Latino/black affinity is rooted in perceived discrimination and shared outsider status" and therefore "Latinos who perceive high levels of anti-Latino discrimination . . . would also be the most likely to sense commonality with blacks."[48]

Nevertheless, for the most part, it was the *idea* of blackness in the US context, not only the personal experience with blacks, that provided a set of symbols and meanings—the civil rights movement, state-sanctioned exclusion, and the symbolism and expectations carried by the first black president—that resonated with contemporary Mexican migrants in Winston-Salem. Importantly, this connection could not be attributed simply to having Afro roots. This Latino community in particular was primarily comprised of undocumented immigrants from Mexico, as many as half from the coastal regions. However, there were also significant numbers of other Latinos in the area, particularly Central Americans, Puerto Ricans and Cubans.

Indeed, many Mexicans I interviewed specifically pointed to divisions in the Latino community between Puerto Ricans and Mexicans, underlining Puerto Ricans' citizenship status as the reason for the division. They frequently noted, unprompted, that Puerto Ricans believed they were better than other immigrants and avoided associating with them. Cubans were often cited in a similar way, with their unique access to legal status in the US highlighted. In this way, access to key resources, like citizenship, was far more important in developing ties than color. Importantly, it was the specific forms of racial exclusion experienced by African Americans in the South that mattered here.

Scholars who examine closeness and linked fate tend to gloss over these distinctions in the Latino community, while simultaneously pointing out that Pan-Latino identity is a strong predictor of a sense of linked fate with African Americans.[49] Whether Latinos identify collectively is an empirical question. Although Mexicans often spoke to the collective plight of Latinos, they also were quick to point out a perceived hierarchy within the Latino community, in which Puerto Ricans and Cubans (Dominicans are also sometimes included here) view themselves as more American, with citizenship status and greater access to resources. Central Americans tend to locate themselves in the middle, with greater access to refugee status and visas, with Mexicans occupying the bottom. In this way, legal status and racial identity played important, mutually constitutive roles in shaping the assimilation process, complicating our current understandings of assimilation, and suggesting a need for caution when analyzing Latinos of distinct national origin as one group.

RACE AND MOBILITY

In this way, I uncovered that being Afro-descendant was not a necessary or a sufficient condition for expressing closeness to African Americans. Rather, I argue that it is the combination of their structural position as Mexicans—as the prototypical symbol of undocumented migration—and their perceived similarities with blacks that shaped their assimilation trajectories into a shared minority or racial status with African Americans as mechanisms for establishing community and accessing resources. That is, a small portal of contact combined with a hostile political structure created a context in which most Mexicans, not just Afro-Mexicans, saw themselves as both politically and socially closer to blacks because of what they understood as the shared experiences of being racialized.

Much of the work on segmented assimilation highlights the two pathways of assimilation and acculturation available to migrants. The first path is predicated on maintaining appropriate traditional ethnic values that are approved of and valued by mainstream society, and developing those values as social capital.[50] The other path, often constrained by social class, is predicated on adopting the behaviors of alienated minorities who develop identities that resist mainstream values (often specifically achievement) and therefore become downwardly mobile or stagnant. However, this view presumes that ethnicity translates into social capital in ways that simply do not exist for undocumented migrants, and that racial identity is about resistance to those values, rather than an alternative set of resources.[51]

It also presumes an overwhelming minority underclass, a condition that is not universally applicable, especially in places like wealthy Winston-Salem. I argue that both Mestizo and Afro-Mexicans are moving away from an ethnic identity and toward a racialized one through which they are developing a minority consciousness that they believe they share with African Americans, but they are doing so in a way that is not necessarily downwardly mobile. In contrast, it is heavily dependent on a more inclusive ideology of racial solidarity and shared political and institutional resources rather than ethnic exceptionalism and individualism.

Much of the literature on political coalition building between African Americans and Latinos highlights what seems to be a spurious lack of connection between the two groups. Frequently examining closeness and affinity through the concepts of linked fate[52] and racial attitudes, scholars find[53] that these two groups often perceive each other in stereotypical ways, and more often than not view themselves as in competition and conflict. Indeed, in both rural and traditional destination centers, these findings may not necessarily be surprising. My study suggests, however, that migration to new economically robust urban and suburban regions in the South, migration from new sending areas and increasingly repressive immigration policies at the state and municipal level can produce the conditions for an alternative assimilation trajectory in which Latinos ally with blacks and achieve greater social standing because of it.

RETHINKING ASSIMILATION

Most Mexicans (and many other Latinos) throughout North Carolina wear the stigma of undocumented status throughout their daily lives and are literally under constant surveillance by the state. For them, it is difficult, if not illogical, for Mexicans here to engage in behaviors similar to Mary Waters's West Indians, in which they achieve mobility by distancing themselves from US minorities.[54] In this case, their ethnic status afforded them no privileges in terms of status or access to economic resources. Thus, instead of asserting a distance from African Americans, I found that Mexicans oriented themselves toward them.

Moreover, I speculate that this orientation will continue to build into the second generation, in part because of a transition to bilingual youth who are more able to establish a material closeness—that is, building social, economic and political relationships with African Americans—and in part because, although they themselves are citizens, they remain part of mixed-status families, whose parents, aunts, uncles, cousins and grandparents are at risk. In addition, because over 80 percent of unauthorized immigrants nationally are from Mexico, and Mexicans account for about 30 percent of the foreign-born[55] it is possible that this case is indicative of a larger trend toward permanent coalitions and greater integration between the two groups. I speculate that this is particularly likely to emerge in new destination areas that lack established immigrant communities.

As a result, we might predict that the continued socialization of Mexicans as minorities and as 'not really citizens' will incentivize them to maintain a strong minority group affinity and ethnic group consciousness. This would be a marked difference from the proposals of some assimilation theorists[56] who view later-generation Latinos as trending toward political views that are most similar to whites. As migration destinations continue to expand throughout the suburbs and small towns of the Midwest and the South, similar distinct racialization patterns may emerge, moving away from the predicted orientation toward honorary whiteness or middle status.

Rather, it is likely that African Americans and Mexicans will share the bottom of racial exclusion, a process that pulls Afro-Mexicans closer to African Americans, but also other Mexicans whose status makes them subject to overracialization. Moreover, this shift is not necessarily without benefits. In contexts in which African Americans have established resource-rich, middle-class communities, Mexicans may access financial, institutional and political resources, as well as upwardly mobile values and strategies already held by the minority community.

In other words, rather than move into an in-between or whitening racial category, my study suggests that certain Latino populations may be more likely to 'brown', rather than to 'whiten'. Whether this will result in a divided population of American Latinos along lines of color and status is unclear, and perhaps unknowable, varying across time and geographic context. Certainly, my findings suggest that there is still much research to be done among various Latino groups and across new destinations. They also caution that it is important for scholars to investigate Latino racialization and immigrant assimilation very carefully, paying attention not only to distinct national and regional backgrounds but also to differences in immigration status, as well as the impact of current immigration policies and labor market contexts in the sites in which we investigate. To obscure these differences can mean the loss of valuable insights into important shifts in the process of US integration.

NOTES

1. This project was made possible with funding from the National Science Foundation and the UC Center for New Racial Studies. Portions of this chapter have previously appeared in Jennifer Jones, "'Blacks May Be Second Class, but They Can't Make Them Leave': Mexican Racial Formation and Immigrant Status," *Latino Studies* 10, no. 1–2 (2012): 60–80.
2. Nathan Glazer and Daniel Moynihan, *Beyond the Melting Pot* (Cambridge, MA: Harvard University Press and MIT, 1963); Milton Gordon, *Assimilation in American Life: The Role of Race, Religion and National Origins* (New York: Oxford University Press, 1964); and Robert Park, *Race and Culture* (Glencoe, IL: Free Press, 1950).
3. Alejandro Portes and Min Zhou, "The New Second Generation: Segmented Assimilation and Its Variants," *ANNALS of the American Academy of Political and Social Science* 530, no. 1 (1992): 74–96; Ruben Rumbaut, "The Crucible Within: Ethnic Identity, Self-Esteem and Segmented Assimilation among Children of Immigrants," *International Migration Review* 28, no. 4 (1994): 748–794; and Scott J. South, Kyle Crowder and Erick Chavez, "Migration and Spatial Assimilation among US Latinos: Classical versus Segmented Trajectories," *Demography* 42, no. 3 (2005): 497–521.
4. Renato Rosaldo, "Cultural Citizenship, Inequality, and Multiculturalism," in *Race, Identity, Citizenship: A Reader*, ed. R. Torres, L. Miron and J. Inda (Malden, MA: Blackwell, 1999), 247–253.
5. Iris Marion Young, "Structure, Difference, and Hispanic/Latino Claims of Justice," in *Hispanics/Latinos in the United States: Ethnicity, Race, and Rights*, ed. J. Garcia and P. DeGreiff (New York: Routledge, 2000), 159.
6. Glazer and Moynihan, *Beyond the Melting Pot*; Gordon, *Assimilation in American Life*; Portes and Zhou, "The New Second Generation"; Rumbaut, "Crucible Within"; and South, Crowder and Chavez, "Migration and Spatial Assimilation among US Latinos."
7. Karen Kaufmann, "Cracks in the Rainbow: Group Commonality as a Basis for Latino and African American Political Coalitions," *Political Research Quarterly* 56, no. 2 (2003): 199–210; Helen Marrow, "Hispanic Immigration, Black Population Size, and Intergroup Relations in the Rural and Small-Town South," in *New Faces in New Places: The Changing Geography*

of American Immigration, ed. Douglas Massey (New York: Russell Sage, 2008), 293–340; and Paula McClain, Niambi Carter, Victoria DeFrancesco Soto, Monique Lyle, Jeffrey Grynaviski, Shayla Nunnally, Thomas Scotto, J. Alan Kendrick, Gerald Lackey and Kendra Cotton, "Racial Distancing in a Southern City: Latino Immigrants' Views of Black Americans," *Journal of Politics* 68, no. 3 (2006): 571–584.

8. For notable exceptions, see Monica McDermott, *Working-Class White: The Making and Unmaking of Race Relations* (Berkeley: University of California Press, 2006); Wendy Roth, "Caribbean Race and American Dreams: How Migration Shapes Dominicans' and Puerto Ricans' Racial Identities and Its Impact on Socioeconomic Mobility" (PhD diss., Harvard University, 2006); and Mary Waters, *Black Identities: West Indian Immigrant Dreams and American Realities* (Cambridge, MA: Harvard University Press, 1999).

9. Nathan Glazer and Daniel Moynihan, *Beyond the Melting Pot* (Cambridge, MA: Harvard University Press and MIT, 1963); Milton Gordon, *Assimilation in American Life: The Role of Race, Religion and National Origins* (New York: Oxford University Press, 1964); and Robert Park, *Race and Culture* (Glencoe, IL: Free Press, 1950).

10. Rumbaut, "Crucible Within"; Waters, *Black Identities*; and Min Zhou, "Segmented Assimilation: Issues, Controversies, and Recent Research on the New Second Generation," *International Migration Review* 31, no. 4 (1997): 975–1008.

11. Noel Ignatiev, *How the Irish Became White* (New York: Routledge, 1999); Peter Kolchin, "Whiteness Studies: The New History of Race in America," *Journal of American History* 89 (2002): 154–173; and David R. Roediger, *Working toward Whiteness: How America's Immigrants Became White: The Strange Journey from Ellis Island to the Suburbs* (New York: Basic Books, 2006).

12. Portes and Zhou, "New Second Generation"; Rumbaut, "Crucible Within"; and Waters, *Black Identities*.

13. Portes and Zhou, "New Second Generation"; Rumbaut, "Crucible Within"; and Waters, *Black Identities*.

14. Waters, *Black Identities*; Philip Kasinitz, *Caribbean New York: Black Immigrants and the Politics of Race* (Ithaca: Cornell University Press, 1992).

15. Waters, *Black Identities*; Roy Simon Bryce-Laporte, "Black Immigrants: The Experience of Invisibility and Inequality," *Journal of Black Studies* 3, no. 1 (1972): 29–56.

16. Reuel Reuben Rogers, *Afro-Caribbean Immigrants and the Politics of Incorporation: Ethnicity, Exception, or Exit* (New York: Cambridge University Press, 2006), 172.

17. Alejandro Portes and Ruben Rumbaut, *Immigrant America: A Portrait* (Berkeley: University of California Press, 1996); Alejandro Portes and Alex Stepick, *City on the Edge: The Transformation of Miami* (Berkeley: University of California Press, 1993); and Rogers, *Afro-Caribbean Immigrants*.

18. Kasinitz, *Caribbean New York*; Constance Sutton and Susan Makiesky, "Migration and West Indian Racial and Ethnic Consciousness," in *Migration and Development: Implications for Identity and Political Conflict*, ed. H. Safa and B. Du Toit (Herndon, VA: Walter de Gruyter, 1975); and Milton Vickerman, *Crosscurrents: West Indian Immigrants and Race* (New York: Oxford University Press, 1999).

19. Rogers, *Afro-Caribbean Immigrants*, 189–191.

20. Alex Stepick and Carol Dutton Stepick, "Diverse Contexts of Reception and Feelings of Belonging," *Forum: Qualitative Social Research*, 10, no. 3 (2009): Article 15, accessed Sept. 8, 2012, http://www.qualitative-research. net/index.php/fqs/article/view/1366/2862.

21. Philip Kasinitz, John Mollenkopf, Mary Waters and Jennifer Holdaway, *Inheriting the City: The Children of Immigrants Come of Age* (Cambridge, MA: Harvard University Press, 2008).

22. Kathryn Neckerman, Prudence Carter and Jennifer Lee, "Segmented Assimilation and Minority Cultures of Mobility," *Ethnic and Racial Studies* 22, no. 6 (1999): 945–965.

23. Neckerman, Carter and Lee, "Segmented Assimilation and Minority Cultures of Mobility," 949.

24. Joel Perlmann and Roger Waldinger, "Second Generation Decline? Children of Immigrants, Past and Present—a Reconsideration," *International Migration Review* 31, no. 4 (1997): 893–922.

25. Mestizaje refers to a national ideology of racial mixing, popular throughout Latin America, although it generally refers exclusively to European and indigenous mixing, regardless of the presence of Afro-descendants in the country. I contrast this orientation with anti-black and racial democracy ideologies, which situate blackness in a particular way, rather than make it invisible, as in the case of mestizaje nations.

26. Patrick Carroll, *Blacks in Colonial Veracruz: Race, Ethnicity, and Regional Development* (Austin: University of Texas Press, 1991).

27. A two-lane coastal highway was built in the 1960s connecting the town of Cuajinicuilapa to larger towns in the north. The majority of towns in the municipality, however, continue to be connected only by dirt roads, maintaining a relative sense of isolation throughout the region. See Laura Lewis, "Of Ships and Saints: History, Memory and Place in the Making of *Moreno* Mexican Identity," *Cultural Anthropology* 16, no. 1 (2000): 64.

28. According to the 2000 census, 16.1 million of the foreign-born population (total of 28.4 million) is from Latin America, a figure that has more than doubled each decade beginning in 1960. Mexicans make up about eight million of that total. Cubans follow most closely at 850,000. See Migration Policy Institute Data Hub, Migration Policy Institute, accessed June 5, 2007, http://www.migrationinformation.org/DataHub/whosresults.cfm.

29. However, the distinct political situation of Puerto Ricans and Cubans as Latinos and immigrants, but also as citizens, or residents with a clear path to citizenship, is well known among Mexican migrants. It is also frequently cited as a source of interethnic discord.

30. Jonathan Fox and Libby Haight, "Synthesis of Findings: Farm Policy Subsidy Trends," in *Subsidizing Inequality: Mexican Corn Policy since NAFTA*, ed. J. Fox and L. Haight (Washington: Woodrow Wilson Center, 2011), 1–2.

31. Jorge Durand, Douglas Massey and R. Zenteno, "Mexican Immigration to the United States: Continuities and Change," *Latin American Research Review* 36, no. 1 (2001): 111.

32. Ibid.

33. Lisa Hoppenjans and Ted Richardson, "Mexican Ways, African Roots: Most of the City's Hispanic Residents Are Natives of a Region Populated by Descendants of Black Slaves," *Winston-Salem Journal*, June 19, 2005.

34. James Kasarda and James Johnson, *The Economic Impact of the Hispanic Population on North Carolina*, (Chapel Hill: T. Kenan-Flager Business School and University of North Carolina, 2006), ii.

35. Ibid.

36. Section 287(g) of the Immigration and Nationality Act (INA) was made law in the US in 1996 as a result of the Illegal Immigration Reform and Immigrant Responsibility Act (IIRIRA). Section 287(g) authorizes the secretary of homeland security to enter into agreements with state and local law enforcement agencies. It permits designated officers to perform immigration law

enforcement functions, pursuant to a memorandum of agreement (MOA), provided that the local law enforcement officers receive appropriate training and function under the supervision of sworn US Immigration and Customs Enforcement officers. Under 287(g), ICE provides state and local law enforcement with the training and subsequent authorization to identify, process and, when appropriate, detain immigration offenders they encounter during their regular, daily law-enforcement activity. See Department of Homeland Security, Fact Sheet: Delegation of Immigration Authority Section 287(g) Immigration and Nationality Act, accessed April 11, 2013, http://www.ice.gov/news/library/factsheets/287g.htm.

37. Mathew Coleman, "The 'Local' Migration State: The Site-Specific Devolution of Immigration Enforcement in the US South," *Law & Policy* 34, no. 2 (2012): 159–190.

38. In 2012, the Obama administration declined to sign up any new municipalities to the 287(g) program and terminated some agreements, and appears to be winding down the program. Instead, these programs will be replaced by the Secure Communities program, which operates similarly to the 287(g) jail-based program, but in a uniform and more cost-effective manner because all information is managed through ICE, not ICE-trained officers in local jurisdictions. Some have reported that this process intends to terminate the 287(g) program within three years, when all of the remaining agreements expire. However, at the time of publication, intentions to terminate the program have not been officially made known. There was, however, a reduction in funding by $17 million for the 2013 287(g) budget and the termination of several task force programs in Arizona. The budget request calls this a realignment and reduction in the program. See Muzaffar Chishti and Claire Bergeron, "Questions Arise with Implementation of Obama Administration's New Prosecutorial Discretion Policy," Migration Information Source, Feb. 29, 2012, Migration Policy Institute, accessed Sept. 6, 2012http://www.migrationinformation.org/USFocus/display.cfm?ID=883.

39. In 2012, North Carolina was down to seven agreements of sixty-four, as three counties, including Guilford, NC (neighboring Greensboro), declined to renew their agreement. See Immigration and Customs Enforcement, "Fact Sheet: Delegation of Immigration Authority Section 287(g) Immigration and Nationality Act," Department of Homeland Security, accessed Sept. 7, 2012, http://www.ice.gov/news/library/factsheets/287g.htm.

40. As of 2008, sixty-six agreements between local municipalities and ICE have been entered into nationwide. In July 2009, eleven new agreements were made, including one in Winston-Salem's neighboring Guilford County, for a total of seventy-seven agreements nationwide, nine of which are in North Carolina. See Department of Homeland Security, "Secretary Napolitano Announces New Agreement for State and Local Immigration Enforcement Partnerships & Adds 11 New Agreements," press release, July 10, 2009, accessed Aug. 20, 2012, http://www.dhs.gov/ynews/releases/pr_1247246453625.shtm, and American Civil Liberties Union of North Carolina Legal (ACLU) and Immigration & Human Rights Clinic of University of North Carolina Chapel Hill, *The Policies and Politics of Local Immigration Enforcement Laws 287(g) Program in North Carolina* (Chapel Hill: UNC, 2009).

41. ACLU and Immigration & Human Rights Clinic of UNC, *Policies and Politics of Local Immigration Enforcement Laws*, 28.

42. Ibid., 46.

43. See Immigration and Customs Enforcement, "Fact Sheet."

44. US Census Bureau, "American Community Survey 2005–2007, Winston-Salem City," *American Fact Finder* (Washington: US Census Bureau, 2008).

45. Sheriff Bill Schatzman recently confirmed in a public forum sponsored by the City of Winston-Salem Human Relations Department that the Forsyth County Sheriff's department requested a 287(g) agreement in 2007 and is currently awaiting review from ICE and funding from the county commissioners to proceed (field notes, May 2009).
46. The City Council of Winston-Salem did pressure local law enforcement to request a 287(g) agreement, even promising funds to account for any additional costs. Ultimately, however, both the sheriff and chief of police declined to participate.
47. Ties appeared to be much stronger in the 1.5- and second-generation youth, who spoke English fluently, grew up in the American culture and attended the same schools and institutions as African American children.
48. Kaufmann, "Cracks in the Rainbow," 202.
49. Ibid.
50. Portes and Zhou, "New Second Generation"; Min Zhou, "Segmented Assimilation," *International Migration Review* 31, no. 4 (1997): 975–1008; and Min Zhou and Carl Bankston, *Growing Up American: How Vietnamese Children Adapt to Life in the United States* (New York: Russell Sage, 1999).
51. In 2008, North Carolina community colleges initiated a total ban on access to community colleges for undocumented persons.
52. Linked fate refers to Dawson's concept in which he highlights how collective experiences of discrimination and racism among African Americans, and presumably other minority groups, create a sense of collective interests that supersede individual interests. Michael Dawson, *Behind the Mule: Race and Class in African American Politics* (Princeton, NJ: Princeton University Press, 1994).
53. Kaufmann, "Cracks in the Rainbow"; Marrow, "Hispanic Immigration"; McClain et al., "Racial Distancing in a Southern City."
54. Waters, *Black Identities*.
55. Migration Policy Institute Data Hub.
56. Lawrence Fuchs, "The Reactions of Black Americans to Immigration," in *Immigration Reconsidered: History, Sociology and Politics*, ed. V. Yans-McLaughlin (New York: Oxford University Press, 1999)293–314, and Gordon, *Assimilation in American Life*.

15 Becoming Black?
Race and Racial Identity among Cape Verdean Youth

P. Khalil Saucier

I love being black and wouldn't change for the world. If I had a choice, I would still choose black. Yeah, I'm Cape Verdean, but regardless of where my family is from, I'm black.

(Informant, 2007)

In *Between Race and Ethnicity* Marilyn Halter clearly illustrates that early Cape Verdean immigrant identities sat between the registers of both race and ethnicity.[1] However, when it comes to understanding second-generation Cape Verdean youth identity in the US, as the epigraph shows, the ambiguity and liminality surrounding race and ethnicity in previous generations have vanished. Cape Verdean youth have come to see themselves both racially as black and ethnically as Cape Verdean. More importantly, they have come to see themselves as minorities in a white-dominated hierarchical social structure. As a result, they experience noteworthy solidarity with nonwhites, particularly African American youth. Further, Cape Verdean youth have come to see themselves as a marginalized population locally and globally. For example, many of my informants informally and formally discussed the hardships their parents and grandparents endured in Cape Verde in relation to the neglected neighborhoods they inhabit, as well as the substandard schools they have attended in the US.

Although Cape Verdean youth often reject monolithic/homogenous definitions of blackness via the performance of their Cape Verdean-ness, their identities are fundamentally structured by racial discourse. Regardless of their phenotype, second-generation Cape Verdean youth, unlike their parent's generation, learn to think of themselves as nonwhite with little hesitation, strongly denouncing their European ancestry.

In the following pages, I map the importance that phenotype, class and cultural practices have in creating black identities out of ethnic difference via interview material.[2] Although identities are never static and immutable, they are never created of their own accord. To this end, we cannot assure that fluidity in matters of racial and ethnic identity is open-ended for all individuals at all times.

DEFINING BLACKNESS AND THE
POLITICS OF RACIAL SINCERITY

Blackness is an elusive concept. It is overdetermined—a constituted fact—and therefore has multiple meanings—meanings rooted diachronically and synchronically. Its elusiveness does not preclude anyone from trying to define it with particular attributes and fix it in time and space. Since the invention of race and by extension racial identity, the quest of authenticating a black identity has been a long, complex and politically contested struggle. As an elusive racial signifier—one that is not always based solely on phenotype—blackness has sometimes been constructed as natural, one-dimensional and static. As Frantz Fanon acknowledged, some, both black and white, see blackness as a universal standpoint.[3] On the other hand, others underscore the multiplicity of blackness and the black experience.

Throughout this chapter, I straddle the dichotomous nature of blackness as fixed and multiple. On the one hand, I tease out the ways in which blackness, conceived as one-dimensional, as conforming to preexisting although updated patterns and stereotypes, continues to reinforce and sustain white supremacy. On the other hand, I repudiate the idea that there is an 'authentic' undifferentiated black identity.

As many have already argued, white hegemonic notions of essentialized blackness are evoked to construct and maintain essentialized notions of whiteness. The discourses of white supremacy have targeted and effectively marked black people as primitive, undeserving, capricious, dangerous, unintelligent, sly, oversexed and violent.[4] In the past, tropes of blackness circulated in the form of Zip Coon, Stepin Fetchit, Jezebel, Sapphire and others.[5] Similarly, the discursive constructions of blackness of today still represent negative and narrow depictions of black people. This enlarged picture of essentialized blackness now includes the welfare queen, prison inmate, prostitute, hedonistic rapper, thug, single mother and pimp.[6] Whiteness is none of these; the trope of whiteness is supreme, pure, moral and good. The fact of whiteness is taken as a sign of everything, rather than a sign of nothingness. In the end, whiteness is everything blackness is not. As Fanon demonstrated, racism and constructions of blackness are interrelated.[7] And David Theo Goldberg is correct when he states, "blackness has been produced in coercive circumstances."[8] Blackness has been constructed within a culture of racialized exclusion.

Essentialized notions of blackness not only come from the outside—from white people themselves—but also from black people. As bell hooks observed in her essay "Postmodern Blackness," many black people uphold essentialized notions of blackness and thus are unwilling to accept the multiplicity of blackness because they "fear that it will cause folks to lose sight of the specific history and experience of African-Americans and the unique sensibilities and culture that arise from that experience."[9] Recently, for example, black and white critics alike have gone to great lengths to debate the blackness of President Barack Obama. Mr. Obama's blackness has been questioned because his life journey is seen as a departure from customary black stereotypes. As Alan Keyes and Stanley Crouch have publicly observed, he is not a descendant of a slave and never lived your 'typical' black life—one filled with hardship and crushing encounters with racism.[10] Other examples include the late Eldridge Cleaver's biting attack on James Baldwin, calling his homosexuality "anti-black."[11] These critiques illustrate that blackness is often manipulated for social, cultural and political purposes. To echo Michel Foucault's ideas on madness and domination, a judgment in blackness is an act of domination.[12] Others see the demarcating of blackness as counterproductive and social and historically incorrect.

Underscoring the multiplicity of blackness is the late Marlon Riggs. Through films like *Tongues Untied* and *Black Is . . . Black Ain't* Riggs showed that when people attempt to define what it is to be black, they restrict the possibilities of what it can be.[13] That is, the pursuit of an authentic blackness confines and restricts black subjects and therefore human potentiality. For Riggs, blackness needs to be seen as a site of endless possibility.

In his illuminating book, *We Who Are Dark: The Philosophical Foundations of Black Solidarity*, Tommie Shelby conceptualizes blackness in two ways, a thin and thick form. Thin blackness is based solely on skin color, phenotype and ancestry. For Shelby, "One cannot simply refuse to be thinly black . . . No amount of wealth, income, social status, or education can ease one's thin blackness."[14] In other words, one is visibly marked. A thick conception of blackness includes physical characteristics, genealogy and more. The 'more' includes ideas about cultural heritage, nationality, ethnicity, kinship and "an identifiable ensemble of beliefs, values, conventions, traditions, and practices that is distinctively black."[15] According to Shelby, persons who satisfy the thin social criteria for blackness can and often do embrace thick conceptions of blackness. However, this embrace varies in intensity, for rejecting thick conceptions of blackness while meeting the thin social criteria of blackness is considered by many as an act of bad faith.[16]

Nonetheless, as Fanon described in *Black Skin, White Masks*, there is 'the fact of blackness'. No matter what, despite his objection to the 'fact' of an essential and thin blackness, Fanon states, "I was responsible at the same time for my body, for my race, for my ancestors . . . I discovered my blackness . . . and I was battered down by tom-toms, cannibalism, intellectual deficiency, fetishism, racial defects, slave ships and above all else, above all: 'Sho' good eatin'."[17]

Despite 'the fact of blackness', black identity relies on the ongoing process of performance. Notions of racial authenticity are achieved through performative practices—that is, through the use of various texts and practices. Racial authenticity involves an assessment of the degree to which someone is 'truly' representative of a particular race and/or ethnic group. Any attempt to speak of black authenticity is an attempt to draw the boundaries of blackness as a racial signifier. To this end, the inclusion and exclusion of subjects from blackness are political and never innocent. Racial authenticity can be read as a way of establishing social credibility while also protecting interests, whatever those interests may be. When we engage in questions around racial authenticity, we are asking what it means to be of a particular race/ethnicity. We are asking how these identities are constructed and by whom.

As Shelly Eversely has observed, "racial authenticity is masquerading as the natural, ontological 'truth' about people of color."[18] Racial authenticity pervades black culture in that the 'real' or 'authentic' becomes a cultural stance, a racial positionality, an index of culture and a barometer of trust of racial group members. As Essex Hemphill explained in *Black Is . . . Black Ain't*, "Perhaps the standard . . . is the inner city for defining what blackness is. That you've got to constantly be up on the changes in the hip language, the hip black fashions, the hip black music. You've got to use your ghetto experience as your American Express Card."[19] In other words, 'the ghetto' is a prerequisite to the 'real' black experience.

It can be argued that racial authenticity as an analytical concept has been overused and as a result scholarly analysis of racialized phenomena is shortsighted because of its reliance on the concept. John Jackson questions the validity of authenticity as a conceptual analytic, stating that it stunts a more thorough understanding of racial identity. "Racial sincerity," he argues, allows for the envisioning of a more complex blackness as well as a more thorough social analysis of how people classified as black get on with their everyday lives, especially their efforts to make themselves appear as legitimate members of that group.[20]

Unlike authenticity, which is bestowed by an observer on an object, sincerity is property of the object. Accordingly, one must take into account the logic, rationales and motives that people attribute to aspects of their own being and to others to grasp how sincerity claims shape what is taken to be appropriate conduct and character for a member of a particular racial group. In other words, 'authenticity', according to Jackson, is about content, and 'sincerity' is about intent.[21] As I will show, when Cape Verdean youth 'become black' they do so with varying intensity. Although all my informants met the social criteria for both thin and thick forms of blackness and perform essentialized and nonessentialized ideas of blackness, they did so with varying degrees of authenticity and sincerity.

THE FACT OF 'CAPE VERDEAN' BLACKNESS

"If I'm not black, then what am I?"
(Informant, 2007)

"Once you have a mix in you. You're black."
(Informant, 2007)

Blackness is often associated with disadvantage and criminality; thus black immigrants have and often seek to distance themselves from such associations. In turn, many use ethnicity as an important marker of distinction. This tactic is particularly useful for black immigrants, for it is difficult to deny thin blackness, but denying thick forms of blackness, especially those rooted in cultural practices, is less difficult. Historically, the children of black immigrants have merged into black American populations.[22] In her study of Afro-Caribbean immigrants in New York City, Waters found that second-generation immigrants from families of higher economic status maintain a strong ethnic-national identity, whereas those from lower-income neighborhoods and poor families adopt African American identities—that is, their language is influenced by black popular culture, as are their cultural tastes and perceptions of race and racism.[23]

For second-generation Cape Verdean youth, race is central to identity formation. Whereas the parents and grandparents of Cape Verdean youth commonly sought to resist racial ascription, today's youth do not. Rather than distance themselves from African American youth, many of my informants have extensive contact with African American youth and black popular culture. Therefore, being Cape Verdean has a very different meaning for the second generation than it does for the first generation. Many Cape Verdean youth understand the 'fact of blackness' as the following interview excerpts illustrate.[24]

Researcher: How do you identify in terms of race and ethnicity?
Antonio: Personally, I identify with being back. I'm black! I'm a black man!
Researcher: Do you identify with any ethnicity?
Antonio: Again, I'm black, but ethnically I'm Cape Verdean. Being Cape Verdean takes a back seat to being black.
Researcher: Why does it take a backseat?
Antonio: Black is first because that is what you see. Look at my skin color and how I dress. People don't know I'm Cape Verdean. Plus, that wouldn't make a difference. Black and white is too powerful of a concept. You look at me, you'll say I'm black.

Another informant, again, when asked how he identifies in terms of race and ethnicity, although loosely identifying with being Cape Verdean, also emphatically stated, "I'm black! Look bro," he said, "you ain't fooling anyone to say you're not black. Yeah, I can say I'm Cape Verdean or African or whatever, but what will that do? Tell the police that shit. The fact is I'm black, if I like it or not."

Despite claiming Cape Verdean identities these two informants understand that it means little in a society where race is at the vortex of its creation. Thus, I am at odds with Halter when she states, "For the Cape Verdean American, social identity can never be assumed and is never given."[25] Despite efforts to transcend racial categorization, Cape Verdeans, whether they approve or disapprove, are sucked into the vortex of the racial state. Black racial identity, it seems, is coercive in part because identity formation is coercive. They suffer from what philosopher Charles Mills has rightfully identified as "the stigmata of subordination."[26]

In a focus group that I conducted, Soraya had this to say about being black: "No one has ever considered me a white person. They always say 'Yeah, that's that black girl.'" Carlos, a proud Cape Verdean, had the following to say after explaining how his parents, especially his mother, ironically identified as black.

Researcher: Do you also consider yourself black?
Carlos: Yes, I do.
Researcher: What's first? Black or Cape Verdean?
Carlos: To me, if you put anything before black in America you're fooling yourself. Because they don't care if you been here ten years or whatever. All they know is you're a nigga!

Being Cape Verdean in a country where race is of central importance simply means being assigned to an unfavorable position in the racial hierarchy. In his concern over the celebration of hybrid identities, Peter McLaren states: "We are not autonomous citizens who can fashionably choose whatever ethnic [and racial] combinations we desire in order to reassemble our identity . . . it is dishonest to assert that pluralized, hybridized identities are options."[27] Despite seeming deterministic, McLaren's observation reflects what many of my informants stated in informal and formal interviews. Throughout many of my interviews, I sensed from my informants a yearning to simply be 'Cape Verdean', but as many noted this is difficult, if not impossible, in a racial state. As Anthony stated: "Society makes you black. Being Cape Verdean is second, if it means anything at all." In short, some Cape Verdean youth treat blackness as totalizing in which ethnicity, culture and ancestry are undifferentiated.

SIMILARITIES, DIFFERENCES AND SOLIDARITY IN BLACKNESS

Although many informants related being black, they were careful to draw a distinction between being African and African American. Many did not identify as African American (or black American), but identified *with* African Americans and their experiences; living in an antiblack social world forces one to see connections and desire group solidarity. Herein I define solidarity loosely, for it is not meant to be a comprehensive political program nor is it meant to address every social problem black people experience. Rather, solidarity, as it is alluded to ahead, is simply based on shared racial oppression and its consequences. I am not suggesting that it cannot mean the former, but herein it does not. Unfortunately, this narrowly conceived form of solidarity is not ideal because it neglects other forms of social oppression.[28]

Luisa offered the following insight into Cape Verdean identity.

Researcher: How do you define yourself?
Luisa: I'm black and Cape Verdean.
Researcher: What makes you black?
Luisa: My ancestors.
Researcher: Anything else?
Luisa: Yeah . . . background, skin color and culture.
Researcher: What do you mean by background and culture?
Luisa: All our dances and rituals come from Africa. For example, batuko and funana are both African. As for background, I'm badius.

Badius are a people on the island of Santiago who have retained a certain degree of African-based distinctiveness in their cultural practices from other Cape Verdeans; the badius were of great symbolic importance during the war of liberation. Offering a rejoinder to her answers, Luisa stated: "I'm black, but I'm not African American. When I think of African Americans, their traditions are different. I mean they have jazz and the blues. We got funana. Do we have similarities? Sure! Like our struggle with racism. It's because of racism that we should unite as a people." Although Luisa accepts her blackness, she is resolute in drawing a distinction between 'black' as a racial identity and African American, seeing the latter as culturally distinct from Cape Verdeans such as herself.

Identifying as African, black and Cape Verdean, not in that order, Carlos offers this lengthy insight into similarities and solidarity with black Americans:

Carlos: Like I said before, I do identify with black Americans . . . Our histories are similar . . . I identify with them [African Americans] in terms of black issues and what should be of concern for us as a people in terms of where we are and where we're lagging. [Pause] I think also being black or feeling black, I think maybe I have a hypersensitivity to race. Sometimes people will say, "You're just looking for prejudice. Maybe they were just having a bad day." But being black you don't have that luxury, being a black person in America, if you're conscious of history. You can walk around with your blinders on and say it's equal. And I'm going to get a job like anybody else and I didn't get it because the other guy was more qualified." Simply put! You can believe that if you want to, but if you are cognizant of the civil rights movement, if you're cognizant of slavery, and anything that has happened since then. I'd rather welcome that and put that in my backpack. Being black is something I can't control. And that's why I think I'm so pro-black . . . I mean I don't believe in racial superiority. I'm not a black supremacist. Me loving black doesn't mean I'm hating anybody else . . . I'm pro-black. That doesn't mean I hate white people or whatever . . .

Carlos's identification with African Americans is based on a historical fact that most African Americans, like Cape Verdeans, know little about which specific parts of Africa their ancestors came from. Further, he highlights the shared structural position of black youth in the US. Due to this he feels he has more in common with African American youth than African youth, despite understanding that structural racism affects both groups equally. Throughout his interview he grouped African Americans and Cape Verdeans by using the first-person plural pronoun of 'we' and 'they'. Carlos's use of the pronoun 'we' is significant and draws attention to the structural and historical similarities of 'black people'. For Carlos, and correctly so, racial discrimination was historically directed uniformly at individuals of African descent, regardless of difference.

Francisco, a twenty-four-year-old second-generation Cape Verdean, also emphasizes experiential similarities and as a result the need for solidarity:

Francisco: small number of Cape Verdeans in America don't seem to like to be identified as Black or African American . . . We should be aware of the fact that as, we say in Crioulo, "a união faz força" [united we are strong] and stop trying not to identify with black people because that is what we are, either black Africans or black Americans for those born in America.

Researcher: Can you say more?

Fransisco: Yes, we are Cape Verdeans, but we are still black people . . . I mean where did we come from? West Africa! What is the predominant race and culture of Cape Verde? African people and African culture! Just because we have some Portuguese blood in us doesn't mean we're not black. How many black people don't have some European blood? So, let's be proud of who we are: black and African!!

Cape Verdean youth experiences with structural and individual racism lead them to see themselves as black and African. Racist culture prompts self-defining cultures of resistance. As a result, they experience solidarity with other marked black bodies, particularly African Americans and continental

Africans, whom they see as inhabiting the same social position in the US and globalized racist structure. Yet, although emphasizing their similarities through time and space, some Cape Verdeans draw cultural distinctions between Cape Verdeans and African Americans, choosing instead to identify with continental Africans. Some informants resist black/white dichotomization, yet they are more sympathetic to black issues. What should also be highlighted is that second-generation Cape Verdean youth deploy ethnicity not to draw a distinction from blackness but to complicate blackness. The deployment of 'Africa' and 'African' is presented only as a political project. Therefore, they are not obfuscating the power relations embedded in processes of racialization. Furthermore, my informants articulate a desire for a pan-African politics of liberation that comes from similar experiences of oppression and racialization.

In the end, my informants express a linked fate, a shared history of oppression rooted in ideologies of white supremacy and racial hierarchy that has motivated these youth to develop a common narrative of exclusion and struggle, and a shared consciousness. Given this, racial group identity is important for group mobilization—social issues become framed as important for the 'black' community, locally and globally, a part of which many of my informants see themselves.

"MY LAST NAME IS RAMOS, BUT I'M NOT SPANISH": A NOTE ON MISTAKEN IDENTITY

Despite identifying with other racially marked subjects like African Americans and continental Africans, the Cape Verdean youth that I interviewed resisted identification with other nonwhite minorities, namely Latinos. More specifically, Cape Verdeans, given their tendency to be light in skin color, are often mistaken as Dominican or Puerto Rican. As one informant noted with slight dismay: "Some people think I'm Hispanic . . . I always get, 'are you Puerto Rican? Are you Dominican?'" In this context, my informants were adamant about defining their Cape Verdeanness and blackness as exhibited by the following statement: "I always let people know I'm Cape Verdean. I don't want to be mistaken for nobody else." In her study on Cape Verdeans in Boston, Sanchez-Gabau suggests that there exist between Cape Verdeans and Latinos great similarities, culturally and socially, which have resulted in a relationship between the Latino population and Cape Verdean diaspora. She speaks of "a sense of affinity in life experiences", based both on foreign status and language issues.[29] This may be the case with previous generations and current immigrants, but for my informants this was not the case. Rather, my informants were resolute in denying any relationship to Latinos. This resistance to being identified as Latino raises questions of immigration and citizenship. Cape Verdean youth of the Greater Boston area resist this form of classification by defining themselves as either black and/or Cape Verdean. Through this act, not only are a black and/or Cape Verdean identities claimed, but also it is a form of citizenship.

I understand the complexities and problems with a word like citizenship, for it is used in a number of different ways in academic and political discourse and social contexts. Herein I am not referencing a citizenship that takes on the specific juridical links between individual and state. Rather, I use citizenship in a tendentious way to mean belonging to a national community and "a set of moral qualities thought to be crucial for the existence of the good citizen."[30]

Unlike assimilation theories of the past, Ramos-Zayas has shown that "becoming American" for Brazilian and Puerto Rican youth of Newark is not necessarily tied with "becoming white."[31] Rather, she shows that migrants from Latin America associated blackness with "American-ness." Given my informants incessant need to draw a distinction between themselves and Latinos, I suggest, much like Ramos-Zayas, that there is an alternative way of exerting and claiming citizenship. According to Ramos-Zayas, this reversal of citizenship or assimilationist logic is a move away from "delinquent forms of citizenship."[32]

Despite suffering from many of the same forms of structural oppression, second-generation Cape Verdean youth are not immune from accepting nativist views of immigrant illegality. Although previous generations attempted to assert their belonging via 'acting white' or drawing a sharp distinction between Cape Verdeans and blacks, today's youth attempt to belong by utilizing in their daily behaviors the texts and practices associated with black youth culture. This is also accomplished by the valorization of blackness and by extension Africanness and the devalorization of whiteness.

According to my informants, Cape Verdean youth are often confused for "being Latino." As Juvenal, who identifies as black and Cape Verdean, stated:

> I get "you're Spanish," "you're Dominican" all the time. In high school all the girls would come up to me speaking Spanish. People will argue with me until the death saying I'm Dominican. But I always make sure I tell people I'm Cape Verdean . . . I don't like being called any other ethnicity.

What this might suggest is the denunciation and adamant responses of distinctiveness from being Latino could be a deliberate way to escape the stigma associated with 'immigrant'. Being an immigrant often conjures images of illegality. Further, it suggests 'backwardness' and 'foreignness'. Denouncing their perceived Latino-ness and aligning themselves with 'black people', Cape Verdean youth escape the negative connotations of immigrant-ness, especially following the heightened nativism of 9/11. Also, in avoiding an immigrant identity one transcends the ambiguity of liminality and not belonging.

BEING HOOD: THE IMPORTANCE OF 'BEING URBAN'

Racial identity, as many scholars have illustrated, is not predicated solely on phenotype, but also other 'things' imbued with social significance like 'space' (locale) and 'place' (the realities of physical terrain). For Murray Forman and others, "the term 'inner-city' implicitly refers to racialized images or racially infected conditions of danger, violence, and depravity that can be contrasted with the ideals of calm, safety, and security attributed to non-urban or suburban space."[33] Interestingly, the relationship between race, particularly blackness, and geography has shifted from largely a rural concern to an urban concern. Du Bois's *The Philadelphia Negro*, which prefigured Drake and Cayton's *Black Metropolis*, signaled a change in the ecological foci of social scientists from the countryside to city.[34] Simultaneously, state policies and racial governmentality shifted their focus of containment and spatial segregation from the rural to the urban. These transformations in concern did not occur out of simple curiosity; rather they were the result of black migration north. The more black urbanization expanded, the more racial segregation and restriction of black residents within cities were extended. As a result, not only were regions becoming racialized, but also neighborhoods were becoming racial and ethnically uniform. As Denton has pointed out, black segregation in urban communities is not the result of black housing preferences but of conscious white avoidance and state design.[35] Through this, what has emerged is a strong connection between blackness and urban space in that the symbolic value of the 'inner city' now illustrates racial authenticity.

For my informants, urban communities are black and brown spaces. When asked where they were from and what their neighborhood was like, many of my participants became extremely specific, identifying specific streets and historical markers (namely, project housing complexes), even recalling house numbers at times. I must admit, at first I thought the hyper-specificity was strange and unimportant, especially given that my informants were to remain anonymous and any reference to where they lived seemed almost in violation of ethical codes. Yet I later realized that the distinctions my informants wanted to seemingly draw were to differentiate who lived where. For instance, if the city itself was not predominantly black or brown, certain streets and sections of town were racialized. The following statements from various informants suggest this:

> I don't live in the good section . . . I live, and have all of my life, lived in the hood. Ya' know the Southside, near the projects.

> I'm not from the best neighborhood. I mean I'm from South Providence. Crime is high and the cops are everywhere.

> Where I'm from, things are difficult. People are surviving day by day. The ghetto is a hard place to grow up in.

My neighborhood . . . is not the best neighborhood in the world; people selling drugs, getting shot. A lot happens! There is a lot of crime . . . Poverty is high. Even the white people in the neighborhood are poor.

I grew up in Dorchester in "Cape Verde-vill" from Bowden Street all the way to Dudley.

Others articulated similar statements of living in marginal places.

Of the participants who moved, many moved from urban community to urban community. Although the place differed, the space remained similar, often highlighting the deep and intimate connect between race and class. Informants seemed to maintain that racialized and ethnic minorities, like Cape Verdeans, live in segregated communities and areas with little interracial contact.[36] For example, despite movement to other locales, racial and class demographics were alike, and housing and school systems comparable. Some informants described circular urban migratory patterns like being born in one urban area, only to move back during adolescence. This phenomenon highlights a reversal in Cape Verdean settlement patterns—that is, Cape Verdeans have gone from voluntary segregation to involuntary segregation.

All, with the exception of two Cape Verdean youth interviewed, lived and continue to live in urban areas. Interestingly—and what made me realize the importance of space, particularly racialized spaces like the 'inner city'—the two who spent some time growing up in a white suburban enclave in Massachusetts often valorized being from 'the hood'—that is, the inner city.

Even those who spent the early part of their childhood in Cape Verde, particularly in the urban cities of Mindelo and Praia, highlighted to me the decrepit conditions into which they were born. As one participant who was born in the area of Praia known as the 'Plateau' stated, "I've always been from the hood." Others born in the urban communities of Cape Verde, or those who have relatives present, would highlight, even though many have not returned since leaving or maintain little contact with family members in the islands, the cities' seemingly worsening harsh conditions. These informants almost fetishized the conditions and realities of Cape Verde's urban enclaves.

Why valorize the hood or 'being urban'? Here Pierre Bourdieu's definition of 'cultural capital' is instructive, for the valorization of 'being urban' is a means of bringing a level of sociocultural distinction to one's identity.[37] However, 'being urban' and from the hood is not the cultural capital lauded by the labor market and mainstream society. In a sense, what many Cape Verdean youth have projected and take pride in is a 'streetwise' presentation of self; being 'streetwise' is a way to navigate the harsh realities of urban America.[38] Although this can be said for those Cape Verdean youth who spent their lives in urban communities, what does it mean when those who have spent time away from urbanity continue to valorize 'being urban'? And why would some participants valorize the harsh conditions of Cape Verdean cities?

What I think this articulates is that 'being urban' is at the vortex of blackness, particularly in the northeast.[39] Acting authentically black is to be of a particular space and by extension specifically classed.[40] In her study on Brazilian and Puerto Rican youth in Newark, New Jersey, Ramos-Zayas cogently observed that one's urbanness was often used to authenticate a black identity.[41] The same can be said for the Cape Verdean youth I interviewed and observed. Many participants pointed out that life is hard in the ghetto. The ghetto in this sense becomes a symbol of authenticity; it becomes the heart of blackness. Life in the streets of Providence, Brockton, Dorchester, etc. becomes valorized, a badge of honor. A ghetto lifestyle helps connect and forge an imagined community of the oppressed.

What cannot be lost in all of this is that the valorization of the hood and the dangers of the inner city were proclamations made by Cape Verdean males. They appeared to embody an imaginary conflation of 'masculinity' and 'blackness' with 'being urban'. Some informants, despite having described the harsh realities of their communities, took great pride in being "from the Southside" or "from Brockton" as if there exists a 'ghetto hierarchy'. Statements from some of my informants like "It's tough out there . . ." almost seemed like badges of honor, a source of intense pride. A comparison can be made with reggae artist Damon Marley's hit record *Welcome to Jamrock*—an album that covers issues such as crime, poverty and political corruption as part of the harsh reality of urban Jamaica—which differs from the Jamaica advertised as a popular tourist destination. One informant boasted that he was "from New Bedrock [New Bedford]." Describing the difficulties of one's hood is intended to sustain a black masculine identity. Evoking street toughness is a form of macho posturing. Unfortunately, such forms of black masculinity fail to challenge marginality and poverty. Further, black masculinity comes across as natural, locking individuals and groups a priori into a genealogy that is fixed and static, not fluid. Black masculinity almost seems to be immutable and intangible in origin. This rigid model allows for little if any flexibility in the construction and performance of black masculinity—hence cultural critic and black male feminist Mark Anthony Neal's call for a "new black man."[42]

In this work, I think that David Harvey's notion that place-bound identities are becoming more important, rather than less important, is correct.[43] Whereas both federal and state governments have divested in urban areas over the last thirty-plus years, the Cape Verdean youth I interviewed and observed have overinvested in their neighborhoods. In other words, policies of 'benign neglect' have seemed to create a 'benign embrace' of dangerous regional localities. As Murray Forman has shown in great detail to "keep it real" or "represent" in hip-hop is always to represent the hood.[44] This phenomenon in effect has trickled down from hip-hop artists and made its way into the everyday lives of young Cape Verdean men. Although I do not doubt the proclaimed dangerousness of the urban communities from which my informants are from, I do wonder how much my male informants seized on and exaggerated many of the sensational aspects of urban living. How much did they exaggerate what neoconservatives and gangsta rappers have been portraying for years?

It is here where 'being urban' can and may support white supremacy, therefore reinforcing the status quo. The ways in which my male informants described their communities tended to reaffirm prejudicial beliefs about predatory inner-city communities and black males and, as a result, reinforced racial stereotypes held by many whites. However, can we blame these youth for perpetuating racial stereotypes? Can we blame them for keeping stereotypes in circulation? As Harvey explains: "Places in the city are dubbed as 'dubious' or 'dangerous,' again leading to patterns of behavior, both public and private, that turn fantasy into reality."[45] Not only do stereotypes become 'common sense', thus reinforcing racial hegemony, but stereotypes also become reality. Unlike the gangsta rappers who have capitalized on the marketing of the hood or ghetto, Cape Verdean youth are unable—for all cannot become hip-hop artists—to exploit 'being urban' for capital gain. Further, exaggerating the dangers of urban locales has a reductive effect, thereby stripping these communities of their sociocultural heterogeneity. In a sense, these communities are far more diverse than their caricatures suggest.[46]

Sartorial tendencies and clothing selection such as wearing regionally specific athletic paraphernalia (e.g., Boston Red Sox hats) are further illustrative of this point. In other words, 'being urban' is protected and authenticated not just through lived experience and spatial residency, but also through 'ghetto fabulous' clothing styles associated with hip-hop culture. The ghetto has become a product—that is, consumed and worn.

Most of the informants whom I talked with, formally or informally, defined themselves as Cape Verdean and by extension black (or African) in terms of the US racial hierarchy—thus highlighting that race is hierarchical whereas ethnicity is not. Cape Verdean identities in the Greater Boston area reflect their socialization in low-income urban American environments. Cape Verdean youth grow up in a context in which their skin color, phenotype, geographical location, history and cultural tendencies mark them as 'black'. Based on these experiences and being classified as black, Cape Verdeans identify and experience solidarity with groups that they see in the same structural position (with the exception of Latinos). However, when push comes to shove, Cape Verdean youth relate to Latinos based on similar experiences with racism. My interviews also suggest that identity is the result of discourse that is organized by the social relations of production. In other words, there is a close correlation between race and class relations. They realize that racism can just as easily be aimed at them as at African Americans and other racially marked subjects, and that the dominant groups in society seldom differentiate among nonwhite groups, giving race a totalizing effect. Many Cape Verdean youth see themselves black, but this is to be understood as a racial identity and not to be confused with being African American (or black American). Therefore, suggestions that the black/white (nonwhite) binary is under radical reconstruction are at best questionable.

Intergenerational conflict exists between Cape Verdeans because the two have been raised in different social contexts. Cape Verdean youth move away from their parents' generation through corporeal contact and social interaction with other black people. Further, they use a different cultural framework to view themselves, which may highlight racial identity, and racial solidarity in an ever-increasing globalized world is sometimes better predicted by generation than skin color or phenotype.

In short, 'being black' is not only based on popular culture and consumption patterns, but also organized around power relations and material conditions. Cape Verdean youth are interpolated, called into constructed racial categories, categories that make sense only in a racial hierarchy. To be black in a world where white power is normative is to always be structured in hierarchical relation to that power. The racial self involves thinking of oneself in terms of the prevailing concepts and performative practices of the sociohistorical order. Although levels of agency are exhibited, these youth exist and act within a set of preexisting assumptions and formulations. In other words, those second-generation Cape Verdean youth who are racialized as black are affected by race and actively structure their existence around the reality of its normalizing paradigms.

NOTES

1. Marilyn Halter, *Between Race and Ethnicity: Cape Verdean American Immigrants* (Urbana: University of Illinois Press, 1993).
2. All interview material is the culmination of ethnographic fieldwork conducted from May 2007 to May 2008. It entailed informal and formal interviewing, participant observation and textual analysis. All informants were 18–25 years old and from the Greater Boston area. As a result, the conclusions I draw are not generalizable to the entire Cape Verdean diaspora. I utilized homogeneous and snowball sampling techniques.
3. Frantz Fanon, *Black Skin/White Masks* (New York: Grove Press, 1967).
4. See Frantz Fanon, *The Wretched of the Earth* (New York: Grove Press, 1963); Janell Hobson, *Venus in the Dark: Blackness and Beauty in Popular Culture* (New York: Routledge, 2005); and T. Denean Sharpley-Whiting, *Black Venus: Sexualized Savages, Primal Fears and Primitive Narratives in French* (Durham: Duke University Press, 1999).
5. See, for example, Eric Lott, *Love and Theft: Blackface Minstrelsy and the American Working Class*, (New York: Oxford University Press, 1993).
6. Herman Gray, *Watching Race: Television and the Struggle for "Blackness"* (Minneapolis: University Minnesota Press, 2004).
7. Fanon, *Black Skin/White Masks*.

8. David Theo Goldberg, *Racial Subjects: Writing on Race in America* (New York: Routledge, 1997), 75.

9. bell hooks, "Postmodern Blackness," in *Yearning: Race, Gender, and Cultural Politics*, ed bell hooks (Boston: South End Press, 1999), 29.

10. Obama's connection to Reverend Jeremiah Wright also brings up questions concerning what blackness is and can be. Wright's inflammatory remarks about the US and its treatment of black people hint at the idea that Obama, because of his perceived blackness, is predisposed to such rage and possibly criminality, whether real or perceived.

11. Eldridge Cleaver, *Soul on Ice* (New York: Random House, 1991), 122–135.

12. Michel Foucault, *Birth of the Clinic: An Archeology of Medical Opinion* (New York: Vintage, 1994).

13. *Black Is . . . Black Ain't*, directed by Marlon Riggs (San Francisco, CA: California NewsReel, 1995) DVD, and *Tongues Untied*, directed by Marlon Riggs (San Francisco, CA: California Newsreel, 1990) DVD.

14. Tommie Shelby, *We Who Are Dark: The Philosophical Foundations of Black Solidarity* (Cambridge, MA: Belknap, 2005), 208.

15. Ibid., 211.

16. Lewis Gordon, *Bad Faith and Antiblack Racism* (Amherst, NY: Humanity Press, 1999).

17. Fanon, *Black Skin/White Masks*, 112.

18. Shelly Eversely, *The Real Negro: The Question of Authenticity in Twentieth-Century African American Literature* (New York: Routledge, 2004), 79.

19. *Black Is . . . Black Ain't*.

20. John Jackson Jr., *Real Black: Adventures in Racial Sincerity* (Chicago: University of Chicago Press, 2005).

21. Ibid.

22. See, for example, Roy Bryce-Laporte and Delores M. Mortimer, eds., *Caribbean Immigration to the United States* (Washington, DC: Research Institute on Immigration and Ethnic Studies, Smithsonian Institution, 1976); Mary Waters, *Black Identities: West Indian Immigrant Dreams and American Realities* (Cambridge, MA: Harvard University Press, 1999); and Raynel Shepard, *Cultural Adaptation of Somali Refugee Youth* (El Paso: LFB Scholarly, 2008).

23. Mary Waters, "Ethnic and Racial Identities of Second-Generation Black Immigrants in New York City," *International Migration Review* 28, no. 4 (1994): 795–820.

24. All informants' names have been changed to protect their anonymity.

25. Halter, *Between Race and Ethnicity*, 174.

26. Charles Mills, *The Racial Contract* (Ithaca: Cornell University Press, 1997).

27. Peter McLaren, *Revolutionary Multi-culturalism: Pedagogies of Dissent for the New Millennium* (Boulder: Westview, 1997), 7.

28. See, for example, Patricia Hill Collins, *From Black Power to Hip Hop: Racism, Nationalism, and Feminism* (Philadelphia: Temple University Press, 2006).

29. Gina Sanchez-Gabau, "Contested Identities: Narratives of Race and Ethnicity in the Cape Verdean Diaspora," *Identities: Global Studies in Culture and Power* 12 (2005): 405–438.

30. Marco Martinello, "Citizenship," in *A Companion to Racial and Ethnic Studies*, ed. David Theo Goldberg and John Solomos (Malden: Blackwell, 2002), 116.

31. Ana Ramos-Zayas, "Becoming American, Becoming Black? Urban Competency, Racialized Spaces, and the Politics of Citizenship among Brazilian and

Puerto Rican Youth in Newark," *Identities: Global Studies in Culture and Power* 14 (2007): 85–109.

32. Ibid.

33. Murray Forman, "'Straight Outta Mogadishu': Prescribed Identities and Performative Practices among Somali Youth in North American High Schools," *Topia* 5 (2001): 43.

34. St. Clair Drake and Horace Cayton, *Black Metropolis: A Study of Negro Life in a Northern City* (New York: Harper and Row, 1962), and W. E. B. Du Bois, *The Philadelphia Negro: A Social Study* (Philadelphia: University of Pennsylvania Press, 1996).

35. Nancy Denton, "Residential Segregation: Challenge to White America," *Journal of Intergroup Relations* 21, no. 2 (1994): 19–35.

36. Douglas Massey and Nancy Denton, "Hypersegregation in U.S. Metropolitan Areas: Black and Hispanic Segregation along Five Dimensions," *Demography* 26 (1989): 373–391.

37. Pierre Bourdieu, *Distinction: A Social Critique of the Judgment of Taste* (Cambridge, MA: Harvard University Press, 1984).

38. See, for example, Elijah Anderson, *Streetwise: Race, Class, and Change in an Urban Community* (Chicago: University of Chicago Press, 1992), and Elijah Anderson, *Code of the Street: Decency, Violence, and the Moral Life of the Inner City* (New York: W. W. Norton, 1999).

39. I make reference to the northeast, for 'being country' as opposed to 'being urban', it can be argued, is at the vortex of southern definitions of blackness. Any number of popular hip-hop songs from the South in the past five years are illustrative of this point.

40. Eithne Quinn, "Black British Cultural Studies and the Rap on Gangsta," *Black Music Research Journal* 20, no. 2 (2000): 195–217.

41. Ramos-Zayas, "Becoming American, Becoming Black?"

42. Mark Anthony Neal, *New Black Man* (New York: Routledge, 2005).

43. David Harvey, "From Space to Place and Back Again: Reflections on the Conditions of Postmodernity," in *Mapping the Futures: Local Cultures, Global Change*, ed. Jon Bod et al. (New York: Routledge, 1993), 3–29.

44. Murray Forman, *The 'Hood Comes First: Race, Space, and Place in Rap and Hip Hop* (Middletown: Wesleyan University Press, 2002).

45. Harvey, "From Space to Place and Back Again," 7.

46. See, for example, John Jackson Jr., *Harlemworld: Doing Race and Class in Contemporary America* (Chicago: University of Chicago Press, 2001), and Robin Kelley, *Yo' Mama's Disfunktional!: Fighting the Culture Wars in Urban America* (Boston: Beacon, 1997).

16 Latino or Hispanic

The Dilemma of Ethno-Racial Classification for Brazilian Immigrants in the US

Tiffany D. Joseph

The ethno-racial composition of the US has changed considerably due to increased migration from Latin America, Asia and Africa. Recent research on immigrants from these regions indicates that they are challenging current US racial conceptions.[1] Because Brazilians are some of America's newest immigrants, less is known about them compared to other Latin American immigrants. Furthermore, comparative research on the social construction of race in the US and Brazil has increased as scholars have explored the subtleties of racial classification and inequality in both places.[2] This chapter merges research on Brazilian immigrants in the US with comparative studies of race in the US and Brazil, combined with an examination of Brazilian immigrants' perceptions of the Latino and Hispanic ethno-racial categories. Relying on data from interviews with forty-nine Brazilian return migrants (Brazilians who immigrated to the US and subsequently returned to Brazil), this chapter argues that three factors influenced their ethno-racial self-classifications: (1) participants' confusion about US racial categories; (2) participants' perception of a difference between Latinos and Hispanics; and (3) participants' external classification as Hispanic by Americans. The following discussion will attempt to provide a better understanding of Brazilian immigrants' US ethno-racial classifications, specifically with regard to the Latino and Hispanic categories. Understanding how and why Brazilian immigrants choose to self-classify using these categories has implications for their personal, social and political relationships with Latinos in the US. This is particularly important now as Latinos are the largest ethnic minority in the US.

THEORETICAL FRAMEWORK

Racial Classification in Brazil and the US

Significant comparative research on racial classification in Brazil and the US suggests that race developed much differently in each country.[3] The rule of hypodescent historically racially classified any individual with black ancestry as black and has indelibly shaped US race relations.[4] Consequently, racial classifications and ethno-racial groups were rigidly defined, facilitating the development of race-based identities among racial minorities in the US.[5] In Brazil, Gilberto Freyre's *Masters and Slaves* introduced the racial democracy ideology, which encouraged Brazilians to embrace their African ancestry and racial miscegenation.[6] Freyre also argued that there could be no distinct racial groups because Brazilians were racially mixed. Thus, racial discrimination was antithetical to racial democracy in Brazil. Due to socially accepted racial mixing and racial democracy, racial classification among Brazilians has been difficult to assess. Brazilians of all phenotypes acknowledge having African ancestry and almost half self-identify as racially mixed, not as solely white or black.

Racial democracy yielded fluid racial classifications for Brazilians who do not see themselves as members of distinct racial groups and have not used race as a basis for legal discrimination since the abolition of slavery. Therefore, Brazil was considered a racial paradise compared to the US, where legally sanctioned racism had oppressed nonwhites for centuries. However, academics have questioned the reality of Brazil's racial democracy as studies have documented extreme racial inequality.[7]

Hispanic Ethnic Categories in the US

Like other Latin American migrants, Brazilians were unaware of the Latino/Hispanic terminology until arriving in the US. The term Hispanic was formulated by the US Census Bureau in response to the 1960s' civil rights movement, when various ethnic groups were competing for political power and recognition. It was developed to suppress ethnic differences between and prevent collective political mobilization among Chicanos, Puerto Ricans and Cubans.[8] However, as more Latin American immigrants arrived, all Spanish-speaking immigrants were classified as Hispanic despite the national, social and linguistic diversity of nearly twenty-five million people.[9]

De Genova and Ramos-Zayas argue that the plurality of politicized 'Hispanic' ethnic identities was minimized to presumably shared cultural elements (e.g., values, beliefs, customs) among all Latin American nationalities.[10] Whereas 'Hispanic' has been externally ascribed to individuals of Latin American descent, they are less fond of this term, perceiving it as Eurocentric and depoliticized.[11] Thus, 'Latino' has been the preferred category because it is similar to the term Latinoamericano, which is more commonly used in Latin America.[12] The Latino label also includes Portuguese-speaking Brazilians who are also Latin American. Although the Latino/Hispanic label is ethnic because Latinos can also racially be black or white, the label is highly racialized in US society. Consequently, Latinos are viewed as members of one racial group despite being from various countries in Latin America.

Brazilian Immigration to the US

Various studies have documented the immigration and assimilation of Latin Americans and Caribbeans in the US.[13] Yet less is known about Brazilian immigrants, whom Margolis refers to as an "invisible minority" due to their small numbers.[14] In recent years, the Brazilian immigrant population has increased, yielding more studies about Brazilians in the US.[15]

Brazilians have been coming to the US in large numbers since Brazil's economic crisis in the 1980s and have continued to into the twenty-first century.[16] Brazilians view immigration as a means of social mobility in their own country, because wages in Brazil, even for the well-educated, are very low. Therefore, Brazilian immigrants come to the US primarily seeking better economic opportunities like other immigrant groups; however, extensive return migration has been documented among Brazilians.[17] The majority intend to stay in the US only two to five years as undocumented immigrants to work, save money and send it back to Brazil to buy a car and house upon returning, a process referred to as 'Fazer à América', which translates to 'making America' in English.[18] The 2010 US Census estimated that 339,000 foreign-born Brazilians are living in the US, mostly in the northeastern US.[19] However, due to their wide-spread undocumented status and difficulty with US ethno-racial categories, Brazilian immigrants are highly undercounted.[20] Historically, Brazilian immigrants have generally been better educated than the Brazilian population, range from working- to middle-class and have been predominantly male.[21] They are generally less than forty years old and lighter in skin tone (than most Brazilians), usually self-classifying as white.[22] However, Jouet-Pastre and Braga argue that these trends may be changing as female, poorer (and probably darker) and less-educated Brazilians come to the US.[23]

US Racial Conceptions among Brazilian Immigrants

Despite the growing amount of research on Brazilian immigrants and comparative studies of race in Brazil and the US, few studies have explored how Brazilians negotiate race in the US. Margolis finds that some Brazilian immigrants in New York City in the 1990s were confused by the Latino/Hispanic categories, and felt superior to and socially distanced themselves from other Latin American immigrants.[24] Marrow finds that first-generation Brazilian immigrants classify themselves using nationality rather than explicit US racial categories.[25] Although Brazilians are from Latin America, they do not identify strongly with the panethnic 'Latino' label.[26] Furthermore, the conflation of the ethnic Hispanic/Latino labels further influences Brazilian immigrants' ethnic identity choices.[27] Brazilians speak Portuguese and do not consider themselves to be Hispanic—a category many Brazilian immigrants strongly resist.[28] But despite the inaccuracy of the Hispanic label, Brazilians are still categorized as such in the US.

Although previous studies of racial conceptions among Brazilian immigrants in the US demonstrate the resistance of this group to classify as Hispanic, to my knowledge, no other study has explored comprehensively Brazilian immigrants' perceptions of the Hispanic/Latino category and their reluctance to identify as Hispanic. Brazilian immigrants' interpretation of the Latino/Hispanic label is significant for understanding how immigrants' internalization of aspects of the US racial system (e.g., discrimination, stereotypes, external classification) influences their ethno-racial classification options. Because such classifications may be tied to coalition building and Brazilians are perceived as Latino/Hispanic, their self-classification choices and interactions with Latinos/Hispanics may have implications for their sociopolitical mobilization in the future, as Latinos are now the largest ethno-racial minority in the US.

METHODS

Data for this discussion come from semistructured interviews conducted with forty-nine Brazilian return migrants in Governador Valadares (GV), Brazil, from October 2007 to October 2008.[29] Studies on Brazil-US migration cite the process beginning in GV, which remains Brazil's largest immigrant-sending city to the US.[30] In a permanent population of 246,000 people, 15 percent of GV residents are estimated to be living in the US.[31] The sample consisted of twenty-six women and twenty-three men between twenty and fifty-seven years of age, whose average length of stay in the US was almost eight years. The majority (76 percent) lived on the East Coast and returned to GV between 1989 and early 2008. In terms of education, 83.7 percent of the sample had at least a high school diploma. Because 61 percent spoke very little or no English, they worked as housecleaners, babysitters, dishwashers, 'busboys/girls' and/or in construction. With regard to reasons for immigrating, 45 percent immigrated primarily to work, 18 percent due to having family in the US and 37 percent immigrated for other reasons. Before immigrating, 80 percent intended to return to Brazil. Even though 63 percent of returnees obtained tourist visas before immigrating, only 25 percent acquired a green card or US citizenship.[32] The racial makeup of the sample can be seen in Figures 16.1 and 16.2.

Whereas Figure 16.1 shows participants' premigration classifications using Brazilian census categories, Figure 16.2 shows the sample's racial self-classifications in the US using US Census–derived categories.[33] From looking at the charts, it is clear that participants' premigration racial classifications in Brazil differ from their US racial classifications. Before immigrating, almost half of the sample classified as white in Brazil, whereas white racial classification in the US was about 30 percent. One-fourth of participants self-classified as 'mixed' premigration. The charts also show a decrease in participants who classified as black in Brazil premigration,

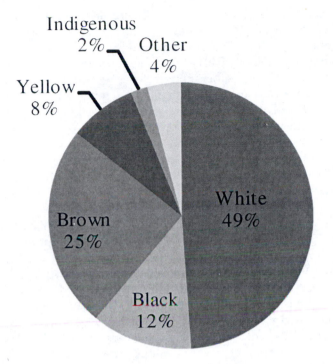

Figure 16.1   Race in Brazil, premigration (Brazilian census).

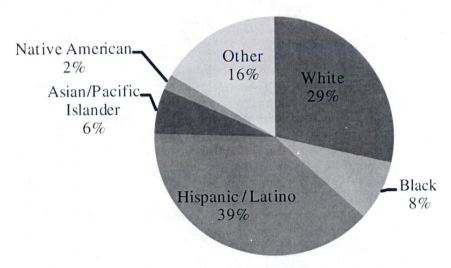

Figure 16.2   Race in the US (US Census).

dropping from 12 percent in Brazil to 8.2 percent in the US. It appears that the lack of an official 'mixed' category and the presence of the Hispanic/Latino category on the US Census absorb a considerable amount of the sample's premigration racial classifications, especially for those who classified as white and brown before immigrating.

Interviews were conducted in Brazilian Portuguese and focused on the following in Brazil and the US: (1) self-ascribed racial classification before, during and after immigration; (2) participants' perceptions of race; (3) experiences of racism; and (4) influence of race on social interactions. In the part of the interview that focused on participants' perceptions of race in the US, I asked specifically about perceptions of the Latino/Hispanic categories, whether returnees would self-classify in either category and about their reasons for doing so.

Participants were recruited primarily through snowball sampling, participant referrals and local contacts (e.g., Brazilian immigration researchers, immigration organizations), which were very effective given GV's extensive US migration history and the significance of social networks for immigration. Interviews were audio-recorded and transcribed for qualitative data analysis. I used focused coding to identify any phrase or sentence that mentioned some aspect of race in the US as it related to racial classification and the Latino/Hispanic categories, paying careful attention to portions of the interviews in which returnees mentioned the words Latino/Hispanic or responded to interview questions about those ethnic categories. From analyzing those data, I noticed there were similarities across participants (of both genders, all skin tones, education levels, premigration social class and time period in the US) regarding their perceptions of the Latino/Hispanic category and why they classified in a certain way.

RESULTS

Although 38.8 percent of the sample racially self-classified as Hispanic/Latino using US Census categories (see Figure 16.2), only 10 percent identified as Hispanic and 6 percent identified as Latino when asked for an open-ended racial classification in the US. Table 16.1 shows the categories and frequencies in which returnees self-classified. Return migrants most frequently self-classified as mixed (26 percent) and white (22 percent) when not given specific racial categories in which to classify. The different percentages using US Census and open-ended classifications reveal a complexity to racial classification before and during the US migration, which demonstrates returnees' attempts to navigate racial classification in both countries.

The range of categories participants used to self-classify themselves when not given specific categories demonstrates Brazilians' less rigid norms of racial classification. However, once asked to classify using US Census categories, the majority of participants classified as Latino/Hispanic. These

Table 16.1 Open-Ended Racial Classification in the US

Category	Frequency	Percent
Mixed/Moreno	13	26
White	11	22
Black	5	10
Hispanic	4	8
Latino	2	4
Not White or Black	2	4
Did Not Classify	2	4
Black/Hispanic	1	2
Brazilian/Latina	1	2
Brazilian	1	2
Foreigner	1	2
Lighter	1	2
Mixed, Yellow, White	1	2
Mulatta	1	2
Not White, or Black Foreigner	1	2
White or Yellow	1	2
White Brazilian	1	2
Yellow	1	2

different numbers reflect returnees' preference not to classify in specific categories, especially the Latino/Hispanic category, unless prompted to do so. In-depth analysis of participants' interviews revealed three particular reasons why return migrants self-classified as Latino, Hispanic, both or neither during their time in the US:

(1) Category confusion: US racial categories confused participants;
(2) Belief in a difference between Latinos and Hispanics; and
(3) External classification by Americans as Latino/Hispanic.

This section will explore each of these perceptions and include some interview quotes to demonstrate returnees' perspectives regarding the Latino/Hispanic category.[34]

Category Confusion

While in the US, many return migrants discussed how US racial categories were sources of confusion. Some returnees mentioned being unsure of how to racially classify on applications (e.g., employment, school enrollment) because they felt none of the common US Census categories applied to them as Brazilians. Such confusion was the result of various factors: the absence of a 'mixed' racial category, recognition that their self-classification differed from how Americans racially perceived them, and external classification by others as Hispanics. The following quotes demonstrate some participants' experiences being confused by US racial categories.

> . . . I think the Brazilian doesn't know what it is to be Latino. They [Brazilians] don't know they are Latinos [when they arrive to the US] . . . I think there [in the US] they know [learn]. It's because they [Brazilians] don't know that languages like Portuguese, French, Spanish, Italian have Latin origin. So, they [Brazilians] think Latino is only Hispanics, just the Hispanics. (Gustavo, white, thirty-seven years old, Massachusetts)

> One time I was talking with a person that had lived there [in the US] many years and I said, "Why do they [Americans] say we are Latinos?" She said, "It's because we are." . . . The Brazilian is classified as Latino, whether he is black, yellow, green, but it's because we are from South America, so we're seen as Latino . . . Latino is Mexican, Spanish, Bolivian, but the Puerto Rican is now American. (Leticia, black, forty-five years old, New York, New Jersey and Massachusetts)

> Now I, at times, I don't understand who the American classifies as Latino. Latino, as I understand it, at least based on the etymology of the word, Latino[s] are people [that speak] Latin languages. Italian is Latino, French is Latino, Spanish is Latino, Portuguese is Latino . . . I am Latin American, now I don't know if they [Americans] use this term to, I don't know how to say, offend or belittle a person or a race . . . So, in that regard, you are less or lower, it is pejorative. I didn't know what their [Americans] intentions were [when they used Latino]. (Thiago, white, forty-nine years old, New York)

Gustavo suggests that Brazilians are uncertain but learn their status as Latinos after arriving to the US. Gustavo believes that Brazilians assume that the Latino label applies only to Hispanics. However, Leticia's quote shows that Brazilians learn that anyone from South America is considered Latino, and Leticia concurs that Brazilians are Latino after a discussion with a friend. Finally, Thiago's final quote also implies some ambivalence regarding the parameters for self-classification in the Latino/Hispanic categories. Thiago was aware that Americans classified certain individuals as Latinos, but was unsure if Brazilians should be included in that category. Although Thiago feels that anyone who speaks a romance language is Latino, he also mentions not knowing if Americans pejoratively ascribe this category to particular individuals.

Each of these quotes demonstrates returnees' personal experiences with being confused by US racial classification, especially the Latino and Hispanic categories. There is a sense of uncertainty regarding exactly who should be classified within those categories. Not only was classifying in a particular ethno-racial group a new experience for many returnees, but also negotiating the meaning of US Census categories compared to Brazilian categories was very daunting.

Even though there are white and black racial categories on the US and Brazilian censuses, the social meanings ascribed to those categories are very different in each country. Although most return migrants self-classified as white before immigrating to the US, some acknowledged that they had racially mixed ancestry, which in the US is a disqualifier for self-classifying as white due to the rule of hypodescent. Because a large percentage of Brazilian whites acknowledge having African ancestry, these individuals would be black in the US.[35] Returnees also noted that being white in Brazil is different from being white in the US, which they describe as 'really white' or very fair and having blonde hair and blue eyes. Furthermore, the absence of an official racially mixed category on the US Census was another source of confusion because returnees felt they had to self-classify using distinct and mutually exclusive racial categories. Another key difference between racial classifications on both censuses is that classifying in a particular category on the Brazilian census does not have the same social significance that it does for individuals in the US. A racial/ethnic identity is not tied to one's racial (or skin tone) classification in Brazil. Thus, returnees were very aware of the social differences that existed between US and Brazil racial categories, which informed their classification choices.

Differences between Brazilians, Latinos and Hispanics

When I asked returnees about their experiences in the US as immigrants and living in particular regions of the US, many returnees talked about Latinos and Hispanics as though they were separate ethno-racial groups. This prompted me to ask return migrants what they perceived as differences between Latinos and Hispanics, and if Brazilians could be classified in either category. The following quotes show some of their responses.

They [Americans] have a way of looking at each other and the Hispanics and we Brazilians recognize this. Because, for example, who[ever] looks at the Brazilian and at the Hispanic sees the difference in the shape of the head, the way they dress, many things . . . They [Hispanics] are very different from us, I think they're different. . . . Because in reality, we [Brazilians] are not Hispanic, not because I have anything against them [Hispanics], but we're different to the point that we [Brazilians] don't have a place [category], we are without a place [category] there. (Juliana, morena/mixed, forty-one years old, Massachusetts)

No, I would never classify in that category [Hispanic], I would always classify myself as Brazilian. [Although] I am classified by others as Latino or Hispanic. (pause) . . . Maybe, but I could be wrong that I can be classified as Latino, but not as Hispanic. I am not Puerto Rican, I am not Dominican, I am not from Costa Rica, I consider myself Brazilian and I will continue to consider myself Brazilian. . . . So, will I say I am Hispanic, no [but] I can be a Latino Brazilian, I am from Latin America, South America. (Ricardo, white fifty years old, New York)

There are always differences you know [between Brazilians and Hispanics]. The things they eat, their ways, the clothes they wear, the music . . . I know a person was Hispanic because of the music they listened to. And the Hispanics liked to accessorize their cars . . . put in those sound systems. The Brazilians, no . . . So we knew when there was a Hispanic [around] you know? Just from looking at their physical features [no], but by their way of being and talking loud, Hispanics talk loud (laughs), they're different [from us]. (Vinicius, white, thirty-one years old, Florida)

These quotes definitely reveal some return migrants' perceptions of differences with regard to language, culture and even physical appearance between themselves and Latinos and/or Hispanics. Although those differences seem important reasons for socially distancing themselves from Latinos/Hispanics, the quotes also demonstrate an internalization regarding the marginalized social position of that particular group in US society. Juliana's first quote mentions specifically how she noticed how Americans perceive Hispanics, whereas Ricardo strongly affirms his Brazilian identity and does not want to be classified as Hispanic in the second quote. He spoke more forcefully at that point of the interview and even listed particular nationalities to further show that he categorized certain nationalities as Hispanic and does not self-identify as Hispanic because he is Brazilian. Ricardo was not the only returnee to classify certain nationalities as Latino or Hispanic.

For the most part, when I asked returnees about differences between Latinos and Hispanics, Mexicans, Puerto Ricans and Dominicans were considered Hispanic whereas returnees considered South American nationalities such as Argentine, Chilean and Brazilian to be Latino. Return migrants most often identified Mexicans as the predominant Hispanic group in the US and did not want to be classified as Hispanic because returnees thought this group was the most stigmatized. Whereas the earlier quotes focus on lack of a category with which to classify and assess which nationalities are Latino and Hispanic, Vinicius's quote provides more specific examples of behavioral and cultural differences between Hispanics and Latinos, suggesting that Hispanics, by virtue of their food, clothing and car accessorizing, are different from Brazilians specifically and Latinos generally.

Some returnees' comments about Hispanics, especially Mexicans, reflected negative stereotypes about Mexicans (foreign- and native-born) in the US, which resulted in social distancing attempts. Brazilians' perceptions of Hispanics are not unlike those of black immigrants (Caribbean and African), who also attempt to distinguish themselves from African Americans, who are perceived as highly marginalized and stigmatized in US society.[36] Recent immigration reform debates have racialized all contemporary immigrants as both Hispanic and Mexican, raising doubts among conservative and other members of US society about their assimilability as poor, Spanish-speaking, undocumented immigrants who absorb taxpayers' resources.[37] With such negative perceptions regarding Hispanics overall and Mexicans specifically, it should not be surprising that Brazilians do not want to be associated with this group, as is reflected in the quotes.

External Classification as Latino/Hispanic

Despite identifying differences between and attempting to distance themselves from Hispanics, returnees were aware that Americans viewed them as Hispanics. Some also expressed concern that negative perceptions of Hispanics would negatively influence Americans' perceptions of Brazilians. The pie chart in Figure 16.3 shows how return migrants felt Americans classified them in the US using US Census categories.

Whereas only 38 percent of returnees self-classified as Hispanic/Latino using US Census categories (see Figure 16.2), 62 percent reported believing that Americans classified them as Latino/Hispanic. Therefore, despite being reluctant to classify as Latino/Hispanic, returnees recognized that they were racialized as Latino/Hispanic during the US migration. Many return migrants mentioned a perception that Americans view all immigrants as Mexican or Hispanic despite nationality differences and that many Americans know very little about Brazil, which also influences Americans' perceptions of Brazilians.

> If the American goes to Mars and encounters ET there, he'll [the American] go to ET and say 'que pasa?' Because he [the American] thinks everyone in the US is Mexican. . . . the American thinks everyone is Hispanic. So, he [the American] doesn't differentiate the Brazilian from the Hispanic, it's not that important to him [the American]. One time I told an American, 'I don't speak Spanish, I speak Portuguese.' And he said 'it's all the same shit.' (Felipe, white, thirty-four years old, Massachusetts and Connecticut)

> I worked in a factory in Elizabeth [New Jersey] . . . and [my coworker] even though he was American, he was of Hungarian descent . . . He was white, with really blonde hair and light eyes and he never talked to me because he thought I was Hispanic. . . . And he ignored me until he

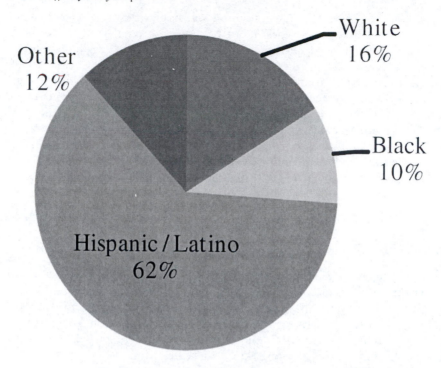

Figure 16.3 How Americans classified returnees in the US (Census categories).

discovered that I was Brazilian. . . . that completely changed everything for me. He doesn't like, he did not like Hispanics . . . So, he came and showed me some photos of Rio de Janeiro, lots of things and became my friend . . . but before this [identifying as Brazilian], I couldn't go near him. (Carolina, morena/mixed forty-four years old, New York and New Jersey)

The only thing I cared about was [being] illegal. So, that was something . . . they'd say, like Latino, it came to my mind, like illegal. That was tough. (pause) You associate, you really associate, like Latino with immigrants and with illegal people. (Amanda, white, thirty-eight years old, Connecticut and Massachusetts)

Felipe's quote demonstrates returnees' perceptions that Americans view all immigrants (at least those from Latin America) as Mexican regardless of nationality or language. Returnees felt that Americans do not recognize ethnic differences between members of the same presumed 'racial' group. Although Felipe attempted to inform an American that he spoke Portuguese, this did not matter for that particular American who responded, "it's all the same shit." This example further implies that Americans are sometimes ignorant or nonchalant when it comes to knowledge of other countries or nationalities.

Carolina's second quote describes her recollection of how being externally classified as Hispanic affected her relationship with a colleague. She discusses in great detail how her white coworker's behavior changed once she identified as Brazilian and not Hispanic. This example shows that some Americans may actually view Brazilians as different from Hispanics. Margolis refers to this as Brazilian exceptionalism, in which Brazilians can sometimes receive better treatment after identifying as Brazilian and making it known that they are not Hispanic.[38] Therefore, in a few cases, returnees mentioned being treated negatively when ascribed as Hispanic and being treated better after identifying as Brazilian. Because most return migrants acknowledged being externally classified as Hispanic and felt negative stereotypes were subsequently ascribed to Brazilians, it is possible some returnees sensed that identifying as Brazilian would result in receiving positive treatment from Americans. Some of those negative stereotypes included affiliation with drug trafficking and undocumented immigration status.

Amanda's quote reveals an awareness of negative characteristics associated with Latinos and Hispanics in the US relating to undocumented status. Amanda directly states that upon hearing the word Latino, she immediately thinks of Latinos as illegal. Even though Amanda and the majority of returnees I interviewed were undocumented, they did not see this as a source of commonality with other undocumented Latinos or Hispanics. Because return migrants recognized the stigma attached to being undocumented, many preferred not to classify as Hispanic.

When asked more specifically about the Latino/Hispanic category, returnees demonstrated less of a resistance to Latino than Hispanic because they recognized that Brazil was a part of Latin America. However, even in those cases, returnees mentioned their preference to be identified as Brazilian to distinguish themselves among Latin American immigrants.

DISCUSSION AND CONCLUSION

Although Brazilians are Latin American and others often classify them as Latino/ Hispanic, Brazilian immigrants in the US do not necessarily self-classify in these categories. This chapter has explored a sample of Brazilian return migrants' perceptions of these categories and how these perceptions influence Brazilians' classification choices in the US. Many returnees resisted the Hispanic classification due to perceived language and cultural differences. Whereas Latino was the preferred category of the two, most returnees wanted to be classified as Brazilian if given a choice.

Brazilian return migrants found negotiating ethno-racial classification in the US to be very confusing. The US system of racial classification seemed very different compared to their home country, where the census includes an official racially mixed category and Brazilians of multiracial ancestry can classify as white. It was clear from the interviews that returnees quickly recognized three things while living in the US: (1) racial classification was important; (2) others would racially classify them in some way; and (3) they would have to find a 'place' to classify as Brazilian immigrants. These three factors are directly related to returnees' perceptions of the Latino/Hispanic category. Although confused by US categories, return migrants felt pressure to identify with the one(s) that has been ascribed to other Latin American immigrants. This negotiation of racial classification demonstrates an internalization of US racial ideals, particularly how negative stereotypes of certain ethno-racial groups, such as Latinos/ Hispanics, influenced returnees' racial classifications and their perceptions of certain categories.

Despite socially distancing themselves from Hispanics, Brazilians' understanding of the Latino/Hispanic labels and experiences with US racial classification are somewhat similar to other Latin American immigrants who are also unfamiliar with US ethno-racial terminology upon arrival.[39] However, language, Brazil's increasing cultural presence in the US (e.g., soccer, capoeira, samba, increased tourism) and Brazil's position as an upcoming global economic powerhouse are factors that distinguish Brazilians from Hispanics and other Latin American immigrants in the US. Because they do not speak Spanish, returnees' rejection of the Hispanic label is more valid than that of other Latin American immigrants. These factors also facilitate a sense of national pride and Brazilian exceptionalism, which some Brazilian immigrants may use in attempts to socially distance themselves from marginalized Hispanics in the US.

Nonetheless, the presumed homogeneity of the Hispanic/Latino labels as referring to all individuals of Latin American ancestry classifies Brazilians, regardless of whether they resist, in those categories. As racialized, (primarily) undocumented and non-English-speaking immigrants working in the service sector, most Brazilian immigrants are marginalized in the US race, class and citizenship hierarchy. Like many other Latin American immigrants in the US, Brazilian immigrants are also concerned about their documentation status, are subjects of racial/anti-immigrant discrimination and live in isolated Latino immigrant communities. Thus, they lack the societal power to categorize themselves in a way that is acknowledged by the larger society. Brazilian immigrants' attempts to socially distance themselves from Hispanics do not prevent them from being associated with this group or experiencing racial or anti-immigrant discrimination.

In the present context of immigration reform debates, the rise of anti-immigrant hate crimes and the sizeable growth of the Latino population, it is very difficult for Brazilian immigrants to claim special immigrant status by virtue of Brazilian exceptionalism because many Americans still think of Brazil as a nonwhite Latin American country. As such, Brazilian immigrants are seen as nonwhite Hispanics in US society and are not in a privileged social position to collectively contest such an identification.

In contemporary US society, Brazilians and other Latin American immigrants are considered nonwhite within the black-white racial binary. However, given that the country's ethnic demographics have shifted, scholarly debates suggest that this binary may become a black/nonblack binary, in which some Latinos will fall on both sides of the racial divide, or that the US will experience a *Latinamericanization* of race, in which skin tone and social class will be more significant than racial group classifications.[40] If these shifts do occur, it is not completely clear where Brazilian immigrants (as a collective) would fall within these nuanced US racial frameworks. However, Brazilian immigrants' racial classification choices in the present, particularly their perceptions of the Latino/Hispanic label, will be crucial in shaping their social and political relationships with other Latinos. As the largest ethnic minority in the US, Latinos are organizing collectively and individually (along national origin lines) to stake their political claim in US society while fighting for recognition within the existing black-white binary. Brazilian immigrants' perceptions of and interactions with Latinos/ Hispanics will have implications for their ability to benefit from political gains that Latinos (as a collective) may have in the future.

NOTES

1. See Mary Waters, *Black Identities: West-Indian Immigrant Dreams and American Realities* (New York: Russell Sage, 1999), and Jose Itzigsohn, Silvia Gorguli and Obed Vazquez, "Immigrant Incorporation and Racial Identity: Racial Self-Identification among Dominican Immigrants," *Ethnic and Racial Studies* 28 (2005): 50–78.
2. Stanley Bailey, *Legacies of Race: Identities, Attitudes, and Politics in Brazil* (Palo Alto: Stanford University, 2009); Antonio Guimarães, "Race, Class, and Color: Behind Brazil's Racial Democracy," *NACLA Report on the Americas* 34 (2001): 28–29; Anthony Marx, *Making Race and Nation: A Comparison of the United States, South Africa, and Brazil* (New York: Cambridge University Press, 1998); Livio Sansone, *Negritude Sem Ethnicidade: O Local e O Global Nas Relações Raciais e Na Produção Cultural Negra do Brasil* (Salvador: Edufba/Pallas, 2003); Luisa Schwartzman, "Does Money Whiten? Intergenerational Changes in Racial Classification in Brazil," *American Sociological Review* 72 (2007): 940–963; and Edward Telles, *Race in Another America: The Significance of Skin Color in Brazil* (Princeton, NJ: Princeton University Press, 2004).
3. Bailey, *Legacies of Race*; Carl Degler, *Neither Black nor White: Slavery and Race Relations in Brazil and the US* (Madison: University of Wisconsin Press, 1986); Marx, *Making Race and Nation*; and Telles, *Race in Another America*.
4. Joe Feagin, *Racist America: Roots, Current Realities, and Future Reparations* (New York: Routledge, 2000), and James Davis, *Who Is Black? One Nation's Definition* (University Park: Pennsylvania State University Press, 1991).
5. Marx, *Making Race and Nation*; Michael Omi and Howard Winant, *Racial Formation in the United States: From the 1960s to the 1990s* (New York: Routledge, 1994); and Telles, *Race in Another America*.
6. Gilberto Freyre, *Casa Grande e Senzala* (Rio de Janeiro: Editora Record, 1933).

7. Anani Dzidzienyo, "The Changing World of Brazilian Race Relations?" in *Neither Enemies nor Friends: Latinos, Blacks, Afro-Latinos*, ed. Anani Dzidzienyo and Suzanne Oboler (New York: Palgrave, 2005), 35–60; Guimarães, "Race, Class, and Color"; and Telles, *Race in Another America*.

8. Nicholas DeGenova and Ana Ramos-Zayas, "Latino Racial Formations in the United States: An Introduction," *Journal of Latin American Anthropology* 8, no. 2 (2003): 2–17.

9. Suzanne Oboler, *Ethnic Labels, Latino Lives: Identity and the Politics of (Re)Presentation in the United States* (Minneapolis: University of Minnesota Press, 1995).

10. De Genova and Ramos-Zayas, "Latino Racial Formations."

11. De Genova and Ramos-Zayas, "Latino Racial Formations"; Michael Jones-Correa and David Leal, "Becoming 'Hispanic': Secondary Panethnic Identification among Latin American-Origin Populations in the United States," *Hispanic Journal of Behavioral Sciences* 18, no. 2 (1996): 214–254; and Oboler, *Ethnic Labels, Latino Lives*.

12. De Genova and Ramos-Zayas, "Latino Racial Formations."

13. Richard Alba and Victor Nee, *Remaking the American Mainstream: Assimilation and Contemporary Immigration* (Cambridge, MA: Harvard University Press, 2003); Nancy Foner, *In a New Land: A Comparative View of Immigration* (New York: New York University Press, 2005); Peggy Levitt, *Transnational Villagers* (Berkeley: UC Press, 2001); and Waters, *Black Identities*.

14. Maxine Margolis, *Little Brazil: An Ethnography of Brazilian Immigrants in New York City* (Princeton, NJ: Princeton University Press, 1994).

15. Margolis, *Little Brazil*; idem, *An Invisible Minority: Brazilians in New York City* (Boston: Allyn and Bacon, 1998); Helen Marrow, "To Be Or Not to Be (Hispanic or Latino): Brazilian Racial and Ethnic Identity in the United States," *Ethnicities* 3 (2003): 427–464; Clemence Jouet-Pastre and Leticia Braga, eds., *Becoming Brazuca: Brazilian Immigration to the United States* (Cambridge, MA: Harvard University, 2008); Teresa Sales, *Brasileiros Longe De Casa* (Sao Paulo: Cortez Editora Ltda, 1999); and Sueli Siqueira, "Emigrants from Governador Valadares: Projects of Return and Investment," in Jouet-Pastre and Braga, *Becoming Brazuca*, 175–210.

16. The current global economy and anti-immigrant sentiment in the US may yield a decrease in these numbers. It is difficult for Brazilians to obtain US tourist visas, and there have been significantly more deportations and voluntary returns to Brazil since 2007. See Nina Bernstein and Elizabeth Dwoskin, "Brazilians Giving Up Their American Dream," *New York Times*, Dec. 4, 2007.

17. (CIAAT) Centro de Informação, Apoio e Amparo à Família e ao Trabalhador no Exterior, "Um Estudo Sobre a Imigração Em Governador Valadares"; Ana Cristina Braga Martes, "The Commitment of Return: Remittances of Brazilian Emigrés," in Jouet-Pastre and Braga, *Becoming Brazuca*, 45–68; and Siqueira, "Emigrants from Governador Valadares."

18. Martes, "Commitment of Return," and Siqueira, "Emigrants from Governador Valadares."

19. Martes, "Commitment of Return," and Carlos Siqueira and Tiago Jansen, "Updating Demographic, Geographic, and Occupational Data on Brazilian in Massachusetts," in Jouet-Pastre and Braga, *Becoming Brazuca*, 105–131.

20. Margolis, *Little Brazil*; Siqueira and Jansen, "Updating Demographic"; and Carlos Siqueira and Cileine Lourenço, "Brazilians in Massachusetts: Migration, Identity, and Work," in *Latinos in New England*, ed. Andres Torres (Philadelphia: Temple University, 2006), 41–68.

21. Franklin Goza, "Immigrant Social Networks: The Brazilian Case," 1999, accessed Aug. 21, 2012, http://iussp2005.princeton.edu/download. aspx?submissionId=50570; Margolis, *Little Brazil*; and Sales, *Brasileiros Longe De Casa*.

22. Goza, "Immigrant Social Networks"; Margolis, *Little Brazil*; and Sales, *Brasileiros Longe De Casa*.

23. Jouet-Pastre and Braga, *Becoming Brazuca*.

24. Margolis, *Little Brazil*.

25. Marrow, "To Be or Not to Be."

26. Ibid.

27. Judith McDonnell and Cileine de Lourenco, "You're Brazilian, Right? What Kind of Brazilian Are You? The Racialization of Brazilian Immigrant Women," *Ethnic and Racial Studies* 32 (2009): 239–256; Martes, Ana Cristina Braga, "Neither Hispanic, Nor Black: "We're Brazilian"," in *The Other Latinos: Central and South Americans in the United States*, eds. J. L. Falconi and J. A. Mazzotti (Cambridge: Harvard University Press, 2007), 231–256.

28. Latinos and Latin American immigrants also resist the Hispanic label. See De Genova and Ramos-Zayas, "Latino Racial Formations"; Marrow, "To Be or Not to Be"; and Oboler, *Ethnic Labels, Latino Lives*.

29. I interchangeably use the terms 'return migrants' and 'returnees' to refer to Brazilian return migrants. A comparison group of twenty-four nonmigrants was also interviewed, but the findings in this chapter reflect those of returnees during the US migration.

30. Goza, "Immigrant Social Networks"; Jouet-Pastre and Braga, *Becoming Brazuca*; Margolis, *Little Brazil*; and Sales, *Brasileiros Longe De Casa*.

31. CIAAT, "Um Estudo Sobre a Imigração Em Governador Valadares," and Margolis, *Invisible Minority*.

32. Although the majority legally entered the US, most returnees became undocumented by working and overstaying tourist visas.

33. In the Brazilian census, yellow (amarela) generally refers to people of Asian ancestry (e.g., Japanese Brazilians). Participants who self-classified as yellow were not of Asian descent, but felt this category most closely described their skin tone. Participants who classified as 'other' generally classified as morena, which is the common term for racially mixed individuals, denoted as pardo in the census. Some participants classified as Asian/Pacific Islander in the US because the Portuguese translation was 'amarela' (yellow). Although the US Census asks individuals of Hispanic origin to classify ethnically as Hispanic and also racially (e.g., black, white), the Latino/Hispanic categories were combined because: (1) literature on Brazilian immigrants indicates that they have exposure to both terms in the US and (2) some returnees used the terms interchangeably during pre-test interviews. See Martes, "Commitment of Return."

34. The quotes include returnees' pseudonyms, racial self-classifications at time of interview (postmigration), age and US state of residence.

35. Telles, *Race in Another America*.

36. Waters, *Black Identities*.

37. Lindsay Huber, Corina Lopez, Maria Malagon, Veronica Velez and Daniel Solorzano, "Getting Beyond the 'Symptom,' Acknowledging the 'Disease': Theorizing Racist Nativism," *Contemporary Justice Review: Issues in Criminal, Social, and Restorative Justice* 11 (2008): 39–51; Charles Jaret, "Troubled by Newcomers: Anti-immigrant Attitudes and Actions during Two Eras of Mass Migration," in *Mass Migrations to the United States: Classical and Contemporary Period*, ed. Pyong Gap Min (Walnut Creek, CA: Altamira Press, 2002), 55–78; Susanne Jonas, "Reflections on the Great

Immigration Battle of 2006 and the Future of the Americas," *Social Justice* 33 (2006): 6–20; and Laura Pulido, "A Day without Immigrants: The Racial and Class Politics of Immigrant Exclusion," *Antipode* 39 (1997): 1–7.

38. Margolis, *Little Brazil*, and idem, *An Invisible Minority*.

39. DeGenova and Ramos-Zayas, "Latino Racial Formations," and Oboler, *Ethnic Labels, Latino Lives*.

40. Eduardo Bonilla-Silva, "From Bi-racial to Tri-racial: Towards a New System of Racial Classification in the USA," *Ethnic and Racial Studies* 27, no. 6 (2004): 931–950; Jennifer Lee and Frank Bean, "America's Changing Color Lines: Immigration, Race/Ethnicity, and Multiracial Identification," *Annual Review of Sociology* 30 (2004): 221–242; and George Yancey, *Who Is White?: Latinos, Asians, and the New Black/NonBlack Divide* (Boulder: Lynne Rienner, 2003).

17 Popular Culture and Immigration

Rachel Rubin and Jeff Melnick

We started our book, *Immigration and American Popular Culture,*[1] with a scene from the Will Smith film vehicle *Men in Black II*—for more than a few reasons. The scene (as we will discuss in a moment) from this 2002 movie had quite a bit to say about immigration, identity, memory, Americanness and otherness. It processed these large concerns with a light touch and a sure sense of purpose. But although we were certainly interested in parsing the content of one particular scene in the movie, more important for us was to begin our study of how popular culture and immigration have been mutually constitutive with a distancing move. For too long we scholars of immigration have contented ourselves with comforting paradigms and overly familiar images: key words and phrases such as 'assimilation' (or even Milton Gordon's more nuanced "Anglo-conformity" in *Assimilation in American Life*[2]) and 'acculturation', and images—say Alfred Stieglitz's "The Steerage"—that have cornered the academic and popular market. The usual problems of saturation and narrowcasting apply here—the 'winning' words and pictures tell at best a partial, and at worst a misleading, story about immigration and American cultural history. (Stieglitz's picture, of course, is of poor people *leaving* the US—'birds of passage' they were, although it seems our collective unconscious processes the photograph in a much different way.) We wanted to start with *Men in Black II*, then, because it hadn't already earned a stop on the Immigration Hit Parade, and was not even obviously about immigration.

Except that it is. Popular culture in general, and science fiction in particular, has long been an important collective processing site for questions related to the politics and ethics of immigration. In fact, our entire book is an argument in favor of the proposal that popular culture might ultimately turn out to have been a more consequential processing site than Ellis and Angel Islands put together. Immigrants to the US come through popular culture: quite often (as with the case of the Jamaican migrants in the Bronx in the 1970s) these new Americans have already had so many elements of American culture beamed at them before leaving their homeland that they are already competent 'readers' of the American languages of popular culture—and sometimes already competent producers too. Putting popular culture into immigration studies is much more than a simple add-on. In many ways it ought to upset the applecart. Conventional wisdom about periodization, assimilation and models of success really cannot survive the challenge.

The new social history of the post–World War era made enormous contributions to the study of everyday people in their 'own' spaces (slum neighborhoods, workplaces and so on) and established an important new paradigm for investigating the past 'from the bottom up'. With hindsight we can easily discover how this generation of well-meaning and often quite progressive historians and sociologists struggled with doing this work from the top down: it would not be hard to find numerous instances of how the blind spots and tin ears of noblesse oblige marred even the most successful of these new histories. But it is still possible to find an intellectual and political thrill here when we see how this generation of scholars insisted on the importance of finding the data of immigrant life in the deeds, words and creations of the immigrants themselves and then demanded that their readers understand that data as central to the telling of American history itself. Emblematic in this respect is Oscar Handlin, who opened his 1951 book *The Uprooted* with these oft-quoted lines: "Once I thought to write a history of the immigrants in America. Then I discovered that the immigrants *were* American history."[3] More than half a century later it is not hard to see that the paradigm shift that Handlin and his colleagues effected—necessary as it was—has put a lid on our imagination when it comes to studying immigration to the US. Handlin's new answer to the question of how to 'place' immigrants in America, that immigrants "were American history,"[4] begs a whole new set of questions—not least of which is, "Just *how* were immigrants American history?"

This is really just another way of saying that studying immigration from the 'bottom up' in a careful positivistic way (as so many valuable contributions have done over the past few decades) often leaves us looking at that rich and complex life on the 'bottom' with Les McCann's old jazz question in mind: compared to what? We don't mean to suggest that other scholars of immigration have never found ways to stitch together the downward pressure of legislative and culture industry control on the one hand, and immigrant innovation and resistance (or capitulation) on the other, but it has been too rare to find this dialectic plotted as central to a field that has been dominated by positivistic sociological and historical studies. The dialectic itself is the subject: our central impulse in bringing culture and immigration together is to try to make sure that all the consequential players are at the table at the same time(s). We realized early on in the research process that if the players did not seem to be in conversation at any particular moment, our job was to tease out what political scientist James Scott has called the "hidden transcript" and explore how it existed in relation to the "public transcript."[5] Most important to us was to keep our eyes on the multifarious ways that immigrants participated with native-born Americans in the discussions that shape American cultural life—where, when and *how* they take the stage. Although far too messy to count as a mantra, we did develop a scholarly 'fight song' of sorts. The words to it were simply "mutually constitutive, mutually constitutive."

We've tried to find a way to insist that the 'and' might be the crucial word in the title, but also the trickiest. We knew that we could simply 'add' immigrants and popular culture in order to develop a neat chronicle of how one clear activity ('immigration') engaged with another (popular culture). But the problem—as we have already hinted here—is that you cannot separate out 'immigration' from popular culture. If we can agree that immigrants have been, for more than a century, at the heart of the production and reception of popular culture imagery and that popular culture helped create and define various key moments in immigration history, then it starts to come clear why our 'and' is both central and more than a little unstable. In order to try to keep ourselves on task, we set out three major sets of questions to remain mindful of in each of our six case studies—case studies that ranged from gangster movies of the 1930s through Asian American cyberzines in the last years of the twentieth century and the first years of the twenty-first century:

1. In what particular ways have immigrants consumed American popular culture? What have these new Americans done with (or done to) the films, songs, fashions and so on that they have found in the US? What does the world of popular culture tell immigrants about what it means to be 'American'?
2. How have immigrants shaped the production of popular culture? How has the influence of particular immigrant groups changed from one generation to the next? What industries or forms have been particularly congenial or hostile to new immigrants? What legislative acts and technological advances have played major roles in the access immigrants have had to mainstream American popular culture?
3. How have immigrants been used as subject matter in American popular culture productions? Which groups have been depicted most frequently—in what contexts, and with what outcomes?

What this boils down to in practice is that we are trying to offer a road map of what we might call the 'cultural imaginary' of immigrant life in America. 'Imaginary' certainly does not mean 'unreal': it is meant to index a series of sites where the real and the representational make and remake each other, where individual lives and creations come into productive conflict with institutional requirements and prescriptions. The cultural geographer Michael Laguerre has written convincingly of how the socialization of immigrant subjects gets constructed in minoritized spaces.[6] This is really just a theoretical updating of the old real estate axiom about the three most important factors in selling a house (location, location and location). What

Laguerre wants us to pay attention to is how physical location shapes the way that immigrants 'read' their surrounding environment, interact with it and, ultimately, change it. Our revision of Laguerre's useful emphasis on location is rooted in our sense that quite often the most consequential interaction of immigrants with the larger surrounding culture has taken place through the multiple vehicles of popular culture.

This is not to say that we are content with an ahistorical vision of the popular culture industries as a machine that constantly grinds up and reconstitutes powerless immigrants in some predetermined way. In fact, we employ a case study method as a strategy to inoculate ourselves (we hope) against the overreaching that often accompanies a too-neat through narrative. Each of our six case studies starts from a time and place in which the relationship of immigrants and popular culture was being worked out in an especially focused and sustained way—the Zoot Suit Riots of 1943, for instance, or the adoption of Indian sitar master Ravi Shankar by young white people at the Monterey Pop festival in 1967. In orienting our case studies around a particular time/space nexus we are borrowing a crucial theoretical insight, the 'chronotope', from the Russian literary theorist Mikhail Bakhtin. Bakhtin's notion of the chronotope describes the site where "knots of narrative are tied and untied."[7] Whereas Bakhtin was interested in narrative form, we adopt his approach for our own purposes: our cultural chronotopes work much as Bakhtin's novelistic ones did, to create a "center for concretizing representation."

With no claims to thematic or chronological neatness, we strive to demonstrate how the triangle formed by immigrants, African Americans and native-born white people organizes a central dynamic of American cultural life. Another way of saying the same thing is that the 'and' of our study anchors a powerful allegory about American life, an allegory about the supposed 'ordinary' goodness of certain groups of immigrants—especially in relation to African Americans. Judith Smith has recently demonstrated in convincing detail how a cohort of American writers and filmmakers in the post–World War II era converted the immigrant family story into *the* story of proper American modern life, and in doing so wrote African American families out of the category of the 'healthy' or 'deserving'.[8] It was a similar approach to that adopted by Oscar Handlin and his 'progressive' colleagues. To domesticate immigrants, to plot them as central actors in a new pluralistic reality, too often meant positioning them, explicitly or not, as a countervailing force to African Americans. Nearly a hundred years after W. E. B. Du Bois asked rhetorically of African Americans how it felt to be a problem in American cultural life, Vijay Prashad turned to South Asians in America to ask how it felt to be a solution.[9] 'Race' is the barely hidden term that structures American immigrant life and culture.

What was fascinating for us to discover was how often concerns about new players on the American scene, about cultural status and belonging, and about the constantly negotiated line that putatively separates black and white in American life have been processed by putting on masks. Since the founding of the American nation (think of colonists getting tricked out in 'Indian' garb for the Boston Tea Party), white people here have habitually—and one might say, obsessively—worked out a variety of concerns about racial difference and likeness through acts of masquerade. Most crucial here is the foundational American popular culture form, blackface minstrelsy. From its most important home in theater, through its articulation in vernacular writing, to the central role it played in early Hollywood sound film, to its later role on the radio and television, minstrelsy has never left the stage for long. Blackface has gotten American audiences, producers and performers used to the idea that the most serious conversations surrounding race and national identity should be hosted on popular culture stages and from behind the mask. The various 'stages' of American popular culture have relied on the masking strategies that energized nineteenth-century blackface practice. The mask has signaled many things—racial derision, cross-racial sympathy, sexual attraction, sexual repulsion, misogyny, confusion about modern life and so on.

Minstrelsy, with its central claim that the complex challenges of racial formation could be profitably turned into entertainments, gave birth to a popular culture in the US that has never been able to shrug off its responsibility to make sense out of racial and ethnic identity. One major story is about how the denizens of America's popular culture stages have put masks on and taken masks off—sometimes ruefully, sometimes gleefully, but almost always with focused purpose. We plot a dynamic in which Americans of the dominant culture and Americans in marginalized immigrant and ethnic groups wear masks as emblems, as weapons, as apologies. From the all-purpose white ethnic slang of the classic 1930s gangster movies we study in our first chapter, through the now-you-see-it-now-you-don't rebellious spectacle of young Latinos wearing Zoot Suits in the 1940s of our second chapter, to the white hippies who wrapped themselves in a kind of sacred Indian dress in the 1960s and the Asian American pranksters playing with all kinds of 'yellowface' ironies in cyberspace around Y2K, 'masks' are a frequent object of our analysis. The tricky thing for us, as for so many teachers and scholars of immigration and popular culture already know, is to find a way to keep in mind the black and white frame that defines American life even as we only occasionally look directly at African American life in the US.

Introducing students to the notion that masquerade is central to the study of immigration and American popular culture is a useful way to emphasize that both historical particularity and interpretive flexibility are necessary tools for getting a handle on this vast subject. For instance, we propose that one dominant genre of Hollywood film in the 1930s, the gangster film, was defined by a kind of ritual masquerade. In this case, the rituals of masquerade turned extraordinary behaviors into a seemingly organic set of practices. The gangsters on screen were double agents, we argue, who held many secrets and told some of them. A few of the most important secrets had to do with 'Jewishness'—the tough talk and urban poses of the gangster were very much the product of a New World Yiddish, as language and culture. The key thing here, though, as we have begun to suggest, is that audiences quickly learned to 'read' the gangsters' many feints and dodges—to become expert, in fact, at decoding the genre-based conventions of speech, dress and action that defined the gangster movie.

It was the masked complexity of the gangster, his ability to be criminal and heroic, stylish and tasteless, bold yet ultimately defeated, that made him so appealing to Jewish producers and consumers in the 1930s. The first movie we discuss in the first chapter of our book, the 1935 film *Let 'Em Have It*, features a brutal gangster on the run from the law. In an attempt to dodge punishment, the gangster and his henchmen capture a plastic surgeon and threaten to kill him unless he surgically alters the gangster's face so that he won't be recognized. The surgeon performs the operation and, not surprisingly, the gangster murders him anyway. This climactic moment, though, comes when the gangster faces a mirror and begins to unwrap the bandages from his face. The surgeon, who knew not to trust a gangster, and who *knew* he would be killed no matter what, has carved the gangster's initials into his face—thereby permanently identifying him. This bizarre scene reminds us to take note of how masks are not simply ready-mades in American popular culture, but sites of negotiation and contestation. By the time of this film, Jews were particularly 'visible' in the larger culture as participants in the culture of plastic surgery (as with the famous case of performer Fanny Brice and her nose job—the operation that led Dorothy Parker to quip that Brice had "cut off her nose to spite her race."[10]

Brice, like the fictional gangster of *Let 'Em Have It*, might have thought she could control the meaning of her 'Jewish' face, but other powerful players in the culture would surely have their say as well. Masquerade has been a remarkably supple device for the creators and audiences who find each other in those overlapping circles of social activity we call "immigration and American popular culture." On the 'face' of things, utilizing masquerade is an admission (or a boast) that there is some deliberate hiding and feinting going on. The work for those of us who want to bring culture to immigration studies is to figure out why dodges were necessary in the first place—what made popular culture workers deploy them? Moreover, we need to know something about how audiences understood these acts of hiding in plain sight. What secrets did masquerade keep and what secrets did they tell? For us, what might have been most exciting about looking at the 'masks' present in Hollywood gangster movies of 1930s was how much light this masquerading could shine on the history of minstrelsy in American cultural life.

What we came to see is that the Jewish masquerades in gangster movies (the set of ritualized behaviors in films that marked the main characters as legibly 'ethnic' but not Jewish) must be understood as a relatively late addition to a long-standing Jewish investment in minstrelsy. By the 1910s or so Jews had more or less taken over the performance and production of stage blackface in the US. For decades they had used the traditions of blackface comedy and music to establish their place at the center of the American entertainment business. Among other innovations, Jews in New York and other major cities devised ways to incorporate minstrelsy into larger vaudeville productions. By the early twentieth century blackface itself came to be widely understood as a variety of Jewish cultural expression.

But Jews in blackface also presided over the final days of the form. The Jews who "invented Hollywood" (to use Neal Gabler's phrase[11]) used blackface, especially in Al Jolson movies, as long as they profitably could. But blackface was becoming less attractive to Hollywood movie producers in the early years of the 1930s for a number of reasons, including that so many people saw it as so obviously a Jewish cultural form. What these producers created to replace blackface was a more diffuse but no less purposeful kind of masquerade, which Jews could continue to use as a way of processing major concerns surrounding their public identities. In short, just as an earlier generation of Jewish actors, comedians and singers established blackface as a recognizably Jewish sphere of cultural activity, so too did the Hollywood industry of the early 1930s translate Jewishness into 'gangster' as a recognizable performative mold. Gangsters were not given Jewish names or Jewish 'back stories': but whether called 'Irish' or 'Italian' onscreen, audiences became quite adept at figuring out how these Jewish actors (who gave themselves names like "Edward G. Robinson," "John Garfield" and "Paul Muni") smuggled Jewish affect and attitude onto the screen. What we now call 'hard-boiled' or 'tough guy' was really a way that gangster film directors and actors (with the complicity of audiences) worked out a New World Jewishness onscreen without admitting that this is what they were doing.

Looking at Jews in gangster movies of the 1930s is an indirect way to remind ourselves of the centrality of African Americans and 'blackness' to the American culture industries. As we have been suggesting, the most powerful institutional forces in American popular culture history and the most influential audiences have relied on the notion that it is somehow fun, useful and/or necessary for white people to 'act' black. We don't want to rehearse here the debates that have followed in the wake of these culture-defining impersonations, but it is important to keep reminding ourselves that the practice of racial masquerade has been employed by Americans for a long, long time to articulate major social concerns and enact 'solutions' (at least on the make-believe level) to those problems. Since its inception, blackface minstrelsy has been much more than simple white/black affair. At the beginning it was dominated by Irish immigrant and Irish American performers; later on (and in early film productions utilizing blackface), Jewish Americans were at the center. The adaptation of black style has been a major forum for white Americans to explain to themselves and to others what 'whiteness' means and how it functions. In related fashion, immigrants to the US and their children have used blackface to figure out what access they have to whiteness and how they will deploy whiteness in the context of their own hyphenated identities.

Donning blackface makeup, acting black and later 'sounding' black on musical recordings and 'dressing' black in daily life have been crucial modalities for white Americans to confront major social changes or cultural challenges. Immigration has itself been a primary flash point for all manner of minstrelized performances since the 1840s or so. The world of popular culture has hosted an ongoing discussion *through* racial impersonation, about the proper shape and content of American identity.

One thing we hope to accomplish by bringing 'culture' to immigration studies is to help explain how racial impersonation has evolved over time and come to act as a major player in those processes we have (somewhat lazily) in the past indexed with names like 'assimilation' and 'Americanization'. Acting black has been joined, of course, by what Philip Deloria has called "playing Indian."[12] Consider the film musical *West Side Story,* for instance, and how four Jewish artists worked together to create what audiences understood to be an apt updating of the intermarriage plot." They did this through a consequential act of ethnic impersonation, converting a familiar story into a new one about the white/Latino dynamics of the Jets and Sharks.

In the context of one hundred years of immigration and American popular culture, this 'use' of Puerto Ricans by Arthur Laurents, Leonard Bernstein, Stephen Sondheim and Jerome Robbins actually feels somewhat 'traditional.' Although certainly cleansed of the most heinous racism of blackface minstrelsy, *West Side Story*'s creators cannot hide that they are 'using' brown people to intensify the feelings attached to their narrative. As film critic Pauline Kael noted, in *West Side Story* "Puerto Ricans are *not* Puerto Ricans and the only real difference between these two gangs . . . is that one group has faces and hair darkened and the other group has gone wild for glittering yellow hair dye."[13]

And how consequential these acts of 'brownface' have been for actual Puerto Ricans! We have only to turn to the nomination of Bronx-born Sonia Sotomayor to the US Supreme Court in 2009 to see how fully *West Side Story* has shaped the production of Puerto Ricanness in public. From editorial cartoons riffing on *West Side Story*, to YouTube parodies criticizing Sotomayor using the song 'America' as the soundtrack, to former presidential Republican candidate Mike Huckabee's 'mistaken' reference to Sotomayor as 'Maria', it was clear more than forty years after the Broadway play's debut that *West Side Story* was still instructing audiences on how to understand Puerto Ricans. (Judith Ortiz Cofer has written with breathtaking power about what it has meant to her to be serenaded as 'Maria' by strangers on the bus, having her cherished and hard-earned subjectivity erased in the process.[14]) *West Side Story* cornered the market on representing the migration of Puerto Ricans from the island to the 'mainland,' displacing virtually all other representations. The play and film created a distinct *ethnic* identity for Puerto Ricans—perhaps most definitively by erasing African Americans from the picture. That erasure is perhaps the single most important and lasting fact about *West Side Story*. All the areas of overlap (geographical and cultural) that linked Puerto Ricans and African Americans in New York were rendered invisible by *West Side Story* in favor of projecting Puerto Ricans onto an available screen of interethnic romantic melodrama. The implicit argument, achieved through this stunning representation, was that Puerto Ricans should be understood as no different from the earlier immigrant groups (Jews above all) that the creators of the show were most familiar with.

This was a 'progressive' bit of cultural work, in one sense, then. If *West Side Story* constructed Puerto Ricans as players in a mildly stimulating ethnic fantasy, what it accomplished most of all was to take this relatively new and threatening migrant group (the newspapers of the 1950s were rife with stories of Puerto Rican family dysfunction, juvenile delinquency and so on) and incorporate it into a familiar story of ethnic succession. The use of brown makeup, dreadful accents and faux-Latin music in *West Side Story* is at once a late-model entry in the American popular culture tradition of minstrelsy *and* a well-intentioned effort made by a group of relatively powerful Jewish men to accept Puerto Ricans into the national family.

This brand of politically 'progressive' cultural work reached a sort of apotheosis in the 1960s through the hippie appropriation of 'Eastern' style, religion and music. Many young (mostly white) Americans used costume and other forms of masquerade, an overall 'turn East' as an expression of their own larger cultural Declaration of Independence and also as a way to demonstrate solidarity with the Asian people then suffering under American military attack. The guiding assumptions that shaped the reception of actual Indian immigrants after 1965 came through the reception of popular icons, styles and religious adaptations, and not through the social realities produced by the large numbers of Indians themselves.

Thousands of young Americans found and constructed in South Asian Indians models of how to live a fuller and spiritually rich life in America. This came at just the moment (as Harvey Cox pointed out long ago[15]) when so many actual Asian Indians, encouraged by new immigration math developed by the Hart-Cellar Act, were turning West. The hippie embrace of the East reached a moment of defining visibility with the ecstatic reception of Indian sitar master Ravi Shankar at the Monterey Pop festival in 1967 and then two years later at Woodstock. Our argument is that Shankar acted as a sort of 'superimmigrant' for young white Americans—an idealized version of the new 'brown' immigrants who were coming to the US in the mid- to late 1960s. Richard Seager has written wisely that the 'big' stories in immigration history do not always involve a "mass phenomenon with dramatic consequences" but sometimes involve a "handful of newcomers" exerting power over a "limited number of individuals."[16] Ravi Shankar acted, to put it too briefly, as an emblem for how South Asians would be converted by white Americans into a 'model minority.' As with *West Side Story*'s vision of Puerto Ricans in New York, this relatively positive vision of the migrant other involved consequential silences surrounding African Americans.

The Woodstock-era career of Ravi Shankar stands as a compact example of how the complicated currents of American minstrelsy, global politics and new patterns of consumption could position young white Americans to fall in love with a certain type of brown immigrant. 'Falling in love' with Ravi Shankar was (among other things) a kind of racial masquerade for young white Americans. By the 1960s, we argue, racial masquerade was a reliable vehicle for young white Americans to ride their anxieties and aspirations on. They demonstrated in this era that racial impersonation and ventriloquism can be prosecuted with numerous complex motives and wildly varying outcomes. Members of the American counterculture did not invent Ravi Shankar, nor did they have much to do with the shape of his career in the late 1960s, but they did *use* him as an important medium for their own explorations of race, identity and world politics.

In their embrace of Shankar along with Eastern religions, visual arts and fashions, the hippies seized an opportunity to develop a nonracist and anti-imperialist relationship to the darker people of the world. This moment of the hippie turn East reminds us that the politics of racial masquerade are unpredictable, and often cleft by contradictory expressive acts. What the hippie embrace of Shankar at Monterey and beyond meant, above all, is that this rising generation of American culture makers was finding a new way to welcome brown people into the center of life in the US. This inclusion came with a steep price: the hippies required of Shankar and the other new immigrants that they relinquish at least some measure of control over their cultural stuff. The incorporation of South Asians was accompanied by an implicit demand that young white Americans be allowed to borrow their clothes, their religion, their music. Ravi Shankar's appearance as a star in American youth culture came to represent a sort of immigration best case scenario: unlike the Chicano youth held responsible for the social unrest that crested in the Zoot Suit Riots of 1943, Shankar seemed unthreatening above all.

Our purpose in exploring the hippie turn East as a species of racial masquerade is not to question the sincerity of any individual American who sought in Eastern religion or visual or musical culture a personal route to salvation, peace, aesthetic pleasure or comfort. But Arjun Appadurai has taught us to take "collective representations" as "social facts"[17]: as such, it becomes necessary to come to terms with the idea that developed in the late 1960s that the cultures and religions of India (and other parts of Asia) could be carved up, packaged and sold, in parcels of varying shapes and sizes. This set up a subject-object relationship, as Harvey Cox has explained, within which Americans could at once flood the East "with

American products" at the same time that Americans began to dress "in their costumes and help ourselves to their religions."[18] The consumers of the 'Indian' style (mostly young white Americans) became producers of cultural goods—from raga rock to Simplicity sewing patterns for Nehru jackets. It is a familiar alchemy, a sleight-of-hand that has almost always accompanied American minstrelsy; the innovation here is that the cultural and racial masquerade was successfully promoted as a kind of ennobling spiritual and political activity.

That said, the 1960s turn East still stands as a form of minstrelsy created (mostly) by and for white people. Ravi Shankar's star presence helped a generation of young white Americans simultaneously to endorse and fend off the implications of the 'new' immigration from Asia. A generation later, on the eve of the twenty-first century, a group of young Asian American writers, artists and activists launched a fascinating challenge to this whole tradition of racial masquerade that has shaped American popular culture since its inception. They did this through the publication and circulation of 'zines'—noncommercial, 'amateur' publications that operated in stark contrast to the mainstream publishing world. Motivated by passion, not profit, makers of zines tend to forego flawless production in favor of 'homemade' flavor. They give voice to the intimate and the oddball, rather than the trendy and conventional. As intimate as zines are, they must be understood as the product of international, national and local processes that have radically altered the technological landscape and the entertainment industries. Asian American young people (women in particular) have found in zines a remarkably congenial venue for self-expression and self-definition.

Our central concern in studying zines, especially cyberzines, is to figure out what happened to the traditions of racial masquerade—how did 'bodies' and 'race' look— when Asian Americans themselves seized control of the means of production and began creating images in cyberspace, where (as some claim) the physical has become all but irrelevant. As our abstract of minstrelsy, immigration and American popular culture should make clear, American identity has been bound up in how physical bodies are evaluated, regulated and interpreted by individuals and institutions. What does this all mean in cyberspace, where no actual bodies are to be seen? This question became even more interesting for us when we considered how regularly pornographic images circulate that promote the stereotype of the physically small and submissive Asian woman and the emasculated Asian man. There has been much academic attention focused on the *gender* implications of pornographic images, but little that focuses on the *racial* or *ethnic* dimensions. This is surprising, given that pornography has long been one of the most prominent cultural locations for the creation and reception of racial fantasies. It seemed useful to us to consider racially themed pornography as a thriving form of minstrelsy: the enactment of racial stereotypes and fantasies in a performative context for the purposes of entertainment, presumably of nonmembers of the group being portrayed.

Cyberzines have proved to be an especially hospitable forum for the cultural needs of Asian American youth because of the way they allow young people to 'talk back' to a cultural industry turning huge profits by selling Asian things. Zine publishing has 'worked' so well for Asian American youth because it is uniquely successful at providing a means of expression that flies directly in the fact of the 'polite Asian' stereotype. For young people chafing under the label of 'model minority' the slaphappy world of zine culture is a significant opportunity for opposition.

We raise the important questions surrounding Asian American zine dialogue with pornography with cognizance of all the complicated power dynamics the word 'minstrelsy' implies: can there ever be power *gained* from wearing the minstrel mask? Are all such performances historically coercive, or can they be undertaken voluntarily? How does being paid—or needing to be paid—change the equation, if at all? If one types 'Asian women' or, even more, 'Asian girls' into an Internet search engine, the search will yield a few zines or political sites—and a vast number of porn sites promising women who are 'mysterious', 'exotic' and 'submissive'. Many Asian American zines are directly confronting the racial aspect of Internet porn. Several zinesters express a kind of annoyed weariness at still having to harp on what one writer referred to as the "'I'm not a geisha' protest." Nonetheless, the zinesters admit, the notions of what it means to be an Asian woman purveyed in standard pornography remain ubiquitous.

In this light, the most daring and oppositional aspect of Kristina Wong's *Big Bad Chinese Mama* might be the fact that she publishes photographs of Asian and Asian American women all looking ugly on purpose. This completely flies in the face of what Asian women are 'supposed' to do with their bodies, as the multimillion-dollar cosmetics industry attests. The captions accompanying the photographs of young women making absurd faces, picking their noses, sitting on the toilet or sticking out their tongues refer to the cultural expectations they are working to thwart: "Not quite a lotus blossom, but the next best thing," one reads. With her zine, Wong deliberately tries to intercept readers expecting one of the many Internet sites promising Asian mail-order brides or Asian women interested in dating white men. (In an interview we draw from in our book she confessed to publicizing her zine on genuine porn and 'dating' sites.) Upon arriving at Wong's web address, readers are greeted with a photograph of Wong eating cheese doodles with her mouth open, grimacing as grotesquely as possible. "Sorry Guys, did I ruin the mood for ya?" reads the caption under her photo.

This generation of Asian American cyberactivists can be understood as working in the fields of 'late minstrelsy'. Aware of the power of racial masquerade in American cultural history, they purposefully construct challenging visions of the Asian American body in virtual reality. Deploying stereotypes and counterstereotypes, this generation of Asian Americans attempts to grab control of the definition of Asian American identity. These constructions of Asian American identity, coupled with the historical acceleration of technological accessibility, have led to a wide-open cultural opportunity of immigrants, the children of immigrants and the grandchildren of immigrants. On this reconstructed stage social stereotypes, generational conflict, personal ambition, intragroup relationships, personal ambition and gender politics are presented and contested.

The Asian American zinesters of the Y2K era allow us to consider not only how they hold up a mirror to the American cultural reliance on minstrelsy and racial ventriloquism but also how their work sits in relation to even broader questions surrounding immigration and American popular culture. The challenges posed by these zines extend beyond the practical: they call into question some fundamental tenets of American cultural hierarchy. Perhaps the most fundamental challenge is to the system of cultural value. There is still a dominant ideal that what is valuable must be lasting, as indicated by the word 'classic'. In order to evaluate zines, 'disposability' must replace 'lasting' as a key concept. The 'indie' aesthetic of zines flies in the face of the 'great artist' vision of literature—although many of the zines themselves are intensely personal. Therefore, incorporation of this body of work into the story of American culture will necessitate a revised value system. Of course the number of creative and heartfelt zines on the Internet continues to grow every day, but so does the number of pop-up ads, spam e-mail messages and online megastores. In short, whatever opportunities the Internet may offer to individuals and groups in search of a workable identity, it can also take away, with its ability to commodify, package and resell.

Whereas the creators of the zines form a recognizable cultural cohort, their work—existing mostly in cyberspace—forces us to think again about how 'place' shapes identity and how audience expectations exert pressure on artistic creation. The vibrant and uncompromising makers of these zines take all of American popular culture history as their text and are in the ongoing process of remaking it in their own image. Their playful, referential and relentless approach to making popular culture at century's end (and century's beginning) offers a glimmer of hope to those of us who worry about corporate control of all media.

We want to end here with a reminder that mutually constitutive circles of experience are, above all, the result of focused social engineering by powerful governmental and industrial forces. Major migrations and new cultural productions usually have obvious and direct causes, and government policies and corporate strategies are usually a good place to look first. American wars have been major factors in the shaping of unforeseen and sometimes 'unwanted' migrations. But 'war' is only one major constituent of what we have come to call 'globalization'—the complex of economic, social and political connections that ring the world and which is always about to be featured on a screen near you!

NOTES

1. Rachel Rubin and Jeffrey Melnick, *Immigration and Popular Culture: An Introduction* (New York: New York University Press, 2006).
2. Milton Gordon, *Assimilation in American Life: The Role of Race, Religion and National Origin* (New York: Oxford University Press, 1964).
3. Oscar Handlin, *The Uprooted: The Epic Story of the Great Migrations That Made the American People* (1951; Philadelphia: University of Pennsylvania Press, 2002), 1.
4. Ibid., 3.
5. James Scott, *Domination and the Arts of Resistance: Hidden Transcripts* (New Haven: Yale University Press, 1990), x.
6. Michael Laguerre, *Minoritized Space: An Inquiry into the Spatial Order of Things* (Berkeley: Institute of Governmental Studies Press, 1999).
7. Mikhail Bakhtin, *The Dialogic Imagination: Four Essays* (Austin: University of Texas Press, 1981), 250.
8. Judith Smith, *Visions of Belonging: Family Stories, Postwar Culture, and Postwar Democracy, 1940–1960* (New York: Columbia University Press, 2006).
9. Vijay Prashad, *The Karma of Brown Folk* (Minneapolis: University of Minnesota Press, 2001).
10. Bernice Shrank, "Cutting Off Your Nose to Spite Your Race: Jewish Stereotypes, Media\Images, Cultural Hybridity," *Shofar* 25, no. 4 (2007): 18–42.
11. Neal Gabler, *An Empire of Their Own: How the Jews Invented Hollywood* (New York: Anchor, 1989).
12. Philip Deloria, *Playing Indian* (New Haven: Yale University Press, 1998).
13. Mary E. Williams, *Readings on West Side Story* (San Diego, CA: Greenhaven, 2001), 133.
14. Judith Ortiz Cofer, *Call Me Maria* (New York: Scholastic Paperbacks, 2006).
15. Harvey Cox, *Turning East: The Promise and Peril of the New Orientalism* (New York: Simon and Schuster, 1977).
16. Richard Seager, *Buddhism in America* (New York: Columbia University Press, 2000).
17. Arjun Appadurai, *Modernity at Large: Cultural Dimensions of Globalization* (Minneapolis: University of Minnesota Press, 1996), 5.
18. Cox, *Turning East*, 155.

Part V

Where To, Beyond the Margin?

18 Toward Decolonizing Methodologies for Immigration Research

Sharif Islam

In this chapter I argue for a decolonizing methodologies approach for immigration research. This is a multivocal, cross-cultural, participatory mode of research that allows both researchers and the participants to carefully examine the normative issues that underlie all research questions. I begin this discussion by arguing for the relevance of moral-ethical considerations in immigration research and in debates over immigration policy and theory. In the latter part of the chapter, I use these moral-ethical considerations to provide a new perspective on immigration research and immigration policy debates, and introduce a decolonizing methodologies approach, as an alternative way of engaging these issues.

The decolonizing methodologies approach requires immigration researchers to reflect on the normative issues guiding their work, instead of 'submerging' them within the research agenda.[1] It also requires them to reflect on the way that the researcher and the researched relate to one another and communicate with another. We cannot assume that these normative considerations will lead to an 'impartial' consensus. But I also want to show that researchers cannot and should not ignore these normative considerations. There is an urgent need to deepen the engagement between immigration research and the broader, transdisciplinary conversation about the normative framework for research methodologies.[2]

The emergent body of writing on the ethics of immigration,[3] which has been largely produced by political theorists, asks some basic questions regarding borders and citizenship. Some of these arguments, such as Jonathan Seglow's,[4] are fueled by a cosmopolitan vision of distributive justice.[5] Legal scholars such as Cox[6] and Motomura[7] have also explored normative questions that pertain to immigration. But all of these investigations have focused primarily on immigration law and policy, leaving aside ethical and normative questions that pertain to research methodologies.

The decolonizing methodologies agenda that I propose here fills in this gap. It is borrowed from the indigenous scholar Linda Tuhiwai Smith,[8] who argues for dismantling the colonial paradigm of knowledge and authority, which is based on texts alone, and in favor of understanding indigenous knowledge systems. In a broader sense, decolonizing research requires us to reflect on the ethical and political dimensions of all research methodologies and promotes multivocal, cross-cultural representations,[9] creating more space for the lives and views of the subjects who are being interpreted and researched.[10] My aim here is to identify some connections between the normative issues raised by immigration research and these decolonizing methodologies.[11]

Over the past couple of decades, the academic discourse on methods and research practices in the social sciences has paved the way for postpositivist, postmodern, critical scholarships,[12] leading many scholars to embrace diverse ontological, epistemological and methodological positions[13] in the spirit of social justice, human rights and inclusive dialogues.[14] These developments have drawn attention to the 'mess' that has been created by the methods we have been using in social science research.[15] Immigration research has been somewhat disconnected from these debates that are questioning and even reinventing the idea of research itself. I want to bridge the divide between immigration research and this broader body of discourse and debate.

RESEARCH, CATEGORIZATION AND REPRESENTATION

Simply put, the idea of research is "to reveal the overarching contexts and (dis)continuities of various human experiences of various environments in which 'relations' are lived, structured and socially reconstructed."[16] However, research, which is often times ethnographic in nature, is sometimes understood as an activity " . . . conducted on foreign cultures in order to capture understanding of the native population—the customs, values, artifacts associated with a given group and its wider culture."[17] In order for such understanding to happen, certain categorizations are necessary.[18] However, not all of these categorizations are accurate. The problem of accurately and faithfully reporting human lives has been labeled a "crisis of representation."[19] As Margarete Sandelowski has explained, "Instead of giving voice to the voiceless, qualitative researchers have too often engaged in 'ventriloquy,' controlling the voices of the voiceless and, thereby, maintaining their voicelessness."[20]

Immigration research is not immune to these problems. Whether talking about the brutal border crossing experience of a Mexican mother or the job placement situation for a highly skilled Indian IT worker, immigration research always runs the risk of creating problematic categorizations and representations—creating voiceless research subjects. Regardless of our position on immigration policy, at the end of the day human migration is about *humans*, about *us*—no matter how we categorize others or ourselves. Shouldn't our theories, methods and practices reflect our humanness?

One way to understand this crisis of representation is to look at the notion of assimilation. Milton Gordon's work conceptually solidified the notion of assimilation in immigration research.[21] His basic argument was that immigrants would move away from ethnic culture and solidarity and immerse themselves in primary group relationships with the majority group.[22] This classical concept of assimilation has been critiqued and modified by recent immigration scholars.[23] Contrary to assimilation theory, multiculturalism "assumes that each ethnic group is endowed with a unique universe of norms and cultural preferences and that these cultures remain largely unaffected by upward social mobility or spatial dispersion."[24] Multiculturalism problematizes many of the underlying assumptions that connect immigration to conventional ideas about assimilation. As Nicholas De Genova has explained, the assumption is that

> . . . migration inevitably leads to "settlement," and settlement inevitably becomes "assimilation" or in other words . . . migration inevitably becomes "immigration" and hence, actual migrants, whatever their heterogeneous socio-historical specificities, are presumed to be already known, reducible to and subsumed by the abstract figure of "the immigrant."[25]

Furthermore the dichotomous legal and political framework of immigrant versus national is also important when it comes to categorization. As Andrea Wimmer explains,

> "Immigration" only emerges as a distinct object of social science analysis and a political problem to be "managed" once a state apparatus assigns individuals passports and thus membership in national communities [. . .], polices the territorial boundaries, and has the administrative capacity to distinguish between desirable and undesirable immigrants . . . Assimilation theory, both old and new, as well as multiculturalism, do not ask about this political genesis and subsequent transfiguration of the immigrant-national distinction, but take it as a given feature of the social world too obvious to need any explanation . . . Thus, the social forces that produce the very phenomenon that migration research is studying and that give it specific, distinct form in each society vanish from sight.[26]

Whether residing in an ethnic neighborhood or becoming hybrid, transnational migrants, diverse groups of people from different parts of the world with different social, cultural and religious backgrounds are homogenized as 'immigrants'. This single categorization thus enables research methodologies and policy debates to form a one-dimensional sense of the immigration debate—*either you are anti- or pro-immigration, either you like immigrants or you don't.*

The critical methodologies articulated by scholars such as Linda Tuhiwai Smith can provide a new way of thinking about the limitations of these categorizations. Most important these critical methodologies challenge us to understand immigration from the perspective of the immigrants. Before elaborating further, I want to briefly discuss the macrocontext for all of these issues and comment on some of the research agendas that have been used to document and conceptualize immigration.

SETTING THE STAGE

According to the United Nations, in 2005 there were two hundred million international migrants[27] worldwide.[28] Overall, the number of international migrants has more than doubled in the last thirty years. This is due to significant changes in the global economic, political and social landscape. In particular, the worldwide economic crisis of the 1970s, the neoliberal restructuring of the 1980s and the technological advancements of the 1990s, along with increasing inequality and several wars in different parts of the world, contributed to this changing dimension of international migration. These transformations shifted the vantage point of scholars in the humanities and the social sciences on the relationship between capitalism, nation-state and society. Terms such as 'globalization' and 'transnational' were introduced precisely at this historical juncture of global economic crisis, technological boom and displacements and movement of increasing numbers of people around the world.

In 2002, approximately thirty-four million foreign-born people lived in the US.[29] According to the 2000 census, Mexicans accounted for 22 percent of the foreign-born, with Filipinos coming in second at 4.6 percent.[30] Although immigration to the US has a long history, more immigrants arrived during the decade of the 1990s than in any other decade on record.[31] The immigration act of 1965[32] opened wide the gates of immigration, and these migration flows expanded further from the late 1980s onward. The immigration reforms of 1965 were followed by other significant changes that occurred in 1986,[33] 1990[34] and 1996.[35] With these changes the political and policy discourse became more concentrated on illegal immigration, mostly from Mexico. After 9/11, with the National Security Entry-Exit Registration System, the Patriot Act and the US Visitor and Immigrant Status Indicator Technology (US-VISIT), attention shifted to terrorism and security issues. Around the same time, thousands of immigrants from the Middle East and South Asia were deported and/or detained. This is just a brief overview that I will be using to help frame my later arguments.

RESEARCH AGENDAS AND METHODOLOGICAL APPROACHES

The field of immigration research is vast and heterogeneous, involving disciplines such as sociology, political science, demography, anthropology, history, economics, legal studies and urban geography, to name a few. In a recent comparative review of immigration and ethnic studies in the US and Europe, Morawska points out that in spite of their multidisciplinary breadth, immigration studies have long been recognized as a specialized field in the US by converging around their own niche agenda, meetings, journals and research clusters. She also observes that this diverse yet specialized field is "nichyfying" [sic] to the extent that it can deter broader participation: " . . . few nonspecialist scholars read the specialty journals or attend thematic meetings. In the meantime, mainstream social scientists take up the issues central to (im)migration research and, based on skewed and truncated readings of the literature in this field, construct theories of immigrants' assimilation, transnationalism, and generally, multicultural society."[36]

As noted earlier, although immigration research is part of broader social science disciplines, it is somewhat disconnected from wider debates and innovations, in particular when it comes to research methodologies. So the question to keep in mind when talking about ethics and research methodologies is, *how are scholars of immigration interpreting and analyzing significantly important aspects of our globalized world?* In other words, *what exactly are we up to in immigration research?*

Keeping these questions in the background, I highlight some major research trends as well as methodological and theoretical approaches. According to Portes and DeWind,[37] three basic questions can summarize the major trends in immigration research:

1) What motivates people to migrate across international boundaries, often at a great financial and psychological cost?
2) How are immigrants changed after arrival?
3) What impact do immigrants have on American life and its economic, sociocultural, and political institutions?[38]

Morawska also highlights three overarching themes that crisscross these questions in a variety of ways: *assimilation/incorporation*, *transnationalism* and issues of *racialized identity*.[39] Although some scholars attest that because of the complexity and breadth of immigration research a grand theory of migration is not possible, there is agreement in the literature that these themes and questions are "basic pillars supporting the study of immigration",[40] at least in the US.

WHY MORALITY?

Questions about the moral and ethical principles guiding migration research and policy are not included in the foregoing list. Although historians and social scientists have dominated the study of migration, philosophers have become more involved in recent years, adding a moral and ethical dimension to debates in migration studies (not to imply here that ethics and morality are solely confined to the domain of philosophy). Many of these philosophical inquiries have raised questions that invoke normative judgments about the priorities guiding immigration research.[41] It is important to point out that normative debates can surface in different research agendas in a variety of ways. However, these moral-ethical considerations have yet to become a significant component of mainstream immigration research.[42]

For example, there is a growing literature on the issue of 'illegality' in the US. Without adding the moral-ethical dimension, however, this debate boils down to an inclusion/exclusion paradigm, or a debate over the economic pros and cons of immigration that fails to show the human factors involved in migration. Joseph Carens[43] elaborates on the issue of "people who have settled without official authorization", for whom he uses the term 'irregular migrants' and makes a moral argument:

> At one extreme are those who frame the issue entirely as a matter of enforcing the law against people who refuse to respect it. From this perspective, states are morally entitled to control the entry of foreigners. The "illegal immigrants" have no standing in the community and no moral basis for making any claims that the state ought to respect. The only important goal of public policy in this area should be to ensure that the state's immigration laws are obeyed. At the other extreme are those who frame the issue entirely in terms of the interests and claims of the migrants. The basic premise here is that the politico-economic system exploits and marginalizes hardworking contributors to the community who happen to lack official documentation. . . . From this perspective, the only morally legitimate policy goal is to find ways to reduce the vulnerability of the "undocumented" and to challenge their official exclusion from the political community.[44]

Carens goes on to argue that, on moral-ethical grounds, even people who have settled without authorized documentation deserve legal rights. These sorts of arguments could provide a more clearly defined normative framework for research and policy debates over immigration, in which all sides seem to be talking past each other.[45] As Clifford Christians explains,

> Because we are all cultural beings—the researched Others, researchers, and the public to whom we communicate—research is not the transmission of specialized data, but in style and content, it reflects moral discernment. Ethnographic research should enable us "to discover moral truths about ourselves"; our research narratives ought to "bring a moral compass into readers' lives" by accounting for things that matter to them. Communities are woven together by their common understanding of good and evil, happiness and reward, the meaning of life

and death. A critical moral consciousness directs the ongoing flow of praxis and reflection in everyday life.[46]

It's also important keep in mind that there is nothing new about using moral arguments to legitimize the expansion of political and legal rights for marginalized populations. Jonathon Moses uses democratic suffrage as an example of such a moral argument:

> At the expense of real political power, enfranchised elites have consistently expanded suffrage to include the workers, the propertyless, women, blacks, youths and others. Although it is often forgotten, initial democratic gains were made in the face of an ingrained antipathy to democratic ideas (before the First World War), and *all* gains were made at the expense of entrenched interests. The motivation for this apparent irrational behavior was mostly moral indignation, a changing economic and social context (that brought with it new ideas concerning sovereignty, legitimacy and citizenship), and a strong (if often implicit) threat of violent overthrow.[47]

Moses goes on to explain how the moral arguments that were used to legitimize democratic suffrage apply to the legal, political and policy issues raised by contemporary migration (similar to the cosmopolitan argument of Seglow[48]):

> First of all, birthplace remains a natural contingency that is morally arbitrary. Second, a small but wealthy elite control the globe's political and economic purse strings, at the expense of the vast majority. Third, the many facets of globalization are radically changing the way in which we experience and think about sovereignty, legitimacy, and citizenship.[49]

Moses concludes that "The purest moral argument for free mobility holds that migration should be recognized as a universal and basic human right."[50] In the next section I elaborate further on this argument.

THE MORALITY OF IMMIGRATION

Mentioned in the foregoing excerpt from Carens's[51] work is the idea that the state has a moral entitlement to control the entry of foreigners. If states are entitled to moral rights such as controlling entry, then what stops foreigners from furnishing a moral claim? Theoretically nothing. Of course, this is easier said than done.

As noted earlier, most immigration scholars often shy away from making moral arguments, and there are many good reasons why they want to avoid the thorny issues raised by debates over moral universalism and relativism. Viet Bader highlights two of these reasons.[52] First, after WWII the world polity tied the meaning of justice to an idealized, national context, presuming that all persons could rely on a nation-state to protect their interests, and ignoring the need for a global paradigm of justice that is not reliant on national membership. Second, the ethical issues raised by global migration are broad and complex.

Despite these complexities, I am making a case for the inclusion of moral considerations *along with* political, economic, social, cultural and environmental aspects in the research and debates about immigration. I argue that moral considerations are a necessary but not sufficient component of immigration research and the broader immigration policy debate.

Within the limited literature on the morality of immigration several major themes emerge. First, let's consider the issue of open borders and the related question of citizenship and nationality. There are moral arguments on both sides of the fence: (more) open and (more) closed borders. Arguments for tighter control of borders often reference the nation-state's right to control the entry of immigrants and the dangers of overpopulation. Also relevant here are welfare issues, crime and terrorism, threats to cultural homogeneity, job losses and wage depression for the local working population.[53]

Michael Walzer, for example, has argued that nation states should retain the right of closure in order to sustain themselves as 'political communities' and in order to justly distribute social goods to the members of said communities.[54] According to this perspective on social justice, migrants have no inherent right to admission.[55]

Some of these assumptions and conclusions have been challenged by other scholars. Joseph Carens and Phillip Cole have convincingly argued that neither domestic cohesiveness nor cultural distinctiveness requires membership controls. In contrast to Walzer's *Spheres of Justice*, Joseph Carens's article "Aliens and Citizens: The Case for Open Borders" provides a cosmopolitan argument in favor of open borders.[56] In a recent contribution, Mathias Risse argues that attempts to understand the constraints that justice imposes on immigration policy ought to begin from the fact that "the earth belongs to humanity in common."[57] Risse goes on to argue that, if you take a global, cross-national look at population density statistics, it appears that "the United States is critically underusing the resources under its control" and that, as a result, "there can be nothing much wrong with illegal immigration."[58]

Of course, these arguments should not just be accepted on face value, but they are worth considering. It's also important to note that moral considerations don't apply just to debates over border control and citizenship; they pertain also to debates over migrant access to education and health services and other questions having to with worker justice and socioeconomic mobility. These concerns bring me to the final argument of this section. How can we understand these moral considerations in a more concrete fashion?

One of the main themes of the moral discourse of any society is that we live in 'shared spaces'—not in the broad sense described by Risse in which, "the earth belongs to humanity in common," but in a more particularistic, localized sense. These are shared spaces located in a specific society or community. For instance, we live in ghettos, suburbs, housing complexes, high-rise buildings and apartments—socially separated and yet living in the same physical space and sharing many of the same ideas about society. When I argue for the morality of immigration, I think of the kinds of shared commitments and collective identities that can emerge in these shared spaces—which bind all local residents together, regardless of legal status, nativity or nationality. This kind of identification is grounded in the understanding that there are multiple moral and social spaces within any particular community and that "every moral act is a contingent accomplishment measured against the ideals of universal respect of dignity of every human being regardless of gender, age, race, or religion."[59]

Border controls and regulations matter. But inside the borders of the nation-state these other kinds of spaces and communities can evolve, which are not defined by the principle of national membership. These spaces allow for shared identifications that stretch beyond the categorical distinction of 'immigrant' and 'citizen'. Keeping this normative foundation in mind, I propose a decolonizing methodologies agenda that would promote research to help us better understand these shared spaces, and how they are connected to the dynamics of global migration.

DECOLONIZING METHODOLOGIES

In a simple and broad sense, decolonizing research is about improving the condition of marginalized groups. It has a political and ethical thrust that rejects hegemonic, universalizing ideologies and methods. The term decolonization is used here as a starting point for laying out an alternative foundation for immigration research. Decolonizing methodologies do not necessarily need to invoke the postcolonial conditions or the colonizer/colonized binary but these methods are still valuable for their critical processes that engage marginalization and oppression at multiple levels and which try to understand the underlying assumptions, motivations and values that inform various research practices. Besides the ethical and political thrust, these methodolgies are commited to "dialogue, community, self-determination, and cultural autonomy" and resist "efforts to confine inquiry to a single paradigm or interpretive strategy."[60] I borrow the concept of decolonizing methodologies from Linda Tuhiwai Smith, who explains that

> decolonization does not mean and has not meant a total rejection of all theory or research or Western knowledge. Rather, it is about centering our concerns and worldviews and then coming to know and

understand theory and research from our own perspectives and for our own purposes.[61]

In her case 'our' is the Maori way of thinking. Tuhiwai Smith foregrounds efforts by Maori researchers to develop methodologies that are grounded in and respond to the values, experiences and needs of Maori people. Inspired by her work, I advance a preliminary proposal for how a decolonizing methodologies approach could apply to immigration research.

Smith defines decolonizing methodologies as a response to the colonizer's model of doing research. Decolonizing methodologies represent collective and varied ways of uncovering the hegemonic effects of colonizing discourses and their foundational assumptions. These colonizing discourses continue to create grand narratives that push non-Western narratives to the periphery.

Tuhiwai Smith summarizes this problem in the following way:

> The ways in which scientific research is implicated in the worst excesses of colonialism remains a powerful remembered history for many of the world's colonized peoples. It is a history that still offends the deepest sense of our humanity. Just knowing that someone measured our "faculties" by filling our skulls of our ancestors with millet seed and compared the amount of millet seeds to the capacity for mental thought offends our sense of who we are. It galls us that Western researchers and intellectuals can assume to know all that it is possible to know of us, on the basis of their brief encounters with some of us. It appalls us that the West can desire, extract, and claim ownership of our ways of knowing, our imagery, the things we create and produce, and then simultaneously reject the people who created and developed those ideas and seek to deny them further opportunities to be creators of their own culture and own nations.[62]

A parallel could be made with the way that the 'immigrant' category erases the complexity and specificity of the migrant experience and self-concept (as described earlier by De Genova). In the same way that Tuhiwai Smith has argued for a decolonized understanding of the 'indigenous' person, I argue that we also need to 'decolonize' our understanding of the 'immigrant'.

A word of caution is in order here. I am not arguing that there is a simple equivalence between the historical experience of the colonized indigene and the present-day migrant. There are similarities and also many striking differences in the situation of the both of these subjects that need to be spelled out carefully. However, what we can borrow from Smith is a research praxis that is modeled after her suggestions for affirming 'indigenous' ways of knowing the world. Put simply, I am arguing for immigration research to place more emphasis on documenting 'immigrant' ways of knowing the world, with the understanding that there is not just one 'immigrant' experience. And as we try to understand people from their own point of view, moral considerations inevitably come in.

Although 'decolonization' might invoke certain aspects of the past and certain modes of colonization, decolonizing research is not necessarily about the history of European colonization. The main idea here is to develop theories, methods and research projects *with* immigrant communities—to develop theories with 'them' instead of about 'them'.

A recent dissertation project that uses such decolonizing methodologies might help us understand this approach a little better. Mariolga Reyes Cruz, in her dissertation "Everyday Challenges of Building Community and Empowerment: An Ethnographic Study of Immigrant Mexican Parents Advocating for School Reform," narrates the experiences of undocumented Mexican immigrant parents working to make schools responsive and accountable to Latino children and their families. She uses critical ethnographic methods to narrate the experiences and perspectives of the parents "within the social context in which their efforts take place, with an eye to understanding how power is played out in the reproduction and contestation of social inequalities and how empowerment processes interface with building a collective sense of community."[63] This is an example that challenges dominant research methods that are usually constructed around authoritative sources. Reyes primarily uses the narratives of parents who are critical of the racially segregated education system. In a similar vein scholars are arguing to acknowledge not only non-Western ways of thinking but also methods of writing and reporting that include multivocal, multilingual texts.[64]

Another variation on the decolonizing methodologies approach is provided by narrative-based immigration research. According to proponents of this method, storytelling provides a tool for different groups to make claims, to express their own thoughts and values and to provide a different perspective on dominant narratives. The process of surfacing new perspectives is a critically important feature of the decolonizing methodologies approach. As Swander and Kagendo have explained, the practice and process of decolonization research methodologies are not about coming up with a 'valid' or a more 'objective' method:

> [W]e see decolonizing research resisting the lures and mires of postcolonial reason that position certain players within postcoloniality as more "valid" postcolonial researchers/scholars. Rather within decolonizing projects, the possibilities of cross-cultural partnerships with, between, and among indigenous researchers and "allied others" and working collaboratively on common goals that reflect anticolonial sensibilities in action are important facets of decolonization.[65]

CONCLUSION

In this chapter, I surveyed some trends in immigration research and argued that we need to develop a stronger, normative framework for this research.

A decolonizing methodologies approach offers one way of strengthening this foundation, which requires researchers not only to reflect on their own moral and ethical priorities but also to think about how to involve immigrants as active participants in their research, at the individual and community levels. In order to deconstruct homogenizing systems of categorization, we need to grasp not only the sociohistorical dimension but also the underlying moral and ethical issues raised by our research methodologies.

My point is not so much that there is a lack of critical research and theory on these matters but that there is a disjuncture between this body of critical inquiry and the broader field of policy debate and research on immigration, in the social sciences and the public sphere. For instance, the last several years have seen a growth in narrative, autobiography-based ethnographic research that highlights migrants' lived experiences, providing us with glimpses of everyday struggles of particular individuals or communities. However, at the same time, there are ongoing debates in social sciences concerning the emic/etic issue, the dialectic relationship between agency and structure, and most importantly questions about representation and legitimation.[66] My contention is that immigration research needs to tap into these debates more thoroughly. A decolonizing methodologies approach can help us move toward a more humane understanding of these issues, getting us to see that migrants are not just another 'unit of analysis' for our research.

NOTES

1. Ryan Pevnick, "Justice in Immigration: Citizenship, Residence & Political Association" (PhD diss., University of Virginia, 2008).
2. See Ewa Morawska, "Research on Immigration/Ethnicity in Europe and United States: A Comparison," *Sociological Quarterly* 49 (2008): 476.
3. Veit Bader, "The Ethics of Immigration," *Constellations* 12, no. 3 (2005): 331–361; Joseph Carens, "Who Should Get In? The Ethics of Immigration Admissions," *Ethics and International Affairs* 17 (2003): 95–110; and Jonathon Seglow, "The Ethics of Immigration," *Political Studies Review* 3 (2005): 317–344.
4. Seglow, "Ethics of Immigration."
5. Seglow's main point: "Cosmopolitan justice (stipulatively defined) concerns the principles governing the fair distribution of basic burdens and benefits that people suffer or enjoy; all the people who may be affected by a putative principle. Immigration controls involve considerations of justice because they plainly greatly affect people's life chances." Ibid., 318.
6. Adam Cox, "Immigration Law's Organizing Principles," *University of Pennsylvania Law Review* 157, no. 2 (2008): 341–393.
7. Hiroshi Motomura, "Immigration outside the Law," *Columbia Law Review* 108, no. 8 (2008): 2037–2097.
8. Linda Tuhiwai Smith, *Decolonizing Methodologies: Research and Indigenous Peoples* (London: Zed Books, 2005).
9. Clifford Christians, "Ethics and Politics in Qualitative Research," in *The Landscape of Qualitative Research*, ed. N. Denzin and Y. Lincoln (New

York: SAGE, 2011), 61–80, and Norman Denzin, *Interpretive Ethnography: Ethnographic Practices for the 21st Century* (Thousand Oaks: SAGE, 1997).

10. In earlier discussions of decolonizing research, the concept has been situated in the context of European decolonization. As a result scholars from formerly colonized nations stepped in to participate in research projects and provide 'indigenous' knowledge. In this chapter, I am using the term decolonization more broadly, while keeping the history of European colonization in mind.

11. The debates in social sciences suggest that our empirical research (whether qualitative or quantitative) is based on our understanding of our ethical world. Thus talking about values is not just abstract philosophizing; it is based on and reflects some particularistic interpretation of facts. This is, in short, my line of thought regarding the relationship between morality and methodologies of immigration research. However, these are not settled issues.

12. Denzin, *Interpretive Ethnography*.

13. Yvonna Lincoln and Gaile Cannella, "Ethics and the Broader Rethinking/Reconceptualization of Research as Construct," *Cultural Studies è Critical Methodologies* 9 (2009): 273–285.

14. Nursing and education are two fields that participated in these debates and deployed some of these methodologies. Also see Norman Denzin and Michael Giardina, *Qualitative Inquiry and Social Justice* (Walnut Creek, CA: Left Coast Press, 2009).

15. John Law, *After Method: Mess in Social Science Research* (London: Routledge, 2004), and Phillip Payne, "Lifeworld and Textualism: Reassembling the Researcher/ed and 'Others'," *Environmental Education Research* 11, no. 4 (2005): 413.

16. Payne, "Lifeworld and Textualism," 428.

17. Sharlene Hesse-Biber and Patricia Leavy, *Approaches to Qualitative Research* (Cambridge: Oxford University Press, 2005), 230.

18. For both qualitative and quantative social science research, data collection and categorization is a necessary component. This could be in the form of surveys, interviews, case studies, archival or narrative research. However, not all areas of research are crtically reflexive about the assumptions underlying different research philiosophies and methods. For more discussion on this topic see, Linda Finlay "Negotiating the swamp: the opportunity and challenge of reflexivity in research practice," *Qualitative Research* 2 (2002): 209–230.

19. Norman Denzin and Yvonna Lincoln, *Handbook of Qualitative Research*, 2nd ed. (Thousand Oaks, CA: SAGE, 2000), 2.

20. Margarete Sandelowski, "'Meta-jeopardy': The Crisis of Representation in Qualitative Metasynthesis," *Nursing Outlook* 54 (2006): 10.

21. Milton Gordon, *Assimilation in American Life: The Role of Race, Religion and National Origins* (New York: Oxford University Press, 1964).

22. Richard Alba and Victor Nee, "Rethinking Assimilation Theory for a New Era of Immigration," *International Migration Review* 31, no. 4 (1997): 829.

23. Alejandro Portes, ed., *The Economic Sociology of Immigration* (New York: Russell Sage, 1995).

24. Andreas Wimmer, "Herder's Heritage and the Boundary-Making Approach: Studying Ethnicity in Immigrant Societies," *Sociological Theory* 27, no. 3 (2009): 248.

25. Nicholas De Genova, *Working the Boundaries: Race, Space, and "Illegality" in Mexican Chicago* (Durham: Duke University Press, 2005), 89.

26. Wimmer, "Herder's Heritage," 255.
27. UN definition: a person who stays outside their usual country of residence for at least a year.
28. Khalid Koser, *International Migration: A Very Short Introduction* (Oxford: Oxford University Press, 2007).
29. Kay Deaux, *To Be an Immigrant* (New York: Russell Sage, 2006).
30. Caroline B. Brettell, ed., *Constructing Borders/Crossing Boundaries: Race, Ethnicity, and Immigration* (New York: Lexington Books, 2007).
31. Singer Audrey, Hardwick Susan and Brettell Caroline, eds., *Twenty-First Century Gateways: Immigration Incorporation in Suburban America* (Washington, DC: Brookings Institution, 2008).
32. The 1965 Immigration Act eliminated the long-standing national quotas that allowed a greater number of immigrants from non-European countries.
33. In 1986, Congress passed the Immigration Reform and Control Act, which provided legal status to approximately three million undocumented immigrants.
34. The Immigration Act of 1990 increased the numbers of family reunification and employment-related visas.
35. The Illegal Immigration Reform and Immigrant Responsibility Act of 1996 addressed the unlawful presence of immigrants in the US.
36. Morawska, "Research on Immigration/Ethnicity," 476.
37. Alejandro Portes and J. DeWind, *Rethinking Migration: New Theoretical and Empirical Perspectives* (New York: Berghahn Books, 2007).
38. Charles Hirschman, P. Kasinitz, and J. DeWind,. *Handbook of International Migration; An American Experience* (New York: Russell Sage Foundation, 1999), quoted in Portes and DeWind, *Rethinking Migration*, 4.
39. Ewa Morawska, "Sociology and History (Im)Migration: Reflections of a Practitioner," in *International Migration Research: Constructions, Omissions, and Promises of Interdisciplinarity*, ed. M. Bommes and E. Morawska (Aldershot, UK: Ashgate, 2005), 203–242.
40. Portes and DeWind, *Rethinking Migration*, 4.
41. Bader, "Ethics of Immigration."
42. Herbert Gans points out the need for further research dealing with the normative aspect of insider-outsider questions in immigration research. See, Herbert Gans, "Filling in Some Holes: Six Areas of Needed Immigration Research," *American Behavioral Scientist*, 42, no 9 (1999): 1302–1313
43. Joseph Carens, "The Rights of Irregular Migrants," *Ethics and International Affairs* 22 (2008): 163–186.
44. Ibid., 163.
45. Pevnick, "Justice in Immigration."
46. Clifford Christians, "Cultural Continuity as an Ethical Imperative," *Qualitative Inquiry* 13 (2007): 443.
47. Jonathon Moses, *International Migration: Globalization's Last Frontier* (London: ZED Books, 2007), 58.
48. Seglow, "Ethics of Immigration." See n7–10.
49. Moses, *International Migration*, 58.
50. Ibid., 59.
51. Carens, "Rights of Irregular Migrants."
52. Bader, "Ethics of Immigration."
53. Nigel Harris, *Thinking the Unthinkable: The Immigration Myth Exposed* (London: I. B. Taurus, 2002); Peter Higgins, "Immigration Justice: A Proposal for Developing Just Admissions Policies," (PhD diss., University of Colorado at Boulder, 2008); James Hudson, "The Ethics of Immigration Restrictions," *Social Theory and Practice* 10 (1984): 201–239; and Peter

Meilaender, *Towards a Theory of Immigration* (Basingstoke: Palgrave, 2001).

54. Michael Walzer, *Spheres of Justice* (New York: Basic Books, 1983), 61.

55. See Seyla Benhabib, *The Rights of Others: Aliens, Residents and Citizens* (Cambridge: Cambridge University Press, 2004), 95–105. The view holds that, in the case of nonrefugee immigrants, state sovereignty trumps any other moral arguments. However, notions of humanitarian crises and human rights complicate this line of thought.

56. Joseph Carens, "Aliens and Citizens: The Case for Open Borders," *Review of Politics* 49, no. 2 (1987): 250–273.

57. Mathias Risse, "On the Morality of Immigration," *Ethics & International Affairs* 22, no. 1 (2008): 25–33.

58. Ibid., 30. Risse's argument is based on the idea of "Egalitarian Ownership." He states, " . . . that all human beings, no matter when and where they were born, are in some sense symmetrically located with regard to the earth's resources and cannot be arbitrarily excluded from them by accidents of space and time." Ibid., 28.

59. Christians, "Ethics and Politics in Qualitative Research," 208; see also Denzin, *Interpretive Ethnography.*

60. Norman K. Denzin and Yvonna S. Lincoln, "Introduction: Critical Methodologies and Indigenous Inquiry," in *Handbook of Critical and Indigenous Methodologies*, ed. N. Denzin, Y. Lincoln, and L. T. Smith (Thousand Oaks, CA: SAGE, 2008), 2.

61. Smith, *Decolonizing Methodologies*, 39.

62. Ibid., 1.

63. Mariolga Reyes Cruz, "Beyond Cultural Barriers: Mexican Immigrant Parents Advocating for School Reform" (PhD diss., University of Illinois, 2005), 1.

64. Elsa González y González and Yvonna Lincoln, "Decolonizing Qualitative Research: Non-traditional Reporting Forms in the Academy," *Forum: Qualitative Social Research* 7, no. 4 (2006), accessed April 10, 2011, http://nbn-resolving.de/urn:nbn:de:0114-fqs060418.

65. Beth Swander and Mutua Kagendo, "Decolonizing Performances: Deconstructing the Global Postcolonial," in *Handbook of Critical and Indigenous Methodologies*, ed. N. Denzin, Y. Lincoln and L. T. Smith (Thousand Oaks, CA: SAGE, 2008), 31.

66. Denzin, *Interpretive Ethnography.*

19 Conclusion
Discourses and Immigrant Identities

Glenn Jacobs

A reviewer of this book could comfortably say that its contents fill in gaps or answer questions concerning the manner in which inter- and transnational immigrants have evoked official governmental and popular discourses, legislation and coercive enforcement by receiving countries. In turn, these have prompted corresponding effects on and responses to them by immigrant populations and groups. Despite the complementary needs of the migrants and host countries for work and labor force replenishment, the contradictions raised by exclusionary governmental practices, conventional discourses and popular sentiments serve punitive-disciplinary agendas that conceal exploitation, deny human and civil rights and check resistance to them. Moreover, the implications of the work herein suggest that, if anything, these articles elicit the *complexity* of the forces, processes and responses that continue to shape immigrant-host relations in all of these nations.

As I see it, this complexity, although confusing in its detail, can be contextualized in terms of three elements of the global forces setting in motion and maintaining the worldwide immigration flow. Although globalization is not the organizing theme of this book, an understanding of a few of its basic principles can help clarify and supply a macrocontext for the themes underlying much of what our authors have said. The first element is that "immigration is one of the constitutive processes of globalization" on the "macro level of global labor markets," and is thereby "one major process through which a new transnational political economy is being constituted."[1] The second element concerns the place of the state in the global context. Although deregulation and privatization have diminished the role of the nation-state, certain 'wings of the state', such as those enforcing immigration law (amply documented herein) and regulating the exporting and importing of workers, "become more, not less powerful due to their functional importance in the global economy."[2] On the other hand, some sending states take an active interest in their emigrants and maintain offices in host countries in order to manage migrants' interests. Put another way, "globalization could be regarded as the reorganization of the state that doesn't reduce its powers at all—actually allowing it to become more centralized in some ways—but not as connected to a national terrain."[3]

Thirdly, as is evident in the work herein, globalization does not obviate the importance of *locality* in terms of available jobs (especially low- and high-paying ones connected with the global economy) and even *resistance* to exploitation, repression and environmental contamination—for example, by immigrant community-based organizations.[4] In this respect, locality, including those aspects associated with immigrants' struggles against marginalization, has become so salient to social scientists that it has already inspired conceptual labels such as "localized globalism,"[5] "glocalization,"[6] "deep governmentality"[7] and "grass roots globalization."[8] And why is this so?

Localized globalism runs against the self-serving, discursive colonizing tendency Sharif Islam criticizes wherein most of the debates about immigration reflect national interests and sentiments. As such, in terms of the rights of immigrant minorities (i.e., marginalized immigrants), for example, there is insufficient questioning of the asymmetry of the predominant right of *emigration* from the nation-state versus the diminutive right of mobility to *immigrate* into it. In other words, mobility is inter- and intranationally unevenly distributed.[9] This is, as discussed ahead, relevant to the matter of citizenship and the framing of national discourses concerning immigrants.

Now, as to a possible thematic infrastructure, the work herein has probed immigrant-host relations in three significant ways: (a) it has elucidated host-governmental policies and legal and enforcement practices toward immigrants in several nations; (b) it has probed the manner in which these formal and informal practices are framed and legitimated by culturally and historically based, popular, conventional attitudes and discourses that work in tandem with them, conditioning and creating dilemmas for immigrant adjustment; and (c) it has clarified the riddles of identification—that is, identity formation—among so-called segmentally assimilated immigrant groups with respect to the question of racial formation/construction. As will become apparent, there are two leitmotifs crosscutting these themes: the construction of identity—often with more or less visible racial undercurrents—in the contexts of immigrant separation, reception and incorporation, and secondly, the emergence of incipient circular migration patterns imparted by the transnational character of contemporary immigration processes, which recursively affect the construction of identities.

With respect to the first of the three themes, item "a," Mark Dow's hard-hitting critique of the US government's immigrant detention system sets a tone for skepticism about conventional wisdom and reverberates as an indictment of its oppressive posture posing as a defense of citizens' peace and prosperity. A portion of the work herein testifies to a set of common cross-national reflexes, which, as Don Mitchell and Neil Smith remind us, locally marginalize the homeless, immigrants and social minorities and have raised blaming/othering the victim and the parallel assault on human rights to the level of national urban policies, and increasingly national immigration policy and its enforcement.[10] Such national reflexes, global as they might be, Linda Bosniak argues, underscore the exclusionary character of the nation-state. Thus the matter of rights reflects the nationalist character of citizenship, and despite the supranationalist sentiments of many democratic theorists' wishful thinking concerning global citizenship, "we face an 'ever greater gap' between the transnational conditions that structure our collective lives and the territorially-constrained reach of our political capacities."[11] Again, this disjuncture has prompted global responses of popular groups in the political sphere seeking to fill that gap and to halt the marginalization of immigrant groups and communities.

Continuing the legal aspect of the governmentality theme, the Alexis, Conlon and Polanco chapters dissect aspects of the legal anatomies of the state regulation of immigrant communities (exacerbating the gap) and immigrant reception. Gwendolyn Alexis's analysis is an eye-opening portrait of the hypocritical manner in which Swedish legal regulation of churches 'Christianizes' Muslim temples and congregants; it details the legal subtleties enshrouding the Lutheran hegemony impregnating Swedish law regulating religion by donning the masks of vaunted 'secularism', 'liberating neutrality' and 'religious-friendly' legislation. Most of all, it debunks the kiss of death democratic liberalism delivers to national and cultural (i.e., especially non-European) minorities in that country. One might speculate on the part played by Swedish social scientists in the framing of the legal-legislative rhetoric defining religious bodies as 'congregations' in order for religious organizations to partake of government subsidization. Thus non-congregational religions like Islam and Hinduism would have to become 'congregations' in order to qualify for such government largesse, and in that process become culturally denatured—that is, assimilated. Here Alexis's analysis comes close to Robert Paul Wolff's critique of tolerance based on the argument that only the *group* that can muster any significant popular and political support is viewed as deserving of tolerance.[12] Thus the veneer of toleration cloaking Swedish legal religious inclusiveness turns out to be, as Herbert Marcuse would say, repressive.

In a similar light, Dierdre Conlon discusses the narratives of asylum seekers in Ireland from Nigeria, Uzbekistan, Iraq and the Democratic Republic of Congo, constituting a numerical minority of the immigration inflow into this country. Focusing on the narrowing down of opportunities for legal residence, Conlon suggests how evolving cultural definitions and perceptions and their formal/legal incarnations socialize and shape immigrants' coping mechanisms while simultaneously marginalizing them. We are presented with how those who are given the designation of 'asylum seeker' "represent and conduct themselves as such subjects." Thus Conlon elucidates the manner in which such identities become 'real' or, as she says, legitimate through neoliberal governmentality. Perhaps a pointed discussion of race and the race issue would even further plumb and elucidate the structural issue of governmentality as it marches to the neoliberal drumbeat!

Looking at asylum seeking from a somewhat different vantage point, Jacqueline Polanco details the social quandaries exacerbated by US legal categorical criteria for qualification for asylum status of Dominican sexual minorities. Her article navigates the intricately dense forest of legal/legislative enactment and application procedures and the underlying social issues framing them, and does double duty with an analysis of the LGBTIQ movement, thereby fulfilling the criteria of what Michael Peter Smith calls "'the politics of simultaneity,' working to gender the political discourse on human rights and the legal framework in which it is deployed internationally and within particular urban and national formations."[13] Due to the lack of a coherent legal definition and visibility of, once again, such a 'social group' in the US national asylum laws and the Geneva Convention, and due to the prevailing socio-legal patriarchy on both the Dominican and US sides, the chances of being granted asylum are hampered: this is particularly critical for lesbians and for male-to-female transgenders. So once again the legal definition of the group assumes critical importance, with its ambiguity stemming from the fact that "the abbreviations, terms and social categories . . . are . . . simplistic and nonexclusive and miss much of the variety of actual human experiences."

In both the sending and the receiving countries where prevailing heteronormativity prompts them to conceal their sexual orientation/gender identity, the difficulty of substantiating proof of asylum seekers' 'associational status' is exacerbated. Ironically, once granted asylum, there is little to no respite from the police brutality, ostracism and fear of persecution prompting Dominican LGBTIQ individuals to seek it. This is due to the fact that "many Dominican LGBTIQ immigrants hide their sexual orientation/gender identity for fear of their family's and society's rejection, and those who eventually come out experience a ghettoization process by being forced out of the conventional Dominican American community."

Polanco analyzes the way in which representation of sexual minorities in the DR "has been seized by two stable, bureaucratic and conformist organizations that receive heavy technical and financial support from international agencies and governmental health care programs." Despite their preservation of an official and conformist LGBTIQ 'line' protecting the status quo of mainstream sexual minorities, she states that the long-standing practice of hiding one's sexual orientation/gender identity has been changing for gays, bisexuals and transgenders in the last couple of years "toward a more visible and open mobilization." A signature of 'localized globalism', it represents a salutary outcome of resistance and transnational awareness spiriting this movement.

Concerning "b," the second, discourse-based theme, several chapters move through a spectrum of emphases in their analyses of how states and societies deal with, or respond to, immigrant newcomers, ranging from the ugly political realities surrounding immigration that are overtly on the surface of national life, to those concealed by a platitudinous ideological veneer of toleration (e.g., multiculturalism). The Faedda, Pagliai, Araujo and Kralj writings clearly underscore Bosniak's implicit critique of the internal contradictions of liberal cosmopolitan, tolerationist and multiculturalist redistributive (i.e., welfare statist) discourses and policies in advanced capitalist countries, for as she says,

> National redistributions depend, first of all, upon the policing of territorial boundaries against outsiders far more desperately needy than those who are able to enjoy redistribution's benefits. They depend, as well, on the availability of enormous economic resources, some of which have been amassed at the expense of former colonies and less developed countries—if no longer through outright plundering, then through more apparently civilized modes of unequal exchange . . . In the past decade, resident noncitizens have been increasingly shut out from the provision of public benefits in this [i.e., the US] and other countries, a development which serves to exacerbate their second-class status within the national society.[14]

Barbara Faedda's analysis detailing the legislation and politics surrounding immigration in Italy sounds a dour note in tracing the trajectory of stricter immigration laws since the 1990s, the development of a more vociferous reactionary and racist political climate, and the corresponding strengthening and rising xenophobia associating immigrants with crime. She argues, "Italy seems to find a renewed unity by rejecting immigrants and forgetting (or pretending to forget) many other social and economic problems that preceded the new immigration, such as (Italian) mafia, unemployment or widespread corruption. The deep divisions among Italians are seemingly erased in order to (re)create a homogeneous community that is united against the Other."

Valentina Pagliai's take on Italian multicultural discourse is slightly more sanguine than Faedda's, and it does not leave one less skeptical, for it analyzes the way "racist claims are hidden under assertions of 'civilizational differences.'" These differences are reified and naturalized to the point that cultural boundaries become hardened and identified with ethnic boundaries, leaving one with the conviction that they are unbridgeable. Having begun her piece with a vignette on a Senegalese dinner feast in Tuscany hosted by leftist Italian activists whose purpose "was to have Italians and immigrants get together and know each other," Pagliai noticed that few Africans showed up, for they understood the party to be merely a stage to display their hosts' 'tolerance'. As for those African immigrants who did attend, it was used to foster personal influence "that they could later use to help other immigrants." Thus, the respected 'imagined communities' of the immigrants and the Italians differed. Moreover, it is argued that community "risks being used as an instrument of control and regimentation." Finally, underlying these conceptions of the varying immigrant cultures is the presumption of their internal compositional homogeneity, which, as Pagliai clearly understands, by reifying culture and community, erases individual immigrants' political agency. As mentioned earlier, such conceptions are not accidental or casual formulations, but mark an inherent tendency of neoliberal nationality.

In a similar fashion, Marta Araújo's analysis of Portugal's genealogy of current narratives on interculturality and harmonious multicultural coexistence demonstrates their anchorage in ideas of national identity that evade the underlying racism shaping that society's rhetoric of harmonious multicultural coexistence. Here Araújo's thorough-going tracing of the lineage of the Portuguese operant myth of 'tolerant conviviality' manifested in the educational system where her research is focused advantageously triangulates discourse analysis with a historical awareness of Portugal's currently operant 'soft' Lusotropicalist colonial heritage, and an ethnomethodogical-like vantage point on the educational manufacture of immigrant identity. Araújo thus notices that the essentialist baggage loaded into teachers' characterizations of their students' aptitudes, and more formally into curricula and textbooks, *naturalizes* students' presumed national homogeneities, thereby stereotyping them. The nation's inability and unwillingness to disabuse itself of the colonialist mythology of so-called 'cultural contact' have made the historically violent nature of that colonialism invisible and further perpetuate the shibboleths energizing Portugal's national self-image as a humane immigration haven. In turn, this overemphasis of the role of immigration "helps to reinforce a binary vision of development: the global South as poor, wrecked by disease and poverty, aspiring to emigrate to the rich, developed and modern North." As Bosniak would have it, the contradictions Pagliai and Araújo critique underscore and betoken "[n]ationalism's fundamentally exclusionary character points" as they grate against the liberal nationalist project's vaunted "[u]niversal regard for persons."[15]

I am not sure that I entirely agree with Ana Kralj's generalization that a shift has occurred in contemporary societies wherein *indirect* expression of prejudice toward or *avoidance* of newcomers as unwelcome residentially proximate neighbors has replaced more overt hostile expression toward them, but her observation that Slovenian ethnic chauvinism toward non-'pan-Europeans' has become grounded in nativist racism certainly rings true for there and elsewhere. Likewise, its expression in terms of its Slovenian characterization as a threatened "autochthonism" has a familiar ring reminding one of Samuel Huntington's blustering rage over the dilution of the American culture by Hispanics.

Capetillo-Ponce and Galanes's analysis of nativist discourse in the US Virgin Islands offers a transition between the preceding immigration discourse material and the writings of the third theme ("c") concerning identity. In seeking to establish hegemony by claimants who are the descendants of slaves, the utopian native narrative has striven to shape and fill in the lineaments of a national imaginary. Thus, a disjuncture underlies the native narrative between the global interests who own and profit from the tourist industry and the native claimants to status honor. In turn, focusing 'downward,' the so-called natives see themselves as being inundated by the heavy influx of largely subaltern, poor black immigrant workers from at least ten other Caribbean islands who are separated from them by social and economic distance, and with whom political consensus is difficult if not impossible to achieve. Thus the irony of being outsiders in their own land is compounded by their intolerance of the invading black wage-workers whom they see as riffraff and whose ancestors were also slaves. In this respect they have much in common with nativists elsewhere whose identities often have rested on a pretended indigenousness predicating the exclusion of rival, frequently racialized poorer others. Adding insult to injury, the natives here are out-classed by the resident (e.g., nonnative local island jewelers and other merchants) and nonresident (i.e., cruise ship and tour package) owners and proprietors to whom, by economic necessity, they are forced to defer. The native claimants to status honor are thus shorn of and/or checked in class and power (e.g., they have not been able to successfully legislate a constitution). Moreover, it would seem that they are falsely conscious of—that is, do not recognize or confront—those who are their most potent threats, ironically their sustainers—namely, the aforementioned global capitalist entrepreneurs commanding tourism, as opposed to the horde of black out-islanders they feel are overrunning them and with whom they deign to build political consensus.

As for the third category grouping ("c"), the issue of identity, Ryan Mann-Hamilton's material on the history of the African American–based community of Samaná in the Dominican Republic leaves one with the sense that the social construction of race has a perennial schizoid quality. Here, the banishment of race in a population of color sharing an island with a nation (Haiti) created by the revolt of slaves is so at odds with what an outsider might take to be 'reality' that it seems surreal. This construction is in fact cut from the larger cloth typifying the historically deracialized consciousness of the larger black and mulatto Dominican population occasioned by an emergent hegemonic notion of a single Ibero-American race synonymous with *nation*. In this case, Samaná, a locale that once served as a haven for and continued to be populated by the descendants of ex-slaves from the US, represented such an obstacle for consolidation of the Dominican state that it became a target for repression under Trujillo, who literally attempted to erase (i.e., in this case *burn*) blackness from the images reflected in the national looking glass. Trujillo had blacks identify themselves on driver's licenses as 'Indios', as if to say 'anything but black!' This pattern resembles Puerto Ricans' obsession with their Taino forebears, who were for all intents and purposes exterminated. Mann-Hamilton sheds light on contemporary Dominicans' oblique attitudes about race. Those interested in examining the larger historical pattern of Dominican racial construction are urged to consult Silvio Torres-Saillant's insightful work on this subject.[16] Ironically, Dominican migrants currently are experiencing the stigma of immigrant otherness in Puerto Rico, to which large numbers, many of them undocumented, are migrating.

So, although this piece does not, strictly speaking, focus on immigration, it examines the racial-historic legacy of African American migrants in a country now experiencing predominantly massive emigration to the US. Ramona Hernández has examined the structural components of Dominican emigration and immigration in detail.[17] Mann-Hamilton underscores with a twist the observation of Kitty Calavita, a seasoned immigration scholar, that "African Americans are the prototype of otherness against which other people of color—including racialized immigrants [and blacks themselves]—are juxtaposed and compared."[18]

Accordingly, several of the works imply the broadened applicability of W. E. B. Du Bois's insights on African American double consciousness to immigrants' contemporary circumstances. Thus the Saucier, Jones and Joseph studies of Cape Verdeans, Afro-Mexican and Brazilian immigrants stand out as exemplary data-based probes of the ways in which the perennial inequality and social stigmata of African Americans (whom they are occasionally taken for) form a perceptible social baseline from which immigrants gauge their social and economic life chances and construct their identities. They demonstrate how immigrant life-worlds produce, on the one hand, multivalent identities and awareness as rational strategies of adjustment, and, on the other, schizoid attempts to iron out the contrary demands placed on immigrants by mixed messages from the (formal and informal) labor market and the oppressive enforcement of immigration law.

It should be noted that the black reference out-group is a familiar presence in US immigration history and theory, and studies outlining its role and importance of immigrant incorporation constitute a genre of immigration research: witness Noel Ignatiev's incisive analysis of the historical origins of Irish American racism as manifestations of the living institution (later followed by the heritage) of slavery and the stigmatization of free and enslaved blacks, wherein the construction and assertion of whiteness lent a competitive advantage to Irish Americans seeking employment.[19] Ignatiev's, *How the Irish Became White,* heads a spate of literature on other nationality groups following it and offers historical examples and concrete reference points for whiteness studies.[20] More recently the work of Stepick et al.[21] underscores the significance of the consistent mistaking of Haitian youth for African Americans and its consequences for the complex intergenerational shifts in Haitian identity.[22] This and Waters'[23] work on the salience of the social stigma of African Americans for the formation of West Indian migrants' identities bear witness to the continuing baseline offered by the African American experience as a societal looking glass for identity formation of these and other groups.[24] Notable too is the significance of, and identification with, the perceived African American oppositional culture among Asian migrants suffering marginalization due to nonconformity with the model minority stereotype.[25]

In this regard, Rachel Rubin and Jeff Melnick's piece on US pop culture offers important clues concerning "how the triangle formed by immigrants,

African Americans and native-born white people organizes a central dynamic of American cultural life." Their analyses of the tropes of popular culture, especially those of black-faced minstrelsy and of the cinematic gangster/tough guy, are penetrating disquisitions on second-generation Jewish reference-pointed journeys of avoidance of blackness, as well as of ostensive construction of their own counterpointed whiteness. Thus, as they say about the mask, it "has signaled many things—racial derision, cross racial sympathy, sexual attraction, sexual repulsion, misogyny, confusion about modern life and so on."

Having said this, the Saucier, Jones and Joseph studies have gone beyond simply surveying the tropistic responses of Cape Verdeans, Afro-Mexicans and Brazilians toward or away from identification with African Americans (and in given cases and conditions, Latinos and/or Hispanics), but rather have probed the social dynamics and dilemmas underlying the construction of immigrant identities. Thus P. Khalil Saucier has carefully etched the calculi by which Cape Verdean youth see themselves as both racially black and ethnically Cape Verdean, concluding they "deploy ethnicity not to draw a distinction from blackness but to complicate blackness." In probing the meaning and role of youthful discourse concerning the sentiment and symbolism surrounding the urban 'hood,' Saucier has also creatively contributed insights to ethno-geography.

In a similar fashion, noticing that blocked mobility has racialized Afro-Mexicans' expressed shared identities with African Americans, Jennifer A. Jones has done more than exoticize this little known component of the Mexican migration. Before migrating, in Mexico black Mexicans are misperceived by their countrymen as immigrants (i.e., from the Caribbean or the US) who are occasionally asked to prove their Mexicanness by singing the national anthem. In the US both their structural position as Mexicans (who are taken to represent 'illegal' immigration) and the perceived stigmata of their blackness prompt their feelings of racial closeness with African Americans. These circumstances set them apart from other Latino groups (especially Puerto Ricans, Cubans and Dominicans) and even other Mexican immigrants. In any case, Calavita again reminds us that, "while some immigrants of color may find it opportunistic to distance themselves from American blacks and others in contrast may embrace racial solidarity with them, neither represents an abstract choice."[26]

Finally, as Jones suggests, the insistence on citizenship or legal residence in North Carolina[27] for getting a driver's license, as we have recently learned, has opened our eyes to the injustices suffered by Mexican migrants and produced labor shortages in construction, wholesale and retail trade, manufacturing and agriculture.[28] As the saying goes, money talks and b———t walks, and so crises of this nature perhaps redound more to economic and social justice, albeit temporarily pending replenishment of the labor supply, than do moral arguments and political rhetoric.

Tiffany D. Joseph's work on Brazilian return migrants has comprehensively explored Brazilian immigrants' perceptions of the conventional Hispanic/Latino category and their reluctance to identify with what they perceive as Hispanic marginality. The focus on return migrants offered the advantage of looking at their perceptual changes and identity transformations at points along the semicircular trajectory from Brazil to the US and back. Apart from indicting the putative inaccuracy of US Census ethno-racial categories and conventional usages (which starkly divide white from black and leave less latitude for racial mixture) her study compares the prevailing ethno-racial usages in both places as they affect reported identity in the sample, and perhaps most significantly underscores the situational determinants of it. Thus it becomes clear that, depending upon location along the circular trajectory, migrants' identity is multivalent.

This incisive study brings to mind (Brazilian American antipathies to Latino-Hispanic identification notwithstanding) the analogous case of the erstwhile Puerto Rican circular migration pattern, an exemplar in this day of ubiquitous remittance-dependent immigrant donor country economies, digital communication and affordable international transportation. Once having starkly been suffused with pathos and conflict by observers, a shift in the meaning of the circular pattern is now in the making as the migrant and ex-migrant Puerto Rican 'diasporic' experience is being reinterpreted: it appears that mainland socialized 'Newyoricans' have shed their diffidence toward islanders and island culture, and the Newyorican experience is becoming transformed, according to Juan Flores, into an allegedly more confident one of "learning and turning."[29]

Such cultural changes bear watching as the outlines of the Latino 'ethnoid' segment and its variants are developed and forged out of the welter of in-migrating nationalities with often widely varying cultures.[30] Processes and instances of immigrant linguistic hybridization (linguistic 'code switching')—for example, as Rosalyn Negrón demonstrates—appear to be moving from outsiders' and even Latino speakers' own perceptions of them as Spanish-English linguistic bastardization (i.e., as 'Spanglish'), but under certain circumstances are more broadly contextualized and connected with individual and group strategies of situationally framed identity cultivation and impression management within the growing cosmopolitan multiethnic and multinational Latino experience.[31] In these connections it will be interesting to assess the further perceptual and identity changes the Brazilian and other migrants treated herein undergo upon completion of their migration circles back to the US.

In regard to the patterning of migration routes, one wonders about the extent to which the incipient circular pattern suggested in Joseph's article will come to characterize immigrant groups and communities. It is certainly now the case with many Caribbean, European, African, South American and South Asian and Asian immigrants in the US and elsewhere, and is clearly typified, augmented and caused—that is, sustained by the remittance flows that are increasingly associated with these groups. In this respect, much of the work in this volume points in the direction of an impending theoretical synthesis or integration of what Portes initially characterized as the three immigration 'contexts' of separation, reception and incorporation. Much of this thinking appears here in the selections by the Zurabishivilis and Solari.

Tamar and Tinatin Zurabishivili's work, focusing on the post-Soviet Georgian immigration from the impoverished Tianeti district, which is overwhelmingly directed toward Western Europe and is largely motivated by the search for jobs, suggests such a circular migration pattern is in the making considering, that emigrants send money, packages and letters via an effective and regular bus connection to Greece, (the most frequent, and largely feminine, migrant destination).[32] The women work mostly as housekeepers, nannies/babysitters and caregivers, and the men work in construction, factory and other manual jobs. Finally, in Greece emigrants rely heavily upon this busy bus connection, which is "reliable and operates on a regular basis and the fees are much lower than using official money transfer orders." This, of course, represents a transnational connection and a circular financial and communication flow.

Cinzia Solari's ongoing global gendered ethnographic work on two migration patterns—resource drain versus constitutive circularity—of post-Soviet Ukrainian migration goes a step further.[33] Here the sending and receiving countries are revealed as dynamic sites that are interacting with and shaping each other with respect to gender as a key element of the mix:

> A confluence of gendered processes of economic transformation and nationalism inside Ukraine has encouraged emigration to Italy and California, the two largest receiving sites of post-1991 Ukrainian emigrants. I suggest, however, that these two migration streams are not simply about two different destinations for migrants, but rather they produce two divergent migration patterns that are not equally tied to Ukraine's gendered processes of transformation.

Finally, in following these migration streams back to Ukraine Solari has discovered that "Ukraine, far from being a variable held constant, had different effects for the lived experiences of migrants in Italy and California and that the reverse was also true; the migration pattern to Italy and California had different effects in Ukraine." Here we learn that the state structure, ideology and policy, already having undergone dramatic transformation, have dramatically shaped emigrant identity patterns.

Given the fact that the world is now in an unprecedented state of global population flux immanently and imminently accompanied by or associated with economic, political and social crises and environmental catastrophe, it is clear from work such as Solari's that sociological immigration research and conceptualization are poised on the edge of a paradigmatic change from one focused, for example, upon linear, unidirectional assimilation-based social processes, to one emphasizing bi- or multidirectional ones shaped by complex sociocultural global, transnational and local gendered economic, political, cultural, governmental-legal and military forces and conflicts.

On the other hand, 'paradigmatic' seems too pretentious an adjective to describe the contemporary conceptual apparatus of immigration research being displaced in a discipline such as sociology, which is often characterized as 'multiparadigmatic' in nature. Still, as the work herein suggests, the interrelatedness of national immigration discourses with international economic, political and social vectors, as these are associated with immigration enforcement efforts, has significant impacts on the shaping of immigrant identities that are part and parcel of immigrant responses and adjustment strategies.

In this regard, a number of scholars are now exploring the interrelations of globalization, the boundaries of citizenship and the construction of identities. Some, such as Aihwa Ong, posit an emergent form of 'flexible citizenship' against a background of "migrations, diasporas, and other transnational flows." In this case, for example, the *huaqiao*—the overseas Chinese—are viewed as co-producers, along with the Chinese state, of a sojourner discourse, which defies the one-sided critique of orientalism. Likewise she examines such complex phenomena as Malaysian 'graduated sovereignty', in which the state defines and regulates through law three ethnic (Malays, Chinese and Indians) zones.[34] Thus, rather than suggest that the national citizenship model has been eclipsed or made obsolete, Ong argues that states adapt to globalism by making creative responses to it. On the other hand, claiming that in the contemporary world rights and identities derive from universalistic discourses of personhood, Yasemin Nuhoglu Soysal posits an emergent form of "postnational citizenship" eclipsing the national form.[35]

Taking a position somewhat midway between the national and postnational models, Linda Bosniak suggests that although the authority of the state-centered framework in which we live limits our capacity to conceive of alternative arrangements, the postnational *claim* (if not the actual state of affairs) "is best read . . . not as a claim advocating the demise of nation-states and nationalism altogether, but on behalf of decentering or 'demoting' the national form from its privileged position in political thought."[36] This is both a more subtle interpretive *and* moral approach for it interrogates the permeable membrane dividing the phenomena of immigration, citizenship and rights from scholars' conceptions of them. Importantly Bosniak adds that "There are good reasons, grounded in commitments to social justice and democratic engagement, to challenge the presumed inevitability and desirability of a statist conception of citizenship and to prefer, instead, a multiple, pluralized understanding of citizenship identities and solidarities."[37]

Due to the devolution of former nationally funded social and other services left by the accelerated retreat of the federal government due to welfare reform, and more recently, the economic debacle of 2008, immigrant responses and adjustment patterns are increasingly leavened by the efforts of immigrant-serving community-based organizations (CBOs)—agents of 'localized globalism'—that fill in the gaps of service provision.[38]

In response to these pressures CBOs have been incorporated into the manifold service and advocacy ensembles dotting the urban landscape. Coupled with this, the increased nativism and intolerance of immigrants by US and European host nations in the post–9/11 period have prompted community-based organizations to engage in more advocacy and to act as defenders of human and civil rights, resistors to exploitation and facilitators of equitable immigrant incorporation in society. By the same token they have suffered an economic crisis as more stress has been placed on philanthropy and foundation funding to fill in the void left by the retreat of government.[39] Thus immigrant-based CBOs are competing for a smaller economic pie in a devolutionary environment, with greater demand being made on their shrinking resources for services to immigrant clients. Consequently, many are faltering and increasing numbers are closing their doors. If the reader's curiosity is aroused, s/he is urged to consult the references noted herein.[40]

We hope that these chapters have alerted the reader to these rapidly changing complex phenomena and that our introductory and concluding chapters suggest useful ways of understanding them in terms of broader theoretical issues. Readers, now alerted to the playing out of similar phenomena in different national contexts, can thereby recognize their patterning and can avail themselves of tools to understand them. Indeed, along with our readers, we look forward to assessing further developments and changes.

NOTES

1. Saskia Sassen, *A Sociology of Globalization* (New York: W. W. Norton, 2007), 106.
2. Ibid., 51, 106, 217–218.
3. Philip A. Kretsedemas, personal communication July 14, 2011.
4. Elsewhere I have written about two Latino community-based organizations' localized global resistance to the economic and political marginalization of immigrants, including despoliation of the environment, in an old industrial suburb of Boston. See Glenn Jacobs, "Localized Globalism and Latino CBO Resistance to Immigrant Marginalization in a Gateway City," *Latino Studies* (forthcoming); also see idem, "Service versus Advocacy?: A Comparison of Two Latino Community-Based Organizations in Chelsea, Massachusetts," *Trotter Review* 19, no. 1 (2010): 55–73.
5. Manuel Castells and Harry Kreisler, "Identity and Change in the Network Society: Conversations with Manuel Castells: Identity in the Network Society," Institute of International Studies, University of California–Berkeley, May 9, 2001, accessed Sept. 8, 2012, http://globetrotter.berkeley.edu/people/Castells/castells-con0.html.

6. Victor Roudometof, "Transnationalism, Cosmopolitanism and Glocalization," *Current Sociology* 53, no. 1 (2005): 202–231; Eric Swyngedouw, "Globalization or 'Glocalization'?: Networks, Territories and Rescaling," *Cambridge Review of International Affairs* 17, no. 1 (2004): 53–75; and Zygmunt Bauman, "On Glocalization: or Globalization for Some, Localization for Some Others," *Thesis Eleven* 54 (1998): 3–25.

7. Arjun Appadurai, "Deep Democracy: Urban Governmentality and the Horizon of Politics," *Public Culture* 14, no. 1 (2002): 112–142.

8. Arjun Appadurai, "Grassroots Globalization and the Research Imagination," *Public Culture* 12, no. 1 (2000): 75–98. Also, Stuart Hall's work, especially his introduction to and two essays in Anthony D. King's edited volume, *Culture, Globalization and the World System: Contemporary Conditions for the Representation of Identity* (Minneapolis: University of Minnesota Press, 1997), 1–18, 19–39, 41–68, is quite perceptive in this regard.

9. Antoine Pécoud and Paul de Guchteneire, "International Migration, Border Controls and Human Rights: Assessing the Relevance of a Right to Mobility," *Journal of Borderlands Studies* 21, no. 1 (2002): 75.

10. Don Mitchell, *The Right to the City* (New York: Guilford, 2003), and Neil Smith, "Giuliani Time: The Revanchist 1990s," *Social Text* 16, no. 4 (1998): 20–46.

11. Linda Bosniak, "Citizenship Denationalized," *Indiana Journal of Global Legal Studies* 7 (2000): 500, 503.

12. Robert Paul Wolff, *A Critique of Pure Tolerance* (Boston: Beacon, 1969).

13. Michael Peter Smith, *Transnational Urbanism: Locating Globalization* (Malden, MA: Blackwell, 2001), 18.

14. Bosniak, "Citizenship Denationalized," 501–502.

15. Ibid., 500–501.

16. Silvio Torres-Saillant, "The Tribulations of Blackness: Stages in Dominican Racial Identity," *Latin American Perspectives* 25, no. 3 (1998): 126–146.

17. Ramona Hernandez, *The Mobility of Workers under Advanced Capitalism* (New York: Columbia University Press, 2002).

18. Kitty Calavita, "Immigration Law, Race, and Identity," *Annual Review of Law and Social Science* 3, no. 1 (2004): 10.

19. Noel Ignatiev, *How the Irish Became White* (New York: Routledge, 1995).

20. The cases of Jews and Italians immediately come to mind. See Karen Brodkin, *How Jews Became White Folks: And What That Says about Race in America* (New Brunswick: Rutgers University Press, 1998), and Jennifer Guglielmo and Sal Restivo, *Are Italians White?: How Race Is Made in America* (New York: Routledge, 2003).

21. Alex Stepick, Carol Dutton Stepick, Emmanuel Eugene, Deborah Teed and Yves Labissiere, "Shifting Identities and Intergenerational Conflict: Growing Up Haitian in Miami," in *Ethnicities: Children of Immigrants in America*, ed. Rubén G. Rumbaut and Alejandro Portes (Berkeley: University of California Press and Russell Sage, 2001), 229–266.

22. Thus as Stepick et al. conclude regarding Haitian youth, "Haitians are becoming American, but in a specifically black ethnic fashion. They are likely to be perceived and treated as African Americans, subject to the prejudice and discrimination that characterizes American society." Stepick et al., "Shifting Identities," 261.

23. Mary C. Waters, *Black Identities: West Indian Immigrant Dreams and American Realities* (Cambridge, MA: Harvard University Press and Russell Sage, 1999).

24. On the other hand, see the following reference for a generationally qualified conspectus of West Indian identity in some respects similar to and in

others contrasting with the Haitian case: Philip Kasinitz, Juan Battle and Inés Iyares, "Fade to Black? The Children of West Indian Migrants in Southern Florida," in *Ethnicities: Children of Immigrants in America*, ed. Rubén G. Rumbaut and Alejandro Portes (Berkeley: University of California Press and Russell Sage, 2001), 267–300.

25. This is particularly salient among Hmong immigrant youth. See Stacey J. Lee, *Up Against Whiteness: Race, School, and Immigrant Youth* (New York: Teachers College Press, 2005), and idem, "The Truth and Myth of the Model Minority: The Case of Hmong Americans," *Narrowing the Achievement Gap: Issue in Children's and Families' Lives* 3 (2007): 171–184. For Asian youth in general, see Angela Reyes, "Appropriation of African American Slang by Asian American Youth," *Journal of Sociolinguistics* 9, no. 7 (2005): 509–522.

26. Calavita, "Immigration Law, Race, and Identity," 12.

27. Because of the ease in securing a driver's license, North Carolina formerly was a magnet destination for undocumented migrants.

28. Edward Martin, "Down Mexico Way: Illegal Immigration Is Suppressing Tar Heel Wages. But This Boon to Business Also Is Creating a New Underclass," *Business North Carolina*, May 2006, accessed Aug. 3, 2011, http://www.businessnc.com/index.php?src.

29. Juan Flores, *The Diaspora Strikes Back: Caribeño Tales of Learning and Turning* (New York: Routledge, 2009).

30. The term "ethnoid segment" was coined by Alfred McClung Lee to refer to the relatively amorphous arrays of former immigrant nationalities "merged . . . at a variety of rates of assimilation" that have become evolving point-of-reference in- and out-groups in the US. What he identified ca. 1966 as white Protestants ("Wasps"), and "Jewish" groups among others, for example, have been joined since then by the current ethnoid segments of Latinos and Asians. See Alfred McClung Lee, *Multivalent Man* (New York: George Braziller, 1966), 255–267.

31. Rosalyn Negrón, *Ethnic Identification among Urban Latinos* (El Paso, TX: LFB Scholarly, 2011).

32. We are told that Tianeti exemplifies a feminine migration pattern, men constituting only 32 percent of the migrants, with women typically working as housekeepers, nannies/babysitters and caregivers. During the Soviet period full-time female participation in the labor force in the 1970s and 1980s reached 85 percent with women occupying 51 percent of all labor force, and even when the salary of a husband was enough to cover all needs of families, women were reluctant to stay at home and quit their jobs.

33. Cinzia Solari, "Between 'Europe' and 'Africa': Building the New Ukraine on the Shoulders of Migrant Women," in *Mapping Difference: The Many Faces of Women in Ukraine*, ed. M. J. Rubchak (New York: Berghahn Books, 2011), 23–46.

34. Aihwa Ong, *Flexible Citizenship: The Cultural Logic of Transnationality* (Durham: Duke University Press, 1999), 8, 36–38, 43–44, 131, 217–218.

35. Yasemin Nuhoglu Soysal, *Limits of Citizenship: Migrants and Postnational Membership in Europe* (Chicago: University of Chicago Press, 1994).

36. Bosniak, "Citizenship Denationalized," 505. This position is essentially the one taken in her more recent book, *The Citizen and the Alien: Dilemmas of Contemporary Membership* (Princeton, NJ: Princeton University Press, 2006).

37. Bosniak, "Citizenship Denationalized," 507.

38. See Nicole P. Marwell, "Privatizing the Welfare State: Nonprofit Community-Based Organizations as Political Actors," *American Sociological Review* 69

(2004): 265–291; Els de Graauw, "Out of the Shadow of the State: Immigrant Nonprofits as Self-Motivated Political Actors in Urban Politics" (working paper, Institute for the Study of Social Change, Berkeley, CA, 2007); and Héctor R. Cordero-Guzman, "Community-Based Organizations and Migration in New York City," *Journal of Ethnic and Migration Studies* 31, no. 5 (2005): 34–56. A different perspective is given by: Irene Bloemrad, "The Limits of de Tocqueville: How Government Facilitates Organisational Capacity in Newcomer Communities," *Journal of Ethnic and Migration Studies* 31, no. 5 (2005): 68–96.

39. Ann Withorn, "Friends or Foes? Nonprofits and the Puzzle of Welfare Reform," *Annals* 577 (2001): 107–117; Sandra K. Danziger, "The Decline of Cash Welfare and Implications for Social Policy and Poverty," *Annual Review of Sociology* 36 (2010): 523–545; Dennis L. Poole, "Scaling Up CBOs for Second-Order Devolution in Welfare Reform," *Nonprofit Management & Leadership* 13 (2003): 325–341; Susan Raymond, Sally Park and Jason Simons, *The Public Finance Crisis: Can Philanthropy Shoulder the Burden?* (New York: Changing Our World, 2011); and Seema Shah, Reina Mukai and Grace McAllister, *Foundation Funding for Hispanics/Latinos in the United States and for Latin America* (New York: Foundation Center, 2011).

40. The reader also will find useful this special issue titled, "Where Is Home? Immigrants of Color in Massachusetts," *Trotter Review* 19, no. 1 (2010), containing five articles written by members of the Trotter Consortium on Immigration at the University of Massachusetts–Boston, devoted to immigrant community-based organizations in the Boston metropolitan area.

Contributors

Gwendolyn Yvonne Alexis is the lead ethics professor in the Business School at Monmouth University in New Jersey. She has a master's degree in ethics from Yale University Divinity School and a PhD in sociology and historical studies from New School for Social Research. The field research for her doctoral dissertation, "Legislative Terrorism: A Primer for the Non-Islamic State; Secularism and Different Believers," was completed in Sweden, where she was a visiting scholar at Lund University. An experienced corporate attorney, she is a graduate of Harvard Law School and a member of the NY, NJ and FL Bars.

Marta Araújo holds a PhD in sociology of education from University of London (2003). She is a full-time researcher at the Centre for Social Studies (CES) Associate Laboratory, where she also lectures on (anti-)racism and Eurocentrism in the PhD program Democracy in the 21st Century (CES/FEUC). She has been the director of the peer-reviewed electronic journal *e-cadernos ces* (www.ces.uc.pt/e-cadernos). Her research interests center on the (re)production and challenging of racism and Eurocentrism, with a particular interest in education. She has published internationally, particularly on the Portuguese and British contexts.

Jorge Capetillo-Ponce is presently the director of Latino Studies, an associate professor of sociology and a research associate at the Mauricio Gaston Institute at University of Massachusetts–Boston. He is the editor of the books *Images of Mexico in the U.S. News Media* (Mexican Cultural Institute of New York, 2000) and *A Foucault for the 21st Century* (with Sam Binkley; Cambridge Scholars, 2009). He has also published numerous journal articles and policy reports on immigration policy, bilingual education, social movements and social theory.

Deirdre Conlon is an assistant professor of sociology and urban studies at St. Peter's College, Jersey City, NJ. Her research focuses on social and legal justice issues surrounding migration and mobility, particularly among asylum seeker and refugee populations, as well as advocacy and activism within this sector. Currently, she is coinvestigator and US coordinator for an ESRC-funded project, Asylum-Network.org. Her publications include articles in *Environment and Planning D: Society and Space*, *Population, Space and Place* and *Gender, Place and Culture*. She has also contributed book chapters for a number of edited volumes on migration and mobility. At present, she is working on a coedited book titled *Carceral Geographies: Mobility and Agency in Spaces of Imprisonment and Detention*.

Mark Dow is the author of *American Gulag: Inside U.S. Immigration Prisons* (California University Press, 2004) and coeditor (with David R. Dow) of *Machinery of Death: The Reality of America's Death Penalty Regime* (Routledge, 2002). He was a finalist for the 2010 *New Issues* Poetry Prize (Western Michigan University). His essays and poems have appeared in a variety of publications, including *Bender's Immigration Bulletin*, *Boston Review*, *Caribbean Review of Books*, *Conjunctions*, *Guardian*, *Los Angeles Times*, *Miami Herald*, *New York Times*, *Paris Review*, *PN Review* (UK), *Prison Legal News* and *Texas Observer*. He teaches English at Hunter College in New York.

Barbara Faedda is the associate director of the Italian Academy for Advanced Studies and an adjunct assistant professor in the Department of Italian at Columbia University. She received her PhD in legal anthropology and social science from S. Orsola Benincasa University in Naples. She is coauthor of the book *Luoghi di frontier: Antropologia delle mediazioni* and author of *I mille volti della moda*, and is a contributor to various books and manuscripts from *Il Mulino* and other publishers. She is a member of the editorial staff of the journal *Gli Stranieri, Rivista di studi, giurisprudenza e legislazione*, and of the law journal *Diritto & Diritti*. Currently, she is writing a book on the Somali-Italian minority.

Luis Galanes is a professor of anthropology at University of Puerto Rico at Cayey. He has done extensive work and publication on the Caribbean, with particular interest in the geographical area of Puerto Rico and the Virgin Islands, both US and British. His areas of theoretical interest are centered around the work ethics of the Caribbean subject, particularly the youth, and on the relationship between work-related values and reproductive values. He has studied patterns of migration into the USVIs, and their relationship to labor-related conflicts in that region.

Sharif Islam is a PhD candidate in sociology at University of Illinois at Urbana-Champaign. He is currently doing fieldwork for his dissertation project, entitled "Sharia in the City: Construction and Negotiation of Moral Spaces," in Chicago.

Glenn Jacobs is a professor of sociology at University of Massachusetts–Boston and head of the Umass–Boston Trotter Institute research consortium on immigrant community-based organizations. His ethnographic research has focused on urban, Latino, community-based organizations, the culture of Afro-Cuban, barrio musicians and Mexican religious subcultures. He is also the author of *Charles Horton Cooley: Imagining Social Reality* (University of Massachusetts Press, 2006).

Jennifer A. Jones received her PhD in sociology from University of California–Berkeley and is currently a SBS Diversity postdoctoral fellow at Ohio State University. Funded by the NSF Dissertation Improvement Grant and the UC Center for New Racial Studies, she is in the process of revising her book manuscript, entitled *Making Race in the New South: Mexican Migration and Race Relations in Winston-Salem, North Carolina*, based on her dissertation work. Her recent work has been published in *Sociological Perspectives* and (with Sandra Smith) in *Ethnic and Racial Studies*.

Tiffany D. Joseph is a Robert Wood Johnson Foundation Health Policy scholar at Harvard University from 2011 to 2013 and assistant professor of sociology at Stony Brook University (on leave 2011–2013). She completed her PhD in sociology (2011) at University of Michigan. Her research interests include: race, ethnicity and migration in the Americas, the influence of immigration on the social construction of race in the US, immigration and health policy, and the experiences of minority faculty in academia. She is currently working on two projects. The first is a book manuscript examining how US migration influenced the racial conceptions for Brazilian return migrants in Governador Valadares, Brazil. The second project explores how documentation status influences the health care access and utilization of Latino immigrants in the Boston metropolitan area. Her work has been published in *Ethnic and Racial Studies*, *Gender and Education*, and *Race and Social Problems*.

Ana Kralj is an associate researcher at the Science and Research Centre of Koper and assistant professor of sociology at the Faculty of Humanities, University of Primorska. Her areas of interest are globalization processes, nationalism, undocumented migration, immigration, asylum and integration policies and microideologies of everyday life. She has published several books and articles, including *Nepovabljeni: Globalizacija, nacionalizem in migracije* [The uninvited: Globalization, nationalism and migration], *When ć Becomes č: Discrimination of Unrecognized National Minorities in Slovenia* and *Meja kot razlika, metafora in diskurz* [Border as distinction, metaphor and discourse] (with Tanja Rener). Her current research projects explore the living and working conditions of migrant workers in Slovenia and interethnic violence in schools.

Philip Kretsedemas is an associate professor of sociology at University of Massachusetts–Boston. His research and writing have examined the dynamics of immigrant racialization, policy outcomes for immigrant populations and the regulation of migrant flows by the state. Some of his journal articles have appeared in *American Quarterly*, *Current Sociology*, *International Migration* and *Stanford Law and Policy Review*. He is also the coeditor of *Keeping Out the Other: A Critical Introduction to Immigration Enforcement Today* (with David Brotherton; Columbia University Press, 2008) and the author of *The Immigration Crucible: Transforming 'Race', Nation and the Limits of the Law* (Columbia University Press, 2012).

Ryan Mann-Hamilton is a PhD candidate at the CUNY Graduate Center Department of Anthropology and board member of the afrolatin@ forum. He has an undergraduate degree in international business and a master's degree in environmental systems with a focus on renewable technologies. He has taught courses in history, anthropology and ethnic studies and given a variety of workshops on social justice, and environmental activism and social constructions of race. He has also spent time as a teaching artist, conducting music and poetry workshops, and has traveled extensively in search of new adventures.

Jeff Melnick teaches in the American Studies Department at University of Massachusetts–Boston. With scholarly interests in Black-Jewish relations, immigration studies and US popular culture in a global context, his published works include *A Right to Sing the Blues: African Americans, Jews, and American Popular Song* (1999), a book on immigration and popular culture cowritten with Rachel Rubin, and *9/11 Culture: America under Construction* (2009). He has just begun a new project, *Creepy Crawling with the Manson Family*.

Valentina Pagliai received her PhD from University of California, Los Angeles (UCLA), in 2000 in linguistic anthropology. Her main areas of research are racial formation processes in discourse, gender and sexuality and argumentative language. She recently guest edited an issue for the *Journal of Linguistic Anthropology* (June 2010) titled "Performing Disputes: Cooperation and Conflict in Argumentative Language." Other recent publications include: "Non-alignment in Footing, Intentionality and Dissent in Talk about Immigrants in Italy" (*Language and Communication*, Fall 2012). She can be contacted at valentina.pagliai@qc.cuny.edu.

Jacqueline Jiménez Polanco currently works as an assistant professor of sociology at Bronx Community College of City University of New York. She has several publications on migration and human rights, the LGBTIQ movement in the Dominican Republic, women in politics, Dominican politics, political parties and elections, and comparative Caribbean and Latin American politics. She holds a PhD in political science and sociology and a JD in law from Complutense University of Madrid.

Rachel Rubin is the chair of the American Studies Department at University of Massachusetts–Boston and has published numerous works in literary, cultural and historical studies, beginning with her 2000 book *Jewish Gangsters of Modern Literature*. Her interests include migration studies, Appalachian cultural history, the history of radicalism in the twentieth-century US and popular culture. She has published essays and books in all these fields (including a book on immigration and popular culture, cowritten with Jeff Melnick, a scholarly edition of Polly Adler's memoir *A House Is Not a Home*, an American studies textbook and a coedited collection titled *Radicalism in the South since Reconstruction*). She is currently completing a book about the Renaissance faire in American cultural history.

P. Khalil Saucier is the director of Africana Studies and an assistant professor of sociology at Rhode Island College. He specializes in identity formation, black popular culture, social thought, and race and ethnicity. His publications are featured in the *Journal of Popular Music Studies*, *Rethinking Marxism: A Journal of Economics, Culture, and Society*, *American Communication Journal*, *Fashion Theory*, *Encyclopedia of African American Music* and others. He has coauthored the *Historical Dictionary of the Republic of Cape Verde* (4th ed.) with Richard A. Lobban Jr. (2007). He is also the editor of *Native Tongues: An African Hip-Hop Reader* (2011).

Cinzia Solari received her PhD in sociology from University of California, Berkeley, and is currently an assistant professor of sociology at University of Massachusetts–Boston. Her book manuscript is based on her ethnographic dissertation, *Exile vs. Exodus: Nationalism and Gendered Migration from Ukraine to Italy and California*. It explores how two contrasting patterns of migration—the exile of grandmothers to Italy and the exodus of families to California—generate distinct practices and subjectivities among migrants abroad and are differentially implicated in nation-building projects back in Ukraine. She has also written on topics such as the construction of motherhood and nation in transnational migrations, the role of religious institutions in the settlement and transnational practices of migrants, and the gendered work identities of immigrant care workers.

Tamar Zurabishvili has been active in research in Georgia from 1999 onward. Since 2009 she has been working at Eurasia Partnership Foundation, focusing on EPF's media programming. She has been publishing regularly, as well as participating in conferences both in Georgia and internationally. She has MA degrees in media studies (New School University, 2005) and sociology (Moscow School of Social and Economic Sciences, 1999), and a PhD in sociology from Ilia Chavchavadze State University (2008). She has been involved in several studies of labor emigration from Georgia, serving as a consultant for the International Organization for Migration and the Caucasian Institute for Peace, Democracy and Development.

Tinatin Zurabishivili holds her PhD in the sociology of journalism from Moscow M. Lomonosov State University (1999). Her academic publications focus on social research methods, sociology of transition, sociology of the media and sociology of migration. She is currently the project coordinator for the Caucasus Research Resource Center's annual regional Caucasus Barometer survey. In the spring semesters between 2004 and 2007 she was an Open Society Institute faculty development fellow at University of California, Los Angeles, in the Department of Sociology. Between 1999 and 2001 she served as junior researcher for Yale University's project Poverty, Ethnicity and Gender in Eastern Europe during the Market Transition. She also worked for five years as a sociologist at the Russian Center for Public Opinion and Market Research.

Index

31; convergence (transnational), 6, 115-16, 190-91, 195; criminal, 107, 114-17, 124, 240, 246-47; detention and deportation, 8, 105-7, 122, 166, 176, 178; economic development, 177, 215-17, 223, 226-28, 305; education, 39; emigration, 142-43, 334; employment,139; foreign, 217; immigration, 2, 3, 6, 7, 8, 27-29, 33, 38, 72, 85-86, 94-96, 100, 105-7, 114-17, 121-22, 124, 166, 175-76, 177-78, 187, 190-91, 198, 209, 215-17, 219, 240, 246-47, 250-51, 253, 305, 309, 310, 311, 312, 313, 314-16, 320, 325; integration, 29, 36, 39-40, 72, 115, 121; local, 240, 246-47, 250-51; migrant, as subject of, 3; multicultural/diversity, 4-6, 27-29, 38, 39, 41, 74, 328; nation-building/modernization, 223, 226-28, 305; racism/anti-discrimination, 33, 41, 73; religious pluralism and, 74, 77; security, 85, 95-96, 100, 114-16, 175, 190-91, 240; urban, 268, 270, 325; welfare state, 328; Western industrialized nations, 7. *See also*, court decisions; law; legal; multiculturalism.
Portes, Alejandro, 242, 313, 334.
Portugal, 3, 5, 15, 27-41, 111, 265, 276-77, 280, 282, 285-86, 329.
Port au Prince, 104, 224.
Postnational, 18, 335.
Post-Soviet. *See* , Soviet.
Poster, Winifred, 134.
Poverty, 10, 37, 93, 149-54, 158, 161, 177, 218, 269-70, 329.
Prashad, Vijay, 296.
Puerto Rico: citizenship status (US), 250; detention center, 105; femicides, 184; racial-ethnic identity, 14, 224, 266-67, 270, 276, 282, 284, 300-302, 330, 332; migrants, 178, 206, 210, 231, 250, 301, 333.

R

Race: assimilation and, 239-40; asylum seekers, 167; black identity, 15, 259-72; class, 269, 288; citizenship and, 288; colonial era,

41, 276; ethnicity/culture and, 49, 56-59, 85, 189, 258, 261-65, 271; geography, 268; ideologies, 30-31, 36; immigration and, 13, 33, 35, 41, 88-89, 218, 239-40, 247, 249, 275-89, 296; Latinamericanization of, 289; migrant identity, 16, 240, 242, 259-72, 275-89; social mobility, 243, 251; nation building and, 223, 227-28, 234-35, 330; performance, 15, 297-98, 303; religion and, 88; scholarship, 8, 13, 42; social construction of, 11, 15, 27, 29-31, 35-36, 38, 41, 239-40, 259-72, 275-89, 297-98, 302; solidarity, 240, 242, 332.
Racism: academic/policy discourse on, 33, 38, 39, 40, 41, 116; anti-black, 5, 12-14, 228, 259-60, 262-64; anti-Haitian racism, 228; anti-immigrant, 7, 9, 16, 50, 100, 119, 124; anti-Latino racism, 14, 16; antiracist, 28, 29, 41-42, 47-48, 50-51, 119, 124; black/Latino shared experience of, 249, 271; Brazilian migrant experience of, 280; Cape Verdean experience of, 51, 259-64; colonial-era roots of, 41, 48; colorblindness, 35; color prejudice, 32; cultural racism, 5, 7, 48-49, 94, 98, 100; in education, 28, 38; evading problem of, 27, 29, 32, 34, 38, 40, 41, 49; institutional/structural racism, 40, 42, 50-51, 59, 72, 124, 248, 265; intensification of, 39, 50; Irish American racism, 331; nativist racism, 329; Nazism/Fascism and, 49, 72, 116; postcolonial dynamics and, 33, 41; minstrelsy and, 300; multicultural discourse and, 27, 47-48, 50-51, 57, 59, 329; US history of, 248, 276; white racism, 12.
Rathzel, Nora, 49.
Ramos-Zayas, Ana, 267, 270, 276.
Reitz, Jeffrey, 1.
Refugee: Bosnian, 86, 97; Central American, 250; credibility of, 176, 187, 192, 194-98; Croatian, 97; female, 10, 168; Haitian, 105; Herzegovinian, 86,